LONGMAN CRITICAL READERS

General Editors:

RAMAN SELDEN, late Emeritus Professor of English, Lancaster University and late Professor of English, Sunderland Polytechnic;

STAN SMITH, Professor of English, University of Dundee

ROMANTICISM

Edited and Introduced by

CYNTHIA CHASE

LONGMAN
LONDON AND NEW YORK

Addison Wesley Longman Limited,
Edinburgh Gate
Harlow, Essex CM20 2JE, England
and Associated Companies throughout the world.

Published in the United States of America
by Addison Wesley Longman Inc, New York

© Longman Group UK Limited 1993

First published 1993
Second impression 1996

ISBN 0–582–05000–6 csd
ISBN 0–582–04799–4 ppr

British Library Cataloguing-in-Publication Data

A catalogue record for this book is
available from the British Library

Library of Congress Cataloging-in-Publication Data

Romanticism / edited and introduced by Cynthia Chase.
    p. cm. – (Longman critical readers)
  Includes bibliographical references and index.
  ISBN 0–582–05000–6 (csd). – ISBN 0–582–04799–4 (ppr).
  1. English literature – 19th century – History and criticism.
  2. Romanticism – Great Britain. I. Chase, Cynthia, 1953–. II. Series.
PR457,R457 1993
820.9′145′09034-dc20   92-14309
                                                                  CIP

Set 9K in 9/11.5 Palatino
Produced by Longman Singapore Publishers (Pte) Ltd.
Printed in Singapore

Contents

140-
183.

General Editors' Preface

The outlines of contemporary critical theory are now often taught as a standard feature of a degree in literary studies. The development of particular theories has seen a thorough transformation of literary criticism. For example, Marxist and Foucauldian theories have revolutionized Shakespeare studies, and 'deconstruction' has led to a complete reassessment of Romantic poetry. Feminist criticism has left scarcely any period of literature unaffected by its searching critiques. Teachers of literary studies can no longer fall back on a standardized, received, methodology.

Lecturers and teachers are now urgently looking for guidance in a rapidly changing critical environment. They need help in understanding the latest revisions in literary theory, and especially in grasping the practical effects of the new theories in the form of theoretically sensitized new readings. A number of volumes in the series anthologize important essays on particular theories. However, in order to grasp the full implications and possible uses of particular theories it is essential to see them put to work. This series provides substantial volumes of new readings, presented in an accessible form and with a significant amount of editorial guidance.

Each volume includes a substantial introduction which explores the theoretical issues and conflicts embodied in the essays selected and locates areas of disagreement between positions. The pluralism of theories has to be put on the agenda of literary studies. We can no longer pretend that we all tacitly accept the same practices in literary studies. Neither is a *laissez-faire* attitude any longer tenable. Literature departments need to go beyond the mere toleration of theoretical differences: it is not enough merely to agree to differ; they need actually to 'stage' the differences openly. The volumes in this series all attempt to dramatize the differences, not necessarily with a view to resolving them but in order to foreground the choices presented by different theories or to argue for a particular route through the impasses the differences present.

The theory 'revolution' has had real effects. It has loosened the grip of traditional empiricist and romantic assumptions about language and literature. It is not always clear what is being proposed as the new agenda for literary studies, and indeed the very notion of 'literature' is questioned by the post-structuralist strain in theory. However, the uncertainties and obscurities of contemporary theories appear much less worrying when we see what the best critics have been able to do with them in practice. This series aims to disseminate the best of recent criticism and to show that it is possible to re-read the canonical texts of literature in new and challenging ways.

RAMAN SELDEN AND STAN SMITH

The Publishers and fellow Series Editor regret to record that Raman Selden died after a short illness in May 1991 at the age of fifty-three. Ray Selden was a fine scholar and a lovely man. All those he has worked with will remember him with much affection and respect.

Acknowledgements

We are grateful to the following for permission to reproduce copyright material:

Basil Blackwell Ltd for extracts from *Keats's Life of Allegory* by Marjorie Levinson (1988); University of Chicago Press and the author, Margaret Homans, for extracts from the chapter 'Bearing Demons: *Frankenstein*'s Circumvention of the Maternal' from *Bearing the Word: Language and Female Experience in Nineteenth-Century Women's Writing* (1986); the author, Jerome Christensen, for his essay 'Byron's *Sardanapalus* and the Triumph of Liberalism'; the author, Geoffrey Hartman and *Centennial Review* for the article 'Romanticism and Anti-Self-Consciousness' from *Centennial Review*, **6** (Autumn 1962) and from *Beyond Formalism* (Yale University Press, 1970), © Geoffrey Hartman; Johns Hopkins University Press for the chapter 'Past Recognition: Narrative Origins in Wordsworth and Freud' from *Empirical Truths and Critical Fictions: Locke, Wordsworth, Kant, Freud* by Cathy Caruth (1990), the chapter 'The Notion of Blockage in the Literature of the Sublime' by Neil Hertz from *Psychoanalysis and the Question of the Text* edited by Geoffrey Hartman (1978), the article 'Time and History in Wordsworth' by Paul de Man from *Diacritics* **17** (Winter 1987), © 1988 Johns Hopkins University Press, and the article 'Literary Gentlemen and Lovely Ladies: The Debate on the character of *Christabel*' by Karen Swann from *English Literary History*, **52** (Spring 1985), © The Johns Hopkins University Press; Johns Hopkins University Press and the author, Carol Jacobs for the abridged chapter 'Unbinding Words: *Prometheus Unbound*' from *Uncontainable Romanticism: Shelley, Bronte, Kleist* (1989); Oxford University Press for the chapter '"Splitting the Race of Man in Twain": Prostitution, Personification, and *The Prelude*' from *Romanticism, Writing, and Sexual Difference: Essays on The Prelude* by Mary Jacobus (1989), © Mary Jacobus 1989.

Introduction

Romanticism our contemporary

Romanticism resists being defined as a period or a set of qualities that can be comfortably ascribed to others and assigned to the historical past. There are several reasons why this is so. One is that major historical changes of the Romantic period still determine basic conditions of our lives: the invention of democracy, the invention of revolution, and the emergence of a reading public. Another reason is one this 'period' perhaps shares with any other: the permanent difficulty of historical interpretation, of knowing in what ways one's interpretive procedures determine one's results or may be determined by one's object, in what respect current assumptions project themselves onto the past or in fact arise from it. In interpreting Romanticism this difficulty is particularly acute. For in the history of 'literature' (a Romantic institution) as in the history of politics, Romanticism is *our* past: 'we carry it within ourselves as the experience of an *act* in which, up to a certain point, we ourselves have participated'.[1] What are still the most widely current assumptions about literature – such as the idea of 'organic form' and the inseparability of form and content, and the conception of good poetry as the fusion of thought and feeling – derive, critics maintain, from Romantic texts. 'The development of literary theory in the lifetime of Coleridge,' M.H. Abrams begins *The Mirror and the Lamp: Romantic Theory and the Critical Tradition*, 'was to a surprising extent the making of the modern critical mind'.[2] Much evidence suggests that this is true. But the very hypothesis sets up a specular or mirroring relation between Romanticism and the present that one cannot be sure of controlling through its conversion into a genetic narrative or history (as in Abrams's opening sentence). The possibility clearly exists that we project onto the Romantics concepts and attitudes that are central in our interpretation but superficial or tangential in their texts.

The range and energy of efforts to criticize and historicize Romantic writing suggest the difficulty of placing it at a historical distance. Irving

Babbitt closes his attack in *Rousseau and Romanticism* (1919) with a chapter entitled 'The Present Outlook' in which he advises a return to works in which the imagination is 'at once disciplined and supreme', and warns:

> Art in which the illusion is not disciplined to the higher reality counts at best on the recreative side of life. 'Imagination', says Poe, 'feeling herself for once unshackled, roamed at will among the ever-changing wonders of a shadowy and unstable land'. To take seriously the creations of this type of imagination is to be on the way towards madness.[3]

Marilyn Butler, introducing her social history of Romantic literature, *Romantics, Rebels, and Reactionaries*, notes that M.H. Abrams (probably the most influential historian of Romanticism), René Wellek (a major scholar of comparative literature) and Harold Bloom (a major Romanticist with a theory of poems' self-defensive 'strong misreadings' of their predecessors) all accept 'the Romantic artists' self-image as formulated by about the 1820s, their veneration for the creative process, and their elevation of their own inner experience over prosaic external "fact"'.[4] Butler cites as the principal impetus for her book the need to counteract the ways in which 'the majority of modern critical works subscribe to the cult of the Romantic writer':

> It is common to read and write biographies and critical studies of single writers, in isolation, which proceed as though the poet alone is the creator of his poetry. We are regularly in danger of treating the relationship between author and text as a closed system, when really the process of literary production must be open at both ends. The writer takes in words, thoughts and structures from a babel around him, and his text is a giving back into the same discussion, part, in short, of a social process. . . . A book is made by its public, the readers it literally finds and the people in the author's mind's eye.[5]

Butler's work belongs to what has come to be called the 'New Historicism', which has arisen in the 1980s in the study of Romanticism and the Renaissance. (The essays included in this volume by Marjorie Levinson, Jerome Christensen and Karen Swann are varieties of New Historical criticism.) Coming after a period in which formalist criticism and 'close reading' came to predominate alongside traditional historical approaches, it is a movement to interpret literary texts' significance in terms of their involvement with other contemporaneous past discourses, especially those of non-literary 'fact' – social, economic and political history. That New Historicism arose among Shakespearians and Romanticists is certainly no accident. It reacts against our intensely identificatory relationship with those historical constructions – 'Shakespeare' and 'Romanticism' – and it seeks to counter some effects of their institutionalization in the curriculum of modern education – in which the study of 'Shakespeare' has meant making it normal to think in universalizing psychological terms, or in which reading the Romantics has meant reinforcing the belief that poetry transcends politics.

The New Historicism is one among a number of recurrent attempts to take a distance from Romantic attitudes or ideologies seen as persisting in the present. To take a final example, the critic and literary theorist Paul de Man, writing from a quite different critical position from Marilyn Butler, and challenging the 'efficacy of a theory of interpretation based on the public reception of a work of art' which her argument promotes, does so by taking issue with principles identified with Romanticism.[6] In identifying linguistic factors in literary works that undercut the notion of the inseparability of form and content, a major premise of modern criticism, de Man differs with what he calls 'the main tenet and crux of all critical philosophies and "Romantic" literatures', namely the continuity of perception with cognition, 'of aesthetic with rational judgement'.[7] That the most varied critiques of modern critical principles should be cast as disengagements from aspects of Romanticism demonstrates the difficulty of treating it as something behind us which we can know independently of our own reading practices and conceptual frameworks.

Is it the case, as Marilyn Butler and Jerome McGann have claimed, that the most influential modern studies of Romantic literature have accepted and adopted Romantic categories and premises rather than submitting them to analysis? This is one way of describing the problem in modern scholarship on Romanticism, put forward by McGann.

> Like Hegel, Abrams offers a program of Romanticism rather than a critical representation of its character; as such, both reify certain key Romantic self-conceptualizations like 'spirituality', 'creativity', 'process', 'uniqueness', 'diversity'. Indeed, the concepts of 'synthesis' and 'reconciliation' as these appear in the received Romantic texts and their commentaries are themselves Romantic concepts whose meaning cannot be taken at face value. They lie at the very heart of Romanticism's self-representation and as such they must be subjected to critical analysis. This analysis is difficult to perform, however, since the ideologies of Romanticism seek to persuade us that such concepts are fundamental, and hence that they need not – cannot – be analyzed.[8]

On the contents of Romantic ideas and values, interestingly, McGann and Abrams largely agree, even though in McGann's view Abrams reached his conclusions about them using mistaken Romantic assumptions. Where they disagree is in their evaluation of these ostensibly Romantic stances, which are ratified by Abrams and criticized by McGann as the mistaken though historically determined 'response to the age's severe political and social dislocations', a reaching 'for solutions in the realm of ideas', such as that of the synthesizing power of aesthetic judgement or poetry. While McGann thinks the problem in accounts of Romanticism has been other critics' approving repetition of Romantic ideas, his own repetition of the same themes, albeit in the mode of disparagement, gives his diagnosis an ironic appropriateness. This suggests another way of describing the situation in Romanticism scholarship. The problem may well be the tendency, marked in New Historicist criticism such as McGann's as well as in earlier scholarship, to repeat the themes and ostensible statements of certain Romantic texts without submitting them to analytical interpretation or rhetorical analysis. One might see such writing as necessarily falling short of genuine historiography or criticism.

The essays assembled in this volume respond to one or both of these diagnoses of Romanticism scholarship, and exemplify two major strategies for moving beyond the impasse. One is to place literary works in a historical context made up of social and political events and discourses (not, as in an earlier history of ideas, in the context of philosophical or other literary works), in the interest of recovering their historical particularity through the details of their reception. (This New Historicist strategy informs the work of Neil Hertz and Mary Jacobus as well as that of Swann, Levinson and Christensen.) The other is to focus on the text's linguistic mode of production and examine its 'inner' workings: the relationships among its themes and statements and its rhetorical structures. Sometimes called 'rhetorical reading', this approach is closely connected with deconstruction – briefly defined as the exploration of how the hierarchical binary oppositions that structure Western thought are undermined, exposed as constructions, by their functioning in the texts that affirm and depend on them.[9] Rhetorical reading is practised in a variety of ways here in the essays by Paul de Man, Cathy Caruth, Neil Hertz and Carol Jacobs. Close attention to the rhetorical modes of texts serves, along with historicizing tactics, to make visible the outlines of Romantic texts' figurations of gender and sexuality in the essays by Mary Jacobus, Margaret Homans, Jerome Christensen and Karen Swann.

Setting an agenda: Romanticism, art and self-consciousness

The opening essay in this volume, Geoffrey Hartman's 'Romanticism and Anti-Self-Consciousness', raises a question that decisively formulates a crucial phase in the study of Romanticism and evokes the wide range of conflicting interpretations attached to a single statement or theme.

> 'The notion of man (as of history) seems to presuppose that of self-consciousness, and art is not the only major reaction to it. . . . The question, therefore, is why the Romantic reaction to the problem of self-consciousness should be in the form of an aggrandizement of art, and why the entire issue should now achieve an urgency and explicitness previously lacking.
>
> (pp. 48-9)*

The question contains a thesis which Hartman's distinguished work on Wordsworth's poetry has made a dominant modern interpretation of Romantic writing, that Romanticism is a response to the problem of self-consciousness. And it shares with countervailing interpretations a question about the Romantics' 'aggrandizement of art'. In the range of descriptions and explanations of this 'aggrandizement' one sees the disparity among modern approaches to the Romantic period – to simplify matters considerably, between approaches by way of social history and by way of the history of thought. If one major precursor among contemporary critics is Geoffrey Hartman, the other is Raymond Williams, whose chapter on the Romantic artist in *Culture and Society 1780–1950* (1958) carefully weighs both the humane and the damaging potential of Romantic thinking on art. Williams sees Romantic thought as initially a compensatory reaction to historically new social ills of a society which 'was coming to think of man as merely a specialized instrument of production'.[10] Hartman describes art as conceived by the Romantics as a remedy for the ills of thought, a cure drawn from consciousness itself for the disintegrative effects of self-consciousness. He gives his own question (why the 'aggrandizement of art' was the Romantics' response to the problem of self-consciousness) a 'historical' answer: 'There clearly comes a time when art frees itself from its subordination to religion or religiously inspired myth and continues or even replaces them' (p. 49). In a gesture that exemplifies the continuity between Romanticism and its criticism, this statement of Hartman's invokes the history of consciousness, which is also the major Romantic idea he describes.

The interpretation of Romantic thought as the secularization of Western religious ('Judaeo-Christian') belief is monumentalized in M.H. Abrams's *Natural Supernaturalism: Tradition and Revolution in Romantic Literature* (1971). Hartman puts less store in that thesis than in a related

---

* Page references in parentheses in the Introduction are cross-references to pages in this volume.

notion: 'the idea of a return, via knowledge, to naïvete', which he with precision terms a 'commonplace' among the German Romantics. (One can then ask: How does it function in their texts? As a fundamental ideal? Or as a tag, or a skeleton, in a work that explores other patterns?) Or rather, Hartman cares for its various modes of statement and performance in poetry, especially Wordsworth's. In beginning an essay with John Stuart Mill's testimony to the curative effect of Wordsworth's poetry and its having led him to a view of life like the 'anti-self-consciousness theory' of Thomas Carlyle, Hartman makes a link between Victorian and modern ways of seeing Wordsworth. Read as a moralist by the Victorians, in the twentieth century he came to be read in a perspective influenced by phenomenological and existential modes of thought, as a poet of the self-reflective consciousness.[11] Hartman's *Wordsworth's Poetry 1787–1814* (1964) was essential in establishing this change of focus. The change takes hold with efforts by W.K. Wimsatt, Earl Wasserman, and other 'New Critics' to show how Romantic poetry managed in practice that bridging of the gap between subject and object which habitually has been identified as Romanticism's principal concern. In 'The Structure of Romantic Nature Imagery' (1949), a remarkable early 'close reading' of sonnets by Coleridge and William Lisle Bowles, Wimsatt contrasts the intense metaphorical writing of the major Romantic poets with earlier eighteenth-century nature poetry. A similar attention to the details of poetic texts distinguishes Earl Wasserman's studies of Romantic epistemology, in books on Keats and Shelley and essays on other Romantic and neoclassical poets which take on the uncomfortable and Romantic commitment to considering poetry as philosophy (further considered below).

Hartman recasts what Wasserman called the 'problem of the transaction between the perceiving mind and the perceived world'[12] as an itinerary or journey of the individual mind, described and carried out in *The Prelude*. *Wordsworth's Poetry 1787–1814* argues that Wordsworth's fundamental experience is a passage from sense-experience, to an obliterating self-consciousness which Hartman calls 'apocalypse' – a confrontation with the productive power of his own imagination – to a renewed awareness of nature accompanied by the sense that it is nature that leads him beyond nature. Such is the trajectory that 'Romanticism and Anti-Self-Consciousness' sums up as 'Nature, Self-Consciousness, and Imagination – the last term . . . involving a kind of return to the first' (p. 50). Hartman's writing derives its authority both from the way it responds to the nuances of poetic language and the way it draws upon philosophical topoi, upon scenarios from Kant and Hegel strongly intuited, if rarely cited, in his interpretations. His story of the mind's movement to and beyond self-consciousness draws upon Wordsworth's narrative ordering in *The Prelude* of 1805 and 1850 of the Crossing of the

Alps in Book VI. Wordsworth's Crossing of the Alps is regularly invoked
along with Kant on the mathematical sublime as one of the principal
accounts of the sublime experience – a major topic in investigations of
Romantic literature. (Its importance in modern criticism could be dated
from A.C. Bradley's Oxford lectures of 1903 and 1905 drawing attention
to how Wordsworth's poetry infuses ordinary experience with the feeling
of the sublime or the uncanny.)

Hartman's analysis of the Crossing of the Alps takes Wordsworth's
interrupted 'crossing' as an experience but designates its structure in
terms that suggest it is a trope. As an experience it is located not only
in the Alps but also, crucially, at the time of the poem's composition (it
was then that the awful power of Imagination 'rose athwart' him).
Exemplifying, in Hartman's interpretation, the trajectory of consciousness
led by nature beyond nature, the 'crossing' is also a topos – the 'negative
way' of nature, nature itself leading beyond nature: '*Via Naturaliter
Negativa*', the title of Hartman's 'synopsis' of *Wordsworth's Poetry* – or a
trope.[13] How are we to read that journey, with its decisive moment of
disorientation?

> Imagination! lifting up itself
> Before the eye and progress of my Song
> Like an unfathered vapour; here that Power,
> In all the might of its endowments, came
> Athwart me; I was lost as in a cloud,
> Halted without an effort to break through.
> And now recovering, to my Soul I say
> I recognize thy glory; in such strength
> Of usurpation, in such visitings
> Of awful promise, when the light of sense
> Goes out in flashes that have shewn to us
> The invisible world, doth Greatness make abode,
> There harbours, whether we be young or old.
> Our destiny, our nature, and our home
> Is with infinitude . . .

> > > (*Prelude* (1805), Book VI, 525–40)

Hartman's double gesture raises the question incisively posed by Neil
Hertz in 'The Notion of Blockage in the Literature of the Sublime',
about that scene of 'the mind blocked in confrontation with an . . .
indeterminate play between two elements . . . that themselves resist
integration', like the arbitrary productive power of the 'Imagination' and
a thwarted natural perception (Wordsworth), or the 'reason's' 'concept of
freedom' and a baffled exercise of the faculty of 'understanding' (Kant).[14]
Is it 'simply a *fact* about the experience of the sublime', or rather a

narrative figure or metaphor, which helps with the task of *representing* the difficulty of integrating an array of disparate elements, by portraying it as a moment of conflict and confrontation? In transposing the rhetorical concept of difficulty into 'the *experiential* concept of blockage', Neil Hertz suggests, the sublime scenario functions to consolidate a notion of the self. And it is the Romantic elaboration of notions of the self – both presuming and putting into question the category of 'experience' – that has occupied the attention of readers from the early nineteenth century on.

The connection between English Romantic poetry and German Idealist philosophy, established through the mediation of Coleridge, has long been a truism of literary scholarship. Some of Wordsworth's philosophical ideas can be traced to Coleridge's reading of Kant and Schelling.[15] Recent criticism establishes another kind of parallel between Wordsworth's and Kant's texts: narcissism, a permanent motive accompanying what Hertz sees as a historical process of consolidating the idea of the 'self'. It can be argued that the effect and function of the topos of the sublime or the 'analogy' between 'the mind' and 'nature' is to establish a coherent image of the mind or the self, one that can be invested in, loved. Analysis of how texts' rhetorical strategies endanger or sustain the narcissistic structure of the self is an important approach in recent criticism. It can be combined with analysis of the social factors in the anxiety or instability the work would be trying to allay, factors such as competing for readership with Gothic fiction and popular romances, or sharing some of the conditions of the urban underclass – prostitutes – or coexisting with a not yet abolished slave trade unthinkable in the terms of an Enlightened humanism. (These are key factors seen by Karen Swann and Mary Jacobus in discussions of Coleridge, De Quincey and Wordsworth in their essays in this volume.) But studies of works' 'narcissism' focus more centrally on threats to the self and the possibility of self-representation posed by the process of representation itself, by the predicament of inhabiting language that may perform actions but does not coincide with things, that consists in conventional signs and holds potential unpredictable meanings. That such threats or anxieties operate in philosophical writing, as well as in autobiographical and fictional works, has been argued in recent critical writing that participates in the kind of work called deconstruction.

Reading Romanticism with Kant, Hegel and Freud

The parallel between Wordsworth's and Kant's postulations of an analogy between the mind and nature is examined in the way I have just described by Mary Jacobus in an outstanding recent interpretation of the final episode of *The Prelude* ('Romantic Analogy, or What the Moon Saw').[16] Wordsworth's ascent of Mount Snowdon, described near the end of *The Prelude*, is followed by his 'meditation' on the scene, which is 'the perfect image of a mighty mind', and of 'a genuine counterpart / And brother of the glorious faculty / Which higher minds bear with them as their own' (*Prelude*, XIII, 69, 88–90):

> above all,
> One function of such mind had Nature there
> Exhibited by putting forth, and that
> With circumstance most awful and sublime:
> That domination which she oftentimes
> Exerts upon the outward face of things,
>
> (*Prelude*, XIII, 73–8)

Reading this passage alongside a passage from the section on genius in Kant's *Third Critique*, which describes imagination as the agent of a process in which 'material can be borrowed by us from nature . . . but worked up by us into something else – namely, what surpasses nature',[17] Jacobus observes that in Kant's text as well as Wordsworth's, the idea of nature offering an analogy or 'counterpart' to the creative mind tends to accompany and so become a sign or figure of the contrary: of 'the workings of an imagination paradoxically driven to exceed the confines of the nature on which it depends'.[18] Jacobus interprets the movement of the Snowdon passage in the same way Hartman does ('Wordsworth sees Imagination by its own light and calls that light Nature's'), but her argument shows all that is gained from deliberate attention to the tropes and figures brought into play in the poem and in the philosophical text. One trope Jacobus sets out to read is Wordsworth's habitual allusion to Nature as 'she'. Nature's role (in *Prelude*, XIII, 73–83) sounds like that of the pre-Oedipal phase called 'primary narcissism', the first differentiation from the mother. Jacobus argues, 'Wordsworth's own interpretation of the Snowdon vision makes nature the mother of imagination; because it has a life of its own, it provides the ground for claiming that the imagination too is autonomous, even though they both obey the same laws.'[19] A certain specific feminine personification is one of *The Prelude*'s resources in establishing an autonomous but nature-like imagination, one might generalize. (And certainly this blessed babe with a mother who has a life of her own is for many contemporary readers easier to love than Irving Babbitt's 'imagination at once disciplined and supreme'.) Jacobus argues that Wordsworth's conclusion of his poem with the representation of Mount Snowdon as 'the image of a mighty mind', and not just the 'image', or metaphor, but 'a genuine counterpart / And brother of the glorious faculty which higher minds bear with them as their own' (*Prelude*, XIII, 86–90) – an actually existing analogy, in nature, for the creative power of Imagination – shares its intent and its strategy with Kant's insistence on an *analogy* enabling a passage from the realm of the sensible to the realm of the supersensible (in Kant's terms, from understanding to reason or the concept of freedom). Wordsworth's analogies are an attempt (like Kant's) to ensure the unity of the mind. What is involved in such analogies is not Romantic poetry's 'natural supernaturalism', not the continuation in secular form of belief in a divine power (God or Nature), but 'the egotistical Sublime in action':[20] the enormously powerful stabilizing of identity brought about by successfully representing the mind as an aesthetic object. As Jacobus concludes, Wordsworth's

> insistence that nature has offered an analogy for the workings of the imagination . . . tends, not so much to endow nature with the power of supernature, as to elevate the mind itself (his mind) as the proper object of aesthetic contemplation. . . . the aestheticized imagination involves the restitution of an imaginary wholeness.[21]

Unlike Hartman (and like Raymond Williams),[22] Jacobus takes up a critical distance from Wordsworth's 'singling out of the individual mind as the unique ground of understanding' and firmly establishes that distance through criticism of the intentional structure of the poem's tropes.

Psychoanalysis has been important in modern criticism of Romantic literature in a variety of forms. Studies such as Richard Onorato's *The Character of the Poet: Wordsworth in 'The Prelude'* (1971) and Thomas McFarland's 'Coleridge's Anxiety' in *Romanticism and the Forms of Ruin* (1981) offer psychoanalytic interpretations of authors. Another kind of study traces syndromes and structures identified by Freud or Lacan (such as the Oedipus complex or the 'mirror stage') in order to determine their functions in the poem.[23] Psychoanalytic and Romantic texts have also been read alongside one another, with attention to their common concerns and patterns, as in Caruth's essay here on 'narrative origins' in Freud and Wordsworth. Can Romantic literature best be understood (and does it 'understand' itself) in psychological or in rhetorical terms? Does Romantic writing respond primarily to sexual, or social, or epistemological anxieties, and how are these related to one another in a particular poem or critical work? These have been important questions for criticism in the 1970s and 1980s. Relating psychological and rhetorical categories has been a fruitful line of approach to Romanticism, particularly to the literature of the sublime, for instance in Neil Hertz's *The End of the Line: Essays on Psychoanalysis and the Sublime* (1985), Thomas

Weiskel's *The Romantic Sublime: The Structure and Psychology of Transcendence* (1976), and Steven Knapp's *Personification and the Sublime: Milton to Coleridge* (1985).

Both psychoanalysis and feminism are enabling for Jacobus's reading of Wordsworth and Kant, as is true of much recent criticism informed by post-structuralism. Feminist readings have looked critically at the Oedipal character of Romantic desire, the focus of most early psychoanalytic criticism. The fundamental role of the Oedipus complex in Romantic literature, in the sense of a contest of each 'strong' poet with an earlier great poet whom he must displace, was argued influentially by Harold Bloom, in *The Anxiety of Influence* (1973) and *Poetry and Repression* (1976). Bloom's work is also important for bringing together psychological and rhetorical descriptions of Romantic poems, in fact recasting his psychology of Romantic poetry as a rhetoric.[24] In the 1980s, critics have turned to examine Romantic literature in the light of the notion of narcissism and the pre-Oedipal phase.[25]

Hegel has been as important in the study of Romanticism as Kant or Freud. Themes and structures from Hegel's *Phenomenology* and *Aesthetics* – the 'sublation' or '*Aufhebung*' whereby something is 'lifted up', at once cancelled and preserved; the pattern of thesis, antithesis and synthesis (as in the triadic scheme Hartman finds in the Romantics: 'Nature, Self-Consciousness, Imagination'); and symbol, as the character of the authentic work of art – have been central in critical writing on Romanticism, perhaps all the more because they have often been unconscious. Recent re-examination of Hegel and of Hegelian models in Romantic writing has reached different conclusions than an earlier, phenomenological criticism (such as Hartman's), earlier comparisons between the Romantics' narrative and Hegel's (such as Abrams's), and Marxist and historicist interpretations implicitly drawing on Hegel. The more recent readings show (in Hegel's own text as well as in others including Freud's and Wordsworth's that present a story comparable with the *Phenomenology*'s) that an indeterminate and irreducible negativity attaches to the process of self-consciousness and the production of identities, rather than the '*determinate* negation' enabling a crossing from one stage or level to another.[26]

Interpreting the aggrandizement of art and the imagination

Some of the most interesting recent criticism of Romantic writing (the work, for instance, of Jerome Christensen, Reeve Parker, and Karen Swann) combines interpretation of the text through close reading of its rhetorical structures with the New Historicist gesture of attention to the text's social functions or reception. There is a real opposition,

nonetheless, between two main competing accounts of the Romantics'
'aggrandizement of art' or poetry.

One of these is given its strongest formulation in the claim that the
institution of literature as we inherit it from Romanticism 'is thoroughly
determined as a response to a certain philosophical "crisis": that 'Kant
opens up the possibility of Romanticism.'[27] This is a historical argument,
concerning the German Romantics at Jena, the so-called 'Frühromantiker'
or 'theoretical Romantics,' and the texts contained in the *Athenaeum*, a
journal which existed for six issues between 1798 and 1800. A.O.
Lovejoy's observation in 1924 of a contrast between the 'anti-naturalism'
of the German Romantics and the 'naturalism' of the English has been
succeeded by readings suggesting the similarity of their concerns,
invoking various reasons why this might be so (similar social crises? the
mediation of Coleridge? both literatures undergoing and making readable
certain tensions inherent in 'literature' as such?).[28] Of the early
Romanticism at Jena, at any rate, it can be argued that the extraordinary
importance Romanticism ascribes to poetry and to the faculty capable of
presenting 'aesthetic ideas', the imagination, is an effect of the disunity
of the subject (the 'I') uncovered in Kant's Critiques.[29] The danger to a
unified subject is time. Kant's *First Critique* – though it finds 'schemata'
and analogies for the ideas of reason, and thus some link between the
sensible and the intelligible or the supersensible – uncovers a division
between two forms *within* the 'sensible' or intuitive itself, time and space.
'The form of time, which is the 'form of the internal sense, permits no
substantial presentation'.[30] The result is that there is no *intuitus originarius*,
no 'original intuition' of the phenomenal world. Moreover, the subject is
unpresentable to itself. All that remains of the subject is an 'empty form'
that 'accompanies my representations'. The emergence of this
problematic of the subject is the principal determinant of the Romantic
idea of art, according to the most incisive account of Romanticism's
historical connection with the 'Kant-Crisis', Jean-Luc Nancy and Philippe
Lacoue-Labarthe's 1978 book *The Literary Absolute*:

> One must set out from this problematic of the subject . . . in order to
> understand what romanticism will receive, not as a bequest but as its
> 'own' most difficult and perhaps insoluble question. From the moment
> the subject is emptied of all substance, the pure form it assumes is
> reduced to nothing more than a *function* of unity or synthesis.
> Transcendental imagination, *Einbildungskraft*, is the function that must
> form (*bilden*) this unity, and that must form it as a *Bild*, as a
> representation or picture . . .[31]

Hartman's acknowledgment that the transition to imagination is 'as
problematic a crossing as that from death to second life . . .' (p. 50) is

resumed here in Lacoue-Labarthe's and Nancy's emphasis that the transcendental imagination's action is for the Romantics a 'question,' not an assured possibility.

Such an emphasis, on Romantic texts 'questioning' or undercutting the unifying action to which they aspire, characterizes an important approach in recent criticism: rhetorical readings that trace the texts' de-construction or unravelling of their (or our) ostensible values or assertions. Inaugurated by Paul de Man, arguably, in the lecture contained in this volume, such rhetorical readings are exemplified here in the essays by Carol Jacobs and Cathy Caruth. The Romantic texts 'themselves' are seen to disclose the conflicting constituents of their principal themes and categories (the self, nature, man, history, knowledge, imagination). Rhetorical readings treat poetry as philosophy; or is it that they treat philosophy as poetry? (Discussing analogy in *The Prelude* and the *Critique of Judgement*, Mary Jacobus reads Kant's, as well as Wordsworth's, tropes.) They implicitly take up a major issue that emerged together with Romantic literature (which marked a crucial moment in the history of 'literature' as such): that of the relations between literature and philosophy. In *The Literary Absolute* Lacoue-Labarthe and Nancy examine the Jena Romantics' insistence that philosophy or theory must *be* literature (as for instance in Friedrich Schlegel's dictum that 'The theory of the novel must be a novel'), and that literature *include* criticism, that the work contain its criticism within itself as its own vital supplement. Beyond specific problems in the philosophical tradition, this insistence responds to these writers' acute awareness of the rhetorical level of language, of what a text says by what it does, or by its form. The insistence on consistency between statement and performance, or the aspiration to systematize their relationship, is the other side of an exacerbated sense of their disjunction.

What is the significance of rhetorical readings that suggest that this very insight, for example, is implicit or explicit in a given literary work? Tracing the way a text constructs its meanings generates knowledge about those meanings on the basis of the text 'itself' – knowledge about the self, man, etc., in the form of knowledge about the forms of discourse that produce the concepts of 'self', 'man', etc. Even the contradictions or incoherencies such a reading may discover, or the omissions to which it may point (for instance the failure to refer to historical events), can be seen as producing meaning and knowledge at a higher level. How to describe the grounds and the status of such knowledge, how to locate its origin – in the primary text, in the criticism it generates, or in the historical and critical distance the interpretation establishes, by its different rhetorical position or by its command of history – is one of the fundamental issues under dispute in debates about critical approaches to Romanticism. An important topic for both post-structuralist criticism and the New Historicism is the risks and values of criticism that draws primarily on facts and ideas it locates outside the text, in a historical reality that can be known independently. At the same time, unavoidable difficulties attend upon textual interpretation. Rhetorical reading and post-structuralist theory that works through textual interpretation run the same risk as Romantic literature, and of literature as such as it has been instituted since the Romantic period: that of claiming that a text *can* control and know its own structures, can (implicitly) describe them fully and thereby programme their performance. Like *literature*, textual interpretation runs the danger of 'Romantic ideology': the claim of achieving absolute knowledge by means of form (or of the structures of language).[32] The extent to which a given Romantic work underwrites and authorizes such an aim or undercuts or qualifies it is a matter for judgment in every reading. Contemporary criticism includes a wide variety of formulations about the extent to which the literary work provides or anticipates the critical understanding brought to it by the reader.[33]

The other major account of the Romantics' elevation of art attributes it to changes in society and their impact on writers. As Williams writes: 'In England, these ideas that we call romantic have to be understood in terms of the problems in experience with which they were advanced to deal.'[34] One could say that the difference between the previous explanation and this one is that the former seeks to include the early Romantics' 'experience' of reading Kant, but the tension between the two accounts is more considerable. How does drastic (or gradual) historical change enter 'experience', and what is the relation of writers' experience to their works? How exactly does literature 'mediate' historical change? These questions (reopened through challenges to and reinterpretations of their Marxist answers) have preoccupied much significant critical writing on the Romantic period, including some New Historicist work, such as Alan Liu's *Wordsworth: The Sense of History* (1989). Rhetorical reading questions whether the production or workings of texts, or, indeed, reading itself, can be conceptualized adequately in terms of 'experience', and sometimes explicitly examines the history and stakes of 'experience' as a concept, which takes on some of its principal features, in fact, from British empiricism before and during the Romantic period. (The issue is addressed in this volume particularly in the essays by Neil Hertz and Cathy Caruth.)

Raymond Williams's chapter 'The Romantic Artist' in *Culture and Society 1780–1950* defines the most important Romantic ideas about art as 'a theory of the "superior reality" of art, as the seat of imaginative truth', and the emphasis on 'the independent creative writer, the autonomous genius'.[35] Like Marilyn Butler, he sees their causes as 'the new conditions, an art marketed rather than an art commissioned'; a newly wary and defensive attitude toward the 'public'; and art's status in industrial capitalism – the fact 'that the production of art was coming to be regarded as one of a number of specialized kinds of production, subject to many of the same conditions as general production'.[36] Williams sees Romantic ideas about art originating as defensive constructions in response to social circumstances – that is, as 'ideological' in the limited and negative sense of the word. At the same time he gives the Romantic writers generous credit for both the courage and the ultimate pertinence of their 'social criticism'. But the social-historical account that he initiated tends also to describe the Romantic 'aggrandizement of art' in a different way, as the *self*-aggrandizement of the Romantic artist (not the same thing as the Romantic text's, e.g. *The Prelude*'s, aggrandizement of the self).[37] Williams suggests, for instance, that Shelley's 'Defence of Poetry' culminates in deeming poets 'the unacknowledged legislators of mankind,' as a defensive reaction against their actual social and political isolation.[38]

A certain identification of literature with philosophy appears in Romanticism not only in the emergence of German Romanticism in response to Kant, and in the Jena Romantics' conception of literature as containing its own criticism. It has been for Romantics and their readers a way of describing a kind of truth value or truth effect of poetry. 'Aristotle, I have been told, has said, that Poetry is the most philosophic of all writing; it is so: its object is truth, not individual and local, but general and operative; not standing upon external testimony, but carried alive into the heart by passion; truth which is its own testimony', begins an eloquent passage in the Preface to *Lyrical Ballads* (1850).[39] It is cited by Williams as 'one of the principal sources of the idea of Culture' examined and criticized in *Culture and Society 1787–1950*: it was on the basis of the notion that the artist was (as Wordsworth had put it) 'an upholder and preserver, carrying everywhere with him relationship and love', that the unfortunate 'association of the idea of the general perfection of humanity with the practice and study of the arts was to be made', in a regrettably narrow localization of the Romantics' 'wider and more substantial acount of human motive and energy than was contained in the philosophy of industrialism.'[40] Williams sees Romantic works' identification of literature with philosophy as a source and a feature of the 'aggrandizement of art'. Their identification can also be viewed differently, however: not as a defensive or reassuring but rather as a disturbing factor. John Stuart Mill's *Autobiography* notwithstanding, such has been also the effect of Wordsworth's poetry, which has offered readers not only the experience of relief from 'the ravage of self-consciousness' (Hartman, p. 44) but the difficulty of deciding whether it was to be taken as 'philosophy' or 'poetry.' In 'Wordsworth and the Victorians,' Paul de Man notes

the somewhat irrelevant but insistent question which has shaped
Wordsworth criticism for generations: is he a poet or philosopher – or,
somewhat less naively put, what is it in his work that forces upon us,
for reasons that philosophy itself may not be able to master, this
question of the compatibility of philosophy and poetry? Common
sense tells us that poetry and philosophy are modes of discourse that
should be kept distinct: to couple such power of seduction with such
authority is to tempt fate itself. Hence the urge to protect, as the most
pressing of moral imperatives, this borderline between both modes of
discourse.[41]

De Man suggests that Wordsworth's writing disturbingly intimates the
interdependency of qualities associated with philosophy and with
literature. 'It is as if his language came from a region in which the most
carefully drawn distinctions between analytic rigor and poetic persuasion
are no longer preserved, at no small risk to either.'[42] Both are revealed to
depend upon tropes such as analogy and upon prosopopoeia, the 'giving
a face' to an absent or deceased entity: most fundamentally, a giving of
'voice' to the indeterminably significant configurations of a text.

The 'urge to protect the borderline' between literature and philosophy
can be seen in their present separation as professional practices and as
subjects of study. A Romantic definition and practice of literature –
philosophy and/as poetry – acquires a defensive, inverted
institutionalization in our own period: the definition of literature as what
is *external to* philosophy and of philosophy as what is *not merely*
literature. Despite the incursions in the 1950s through the 1980s of
rhetorical reading, deconstruction and 'theory' (the critical reading of an
undiscriminated variety of 'texts'), that institutionalization of literature
still dominates study in the humanities. Writing or readings that efface
the borderline between literature and philosophy, to the extent that they
work against these institutional structures and definitions, work against
the 'aggrandizement of art' that Williams deplores.

There is some similarity, then, between the critical aims or targets of
the very different critical approaches exemplified in de Man's *The
Rhetoric of Romanticism* and Williams's *Culture and Society 1787–1950*,
linked with virtually opposite interpretations of the identification in
Wordsworth of literature and philosophy. The association that Williams
refers to as 'one of the principal sources of the idea of Culture', the
association of the general perfection of humanity with the practice and
study of the arts',[43] is an element of what Paul de Man terms 'the
aesthetic ideology,' which he traces to the typical and widely received
misreading of Kant exemplified in Schiller's *Letters on the Aesthetic
Education of Mankind*.[44]

Rhetorical reading

What we have seen is the possible convergence between two principal contemporary approaches to the problem of attaining historical distance from Romanticism. A historicist approach informed by Marxism, though not always Marxist, essentially proceeds by *recognizing* received ideas present in Romantic texts and postulating their social functions. Another approach – rhetorical reading – analyses the text's workings to show the actual contents and status of received ideas – an 'actual contents' defined as their linguistic make-up, the movements of their thought and language, rather than the social and economic conditions they are not, in this line of approach, presumed to reflect or signify. Since it is a major form of post-structuralist thought and has had decisive consequences for the interpretation and evaluation of Romanticism, we would do well to look at some of the factors that impel rhetorical reading. They are shown particularly clearly in the essay here by de Man, 'Time and History in Wordsworth', actually a lecture first delivered in 1967 and then again in 1971 or 1972, when de Man recontextualized the readings of Wordsworth within the question of what it means to read, and recast the essay's terminology of authentic temporality and finitude in explicitly rhetorical terms.[45] (The revisions and additions to the essay are included in five footnotes.)

De Man's lecture consists mainly in a reading of two Wordsworth poems, the lines on the Boy of Winander (*Prelude* (1805), V, 389–423) and a late sonnet on the River Duddon. The Winander Boy poem allows a peculiarly vivid illustration of the fact that language does not directly reflect experience, for although it refers to the boy's death, the earliest version of the poem was written in the first person. It concerns an event which is not an 'experience': one's own death. Focusing on the autobiographical aspect of the poem is a way for de Man to argue that Wordsworth's language is not and cannot be representational, a reflection or representation of a world that exists prior to it. Rather, language is what makes possible some kind of reflection upon a non-empirical event, upon what cannot be an experience, yet defines the human condition. It is a device for repeating what is necessarily *missed*; trying to 'anticipate', by treating as *past*, what cannot be present to the self. One can only recount the event of one's own death by means of 'a linguistic sleight-of-hand', as de Man observes in note 9, such as the poem's replacement of a first-person subject by a third-person subject and its substitution of a recollection for an anticipation, of a retrospective structure for a proleptic one.

De Man's reading of the poem begins by observing that its theme is 'a central Wordsworthian experience' – the suspension of the analogy or correspondence 'between ourselves and nature'. ('It chanced / That

pauses of deep silence mock'd his skill': the 'mimic hootings' between
the boy and the owls are interrupted.) When 'in the second part of the
poem we are told, without any embellishment or preparation, that the
boy died, we . . . understand that the moment of silence, when the
analogical stability of a world in which mind and nature reflect each
other was shattered, was in fact a prefiguration of his death' (p. 61). The
death that is prefigured, the boy's death, is a figure for Wordsworth's
death – for the death of the 'I' of whom, as Wordsworth initially wrote,
'pauses of deep silence mock'd *my* skill'. In the course of de Man's
reading, that 'death' comes to be understood as a figure, or name, for the
closing off of the possibility of saying 'I': for the impossibility of claiming
as an intention or experience of a self, a recourse to figurative language
which is inevitable. It is inevitable given the necessity of speaking about
death, given the intention 'to reflect on an event that is, in fact,
unimaginable. For this is the real terror of death, that it lies truly beyond
the reach of reflection' (p. 63). Reflection upon it can take place only
through the mechanical devices of metaphor and metalepsis that de
Man's second version of his lecture emphasizes. In the course of defining
more precisely the *way* the poem achieves its meaning – the rhetorical
figures through which it succeeds in 'nam[ing] the moment of death in a
reflective mood' (p. 63) – de Man's revisions redefine the poem's
meaning. The 'metalepsis' or reversal of past and present by which the
past death of the boy is a figure for the future death of Wordsworth 'is in
fact metalepsis' in another sense, 'a leap outside thematic reality into the
rhetorical fiction of the sign. This leap cannot be represented, nor can it
be reflected upon from within the inwardness of a subject.' It can only be
written, or read.

> The reassurance expressed in the poem . . . is based on the rhetorical
> and not on thematic resources of language. It has no value as truth,
> only as figure. The poem does not reflect on death but on the rhetorical
> power of language that can make it seem as if we could anticipate the
> unimaginable.
>
> [Note 9]

As de Man will write in a later essay on Wordsworth's *Essays upon
Epitaphs*, 'Death is a displaced name for a linguistic predicament.'[46]

In de Man's earlier essay with its two versions, the process of arriving
at such a conclusion is made legible in a rather immediate way. De Man
finds himself distinguishing between 'thematic' and 'rhetorical'
structures in the poem, between 'themes' and 'figures,' and between 'a
thematic concept' and 'a rhetorical fiction'. The 'thematic concept' of the
Winander Boy's death (which as another's, not my, death is an empirical
event which can be anticipated and stated) is in fact a 'rhetorical fiction'

for the death of the one who says 'I', a substitute for the impossible grammatical construction 'I dies'. In the course of his reading (including the later revisions), de Man is led to describe the poem in two inverse ways: first, as a movement in which the theme or 'experience' of the suspension of the mirroring relationship between ourselves and nature is revealed to figure or 'prefigure' death, and then as an operation in which the theme of death is revealed as a figure for a linguistic operation – the 'leap' into rhetorical figuration, out of mimetic language basing itself on a mirroring of nature; a 'leap' de Man conceives no longer as an 'experience' (a 'central Wordsworthian experience') but as the constitutive limit of experience, memory or reflection. In these two descriptions, the 'theme' turns out to be a figure, and 'figure' turns out to be the theme. Or as de Man writes, 'the thematic turns rhetorical and the rhetorical turns thematic, while revealing that their apparent complicity is in fact *hiding* rather than revealing meaning' (note 9). The poem seems to offer reassurance of a continuity beyond death; in fact it offers reflection upon the operations of language that establish that continuity as merely fictional. Theme and figure are in tension, they conflict rather than mutually reinforce one another; the poem is a construct in which 'what seems to be a theme, a statement, a truth-referent, has substituted itself for a figure' (note 4). De Man's rhetorical reading differs crucially in this respect from 'close readings,' familiar since the New Critics, tracing the harmonious interplay of form and content. Instead of furthering the expression of meaning, the interplay of rhetorical and thematic structures checks or thwarts it – suspends it in the 'thematization' of this very interplay.

'Time and History in Wordsworth' differs decisively both from Hartman's account of Wordsworth and from historicist conceptions of Romantic poetry. De Man locates the key to an understanding of Wordsworth in the relationship of imagination not to nature, but to time (p. 68). This means that the poetic consciousness does not 'return' to nature – to correspondence with the natural world, to a language of imitation or representation – 'after' the interruption of that correspondence by the imagination's power of *positing* entities and relationships through language. The imagination is not in the service of the representation of a given world; figurative language cannot ultimately be brought home to the function of indirectly representing empirical reality. It is in these terms that one can describe de Man's differing *on the same grounds* with both Hartman and historicist critics, unlike though they seem. De Man identifies in Wordsworth a powerful resistance to the Romantic (or is it rather the post-Romantic?) ideology, a certain kind of 'aggrandizement of art': in Jerome McGann's words, the belief in 'the power of imagination to effect an unmediated (that is, an aesthetic) contact with noumenal levels of reality'; in Geoffrey Hartman's terms, the autonomous imagination's risk of 'apocalypse' or 'unmediated vision'. De Man stresses to the contrary that Wordsworth's poetry does not involve any movement toward 'unmediated contact with a divine principle'. Rather, the heightening of pitch in a passage such as the apostrophe to Imagination in the Crossing of the Alps results from 'another mediation, in which the consciousness does not relate itself any longer to nature but to a temporal entity', which 'could, with proper qualifications, be called history'. The second half of de Man's lecture is given over to explaining in what sense he means that consciousness or imagination relates itself to history – and distinguishing this statement from various apparently closely similar ones, including the ostensible theme of the second Wordsworth poem he examines in detail, one of the sonnets on the River Duddon, published in 1820.

This sonnet describes the river's progression from a natural and pastoral to an urban and historical landscape. Taking the river as an emblem for consciousness makes the sonnet, like *The Prelude*, a poem on the growth of a mind, a story about 'a consciousness that is able to contain origin and end into a single awareness'. In the river's itinerary, 'the order of nature seems to open up naturally into the order of history' – like 'Love of Nature leading to Love of Mankind', in the words of the title for Book VIII of *The Prelude*. De Man's argument that this is not the case, that the poem in fact subordinates this theme to another movement, involving discontinuities and decay or dissolution of the identity of consciousness or self, is implicitly an argument also against current critical models for which 'the order of nature seems to open up naturally into the order of history': for example, interpretations according to which Wordsworth's personal disillusionment with the French Revolution causes (and constitutes) his texts' conception of history; or the view that the Romantics' poetry falls short insofar as it fails to make the requisite progression from representation of nature and the self to representation of history and society.[47] De Man conceives Wordsworth's relation to history in another way. His imagination 'relates itself' to 'history' in the sense of 'the retrospective recording of man's failure to overcome the power of time'. It relates itself, that is, to the *recording* of a temporal predicament which consists in the necessity and the gratuitousness or groundlessness of the figures or devices of language by which the self constructs its historical continuity. Those devices have to do, as we saw de Man argue in reading the Winander Boy poem, with events, such as death, not susceptible of empirical *experience*. Such events are of the essence of 'history', in the usual sense of the word; de Man's thinking rejoins recent clinical and theoretical work on history as trauma, as traumatic changes or events accessible only to retrospective construction or repetition, not to perception.[48]

Wordsworth's text carries out the task of recording historicity of this kind, according to de Man, by means of a specific figural construction. 'History', the linear progression of causally connected events, is set up as the overarching structure or container in which take place the self's discontinuities and dissolution through *time*. The achievement of Wordsworth's poem is to make legible the inversion or reversal that this construction entails – to reveal that linear history is in fact rather the contents, or 'theme', of the non-linear discontinuous structure of time, or of history as dissolution of the self. Thus de Man comments on how the opening and middle lines of the poem (on first reading, the 'contained' within the 'container' made up by its trajectory from first lines to last), which describe the river initially 'hurled precipitous from steep to steep' and running toward a 'deep' where 'mightiest rivers into powerless sleep / Sink, and forget their nature' (ll, 1, 5–6), remain unassimilable to the continuous progress evoked by the river's itinerary from pastoral landscapes to a cultural and historical realm of 'hamlets, towers, and towns', to where it is 'to sovereign Thames allied, Spreading his bosom under Kentish downs, / With Commerce freighted or triumphant War' (ll. 10, 13–14). That progression is in fact subordinated by the poem to a different movement, 'away from nature toward pure nothingness' (l. 12) – the movement toward a 'deep' where 'mightiest rivers into powerless sleep / Sink, and forget their nature' (ll. 5–6). This is the permanent fall of the self or consciousness into the negativity of its social, historical, *linguistic* condition – entailing, as de Man writes, 'a loss of self, the loss of the *name* that designates the river and allows it to take on the dignity of an autonomous subject' (p. 67). Wordsworth's poem reflects upon this condition and upon the complex figural structure (itself a 'temporal entity') that allows it to be represented.

Progression from nature to history is associated in the poem with historical progress and historical 'triumphs' ('Commerce . . . or triumphant War'), indeed with the triumphs, as it happens, of a counter-revolutionary and imperialist Britain. A thematic reading of the sonnet would tend to interpret it as taking a positive attitude toward both these themes, thereby reflecting the conservative liberalism that can be ascribed to Wordsworth after 1803. De Man's reading implies another way of interpreting the association of these themes: as a critique of the notion of historical progress and of the very assumption of a natural progression from nature to history. Wordsworth's poem associates the domination of 'history' with historical domination. The poem positions these as narrative themes and contents of a fundamentally different order of time or history, one of radical discontinuities and a negativity in all 'identities' that is the possibility of the future or of historical change. It could be argued that in failing to read this dimension of the poem, thematic interpretations of the poem align themselves not only with the notions of progression towards history and history as progress, but with domination and the historical 'triumphs' and conservative politics that such interpretations often would explicitly deplore.

Can rhetorical reading such as de Man's, which generalizes its findings ('there are *no poems that are not*, at the limit, about this paradoxical and deceptive interplay between theme and figure', declare the notes for this lecture's second delivery), place its subject historically? Placement of a kind is implicit in 'Time and History in Wordsworth' in the terms in which de Man describes how the imagination in Wordsworth eludes the 'existential danger' of its radical autonomy – by relating itself, not once again to nature, but to history in the specific sense of 'the retrospective recording of man's failure to overcome the power of time'.[49] It is 'in connection with historical events (the French Revolution)', de Man remarks, that the apostrophe to Imagination comes to be written'. The drastic discontinuity of history is what allows the imagination to originate, as 'a sense of irreparable loss linked with the assertion of a persistent consciousness, and not as 'a memory of a unity that never existed'. This is to say that Wordsworth's imagination does not primarily identify itself with historical *action*. The 'existential danger' Wordsworth's text confronts and averts is that of embracing the power of language to posit – embracing language *as* power: the way rhetorical language functioned during the Terror – the transitory but quintessential phase of the French Revolution in which political power exactly coincided with the successful performance of a rhetorical gesture, the claim to speak with the voice of 'the people'. The historical action of revolution in this sense depended upon the power to negate an existing or 'literal' meaning in favour of an invented one. Through 'the excess of its interiority', de Man writes, such historical action fails.[50] The exertion of the imagination is defined by Wordsworth in the Preface of 1815 as the deliberate use of words in a non-literal sense.[51] An inhabiting of figurative language which is *not* the deliberate act of a subject is (on de Man's reading) the 'experience' of imagination in Wordsworth's poetry. Unlike the Terror, Wordsworth's language avoids the error of claiming total transparency (complete absence of rhetoric or figuration) while bringing into play the power of figuration.[52]

I have chosen not to include Paul de Man's best known essay on Romanticism ('The Rhetoric of Temporality'), because it has been frequently reprinted and discussed, but rather have selected what seems to me his more intriguing discussion of precisely that articulation of rhetoric and historicity with which I am concerned in these pages.

Two stories to a text

De Man's essays state directly the challenge they pose to received accounts of Romantic thought. Cathy Caruth's essay 'Past Recognition:

Narrative Origins in Wordsworth and Freud', without announcing it, carries out a similar challenge to received ideas of Romantic thought, by dint of extremely close reading of passages where those ideas would find their source. The result is a remarkable gain in precision in the paraphrase of the primary texts' statement, and the elaboration of a range of conceptual and discursive possibilities which remain those of current critical (and uncritical) thought.

Caruth's essay examines, in effect, the mediation between 'mind' and 'nature' so central to most accounts of Romanticism. Caruth reads closely a set of passages in *The Prelude* that constitute a principal statement of that theme, passages on the poetic imagination, beginning from the identification of 'our first poetic spirit', in the Blessed Babe passage in Book II. No doubt it is significant that the complexities uncovered by Caruth find their full elaboration in passages of Wordsworth's text which describe the origins of that 'spirit' in the infant's relation to the mother (as if the thinking through of that relationship put the notion of 'the marriage of the Mind and Nature' to the test). As described in *The Prelude*, that relation in fact poses in a particular way the question (posed to all writing on Romanticism) of how language reflects or relates to history: How does 'an empirically situated event', such as the physical relation of the mother and the nursing baby, relate to 'the dynamics of a self that cannot be called empirical' – such as the 'poetic spirit' or a being that inhabits not only a physical world but language? (p. 99). The 'larger' issue treated here, in other words, is the nature of the relationship between history or language as empirically situated events and history or language as conditions of a self or a structure that is not empirical. The productiveness of feminist criticism (in the sense of criticism that deliberately focuses on themes of gender and sexuality) shows up in the way that focus provides a sharp outline of a question concerning language and history.

Caruth's essay deals also with a second text on the origin of a non-empirical self in the empirically situated relationship between infant and mother: Freud's explanation, in *Three Essays on Sexuality*, of the origin of the sexual drive. Psychoanalysis belongs to this investigation as an element in current critical discourse, as part of 'our self-understanding' (p. 99). The effort to understand that understanding historically (for instance, to reflect on the provenance of a phrase such as 'the Romantic ego') involves a move which is in fact an important gesture, and topic, of many Romantic texts – 'the representation of self-knowledge as a history of its evolving discourses' (p. 99). The Blessed Babe passage in *The Prelude* defines the 'poetic spirit' as a being whose history moves from one kind of discourse to another: from 'mute dialogues with my mother's heart' to '"conjectures" which "trace" this progress' (p. 99). Caruth observes that Freud's *Three Essays* similarly defines another sort of 'self which cannot be called empirical', the being that has a sexual drive. Freud's text evokes a self that is defined by its movement between a mother tongue of unconscious thoughts and wishes and their distortion or translation in neurotic symptoms; and that shares with the psychoanalyst, whose language is not fundamentally different from his patient's, conjectures tracing the process of that translation. Like the being described by Wordsworth, the one described by Freud is a being 'whose history is the mediation of two discourses, or who defines the difference between two discourses as its own history' (p. 99).

What is gained by pinpointing as 'discourses' the elements between which a major Romantic work and a major post-Romantic mode of explanation (psychoanalysis) imagine a mediation? What is changed by the close reading that can redefine in this way the theme of 'reconciliation between the Mind and Nature' (like recent re-readings of Hegel's *Phenomenology* conceiving 'Mind' and 'Nature' – in Hegel's terms, 'consciousness' and 'natural consciousness' – as related discourses)?[53] As Caruth emphasizes, this is the gesture made by the primary texts themselves. Starting with that observation, Caruth's essay develops a complex image of Romanticism (and of the conditions of our own self-understanding), by finding that Wordsworth's and Freud's texts tell two stories about this mediation rather than one. The more familiar story (though it may not look familiar here, because of the way Caruth's careful reading maintains its complexity) is that of the loss or sacrifice of a natural relation and gain of a spiritual one. Freud and Wordsworth present this fundamental plot as a story about affect. What Caruth calls 'the affective story' is the strand in both Freud's and Wordsworth's texts which describes the affect of love linking the baby to the mother's body and the separation suffered through loss of the breast or the mother's death. In Freud's *Three Essays on Sexuality*, one account of the origin of the sexual drive explains it as a quest for the original sexual object, the mother's breast. Freud concludes, 'The finding of an object is in fact a refinding of it.'[54] The outcome of a psychoanalysis is defined similarly: as a *refinding* of the original desires behind the neurotic symptoms, their translation back into the mother tongue of unconscious desire. This is the story of 'repression'. Its central action is the *negation* of a given reality involving its transformation into another form, one accessible to interpretation as a transformation of the original.[55] In this strand of Freud's account, he tells the same story of alienation from and return (at a higher level) to nature seen by Abrams and Hartman as the principal theme and movement of Romantic thought, and (so one can argue) assumed as their underlying model by thematic or historicist readings that would translate texts back into the references or reflection of the world from which they arose. It is according to the same model that literature and cultural phenomena generally, and rhetorical and figurative language, are held to be 'symptoms' – of a disorder involving distortion of an originally or ideally direct or literal perception of reality. Such is the premise, in other words, of the kind of cultural criticism called ideology critique, as well as other prevalent ways of thinking about selves and language. Caruth's own essay (and this may be said to define deconstructions and rhetorical readings as such) differs from ideology critique mainly in so far as it does not presume the possibility of dispensing with the 'symptomatic' models and themes it identifies. Her essay shows how difficult it would be to do without any investment whatever in the idea of nature and its loss or in the rhetorical (and social and political) institutions this model sustains.

Another story, however, accompanies this one in Wordsworth's and Freud's texts, a story overlooked in phenomenological and historicist interpretations of Romanticism. This story describes the relationship with the mother (and an original 'discourse', a mother tongue) in terms of a mechanical device or 'propping' function. Wordsworth writes (disconcertingly, in a passage seemingly referring to his mother's death), 'The props of my affections were removed, / And yet the building stood . . . / All that I beheld / Was dear to me . . .' (*Prelude* (1805), II, 295–6); and a key passage in Freud's text reads (in a recent English translation) 'To begin with, sexual activity attaches itself to [props itself upon] functions serving the purpose of self-preservation and does not become independent of them until later. . . . At its origin it has as yet no sexual object.'[56] The first story – the 'affective' story – describes an empirical relationship between infant and mother, or drive and physical object (the mother's breast). The loss of the first meaningful relationship and sexual object, that of the baby 'Nursed in his Mother's arms, who . . . with his soul / Drinks in the feelings of his Mother's eye' (*Prelude* (1850), II, 235–7), issues in the gain of a second meaningful relationship, with the visible world, and a second object of love, Nature (and in Freud's story, the woman who will be the object of mature sexual love). The second story, the 'propping' story, describes the displacement of a non-sexual and in some sense non-meaningful relation – an 'instinct', or mere need – by a sexual one, a 'drive', of an altogether different order. While the object of the instinct is a physical object (milk), the object of the drive is an imaginary object – a fantasized breast. The two objects and the two kinds of relation (instinct and drive) are radically different; one does not and could not replace the other; as Caruth puts it, this is 'a displacement which is not a substitution' (p. 101). This second account of the origin of the self is recounted in *The Prelude* by means of passages that describe how a 'breast'-like entity and an arbitrary combining-together, such as the baby's 'gathering' of passion from his mother's eye, continue to support or 'prop' the poet's activity of imagination and memory. Unlike the first, the second story involves no logic of sacrifice. Instead of the *loss* of a literal object (the mother or the mother's breast) and the *gain* of a proper sexual object, a substitute for the mother (in Freud's first story, a woman, in Wordsworth's first story, Nature), this second story describes the persistence alongside each other of two completely incommensurate modes – one that does not involve meaning ('instinct' or 'need') and one that does ('drive' or 'desire'). To speak of the 'propping' of one upon the other is to designate – while leaving unresolved – the enigma of how one mode relates to the other: to affirm that it happens, without inferring that one mode or object is the goal or meaning 'of' the other.

In a carefully detailed reading, Caruth's essay follows both the 'affective' and the 'propping' story in passages of *The Prelude* that carry on with the words and themes of the Blessed Babe passage. Both are stories about the mediation between two different discourses or forms of language. The first recounts the loss of literal language and its replacement by figural language. (This replacement is represented sometimes as a loss, sometimes as a gain of meaning. The emergence of the 'poetic spirit' or of the matured baby, the 'Child [who] is the Father of the Man', for instance, is represented as the replacement of literal signs by figural meanings,[57] and as a gain. The emergence of a neurosis or of the propensity to emulate Pope or use specialized 'poetic diction' (for Wordsworth a deplorable syndrome) are represented as the replacement of literal meanings by figural signs, and as a loss of meaning).[58] The 'propping' story describes, instead, the relation between the syntactical and the semantic dimensions of language. The mediation that is at stake in the origination of a self with a history is not, finally, in this second story, the relationship between two discourses (the progression or regression between a literal and a figurative discourse), but rather the relationship between two incommensurable aspects of language. The 'propping' story describes the persistence of *material* elements of language not subsumed by the representational (or more exactly, the semantic) function of phenomenalizing a meaning, though also not separable from it. Like 'need' in relation to 'desire', 'a syntax', as Caruth writes, 'is not itself a function of meaning but rather the prop upon which meaning leans, and with which it is immediately confused' (p. 107). This kind of relationship or mediation – vital if there is to be a 'language' in any sense – is not a binary opposition, nor is it a dialectical opposition between a subject and an object or a content and a form. Alongside and in tension with the first story, the account of this relationship, a story which admits of no resolution, no transcendence of materiality, is recounted and played out in Wordsworth's and Freud's texts. They thus define in two different ways the shape or the predicament of *history* (the history of not merely empirical selves): as the distance between figuration and literalness (a distance that can be traversed, if only by radical loss such as the death of the mother or loss

of the mother tongue), and as the permanently uncertain connection
between meaning and the material conditions of meaning.

Caruth's reading leaves us with a more complex and equivocal picture
of the 'narrative origins', in the plural, of the self in Romantic thought.
Her essay poses the question of the relationship between these two
accounts of the relation between empirically situable events and entities
that are not strictly speaking empirical (such as a self that dies or that
speaks). Histories of self-knowledge like Wordsworth's and Freud's, she
suggests, are the *narrativization* of 'a less knowable relation' such as that
between syntax and semantics or what is described as the relation
between trace and symbol in Freud's trauma theory (p. 108). Thinking
along these lines appears in some of the most interesting recent writing
on Romanticism, such as Paul de Man's 'Shelley Disfigured', Neil Hertz's
'Lurid Figures', Alan Liu's *Wordsworth: The Sense of History*, and Carol
Jacobs's 'Unbinding Words' (included here).

Feminist criticisms

A valuable quality of Caruth's chosen texts – or of the reading that brings
out their exemplary as well as peculiar features – is that they reveal the
gendered dimension of those fundamental accounts of language and self-
knowledge that until recently seemed of an abstract order of thought
remote from gender and sexuality or else cast in terms of an insignificant
because 'natural' metaphor of masculine Subject and feminine Object.
Caruth's reading brings to the fore a topic investigated in important
recent feminist work on Romanticism: the association with the mother, or
with femininity, of particular aspects or dimensions of language. This is a
major subject of Margaret Homans's *Bearing the Word: Language and Female
Experience in Nineteenth-Century Women's Writing* (1986) and of Mary
Jacobus's *Romanticism, Writing, and Sexual Difference* (1989), chapters of
which are included in this volume. 'Why should language and culture
depend on the death or absence of the mother and on the quest for
substitutes for her . . .?' Homans asks, invoking Aeschylus' *Oresteia* and
Wordsworth's association of his accession to representational language
with his mother's death, and 'what does it mean to women writers that
the dominant myths of our culture . . . present language and culture as
constructed in this way?'[59] The dominant conception of language, which
assumes the speaker to be masculine, identifies women 'with the literal,
the absent referent', Homans argues.

> From the point of view of this myth, the literal both makes possible
> and endangers the figurative structures of literature. That we might
> have access to some original ground of meaning is the necessary

illusion that empowers the acts of figuration that constitute literature
. . . At the same time, literal meaning would hypothetically destroy
any text it actually entered by making superfluous those very figures
. . . This possibility is always, but never more than, a threat, since
literal meaning cannot be present in a text: it is always elsewhere. This
positioning of the literal poses special problems for women readers and
writers because literal language, together with nature and matter to
which it is epistemologically linked, is traditionally classified as
feminine. . . . A dualism of presence and absence, of subject and
object, structures everything our culture considers thinkable; yet
women cannot participate in it as subjects as easily as can men because
of the powerful, persuasive way in which the feminine is again and
again said to be on the object's side of that dyad.[60]

The identification of women with the literal has to do with the mother's
bearing of the child. Women are associated with embodiment, which is
threatening to men both because it recalls the 'powerful and forbidden'
body of the mother (the Oedipus complex) and because it evokes a
literality threatening to language (Homans, p. 163). These compelling
motives for denying or circumventing the fact of maternity, and for
getting rid of mothers, are at work in Victor Frankenstein's creation of his
monster and in the fictional male first-person narratives invented in Mary
Shelley's novel, Homans suggests. The monster (for whom the novel
elicits our sympathy and identification as well as our disgust) represents
'what it feels like to be the undesired embodiment of romantic
imaginative desire', in accord with our culture's self-contradictory
requirement that the substitute for the 'lost' (dead or obviated) mother 'at
once embody and not embody the object of desire' (pp. 171, 163). In her
explanation of why the Eve created by Victor Frankenstein is male,
Homans's essay joins other recent criticism in invoking narcissism:
Frankenstein's male creation is the form of 'the narcissism that
constitutes the safety of the ego for whose sake the mother is denied'
(pp. 168–9). Like the Poet of Shelley's 'Alastor' (which Homans rather
questionably sees as a direct reflection of Shelley's experience – as Percy
Shelley's uncritical, unselfconscious representation of the narcissism
characteristic of his own relation to Mary), Frankenstein desires his own
imaginings rather than an actual woman.

Frankenstein has proven to have suggestive and critical power equal to
that of any Romantic work. Homans's theoretical argument, that women
have been associated with the literal and that the literal has been
devalued and dreaded, enables her to give Mary Shelley full credit for
her novel's effects; Homans sees the novel as a deliberate literalization of
that myth of the literal, a scary enactment of a male myth – a 'strategy'
signalled and reinforced by Mary Shelley's deliberate presentation of her

own role as the passive (feminine) one of merely adding 'the machinery of a story' to an image that came to her in a nightmare. Unlike other post-structuralist criticism, Homans's feminist criticism imputes a unitary consciousness to the individual author and identifies a work's meaning with the intentions of its author; that the authors she chiefly treats are women makes this, arguably, a politically appropriate move (since women have been considered as passive, as non-subjects). Homans draws upon an account of women's development in American ego psychology – that of Nancy Chodorow – to suggest factors at work in how women, as opposed to men, experience entry into language. The assumptions that this 'entry' is best conceptualized as an 'experience' and that it is experienced by individual subjects who are gendered right from the start are disputed by Mary Jacobus (in the essay included here), and implicitly undercut by the readings of Caruth, de Man and Hertz. Yet Homans has produced a telling account of effects of the conception of language that Caruth's essay finds to be one of the principal 'stories' of self-knowledge in two of our culture's major texts (Wordworth's and Freud's).

The myth of language Homans describes and rebels against is the 'affective' story in Freud's and Wordsworth's texts. With one difference: as Caruth says, their texts describe as a *discourse,* not as a referent or an entity *external* to language, what Homans's 'myth' casts as the feminine pole in a dialectic of subject and object; Wordsworth's 'poetic spirit' begins in 'mute dialogues . . . with his mother's heart'. To this extent, Wordsworth's and Freud's texts are free of the illusion that Homans ascribes to all literature, that of an original meaning or referent outside language. Moreover, the mother is conceived in another way in the second story Caruth shows informing these texts: as the site of a 'propping' that sets up meaning as indistinguishable from the non-meaningful material devices it entails, rather than as a symbolic order transcending them. Yet since many, if not all, texts of our culture, including literary criticism on Romanticism, *have* told and retold story number one, not necessarily framing it as a story, the critique Homans carries out and finds performed in Mary Shelley's *Frankenstein* would seem to be vital.

Homans's work exemplifies an important variety of feminist criticism (inaugurated by Susan Gubar and Sandra Gilbert's *The Madwoman in the Attic*) which focuses on the effects of the dominant literary tradition and conception of language, and specifically, of Romantic desire and figurative language, on the experience of nineteenth-century women writers as reflected and interpreted in their writing. Other recent feminist criticism focuses on the rhetorical, psychological and ideological functions of various sorts of feminine figures in Romantic literature (mainly men's): of genres and of kinds of figurative language habitually characterized as feminine, as well as of female characters. Femininity is often used to personify not only, as Homans's analysis finds, literal language or nature, but rather the figurative elements of language – especially when they are suggested to be expendable or untrustworthy. Prosopopoeia, the gesture of giving a face or a voice (upon which all literal and conceptual language might be seen to depend, as de Man suggests), is disturbing in its implication that 'experience' has to be constructed by linguistic gestures. Prosopopoeia is therefore thematized or personified (in nineteenth-century texts) as a woman, and in one way or another 'abjected' or cast out.[61] Neil Hertz has argued that in nineteenth-century literature, setting up and casting out a female figure is part of the operation of stabilizing the difference between representor and represented, a recurrent necessity for literary or interpretive texts.[62] Such characters include the redeemed or unredeemed 'ruined' women of *The Prelude* and De Quincey's *Confessions*, and metamorphic female figures such as Keats's 'Lamia' or Coleridge's Geraldine and Christabel. They represent and help to control writers' epistemological 'anxieties' – difficulties in the construction of meaning – as well as anxieties about sexual difference, which itself involves an epistemological problem, a matter of interpretation, but one which can be represented and thereby (in some sense) resolved.[63] Epistemological and social 'anxieties' are conceived as substituting for one another in a variety of different ways in recent critical writing on the Romantics. (Evoking 'anxieties', as much recent criticism does, invokes but leaves suspended the question of the relation to 'experience' of literary texts.) Thus it can also be argued that Romantic texts' centring on prosopopoeia – its very prominence in the construction of the identity of the fictional self (Wordsworth's, for example, in his own and De Quincey's texts) – has the function of 'concealing the representational and economic structures which produce . . . a person' (Jacobus, p. 135).

Femininity can also be seen as personifying another kind of threat to the Romantic work's integrity and autonomy, that of the lower genres of popular literature, or the kinds of pleasure – in fantasy, in stereotypes, in repetition – ascribed to them. Certain genres (memorably deplored in the Preface to *Lyrical Ballads* (1800) as 'frantic novels, sickly and stupid German Tragedies, and deluges of idle and extravagant stories in verse',[64] the literature made available through lending libraries, are regularly denigrated by Romantic poets and critics as playing upon mechanical, involuntary, or stereotyped responses, and are regularly characterized as feminine.[65] What if all literary production involved the repetitive, mechanical, involuntary consumption and reproduction of signs that 'literary gentlemen' (including Coleridge and Wordsworth) like to represent as typical of degraded forms of popular literature? In this particular 'anxiety', both the crucial 'new conditions' of Romantic writing identified by new historicist Marilyn Butler – 'an art marketed rather than an art commissioned' – and the perennial conditions of the production of literature (stressed in rhetorical reading and psychoanalytic criticism) play a part. Karen Swann's essay here (in which these two critical approaches successfully coexist) argues that what is at stake in the personification of certain genres and texts as feminine, which helps distinguish them from the literary forms the Romantics were trying to establish as serious (such as lyrical ballads), is 'the identity and autonomy of the subject in relation to cultural forms' (p. 143). As Wordsworth writes in another connection (about the impact on him of first entering London, rather than of standardized popular literature), 'great God! / That aught *external* to the living mind / Should have such mighty sway' (*Prelude*, VIII, 700–2). For Wordsworth and Coleridge, the personification of popular genres as feminine serves not only to differentiate their own writing from what would come to be called mass culture, but also to enable them to borrow its themes and devices: to incorporate and represent (to accept, if also to contain) aspects of the writing process, and of pleasure in reading poetry, akin to sexual pleasure and bound up with stereotyped fantasies and repetition.[66]

Romanticism our history: the politics of style and literature's relation to historical change

Setting Romantic works in the context of contemporary exchanges about them – and examining such exchanges for what their figures of speech, and sexual as well as political allusions, may reveal about how the literary work in question accords or conflicts with established discourses and interests – has been a fruitful approach in recent criticism. Interpreting ways in which (to state this in the most general terms) a work engages with sexuality is an important move in recent interpretations of the ideology or politics of Romantic literature. Literary works participate in and disclose (rather than sublimate or rise above) the fantasies in which ideology consists, and fantasies are sexual – so might run the theoretical argument behind studies such as Swann's, Levinson's, or Christensen's, each of which touches upon the sexual fantasy mobilized by Coleridge's, Keats's or Byron's motifs and styles. Critics have dwelt upon Romantic works' relations to fantasies of wholeness – the Oedipus complex and narcissism. The late 1980s have seen critics paying attention, in tracing such fantasies, to their sexual edge, and asking what particular social and political developments they participated in. Although their conclusions sometimes converge with those of more traditional studies in which the interpretation of the texts themselves is continually orientated by reference to the known political activities or sympathies of their author, such interpretations – analyses of the ideology of style – make for a very different kind of account of the politics of Romantic texts. (Important statements in the older mode include E.P. Thompson's 'Disenchantment or Default: A Lay Sermon' (on Wordsworth and Coleridge); Carl Woodring's *Politics in English Romantic Poetry*, 1970; P.M.S. Dawson's *The Unacknowledged Legislator: Shelley and Politics*, 1980; and Nicholas Roe's *Wordsworth and Coleridge: The Radical Years*, 1988.)[67]

Marjorie Levinson's work on Wordsworth and Keats, and Jerome Christensen's work on Byron suggest the differences and convergences among recent analyses of the politics of style. Levinson's early work on Wordsworth, notably her essay on 'Lines Composed a few miles above Tintern Abbey . . .', faults the poetry for focusing on self-reflection and an artificially framed natural landscape and repressing the historical and social crises indicated by the date of the poem's composition and the presence at Tintern Abbey of homeless unemployed who camped out on the Abbey's grounds.[68] Criticism of this kind – indicting Romantic poetry for its lack of 'historical referentiality' – wants to forget about the figurative character of the language of literary texts, as well as to insist on the importance of a particular subject matter (social injustice). It can be rejected not on the ground that poetic language transcends such concerns or that Wordsworth's themes (nature, inner experience) are of greater value, but that literary language means in another way, and that engagement with historical and political realities does not necessarily take the form of literal statements about empirical facts. Levinson's own work includes reflection on this problem, and her later interpretations of Wordsworth have argued that his poetry makes visible and available for critical judgement (and so helps to make possible a passage beyond) the impasses of the anti-Jacobin attitudes that a poem such as 'The world is too much with us' participates in and rhetorically expresses.[69] Levinson's *Keats's Life of Allegory: The Origins of a Style* (1988), the first chapter of which is included here, gives sustained attention to the poetry's formal features, and, like Swann and Christensen, carries out a reading of contemporary exchanges about the poets' texts, taking the figures of speech in those exchanges as the starting point for the literary text's interpretation. Coleridge's identification with 'Christabel' (his poem as 'lovely lady') put up for sale, Byron's threatened 'despotism' over his public, Keats's 'frigging his own *Imagination*' (in Byron's words), prove in these interpretations to hold the clue to the works' poetic and ideological significance.

Levinson argues that Keats's poetry represents and exposes the contradiction in the 'style' of the middle class, its self-representation as 'an *eternally coming* class, in motion / in place forever' (p. 204). Keats's characteristic motifs and diction evoke the idea of effortful ease; his poetry thereby makes visible 'the *display* of ease, a contradiction in terms', which was a crucial source of value for the middle classes: of economic wealth, and of social prestige and predominance as a class. Hence the discomfiture and hostility which first greeted Keats's poetry. It stemmed also from Keats's 'demystification of a prestigious idea of literary production', the idea of the production of poetry through a spontaneous or casual process like feeling and thinking or like talk – the effect achieved by Wordsworth's and Byron's poetry. With a bravura not unlike Keats's own (zestfully appropriating cultural materials withheld from him), Levinson takes up Byron's notorious description of Keats's poetry as 'a sort of mental masturbation' and makes it into a telling interpretation of 'the mode of social and ideological production' of the middle class (p. 203), which Keats's poetry flagrantly rehearses. Levinson develops the idea that the concept of masturbation captures the essential elements of the fantasy evoked by Keats's style, the fantasy of a 'suspensive poise' that combines fulfillment and anticipation. 'Masturbation, that unnaturally hasty act, dreams of a "slow time": a duration which neither wastes nor realizes, at once history's negation and its fulfillment' (p. 205).

The sense of arrival at 'the end of history' or 'the end of ideology' is a major theme of nineteenth-century liberalism as well as post-war and post-Cold War liberal ideology.[70] In *Lord Byron's Strength: Romantic Writing and Commercial Society* (1992) Jerome Christensen finds the premises of liberalism strongly ironized in Byron's writing and career. Christensen's work takes a different inspiration from Marx than Levinson's assumption that classes are the principal social agents; he takes up the critique of 'political economy' (inaugurated in Marx's reply to Adam Smith).[71] Levinson sees an economically determined 'style', that of the middle classes, reflected in Keats's poetic style. Christensen sees a politically determined economics – consumerism – and a denounced, but continued, discourse and mode of power – despotism – thematized in Byron's drama *Sardanapalus*, and finds that the play both enacts and deconstructs the glorification of commodity consumption. The fantasy of every man his own despot, constantly able to gratify desires which through that very process are constantly rearoused, energizes liberal discourse, together with the notion that 'despotism' (or fascism or totalitarianism) or any illiberal form of government is an anachronism – for Benjamin Constant, in *The Spirit of Conquest and Usurpation and their Relation to European Civilization* (1813), a throwback to 'African' forms, rendered obsolete by the march of history made manifest in Napoleon's downfall. Christensen shows how a Romantic text, Byron's *Sardanapalus*, exposes the fantastic character of such assumptions. The critical potential of literature and the critical power of historicization (both Romantic ideas, as some very diverse critics would agree) are demonstrated by Christensen's work. His essay achieves its critique by demonstrating in detail how Byron's play *participates in* the historical shift it ultimately eludes: from politics to economics, from the dangerously conflictual and contingent sphere of politics to the predictability of 'political economy' (as liberal thought envisaged them), and the habit of thinking of motive in terms of 'interests'. Sardanapalus' Assyria is a 'theatre-state' (a state like Elizabethan England in which staged representations are a crucial locus of political conflict and domination), of a peculiarly ineffectual ('oriental') kind. In the play the ineffectiveness of representations in maintaining power in a state of this kind is by implication generalized, Christensen argues, to the ineffectiveness of politics as such, of sway achieved by representation and persuasion. '*Sardanapalus*' critique of theatrical representation is hand in glove with political economy's assault on the realm of the political as dangerously contingent' (p. 222). But the play *undercuts* the dominion of political economy by displaying the repetitive drive of the consumerism on which its control would have to rest. The supposedly rational rule of political economy is that of a political discourse, liberalism, which in fact rules despotically by means of consumerism (as much an ideological as an economic instance) – and consumerism functions by breaking down the very difference between production and consumption that political economy presumes. Such would be the complex historical and political significance of the moment of consumption that 'displays both expectation and fulfillment', luridly staged by Byron, alluringly evoked by Keats (p. 230). Fulfilling the fantasy of consumerism and deconstructing the fantasy of political economy, this motif is linked, Christensen suggests, to a Romantic argument for the irreducibility of the political and the impossibility of a closure of history.

Among a wide range of critical works orientated by attention to particular genres (romance, lyric, and that non-genre, autobiography), studies of Romantic drama have been especially productive of insights into Romanticism's historical context and political significance. Reeve Parker, like Jerome Christensen, interprets the political valence given by Romantic dramas to theatricality itself. For Wordsworth it is associated with the French Revolution and with a rhetoric that has the power to enslave or feminize its audience. Parker interprets Wordsworth's *The Borderers* and Coleridge's *The Fall of Robespierre* and *Osorio* in the context of events in the 1790s that Coleridge and Wordsworth followed through newspapers or on the spot, including theatrical performances in Paris, of a version of Schiller's *The Robbers*, for instance, that were part of the struggles for power also taking place on the floor of the National Convention. *The Borderers* has always been read as a disavowal of Wordsworth's own earlier Godwinism, deploring disastrous confidence in 'the immediate law / Flashed from the light of circumstances / Upon an independent intellect', the creed declared by the play's villain.[72] In Parker's reading, the play is a critique of revolutionary heroism and sentimental theatre alike, and more, of rhetorical strategies and theories that continue to authorize forms of domination.[73] The play dramatizes and criticizes the seductive power of narrative, especially narratives of sacrifice, and the delusive ideal of a speaking voice fully self-present and present to its occasion – like the 'notion of the hero as the embodiment of vocal power, of capable speech as the index of moral and political *presence*, the dream of words-worthiness' that Wordsworth had engaged in when he wished that

> The gift of tongues might fall, and men arrive
> From the four quarters of the winds to do
> For France what without help she could not do,
> A work of honour.
>
> (*Prelude* (1805), X, 117–27)[74]

A study of this kind, which reads both historical data and the literary text's rhetorical stances, interpreting the text's attitudes toward the kinds of discourse it deploys, offers a detailed and nuanced account of the work's historical situation and political meanings. Such an account not only is richer than historical categorizations like the description of Wordsworth as a 'Burkean' (when that means more or less simply, a conservative, and leaves aside the array of critical and rhetorical stances composing *Reflections on the Revolution in France*), but also occupies a different relation to the Romantic text's politics. These appear as the critical genealogy of current ideologies and the criticism of recurrent ways of exercising domination in a 'political' sphere including all social relationships. Romantic literature is thus seen to belong to a political life still in the making, rather than to a literary or political history 'Exposed, and lifeless as a written book' (*Prelude* (1805), VIII, 727).

The various ways of reading the political significance of Romantic literature that are exemplified in many of the essays collected here imply in practice various answers to a question that critics have also raised directly: what is the relation of Romantic writing to history, to the historical events with which it chronologically coincided (above all, the industrial revolution and the French Revolution)? De Man's claim to locate a crucial conception of historicity in Wordsworth's own texts is a line of approach to this question that defers or displaces the question of the poetry's mediation of particular historical events. If history is radical 'dissolution' or discontinuity, according to Wordsworth's text, history's effect in the text is no more nor less than the disjunctions and contradictions between theme and structure on which rhetorical reading focuses. To relate such disjunctions of figurative language to specific historical data is the effort of some of the most challenging recent writing on Romantic literature, New Historicist in a distinctive way, the work, for instance, of Alan Liu, in *Wordsworth: The Sense of History* (1989). Liu suggests that Wordsworth's poetry can be read as determinate negations of his experience of history. The crossing of the Alps passage, for example, could be seen as the effect of imposing on the amorphous, baffling, never directly available experience of history (or of *asking* 'What is history?' – say, in Paris in the 1790s) the triadic structure of a conversion experience, organizing a narrative of eager ascent, disappointment and ordeal, and ultimate vision of 'Characters of the great apocalypse, . . . Of first, and last and midst, and without end' (*Prelude*, VI, 570–2).[75] The crossing could be seen as being 'about' the intensified sense of history Wordsworth records having had in his Paris hotel room in late 1792 (*Prelude* (1805), X, 38–77), and as recasting in the opposite terms an experience that could be formulated, as Liu proceeds to do:

> Imagination! lifting up itself
> Before the eye and progress of my Song
> Like a *father'd* vapour; here that Power,
> In all the might of its endowments, came
> Athwart me; I was lost as in a cloud,
> Halted, without a struggle to break through.
> And now recovering, to *the World* I say
> I recognize thy glory; in such strength
> Of usurpation, in such visitings
> Of awful promise, when the light of *Mind*
> Goes out in flashes that have shewn to us
> The *visible* world, doth Greatness make abode,
> There harbours whether we be young or old.
> Our destiny, our nature, and our home
> Is with *finitude*.

The italicized words are Liu's substitutions: he has replaced with their opposites certain words in the actual text (ll. 525–39 in Book VI of the 1805 *Prelude*) – 'unfather'd', 'my soul', 'sense', 'invisible', 'infinitude' – which make transcendence the theme of the passage. The result, he observes, aside from the defects in the metre leaves the power of the passage intact. The lines come to state what the poem's displacements and denials dramatize: that 'reference to history . . . is the only "power" of Wordsworth's Imagination'.[76] Liu's gesture of rewriting the text so that it says the opposite of what it seemed to say is a striking way of confronting us with the implications of interpretively reading a literary text, or any text of which one acknowledges the figurative or rhetorical aspect. The resulting unpredictable and disorientating reconfigurations of meaning Liu, like de Man, calls the text's relation to history. Romantic poetry's figurations of transcendence and apocalypse, Liu argues, are signs precisely of the intense vulnerability to history that such figurations negate and deny, and 'such denial is also the strongest kind of engagement with history.'[77]

That revolution in the modern sense of the term was the history with which Romanticism temporally coincided lends force to the notion that history exists for Romantic texts as trauma: as 'experiences' not available for 'experience', but mediated through their repetition (not representation) in writing. No doubt exact inversions or symmetrical reversals of meaning account for few of the intricate mediations in *The Prelude* and other Romantic works, which Liu and other contemporary critics informed by new historicism, psychoanalysis and rhetorical reading trace in a variety of complex textual structures. It looks as though, in any event, exploring the Romantics' relation to history will be for some time to come a significant way of exploring what our history might be.

Notes

1. PAUL DE MAN, *The Rhetoric of Romanticism* (New York: Columbia University Press, 1984), p. 50.

2. M. H. ABRAMS, *The Mirror and the Lamp: Romantic Theory and the Critical Tradition* (New York: Oxford University Press, 1953), p. vii.

3. IRVING BABBITT, *Rousseau and Romanticism* (Boston: Houghton Mifflin, 1919), p. 354.

4. MARILYN BUTLER, *Romantics, Rebels, and Reactionaries: English Literature and its Background, 1860–1830* (Oxford: Oxford University Press, 1981), p. 9.

5. Idem.

6. PAUL DE MAN, *The Resistance to Theory* (Minneapolis: University of Minnesota Press, 1986), p. 61.

7. DE MAN, *The Rhetoric of Romanticism*, p. 239.

8. JEROME McGANN, *The Romantic Ideology* (Chicago: University of Chicago Press, 1983), pp. 32–2.

9. See JONATHAN CULLER, *On Deconstruction: Theory and Criticism After Structuralism* (London: Routledge, 1982).

10. RAYMOND WILLIAMS, *Culture and Society, 1780–1950* (London: Chatto, 1958), p. 42.

11. On the difference between Victorian and twentieth-century interpretations and

the limits upon interpretation of Wordsworth as a poet of consciousness, see PAUL DE MAN, 'Wordsworth and the Victorians', *The Rhetoric of Romanticism*.

12. EARL WASSERMAN, 'The English Romantics: Grounds of Knowledge', *Studies in Romanticism*, **4** (1964): 18.

13. HARTMAN, *Wordsworth's Poetry, 1787–1814* (New Haven: Yale University Press, 1964), p. 33.

14. HERTZ, 'The Notion of Blockage in the Literature of the Sublime', collected here, pp. 82–3.

15. On the philosophical traditions in Germany and England that Coleridge sought to bring together, and his appropriations of Schelling, Maas, Jacobi, Kant and Fichte, see the Introduction to his *Biographia Literaria*, ed. James Engell and Walter Jackson Bate (London: Routledge, 1983), pp. lxvii–cxxxvi. The texts of Kant read by Coleridge are examined in G.N.G. ORSINI, *Coleridge and German Idealism* (Carbondale: Southern Illinois University Press, 1969).

16. MARY JACOBUS, 'Romantic Analogy, or What the Moon Saw', Afterword to *Romanticism, Writing, and Sexual Difference: Essays on 'The Prelude'* (Oxford: Oxford University Press, 1989).

17. *Kant's Critique of Aesthetic Judgement*, trans. J.C. Meredith (Oxford: Clarendon Press, 1911), p. 176.

18. JACOBUS, *Romanticism, Writing, and Sexual Difference*, p. 291.

19. Ibid., p. 278.

20. Keats alludes to 'the Wordsworthian or egotistical sublime' in his letter of 27 October 1818 to Richard Woodhouse. *The Letters of John Keats*, ed. Hyder E. Rollins (Cambridge: Harvard University Press, 1958), vol. 1, p. 387.

21. JACOBUS, *Romanticism, Writing, and Sexual Difference*, p. 292.

22. WILLIAMS, *Culture and Society*, pp. 30–49.

23. Some good examples are ROBERT YOUNG, 'The Eye and Progress of his Song: A Lacanian Reading of *The Prelude*', *Oxford Literary Review*, **4** (Spring 1979): 78–97; GAYATRI SPIVAK, 'Sex and History in *The Prelude*', *In Other Worlds: Essays in Cultural Politics* (Routledge: New York, 1987), pp. 46–76; and CHARLES J. RZEPKA, 'Christabel's "Wandering Mother" and the Discourse of the Self: A Lacanian Reading of Repressed Narration', *Romanticism Past and Present*, **10**, **1** (Winter 1986): 19–41.

24. *Poetry and Repression*, which introduces Bloom's thereafter characteristic recourse to rhetorical terminology, was written in response to Paul de Man's review of *The Anxiety of Influence* (reprinted in *Blindness and Insight*, revised edn, (Minneapolis: University of Minnesota Press, 1983)).

25. See BARBARA SCHAPIRO, *The Romantic Mother: Narcissistic Patterns in Romantic Poetry* (Baltimore: Johns Hopkins University Press, 1983); NEIL HERTZ, 'Afterword: The End of the Line', in *The End of the Line* (New York: Columbia University Press, 1985); CYNTHIA CHASE, 'Primary Narcissism and the Giving of Figure', in *Abjection, Melancholia, and Love: The Work of Julia Kristeva*, ed. John Fletcher and Andrew Benjamin (Routledge: London, 1990), and the essays in this volume by Caruth and Jacobus.

26. See PAUL DE MAN, 'Hypogram and Inscription', in *The Resistance to Theory* and

'Sign and Symbol in Hegel's *Aesthetics*', *Critical Inquiry*, **8** (1982): 761–75; and ANDRZEJ WARMINSKI, *Readings in Interpretation: Hölderlin, Hegel, Heidegger* (Minneapolis: University of Minnesota Press, 1985) and 'Dreadful Reading: Blanchot on Hegel', *Yale French Studies*, **69** (1985): 267–76.

27. PHILIPPE LACOUE-LABARTHE and JEAN-LUC NANCY, *The Literary Absolute*, trans. Philip Barnard and Cheryl Lester (Albany: State University of New York Press, 1988), pp. xiv, 29.

28. A.J. LOVEJOY, 'On the Discrimination of Romanticisms', *PMLA*, **39** (1924): 235–49.

29. *Critique of Pure Reason* (1781); *Critique of Practical Reason* (1788); *Critique of Judgement* (1790).

30. LACOUE-LABARTHE and NANCY, *Literary Absolute*, p. 30.

31. Idem.

32. Consciousness arrives at 'absolute knowledge' at the conclusion of HEGEL's *Phenomenology of the Spirit*. That Hegel's text employs these terms does not mean that it exemplifies Romantic ideology. It *is* the case that the *Phenomenology* poses the same questions for critical reading as Romantic literary and theoritical texts.

33. These range from JEROME MCGANN's claim in his polemical *The Romantic Ideology* that the writings of Wordsworth and Coleridge epitomize the transformation of experience into ideology, to PAUL DE MAN's claim in 'Time and History in Wordsworth' (included here) and 'The Rhetoric of Blindness' (*Blindness and Insight*) that Wordsworth's and Rousseau's texts are not blind to the drastic incompletion and discontinuity of the language and the history that they inhabit. See MARY JACOBUS, 'Geometric Science and Romantic History: Wordsworth, Newton and the Slave Trade' (in *Romanticism, Writing, and Sexual Difference*) and MARJORIE LEVINSON, 'Back to the Future' (in Levinson et al., *Rethinking Historicism* (Oxford: Basil Blackwell, 1989), for interesting different formulations about how the poetic text inhabits specific contemporary discourses and how through its very omissions or contradictions it 'anticipates this reading', in Levinson's words (p. 43).

34. WILLIAMS, *Culture and Society*, p. 36.

35. Ibid., p. 32.

36. BUTLER, *Romantics, Rebels, and Reactionaries*, p. 71; WILLIAMS, pp. 47, 40, 31–2.

37. See for instance for MARILYN BUTLER in 'The Rise of the Man of Letters: Coleridge', *Romantics, Rebels, and Reactionaries*, p. 72. A synopsis like Butler's is not the only way of covering the same ground. The relationship to *economy* of the idea of genius and the hierarchy of the arts in the Romantic period is demonstrated in detail, for instance, in one of Jacques Derrida's essays on Kant's *Critique of Judgement*, 'Economimesis' in SYVIANE AGACINSKI et al., *Mimesis des articulations* (Paris: Flammarion, 1975).

38. WILLIAMS, *Culture and Society*, p. 285.

39. *The Prose Works of William Wordsworth*, ed. W.J.B. Owen and Jane Worthington Smyser (Oxford, 1974), vol. 3, p. 139.

40. WILLIAMS, *Culture and Society*, pp. 280–1.

41. DE MAN, *The Rhetoric of Romanticism*, p. 85. See pp. 83–92 and, for discussion of de Man's own language and claims, NEIL HERTZ, 'More Lurid Figures', *Diacritics*, **20** (Fall 1990). On the received idea of literature as external to philosophy, and on the origin of modern literary theory in Romanticism, see LACOUE-LABARTHE and NANCY, *The Literary Absolute*, especially pp. xiv, xviii, 2.

42. Idem.

43. WILLIAMS, *Culture and Society*, p. 42.

44. See DE MAN, 'Kant and Schiller', in *Aesthetic Ideology*, ed. Andrzej Warminski (Minneapolis: University of Minnesota Press, 1993); CHRISTOPHER NORRIS, *Paul de Man: Deconstruction and the Critique of Aesthetic Ideology* (Routledge: London, 1988); MARC REDFIELD, 'Humanizing de Man' (review of Norris) *Diacritics*, **19**, **2** (Spring 1989): 35–53, and 'De Man, Schiller, and the Politics of Reception', *Diacritics*, **20**, **3** (Summer 1990): 50–70; and PHILIPPE LACOUE-LABARTHE, 'Hölderlin and the Greeks', *Typographies: Mimesis, Philosophy, Politics* (Cambridge: Harvard University Press, 1989).

45. See ANDRZEJ WARMINSKI and CYNTHIA CHASE, 'Wordsworth and the Production of Poetry', *Diacritics*, **17**, **4** (Winter 1987): 2–3.

46. DE MAN, 'Autobiography as De-facement', *The Rhetoric of Romanticism*, p. 81.

47. MARJORIE LEVINSON, *Wordsworth's Great Poems: Four Essays* (Cambridge: Cambridge University Press, 1986); JEROME McGANN, *The Romantic Ideology*.

48. See especially WALTER BENJAMIN, 'On Some Motifs in Baudelaire' and 'The Work of Art in the Age of Mechanical Reproduction', *Illuminations*, trans. Harry Zohn (New York: Schocken, 1969), and 'Psychoanalysis, Culture, Trauma', ed. Cathy Caruth, *American Imago*, **48**, **1** and **48**, **4** (March and December 1991), (as well as concluding remarks in Caruth's essay in this volume). See also ALAN LIU, *Wordsworth: The Sense of History* (Stanford: Stanford University Press, 1989), p. 35.

49. More explicit historical placement of Wordsworth's poetry is found in DE MAN's essays 'The Intentional Structure of the Romantic Image', and 'Wordsworth and Hölderlin', both in *The Rhetoric of Romanticism* (pp. 1–17, 47–66), and 'The Rhetoric of Temporality' in *Blindness and Insight*, pp. 187–228.

50. DE MAN, 'Wordsworth and Hölderlin', p. 59.

51. WORDSWORTH, Preface of 1815, *The Prose Works of William Wordsworth*, vol. 3, p. 31.

52. Compare Maurice Blanchot's suggestion, in a brief but important interpretation of early Romanticism, that the Revolution was a model for Romantic writing: 'The Athenaeum', *Studies in Romanticism*, **22** (1983): 163–72. On 'transparency' as an ideal, see JEAN STAROBINSKI's study of Rousseau, *La Transparence et l'obstacle* (Paris: Gallimard, 1971) and, on the stances that Wordsworth and Coleridge's texts take up in relation to transparency as the ideal of revolutionary eloquence, see REEVE PARKER, '"Oh could you hear his voice!": Wordsworth, Coleridge, and Ventriloquism', in *Romanticism and Language*, ed. Arden Reed (Ithaca: Cornell University Press, 1985), pp. 125–43; and 'Reading Wordsworth's Power: Narrative and Usurpation in *The Borderers*', *ELH*, **54** (1987): 299–331.

53. Re-readings of Hegel's *Phenomenology of the Spirit* linked with interpretation of Romantic literature are ANDRZEJ WARMINSKI's 'Reading for Example', in

Readings in Interpretation and PAUL DE MAN's 'Hypogram and Inscription', in *The Resistance to Theory*.

54. SIGMUND FREUD, *Three Essays on Sexuality, Complete Psychological Works*, ed. J. Strachey (London: Hogarth Press, 1966), vol. 7, p. 222.

55. A critique of the concept of repression in some ways compatible with Caruth's and other deconstructive analyses of this model is that of MICHEL FOUCAULT, in, especially, *History of Sexuality, An Introduction* (New York: Random House, 1978). Foucault's work has been the inspiration of some important new historicist criticism.

56. JEAN LAPLANCHE, *Life and Death in Psychoanalysis*, trans. Jeffrey Mehlman (Baltimore: Johns Hopkins University Press, 1976), pp. 18, 15; See Caruth's note 7.

57. The phrase is Wordsworth's, in the epigraph of 'Ode: Intimations of Immortality from Recollections of Early Childhood'.

58. WORDSWORTH, Preface to *Lyrical Ballads* (1800), *Prose Works*, vol. 1, pp. 132–7, and *Essays upon Epitaphs, Prose Works*, vol. 2, pp. 80–96.

59. MARGARET HOMANS, *Bearing the Word: Language and Female Experience in Nineteenth-Century Women's Writing*, (Chicago: University of Chicago Press, 1986), p. 4.

60. Ibid., pp. 4–5.

61. See CHASE, 'Primary Narcissism and the Giving of Figure'.

62. HERTZ, *The End of the Line*, pp. 217–39.

63. JEAN LAPLANCHE and J–B. PONTALIS, *The Language of Psychoanalysis*, trans. D. Nicholson-Smith (New York: Norton, 1973), pp. 56–60.

64. *The Prose Works of William Wordsworth*, vol. 1, p. 128.

65. On who read what, where, see JON P. KLANCHER, *The Making of English Reading Audiences, 1790–1832* (Madison: University of Wisconsin Press, 1987).

66. ADELA PINCH, 'Female Chatter: Meter, Masochism, and the *Lyrical Ballads*', *ELH*, 55 (1988): 832–52.

67. THOMPSON's 'Disenchantment or Default? A Lay Sermon', on Wordsworth and Coleridge's contact with an English radical, appears in *Power and Consciousness*, ed. Conor Cruise O'Brien and William Vanek (New York: Oxford University Press, 1969), pp. 149–82.

68. LEVINSON, *Wordsworth's Great Period Poems*, pp. 20–57.

69. See LEVINSON, 'Back to the Future'.

70. See for example, FRANCIS FUKUYAMA, 'The End of History', *The National Interest*, 16 (Summer 1989): 3–18; and DANIEL BELL, *The End of Ideology: On the Exhaustion of Political Ideas in the Fifties* (Cambridge, Mass.: Harvard University Press, 1988).

71. KARL MARX, *A Contribution to the Critique of Political Economy* (1859; New York: International Publishers, 1970).

72. *The Poetical Works of William Wordsworth*, ed. E. de Selincourt and Helen Darbyshire (Oxford: Clarendon Press, 1940–49), vol. 1, p. 187. William

Godwin (1756–1836) wrote *An Enquiry Concerning Political Justice* (1792), which sought to ground man's hope for a just society upon human reason rather than emotion.

73. REEVE PARKER, '"Oh could you hear his voice!"', pp. 125–43, and 'Reading Wordsworth's Power', pp. 299–331.

74. REEVE PARKER, '"In some sort seeing with my proper eyes": Wordsworth and the Spectacles of Paris', *Studies in Romanticism* **27** (Fall 1988): p. 388.

75. ALAN LIU, *Wordsworth*, pp. 33–4.

76. Ibid., p. 35.

77. Idem.

1 Romanticism and Anti-Self-Consciousness*

GEOFFREY HARTMAN

Geoffrey Hartman's work concerns the aspirations of modern poetry, the idea of literary history, and the history of interpretation, as well as the poetry of Wordsworth. He has tried to grasp and characterize a distinctively literary kind of 'mediation', of deliberately produced relation to the real. What resources enable Wordsworth or Marvell or Rilke – or Freud or Derrida – to temporize with the inescapable 'wish to put ourselves into an unmediated relation to whatever "really is" is'? Hartman's first book, *The Unmediated Vision: An Interpretation of Wordsworth, Hopkins, Rilke, and Valery* (1954), examined the effects of the gesture which for him defined poetry (including Romantic poetry) as 'modern': doing without the role of mediator of received religion or of a unified authoritative literary tradition and making 'the attempt to find and represent things *immediately* significant, *aesthetic* things, signs of the creative nature of perception' (p. 163). 'The unmediated vision' names both a desire and a particularly desired, properly aesthetic kind of mediation: the immediate or intuitive conveying, through forms and images, of the fact of mediation, of self-reflexive subjectivity or consciousness. Hartman finds a dialectic of this sort in Romanticism, in the essay included here. In asserting the 'precariousness' of 'the transition from self-consciousness to imagination', he indicates difficulties and disruptions of aesthetic mediation through language which are traced in detail in close readings such as Andrzej Warminski's 'Missed Crossing: Wordsworth's Apocalypses' (see Further Reading) or de Man's 'Time and History in Wordsworth' (in this volume).

Taking 'imagination' and 'self-consciousness' as fundamental terms

* Reprinted from *Centennial Review*, **6** (Autumn, 1962): 553–65. This essay also appears in Geoffrey Hartman, *Beyond Formalism* (New Haven: Yale University Press, 1970).

43

and concerns, Hartman has himself mediated between Romanticism and modern criticism. *Wordsworth's Poetry: 1798–1814* (1964) deeply influenced a generation of critics through its description of a dialectic between nature and consciousness but also its attentiveness to the nuances of Wordsworth's text. Equally important in pinpointing aspects of Wordsworth that seem both to epitomize English Romantic poetry and to convey aspirations inseparable from the activity of writing are essays published in *The Unremarkable Wordsworth* (1987), especially those on the *genius loci*, or spirit of place, and on inscriptions and Romantic nature poetry. Among several important essays on Romanticism (among them the one printed below), *Beyond Formalism* (1970) includes 'Poem and Ideology', an essay on Keats's ode 'To Autumn' examining its ideas of Englishness and of the movement of literary history. Hartman's critical writing draws power from his ear for the play of meanings in a given word and his flair for the idioms of more than one language. He treats the texts he reads, even those which are perhaps essentially religious (like midrash or scripture) and those which are philosophical (Derrida), as *essentially* literary – trying to save, rather than translate, their 'veiled but irreducible terms'.

The dejection afflicting John Stuart Mill in his twentieth year was alleviated by two important events. He read Wordsworth, and he discovered for himself a view of life resembling the 'anti-self-consciousness theory' of Carlyle. Mill describes this strangely named theory in his *Autobiography*: 'Ask yourself whether you are happy, and you cease to be so. The only chance is to treat, not happiness, but some end external to it as the purpose of life. Let your self-consciousness, your scrutiny, your self-interrogation exhaust themselves on that.'[1]

It is not surprising that Wordsworth's poetry should also have served to protect Mill from the morbidity of his intellect. Like many Romantics, Wordsworth had passed through a depression clearly linked to the ravage of self-consciousness and the 'strong disease' of self-analysis.[2] Book XI of *The Prelude*, Chapter 5 of Mill's *Autobiography*, Carlyle's *Sartor Resartus*, and other great confessional works of the Romantic period show how crucial these maladies are for the adolescent mind. Endemic, perhaps, to every stage of life, they especially affect the transition from adolescence to maturity; and it is interesting to observe how man's attention has shifted from the fact of death and its rites of passage, to these trials in what Keats called 'the Chamber of Maiden-Thought' and, more recently still, to the perils of childhood. We can say, taking a metaphor from Donne, that 'streights, and none but streights' are ways

to whatever changes the mind must undergo, and that it is the
Romantics who first explored the dangerous passageways of maturation.

Two trials or perils of the soul deserve special mention. We learn that
every increase in consciousness is accompanied by an increase in self-
consciousness, and that analysis can easily become a passion that
'murders to dissect'.[3] These difficulties of thought in its strength question
the ideal of absolute lucidity. The issue is raised of whether there exist
what might be called *remedia intellectus:* remedies for the corrosive power
of analysis and the fixated self-consciousness.

There is one remedy of great importance which is almost conterminous
with art itself in the Romantic period. This remedy differs from certain
traditional proposals linked to the religious control of the intellect – the
wild, living intellect of man, as Newman calls it in his *Apologia*.[4] A
particularly Romantic remedy, it is nonlimiting with respect to the mind.
It seeks to draw the antidote to self-consciousness from consciousness
itself. A way is to be found not to escape from or limit knowledge, but to
convert it into an energy finer than intellectual. It is some such thought
which makes Wordsworth in the preface to *Lyrical Ballads* describe poetry
as the 'breath and finer spirit of all knowledge', able to carry sensation
into the midst of the most abstract or remotest objects of science. A more
absolute figure for this cure, which is, strictly speaking, less a cure than a
paradoxical faith, is given by Kleist: 'Paradise is locked . . . yet to return
to the state of innocence we must eat once more of the tree of
knowledge.' It is not by accident that Kleist is quoted by Adrian at a
significant point in Mann's *Doktor Faustus*, which is *the* novel about self-
consciousness and its relation to art.

This idea of a return, via knowledge, to naïveté – to a second naïveté –
is a commonplace among the German Romantics. Yet its presence is
perhaps more exciting, because suitably oblique, among the English and
French Romantics. A.O. Lovejoy, of course, in his famous essay 'On the
Discrimination of Romanticisms' (1924), questions the possibility of
unifying the various national movements. He rightly points out that the
German Romantics insist on an art that rises from the plenitude of
consciousness to absorb progressively the most sophisticated as well as
the most naïve experience. But his claim that English Romanticism is
marked by a more primitivistic 'return to nature' is weakened by his use
of second-rate poetry and isolated passages. One can show that the
practice of the greater English Romantics is involved with a problematical
self-consciousness similar to that of the Germans and that, in the main,
no primitivism or 'sacrifice of intellect' is found. I do not mean to deny
the obvious, that there are primitivistic passages in Chateaubriand and
even Wordsworth, but the primary tendency should be distinguished
from errors and epiphenomena. The desire of the Romantics is perhaps
for what Blake calls 'organized innocence', but never for a mere return to

the state of nature. The German Romantics, however, for a reason mentioned later and because of the contemporaneous philsophical tradition which centered on the relations between consciousness and consciousness of self (Fichte, Schelling, Hegel), gained in some respects a clearer though not more fruitful understanding of the problem. I cannot consider in detail the case of French Romanticism. But Shelley's visionary despair, Keats's understanding of the poetical character, and Blake's doctrine of the contraries reveal that self-consciousness cannot be overcome; and the very desire to overcome it, which poetry and imagination encourage, is part of a vital, dialectical movement of soul-making.

The link between consciousness and self-consciousness, or knowledge and guilt, is already expressed in the story of the expulsion from Eden. Having tasted knowledge, man realizes his nakedness, his sheer separateness of self. I have quoted Kleist's reflection; and Hegel, in his interpretation of the Fall, argues that the way back to Eden is via contraries: the naïvely sensuous mind must pass through separation and selfhood to become spiritually perfect. It is the destiny of consciousness or, as the English Romantics would have said, of imagination, to separate from nature so that it can finally transcend not only nature but also its own lesser forms. Hegel in his *Logic* puts it as follows:

> The first reflection of awakened consciousness in men told them they were naked . . . The hour that man leaves the path of mere natural being marks the difference between him, a self-conscious agent, and the natural world. The spiritual is distinguished from the natural . . . in that it does not continue a mere stream of tendency, but sunders itself to self-realization. But this position of severed life has in its turn to be overcome, and the spirit must, by its own act, achieve concord once more. . . . The principle of restoration is found in thought, and thought only: the hand that inflicts the wound is also the hand that heals it.[5]

The last sentence states unequivocally where the remedy lies. Hegel, however, does not honor the fact that the meaning he derives from the Fall was originally in the form of myth. And the attempt to think mythically is itself part of a crucial defense against the self-conscious intellect. Bergson in *The Two Sources of Morality and Religion* sees both myth and religion as products of an intellectual instinct created by nature itself to oppose the analytic intellect, to preserve human spontaneities despite the hesitant and complicated mind.[6] Whether myth-making is still possible, whether the mind can find an unselfconscious medium for itself or maintain something of the interacting unity of self and life, is a central concern of the Romantic poets.

Romantic art as myth-making has been discussed convincingly in recent years, and Friedrich Schlegel's call in 'Rede über die Mythologie' (1800) for a modern mythology is well known. The question of the renewal of myth is, nevertheless, a rather special response to the larger perplexities of reflective thought. 'The poet', says Wallace Stevens in 'Adagia', 'represents the mind in the act of defending us against itself.' Starting with the Romantics, this act is clearly focused, and poetry begins to be valued in contra-distinction to directly analytic or purely conceptual modes of thought. The intelligence is seen as a perverse though necessary specialization of the whole soul of man, and art as a means to resist the intelligence intelligently.

It must be admitted, at the same time, that the Romantics themselves do not give (in their conceptual moments) an adequate definition of the function of art. Their criterion of pleasure or expressive emotion leads to some kind of art for art's sake formula, or to the sentimentalism which Mill still shared and which marks the shift in sensibility from Neoclassic to Romantic. That Mill wept over the memoirs of Marmontel and felt his selfhood lightened by this evidence of his ability to feel, or that Lamartine saw the life of the poet as 'tears and love', suggests that the *larmoyant* vein of the later eighteenth century persisted for some time but also helped, when tears or even joy were translated into theory, to falsify the Romantic achievement and make Irving Babbitt's criticism possible.

The art of the Romantics, on the other hand, is often in advance of even their best thoughts. Neither a mere increase in sensibility nor a mere widening of self-knowledge constitutes its purpose. The Romantic poets do not exalt consciousness *per se*. They have recognized it as a kind of death-in-life, as the product of a division in the self. The mind which acknowledges the existence or past existence of immediate life knows that its present strength is based on a separation from that life. A creative mind desires not mere increase of knowledge, but 'knowledge not purchased by the loss of power' (*Prelude*, V). Life, says Ruskin, is the only wealth; yet childhood, or certain irrevocable moments, confront the poet sharply and give him the sense of having purchased with death the life of the mind. Constructing what Yeats calls an anti-self, or recovering deeply buried experience, the poet seeks a return to 'Unity of Being'. Consciousness is only a middle term, the strait through which everything must pass; and the artist plots to have everything pass through whole, without sacrifice to abstraction.

One of the themes which best expresses this perilous nature of consciousness and which has haunted literature since the Romantic period is that of the Solitary, or Wandering Jew. He may appear as Cain, Ahasuerus, Ancient Mariner, and even Faust. He also resembles the later (and more static) figures of Tithonus, Gerontion, and *poète maudit*. These solitaries are separated from life in the midst of life, yet cannot die. They are doomed to live a middle or purgatorial existence which is neither life nor death, and as their knowledge increases so does their solitude.[7] It is, ultimately, consciousness that alienates them from life and imposes the burden of a self which religion or death or a return to the state of nature might dissolve. Yet their heroism, or else their doom, is not to obtain this release. Rebels against God, like Cain, and men of God, like Vigny's Moses, are equally denied 'le sommeil de la terre' and are shown to suffer the same despair, namely, 'the self . . . whose worm dieth not, and whose fire is not quenched' (Kierkegaard). And in Coleridge's Mariner, as in Conrad's Marlow, the figure of the wanderer approaches that of the poet. Both are storytellers who resubmit themselves to temporality and are compelled to repeat their experiences in the purgatorial form of words. Yeats, deeply affected by the theme of the Wandering Jew, records a marvelous comment of Mme Blavatsky's: 'I write, write, write, as the Wandering Jew walks, walks, walks.'

The Solitary may also be said to create his own, peculiarly Romantic genre of poetry. In 'Tintern Abbey', or 'X Revisited', the poet looks back at a transcended stage and comes to grips with the fact of self-alienation. The retrospective movement may be visionary, as often in Hölderlin; or antiquarian, as in Scott; or deeply oblique, as in lyrical ballad and monologue. In every case, however, there is some confrontation of person with shadow or self with self. The intense lyricism of the Romantics may well be related to this confrontation. For the Romantic 'I' emerges nostalgically when certainty and simplicity of self are lost. In a lyric poem it is clearly not the first-person form that moves us (the poem need not be in the first person) but rather the I toward which that I reaches. The very confusion in modern literary theory concerning the fictive I, whether it represents the writer as person or only as persona, may reflect a dialectic inherent in poetry between the relatively self-conscious self and that self within the self which resembles Blake's 'emanation' and Shelley's 'epipsyche'.

It is true, of course, that this dialectic is found in every age and not restricted to the Romantic. The notion of man (as of history) seems to presuppose that of self-consciousness, and art is not the only major reaction to it. Mircea Eliade, following Nietzsche, has recently linked art to religion by interpreting the latter as originating in a periodic and ritually controlled abolition of the burden of self, or rather of this burden in the form of a nascent historical sense. It is not true, according to Eliade, that primitive man has no sense of history; on the contrary, his sense of it is too acute, he cannot tolerate the weight of responsibility accruing through memory and individuation, and only gradually does religious myth, and especially the Judaeo-Christian revelation, teach him to become a more conscious historical being. The question, therefore, is why the Romantic reaction to the problem of self-consciousness should be in the form of an aggrandizement of art, and why the entire issue should now achieve an urgency and explicitness previously lacking.

The answer requires a distinction between religion and art. This distinction can take a purely historical form. There clearly comes a time when art frees itself from its subordination to religion or religiously inspired myth and continues or even replaces them. This time seems to coincide with what is generally called the Romantic period: the latter, at least, is a good *terminus a quo*. Though every age may find its own means to convert self-consciousness into the larger energy of imagination, in the Romantic period it is primarily art on which this crucial function devolves. Thus, for Blake, all religion is a derivation of the Poetic Genius; and Matthew Arnold is already matter-of-fact rather than prophetic about a new age in which the religious passion is preserved chiefly by poetry. If Romantic poetry appears to the orthodox as misplaced religious feeling ('spilt religion'), to the Romantics themselves it redeems religion.[8]

Yet as soon as poetry is separated from imposed religions or communal ends it becomes as problematic as the individual himself. The question of how art is possible, though post-Romantic in its explicitness, has its origin here, for the artist is caught up in a serious paradox. His art is linked to the autonomous and individual; yet that same art, in the absence of an authoritative myth, must bear the entire weight of having to transcend or ritually limit these tendencies. No wonder the problem of the subjective, the isolated, the individual, grows particularly acute. Subjectivity – even solipsism – becomes the subject of poems which *qua* poetry seek to transmute it.

This paradox seems to inhere in all the seminal works of the Romantic period. 'Thus my days are passed / In contradiction', Wordsworth writes sadly at the beginning of *The Prelude*. He cannot decide whether he is fit to be a poet on an epic scale. The great longing is there; the great (objective) theme eludes him. Wordsworth cannot find his theme because he already has it: himself. Yet he knows self-consciousness to be at once necessary and opposed to poetry. It will take him the whole of *The Prelude* to be satisfied *in actu* that he is a poet. His poem, beginning in the vortex of self-consciousness, is carried to epic length in the desire to prove that his former imaginative powers are not dead.

I have already confessed to understanding the *Ancient Mariner* as a poem that depicts the soul after its birth to the sense of separate (and segregated) being. In one of the really magical poems in the language, which, generically, converts self-consciousness into imagination, Coleridge describes the travail of a soul passing from self-consciousness to imagination. The slaying of an innocent creature, the horror of stasis, the weight of conscience or of the vertical eye (the sun), the appearance of the theme of deathlessness, and the terrible repetitive process of penitence whereby the wanderer becomes aware through the spirits above and the creatures below of his focal solitude between both – these point with archetypal force to the burden of selfhood, the straits of solitude, and the compensating plenary imagination that grows inwardly. The poem opens by evoking that rite de passage we call a wedding and which leads to full human communion, but the Mariner's story interposes itself as a reminder of human separateness and of the intellectual love (in Spinoza's sense) made possible by it.

To explore the transition from self-consciousness to imagination and to achieve that transition while exploring it (and so to prove it still possible) is the Romantic purpose I find most crucial. The precariousness of that transition naturally evokes the idea of a journey; and in some later poets, like Rimbaud and Hart Crane, the motif of the journey has actually become a sustained metaphor for the experience of the artist during creation. This journey, of course, does not lead to what is generally called a truth: some final station for the mind. It remains as problematic a crossing as that from death to second life or from exile to redemption. These religious concepts, moreover, are often blended in and remind us that Romantic art has a function analogous to that of religion. The traditional scheme of Eden, Fall, and Redemption merges with the new triad of Nature, Self-Consciousness, and Imagination – the last term in both involving a kind of return to the first.

Yet everything depends on whether it is the right and fruitful return. For the journey beyond self-consciousness is shadowed by cyclicity, by paralysis before the endlessness of introspection, and by the lure of false ultimates. Blake's 'Mental Traveller', Browning's 'Childe Roland to The Dark Tower Came', and Emily Dickinson's 'Our journey had advanced' show these dangers in some of their forms. Nature in its childhood or sensuous radiance (Blake's 'Beulah') exerts an especially deceptive lure. The desire to gain truth, finality, or revelation generates a thousand such enchantments. Mind has its blissful islands as well as its mountains, its deeps, and its treacherous crossroads. Depicting these trials by horror and by enchantment, Romanticism is genuinely a rebirth of Romance.

In the years following World War I it became customary to see Classicism and Romanticism as two radically different philosophies of life and to place modernism on the side of the anti-romantic. André Malraux defined the classical element in modern art as a 'lucid horror of seduction'. Today it is clear that Romantic art shared that lucidity. Romanticism at its most profound reveals the depth of the enchantments in which we live. We dream, we wake on the cold hillside, and our sole self pursues the dream once more. In the beginning was the dream, and the task of disenchantment never ends.

The nature poetry of the Romantics is a case in point. Far from being an indulgence in dewy moments, it is the exploration of enchanted ground. The Romantic poets, like the Impressionist painters, refuse to 'simplify the ghost' of nature. They begin to look steadfastly at all sensuous experience, penetrating its veils and facing its seductions. Shelley's 'Mont Blanc' is not an enthusiastic nature poem but a spirit-drama in which the poet's mind seeks to release itself from an overwhelming impression and to reaffirm its autonomy *vis-à-vis* nature. Keats also goes far in respecting illusions without being deluded. His starting-point is the dream of nature fostered by Romance; he agrees to this as consciously as we lie down to sleep. But he intends such dreaming 'beyond self' to unfold its own progressions and to wake into truth. To this end he passes from a gentler to a severer dream-mode: from the romance of *Endymion* to the more austere *Hyperion*. Yet he is forced to give up the *Hyperion* because Saturn, Apollo, and others behave like quest heroes instead of gods. Having stepped beyond romance into a sublimer mode, Keats finds the quest for self-identity elated rather than effaced. It has merely raised itself to a divine level. He cannot reconcile Miltonic sublimity with the utterly human pathos that keeps breaking through. The 'egotistical sublime' remains.

It was Wordsworth, of course, whose poetry Keats had tried to escape by adhering to a less self-centered kind of sublimity: 'Let us have the old Poets, and Robin Hood.' Wordsworth had subdued poetry to the theme of nature's role in the growth of the individual mind. The dream of nature, in Wordsworth, does not lead to formal Romance but is an early, developmental step in converting the solipsistic into the sympathetic imagination. It entices the brooding soul out of itself, toward nature first, then toward humanity. Wordsworth knew the weight of self-consciousness:

> It seemed the very garments that I wore
> Preyed on my strength, and stopped the quiet stream
> Of self-forgetfulness.
>
> (Prelude (1850), V, 294ff.)

The wound of self is healed, however, by 'unconscious intercourse' with a nature 'old as creation'. Nature makes the 'quiet stream' flow on. Wordsworth evokes a type of consciousness more integrated than ordinary consciousness, though deeply dependent on its early – and continuing – life in rural surroundings.[9]

The Romantic emphasis on unconsciousness and organic form is significant in this light. *Unconsciousness* remains an ambiguous term in the Romantic and Victorian periods, referring to a state distinctly other than consciousness or simply to unselfconsciousness. The characteristic of right performance, says Carlyle in *Characteristics* (1831), is an unconsciousness – 'the healthy know not of their health, but only the sick'. The term clearly approaches here its alternate meaning of unselfconsciousness, and it is to such statements that Mill must be indebted when he mentions the 'anti-self-consciousness theory' of Carlyle. In America, Thoreau perpetuates the ambiguity. He also prescribes unconsciousness for his sophisticated age and uses the word as an equivalent of vision: 'the absence of the speaker from his speech'. It does seem to me that the personal and expressive theory of poetry, ascribed to the Romantics, and the impersonal theory of poetry, claimed in reaction by the moderns, answer to the same problem and are quietly linked by the ambiguity in *unconsciousness*. Both theories value art as thought recreated into feeling or self-consciousness into a more communal power of vision. Yet can the modern poet, whom Schiller called 'sentimental' (reflective) and whom we would describe as alienated, achieve the immediacy of all great verse, whatever its personal or historical dilemma?

This is as crucial a matter today as when Wordsworth and Coleridge wrote *Lyrical Ballads* and Hölderlin pondered the fate of poetry in 'Der Rhein'. Is visionary poetry a thing of the past, or can it coexist with the modern temper? Is it an archaic revelation, or a universal mode springing from every real contact with nature? 'To interest or benefit us', says a Victorian writer, 'poetry must be sentimental, subjective; it must accord with the conscious, analytical spirit of present men.'[10] The difficulties surrounding a modern poetry of vision vary with each national literature. In England the loss of 'poesy' is attributed by most Romantics to a historical though not irreversible fact – to the preceding century's infidelity to the line of Chaucer, Spenser, Shakespeare, and Milton. 'Let us have the old Poets, and Robin Hood', as Keats said. Yet for the German and the French there was no easy return to a tradition deriving its strength from both learned and popular sources. 'How much further along we would be', Herder remarks, 'if we had used popular beliefs and myths like the British, if our poetry had built upon them as whole-heartedly as Chaucer, Spenser and Shakespeare did'.[11] In the absence of this English kind of literary mediation, the gap between medieval romance and the modern spirit seemed too great. Goethe's *Faust* tried to bridge it but, like *Wilhelm Meister*, anticipated a new type of literature which subsumed the philosophical character of the age and merged myth and irony into a 'progressive' mode. The future belongs to the analytic spirit, to irony, to prose. The death of poetry had certainly occurred to the Romantics in idea, and Hegel's prediction of it was simply the overt expression of their own despair. Yet against this despair the greater Romantic poets staked their art and often their sanity.

Notes

1. *Autobiography* (1873), Chapter 5. Mill says that he had not heard, at the time, Carlyle's theory. The first meeting between the writers took place in 1831; Mill's depression lasted, approximately, from autumn 1826 to autumn 1828. Mill called self-consciousness 'that demon of the men of genius of our time from Wordsworth to Byron, from Goethe to Chateaubriand'. See WAYNE SHUMAKER, *English Autobiography* (Berkeley and Los Angeles, 1954), Chapter 4.

2. Thought as a disease is an open as well as submerged metaphor among the Romantics. There are many hints in Novalis; Schelling pronounces naked reflection (analysis) to be a spiritual sickness of man (*Schellings Sämtliche Werke*, ed. K.F. Schelling (Stuttgart, 1856–61) 2, pp. 13–14); the metaphor is explicit in Carlyle's *Characteristics* (1831) and commonplace by the time that E.S. Dallas in *The Gay Science* (1866) attributes the 'modern disease' to 'excessive civilization and overstrained consciousness'. The *mal du siècle* is not unrelated to the malady we are describing. Goethe's *Die Leiden des Jungen Werthers* (1774) may be seen as its *terminus a quo*, and Kierkegaard's *Sickness unto Death* (1849) as its noonday point of clarity.

3. Wordsworth, 'The Tables Turned' (1798). For the first peril, see Kierkegaard's *Sickness unto Death*, and Blake: 'The Negation is the Spectre, the Reasoning Power in Man; / This is a false Body, an Incrustation over my Immortal / Spirit, a Selfhood which must be put off & annihilated alway' (*Milton*, Bk. 2). This last quotation, like Wordsworth's 'A reasoning, self-sufficient thing, / An intellectual All-in-All' ('A Poet's Epitaph'), shows the closeness of the two perils. For the second, see also Coleridge: 'All the products of the mere reflective faculty [viz. the 'understanding' contradistinguished from what Coleridge will call the 'reason'] partook of DEATH' (*Biographia Literaria*, Chapter 9): Benjamin Constant's definition of one of the moral maladies of the age as 'the fatigue, the lack of strength, the perpetual analysis that saps the spontaneity of every feeling' (draft preface to *Adolphe*); and Hegel's preface to *The Phenomenology of Mind* (1807). Hegel observes that ordinary analysis leads to a hardening of data, and he attributes this to a persistence of the ego, whereas his dialectic is thought to reveal the true fluency of concepts. Carlyle most apodictically said: 'Had Adam remained in Paradise, there had been no Anatomy and no Metaphysics' (*Characteristics*, 1831).

4. *Apologia Pro Vita Sua* (1864), Chapter 5. In the same chapter Newman calls reason 'that universal solvent'. Concerning Victorian remedies for 'this disease / My Self' (Marianne Moore), see also A. DWIGHT CULLER, *The Imperial Intellect* (New Haven, 1955), pp. 234–7.

5. *The Logic of Hegel*, trans. from the *Encyclopedia of the Sciences* by W. Wallace, 2nd edn (Oxford, 1904), pp. 54–7. The first sentences given here come from passages in the original later than the remainder of the quotation.

6. *Les Deux Sources de la Morale et de la Réligion* (1933), Chapter 2. Both religion and 'la fonction fabulatrice' are 'une reaction défensive de la nature contre le pouvoir dissolvant de l'intelligence'. (Cf. Newman calling the intellect 'that universal solvent'.) As Romanticism shades into modernism, a third peril of over-consciousness comes strongly to the fore – that it leads to a Hamlet-like incapacity for action. Bergson, like Kierkegaard, tries to counter this aspect especially.

7. 'I lost the love of heaven above, / I spurned the lust of earth below' (John

Clare, 'A Vision'). By this double exile and their final madness, two poets as different as Clare and Hölderlin are joined. See Coleridge's intense realization of man's 'between-ness', which increases rather than chastens the apocalyptic passion: 'O Nature! I would rather not have been – let that which is to come so soon, come now – for what is all the intermediate space, but sense of utter worthlessness? . . . Man is truly and solely an immortal series of conscious mortalities and inherent Disappointments' (*Inquiring Spirit*, ed. K. Coburn (London, 1951), p. 142). But to ask death instead of life of nature is still to ask for finality, for some metal quietus: it is the bitter obverse, also met at the beginning of Goethe's *Faust*, of the quest for absolute truth.

8. I have omitted here the important role played by the French Revolution. The aggrandizement of art is due in no small measure to the fact that poets like Wordsworth and Blake cannot give up one hope raised by the Revolution – that a terrestrial paradise is possible – yet are eventually forced to give up a second hope – that it can be attained by direct political action. The shift from faith in the reformation of man through the prior reformation of society to that in the prior reformation of man through vision and art has often been noted. The failure of the French Revolution anchors the Romantic movement or is the consolidating rather than primary cause. It closes, perhaps until the advent of Communism, the possibility that politics rather than art should be invested with a passion previously subsumed by religion.

9. Mill, Hazlitt, and Arnold came to approximately the same estimate of Wordsworth's poetry. Comparing it to Byron's, they found that the latter had too much fever of self in it to be remedial; they did not want their image cast back at them magnified. Carlyle prefers to compare Goethe and Byron ('Close your Byron, open your Goethe'), yet his point is the same: Goethe retains a strong simplicity in a tormented and divided age, while Byron seems to him a 'spasmodically bellowing self-worshipper'.

10. R.M. MILNES, *Palm Leaves* (London, 1844).

11. *Von Ähnlichkeit der mittlern englischen und deutschen Dichtkunst* (1777). Cf. Louis Cazamian on French Romanticism: 'Le romantisme n'a donc pas été pour la France, comme pour l'Angleterre, un retour facile et naturel à une tradition nationale, selon la pente du tempérament le plus profond' (*Essais en Deux Langues*, Paris, 1938, p. 170).

2 Time and History in Wordsworth*

PAUL DE MAN

This essay was the third lecture on the topic of 'Romanticism and Contemporary Criticism' that de Man delivered as the Gauss Lectures at Princeton University in 1967. It is thus a rather early essay of de Man's, which has the exceptional interest of containing a second 'layer', revisions and additions made in 1971, which allow one to see de Man's introduction of linguistic and rhetorical terminology and explicit focus on the question of reading. It also explicitly engages Geoffrey Hartman's interpretation of Wordsworth. The essay approaches Wordsworth by way of one of the passages of *The Prelude* already singled out as remarkable by De Quincey and Coleridge, the lines on the Boy of Winander.

De Man's best-known essay on Romanticism is 'The Rhetoric of Temporality' (1969). Re-examining the supposed shift from allegorical to symbolical imagery in late eighteenth-century poetry, this essay challenged the critical commonplace that Romanticism is committed to the symbol as the most authentic and expressive kind of figurative language. Coleridge, making a judgement subsequently presumed by most modern literary criticism and shared by Hegel's *Lectures on Aesthetics*, identified allegory as inferior to symbol, as a product of the fancy rather than the imagination. But in their 'most original and profound moments', de Man writes, the texts of late eighteenth- and early nineteenth-century European literature present not symbols, but allegorical structures, which expose the disjunction between the origin and the meaning of a sign and reveal the disjunctive temporal structure of signification. The other rhetorical structure de Man uncovers in Romantic texts is irony, also a disjunction between sign and meaning. Like 'Time and History in Wordsworth', 'The Rhetoric of Temporality' discusses rhetorical structures in terms of their

---

* Reprinted from *Diacritics*, **17**:4 (Winter, 1987): 4–17.

evasion or their unveiling of 'an authentically temporal destiny'; of allegory de Man writes, 'this unveiling takes place in a subject that has sought refuge from the impact of time in a natural world to which, in truth, it bears no resemblance' (p. 206). Allegory, in de Man's description, unlike symbol does not carry the illusion of coming to rest in a truth independent of the relay of signs, for 'it remains necessary, if there is to be allegory, that the allegorical sign refer to another sign that precedes it' (p. 207). Post-Coleridgean criticism has seen the symbol as predominant in successful poetry and the coming together of 'mind' and 'nature' or subject and object through the symbol as Romanticism's principal aim. De Man's focus on the problematic of signification enables him to argue that, to the contrary, 'the dialectic between subject and object does not designate the main romantic experience, but only one passing moment in a dialectic, and a negative moment at that, since it represents a temptation that has to be overcome', that of aiming toward an interchange between the order of time and history and the natural order from which it differs entirely (p. 205).

The second version of 'Time and History in Wordsworth' examines more technically what the title of an early essay of de Man's called 'The Intentional Structure of the Romantic Image' (collected in *The Rhetoric of Romanticism*, 1984). Thus de Man makes the point that the description of the River Duddon's progress is a narrative (one kind of figure), which depends upon metonymy. Metonymy substitutes for one thing something that is related to it merely by contiguity, rather than resemblance or shared substance as in the case of symbol or synecdoche. Metonymy thus implies or admits a sheerly contingent or arbitrary connection between sign and meaning, and implies the 'disjunction of faculties' which in the symbol (as Coleridge observes) seem to function together and form a whole.

Problems touched on in the second version of 'Time and History in Wordsworth' are investigated in important later essays in *The Rhetoric of Romanticism*: among them 'Autobiography as Defacement'; 'Wordsworth and the Victorians' (on prosopopoeia, or the giving of a face or a voice, as the principal figurative structure of Wordsworth's poetry); and 'Shelley Disfigured' (the essay which in de Man's own judgement most fully engages the problem of history).

Up till now, the double-barrelled topic of these lectures[1] has rather prevented us from reading our romantic authors with the kind of receptivity, the self-forgetting concentration, that we have been describing (in the case of Rousseau) as the proper state of mind for critical insights. The need to keep one eye on the text and another eye on the critical commentator has forced us into the rather tiresome grimace well known to anyone who has ever played in an orchestra – where one has to keep track simultaneously of the score and of the conductor. The grimace becomes even more painful when the directives of the score and those of the interpreter are pulling in different directions, as we found to be the case, to some extent, in the three preceding examples. The result often is that because of the unavoidable simplifications involved in a polemical discussion, one fails to do justice to both the writer and the critic. I probably had to overstate the degree of my disagreement with Girard and Starobinski, critics for whom I have a great deal of sympathy and admiration – and I was clearly not being critical enough, to your taste, with Heidegger, when I suggested that there might be perhaps something of merit in an imaginary figure, one that never existed in the flesh, who would have approached literature with some of the insights that appear in *Sein und Zeit*.[2] More distressing are the one-sided readings given to some of the texts, in order to use them as a rebuttal of methodological assertions. Such over-analytical approaches are certainly not attuned to catch the subtle nuances of temporality and intent that a valid commentary should bring out.

Fortunately, my topic today will allow for a more relaxed kind of presentation, in which the voice of the poet might come through in a less garbled manner. Geoffrey Hartman's study of Wordsworth awakens in me no trace of methodological disagreement.[3] I read whole parts of it with the profound satisfaction of full agreement, only marred by the slight feeling of jealousy that I did not write them myself. The much hoped-for synthesis between the best qualities of American and Continental criticism certainly begins to come true in a book like this. It is based on a wide knowledge of the tradition in which the poet is writing, in this case true familiarity with Wordsworth's antecedents in Milton and in eighteenth-century poetry, combined with an ear that is finely attuned to the slightest nuances of Wordsworth's language. Moreover, by interpreting Wordsworth from the inside, from the phenomenological point of view of his own consciousness, Hartman can trace a coherent itinerary of Wordsworth's poetic development. His achievement will make it possible for us to limit ourselves to some indications derived from the reading of a few very short but characteristic texts, thus tracing, in turn, an itinerary through Wordsworth by means of some of those larger themes that Hartman has pursued. These themes, in the case of Wordsworth and Wordsworth scholarship, are quite obvious, and Hartman does not depart from a well-established custom when he makes the relationship between nature and the imagination into Wordsworth's central problem. The Arnoldian tradition of reading Wordsworth as a moralist has, for quite a while now, been superseded by a concern for the implicit poetics that are present in his writing, and that have to be understood prior to the interpretation of a moral statement that seems conventional. This leads inevitably to such abstractions as nature, the imagination, self-knowledge, and poetry as a means of self-knowledge, all of which figure prominently in recent Wordsworth studies, not only because Wordsworth himself talks at times openly about them, but because his poetry, even at its most trivial, always seems to be supported by and to relate back to them.

As will be clear to all of you, the path I'll try to trace by this direct commentary overlaps with that proposed by Hartman in more places than I will have time to mention. It diverges from it in at least one point of some importance, and I will comment on this disagreement later, as a way to summarize a tentative view of Wordsworth's poetry.[4]

Let me start out with a very well-known poem to which Hartman devotes a chapter, the text that Wordsworth placed at the head of the section of his *Collected Poems* entitled 'Poems of the Imagination'. He later incorporated it into *The Prelude* and seems to have, in general, attached a special importance to it. It was written in Goslar, during his stay in Germany, together with several other of the childhood memories that went into the two first books of *The Prelude*. 'The Winander Boy' is divided into two sections separated by a blank space, and all readers of the poem have been struck by the abruptness of the transition that leads from the first to the second part. Problems of interpretation tend to focus on the relationship between the two parts. (I would add that these problems were solved in a definitive but somewhat peremptory fashion in a fine recent anthology of English literature, in which the second part has simply been suppressed.)

> There was a Boy, ye knew him well, ye Cliffs
> And islands of Winander! many a time
> At evening, when the stars had just begun
> To move along the edges of the hills,
> 5 Rising or setting, would he stand alone
> Beneath the trees, or by the glimmering Lake,
> And there, with fingers interwoven, both hands
> Press'd closely, palm to palm, and to his mouth
> Uplifted, he, as through an instrument,
> 10 Blew mimic hootings to the silent owls
> That they might answer him. – And they would shout
> Across the watery Vale, and shout again,
> Responsive to his call, with quivering peals,
> And long halloos, and screams, and echoes loud
> 15 Redoubled and redoubled; concourse wild

Of mirth and jocund din! And when it chanced
That pauses of deep silence mock'd his skill,
Then, sometimes, in that silence, while he hung
Listening, a gentle shock of mild surprise
20 Has carried far into his heart the voice
Of mountain torrents; or the visible scene
Would enter unawares into his mind
With all its solemn imagery, its rocks,
Its woods, and that uncertain Heaven, receiv'd
25 Into the bosom of the steady Lake.

This Boy was taken from his Mates, and died
In childhood, ere he was full ten years old.
– Fair are the woods, and beauteous is the spot,
The Vale where he was born; the Churchyard hangs
30 Upon a Slope above the Village School,
And, there, along the bank, when I have pass'd
At evening, I believe that oftentimes
A full half-hour together I have stood
Mute – looking at the Grave in which he lies.[5]

The first part of the poem introduces us into a world that is, in the words
of the text, both 'responsive' and, as in the gesture of the hands,
'interwoven'. Voice and nature echo each other in an exchange of which
the exuberance expresses a stability, a firm hold on a universe that has
the vastness of rising and setting stars, but nevertheless allows for an
intimate and sympathetic contact between human and natural elements.
Not the 'vaste et profonde unité' of Baudelaire's *Correspondances* should
come to mind, but a more innocent, more playful, pleasure at finding
responses, satisfying possibilities of relationship even for someone who,
like the boy, 'stands alone'. The 'watery Vale' that might separate him
from an alien natural presence is easily bridged by the cry of the owls; it
is, by itself, an eerie noise enough on a dark night, but little of this
eeriness is allowed to enter the poem. If we mimic it well enough to
engage the response of its originators, the gulf between ourselves and
nature need not be unbridgeable. 'The poet . . . considers man and
nature as essentially adapted to each other, and the mind of man as
naturally the mirror of the fairest and most interesting qualities of nature'
– this statement from the Preface to the *Lyrical Ballads* would be a good
commentary on the opening scene of the poem.[6] Much Wordsworth
criticism, still today, considers this frequently as the fundamental
statement not just of Wordsworth, but of romantic naturalism as a
whole, and refuses to go beyond it. Yet, even in this first section of the
poem, one finds some strain at keeping up a belief in such an

'interwoven' world. 'Mimic hootings' is not the highest characterization imaginable for the human voice, and we have somehow to be told explicitly that this is 'concourse wild / Of mirth and jocund din . . .' to convince us of the persistent cheer of the scene.

As soon as the silence of the owls allows for the noise to subside, what becomes audible is poetically much more suggestive than what went before. The deepening of the imaginative level is not announced with any fanfare or pointed dramatic gesture. The 'surprises' that Wordsworth's language gives are indeed such *'gentle* shocks of *mild* surprise' that the transition from stability to suspense can be accomplished almost without our being aware of it. Yet certainly, by the time we come to *'uncertain* Heaven', we must realize that we have entered a precarious world in which the relationship between noun and epithet can be quite surprising. Coleridge singled out the line for comment, as being most unmistakably Wordsworth's: 'Had I met these lines running wild in the deserts of Arabia, I should instantly have screamed out, "Wordsworth".'[7] The line is indeed bound to engender wonder and meditation. The movements of the stars, in the opening lines, had seemed 'certain' enough, and their reflection in the lake was hardly needed to steady the majesty of their imperceptible motion. But the precariousness that is here being introduced had been announced before, as when, a little earlier, in lines 18 and 19, it was said that when 'pauses of deep silence mock'd his skill, / Then, sometimes, in that silence, while he [the boy] *hung* / Listening, a gentle shock of mild surprise. . . .' We would have expected 'stood Listening' instead of the unusual 'hung / Listening'. This word, 'hung', plays an important part in the poem. It appears in the second part, when it is said that the graveyard in which the boy is buried *'hangs* / Upon a Slope above the Village School'. It establishes the thematic link between the two parts and names a central Wordsworthian experience. At the moment when the analogical correspondence with nature no longer asserts itself, we discover that the earth under our feet is not the stable base in which we can believe ourselves to be anchored. It is as if the solidity of earth were suddenly pulled away from under our feet and that we were left 'hanging' from the sky instead of standing on the ground. The fundamental spatial perspective is reversed; instead of being centered on the earth, we are suddenly related to a sky that has its own movements, alien to those of earth and its creatures. The experience hits as a sudden feeling of dizziness, a falling or a threat of falling, a *vertige* of which there are many examples in Wordsworth. The nest robbing scene from Book I of *The Prelude* comes to mind, where the experience is a literal moment of absolute dizziness which disjoins the familiar perspective of the spatial relationship between heaven and earth, in which the heavens are seen as a safe dome that confirms at all times the earth's and our own centrality, the steadfastness of our orientation towards the center which makes us creatures *of* earth. But here, suddenly, the sky no longer relates to the earth.

> Oh! at that time,
> While on the perilous ridge I *hung* alone,
> With what strange utterance did the loud dry wind
> Blow through my ears! the sky *seem'd not a sky*
> *Of earth*, and with what motion moved the clouds!
>
> (1805 Prelude, I, 335–9; p. 291)

Later, when in the Preface to the 1815 edition of his *Poems* Wordsworth gives examples of the workings of the highest poetic faculty, the imagination, as it shapes poetic diction, he chooses three passages, from Virgil, Shakespeare, and Milton, in which the italicized key-word is the same word, 'hang', not used literally as in the last instance from *The Prelude*, but used imaginatively. The Milton passage being:

> As when far off at Sea a Fleet descried
> *Hangs* in the clouds, by equinoxial winds
> Close sailing from Bengala . . .
>   . . . so seem'd
> Far off the flying Fiend.
>
> (Preface to *Poems*, (1815), p.248)

Wordsworth comments:

> Here is the full strength of the imagination involved in the word *hangs*, and exerted upon the whole image: First, the Fleet, an aggregate of many Ships, is represented as one mighty Person, whose track, we know and feel, is upon the waters; but, taking advantage of its appearance to the senses, the Poet dares to represent it as *hanging in the clouds*, both for the gratification of the mind in contemplating the image itself, and in reference to the motion and appearance of the sublime object to which it is compared.
>
> (p. 248)

This *daring* movement of the language, an act of pure mind, corresponds to the *danger*, the anxiety of the moment when the sudden silence leaves the boy *hanging*/listening. In the second part of the poem, we are told, without any embellishment or preparation, that the boy died, and we now understand that the moment of silence, when the analogical stability of a world in which mind and nature reflect each other was shattered, was in fact a prefiguration of his death. The turning away of his mind

61

from a responsive nature towards a nature that is not quite 'of earth' and that ultimately is called an 'uncertain Heaven' is in fact an orientation of his consciousness towards a preknowledge of his mortality. The spatial heaven of the first five lines with its orderly moving stars has become the temporal heaven of line 24, 'uncertain' and precarious since it appears in the form of a pre-consciousness of death.

The uncertainty or anxiety is not allowed, however, to go unrelieved. In the prefigurative first section the uncertain heaven is, with a suggestion of appeasement, 'receiv'd / Into the bosom of the steady Lake', and in the second part, at the moment when we would have expected an elegiac lament on the death of the boy, we hear instead a characteristically Wordsworthian song of praise to a particular place, the kind of ode to spirit of place of which Hartman has traced the antecedents in eighteenth-century nature poetry:

> Fair are the woods, and beauteous is the spot,
> The Vale where he was born; the Churchyard *hangs*
> Upon a Slope above the Village School,
> And, there, along that bank, when I have pass'd
> At evening, I believe that oftentimes
> A full half-hour together I have stood
> Mute – looking at the Grave in which he lies.

The dizziness revealed in the 'hung/Listening . . .' has indeed resulted in a fall, has been the discovery of a state of falling which itself anticipated a fall into death. Now become part of earth in the graveyard, the boy is part of an earth that is itself falling into a sky that is not 'of earth'. But the movement is steadied, the fall cushioned, as it were, when the uncertain heaven is received into the lake, when sheer dizziness is changed into reflection. The corresponding moment in the second part is the meditative half-hour which introduces a long, extended period of continuous duration that exists outside of the ordinary time of daily activity, at the moment of a privileged encounter with a scene that merges the youth of the village school with the death of the graveyard, as boyhood and death merged in the figure of the Winander boy.

We understand the particular temporal quality of this slow half-hour better when we remember that the earliest version of this poem was written throughout in the first person and was referring to Wordsworth himself as a boy. The text went: 'When it chanced / That pauses of deep silence mocked *my* skill . . .' The poem is, in a curious sense, autobiographical, but it is the autobiography of someone who no longer lives written by someone who is speaking, in a sense, from beyond the grave. It would be banal and inadequate to say that Wordsworth is praising and mourning, in the poem, his own youth, the boy he used to be. The movement is more radical, more complex. The structure of the poem, although it seems retrospective, is in fact proleptic. In the second part, Wordsworth is reflecting on his own death, which lies of course in the future and can only be anticipated. But to be able to imagine, to convey the experience, the consciousness of mortality, he can only represent death as something that happened to another person, in the past. Dead men,[8] as we all know, tell no tales, but they have an assertive way of reminding us of mortality, or bringing us eventually face to face with our own finitude. Wordsworth is thus anticipating a future event as if it existed in the past. Seeming to be remembering, to be moving to a past, he is in fact anticipating a future. The objectification of the past self, as that of a consciousness that unwittingly experiences an anticipation of its own death, allows him to reflect on an event that is, in fact, unimaginable. For this is the real terror of death, that it lies truly beyond the reach of reflection. Yet the poem names the moment of death in a reflective mood, and it is this reflective mood that makes it possible to transform what would otherwise be an experience of terror into the relative appeasement of the lines

> that uncertain Heaven, receiv'd
> Into the bosom of the steady Lake.

Another way of putting it is that what Wordsworth strives to conquer, on the relentless fall into death, is the time, the surmise that would allow one to reflect upon the event that, of all events, is most worth reflecting upon but hardest to face. This time is conquered at the end of the poem, in the curiously exact full half-hour that becomes available to him, a purely meditative time proportionate to the time it takes us to understand meditatively Wordsworth's own poem. But the strategy that allows for this conquest is temporally complex: it demands the description of a future experience by means of the fiction of a past experience which is itself anticipatory or prefigurative. Since it is a fiction, it can only exist in the form of a language, since it is by means of language that the fiction can be objectified and made to act as a living person. The reflection is not separable from the language that describes it, and the half-hour of the end also clocks the time during which Wordsworth, or ourselves, are in real contact with the poem. Hartman is quite right in saying that the poem 'becomes an . . . extended epitaph'(p.20), though one might want to add that it is the epitaph written by the poet for himself, from a perspective that stems, so to speak, from beyond the grave. This temporal perspective is characteristic for all Wordsworth's poetry – even if it obliges us to imagine a tombstone large enough to hold the entire *Prelude*.[9]

Wordsworth himself gives us sufficient evidence to defend this kind of understanding. The first of the *Essays upon Epitaphs* describes, in prose, insights that are very close to what we have found in 'The Winander Boy'. What seems to start out as a simply pious statement about the consolatory power of a belief in the immortality of the soul turns very swiftly into a meditation on the temporality that characterizes the consciousness of beings capable of reflecting on their own death. The first characteristic of such a consciousness is its power to anticipate: 'The Dog or Horse perishes in the field, or in the stall, by the side of his Companions, and is incapable of *anticipating* the sorrow with which his surrounding Associates shall bemoan his death, or pine for his loss; he cannot *pre-conceive* this regret, he can form no thought of it; and therefore cannot possibly have a desire to leave such regret or remembrance behind him' (p.605). And Wordsworth characterizes a human being that, not unlike the Winander Boy at the beginning of the poem, would have chosen to remain in a state of nature by an 'inability arising from the imperfect state of his faculties to come, in any point of his being, into contact with a notion of death; or to an *unreflecting* acquiescence in what had been instilled in him' (p. 606). Very soon in the same essay, however, it becomes clear that the power to anticipate is so closely connected with the power to remember that it is almost impossible to distinguish them from each other. They seem like opposites, and are indeed at opposite poles if we think of time as a continual movement from birth to death. In this perspective, the source is at a maximal remove from the final point of destination, and it would be impossible to reach the one by way of the other. In a more reflective, more conscious concept of temporality, however, the two poles will, in Wordsworth's phrasing, 'have another and finer connection than that of contrast' (p. 608). 'Origin and tendency are notions inseparably co-relative' (p. 606), he writes, and the essay develops this notion in an extended voyage image:

As, in sailing upon the orb of this Planet, a voyage, towards the regions where the sun sets, conducts gradually to the quarter where we have been accustomed to behold it come forth at its rising; and, in like manner, a voyage towards the east, the birth-place in our imagination of the morning, leads finally to the quarter where the Sun is last seen when he departs from our eyes; so, the contemplative Soul, travelling in the direction of mortality, advances to the Country of everlasting Life; and, in like manner, may she continue to explore those cheerful tracts, till she is brought back, for her advantage and benefit, to the land of transitory things – of sorrow and of tears.

(p. 608)

Stripped of whatever remnants of piety still cling to this language,[10] the passage summarizes the temporality of the 'Winander Boy' poem. In this poem, the reflection on death takes on the form, at first sight contradictory, of a remembrance of childhood. Similarly, in Wordsworth, evocations of natural, childlike, or apocalyptic states of unity with nature often acquire the curiously barren, dead-obsessed emptiness of non-being.[11] The poetic imagination, what is here called the contemplative soul, realizes this and thus encompasses source and death, origin and end within the space of its language, by means of complex temporal[12] structurizations of which we found an example in 'The Winander Boy'.[13]

Another brief poem of Wordsworth's will allow us to take one further step in an understanding of his temporality; it may also make the concept less abstract by linking it to its more empirical mode of manifestation, namely history. The poem belongs to the later sonnet cycle entitled *The River Duddon* that appeared in 1820.

> Not hurled precipitous from steep to steep;
> Lingering no more mid flower-enamelled lands
> And blooming thickets; nor by rocky bands
> Held; – but in radiant progress tow'rd the Deep
> 5 Where mightiest rivers into powerless sleep
> Sink, and forget their nature; now expands
> Majestic Duddon, over smooth flat sands,
> Gliding in silence with unfettered sweep!
> Beneath an ampler sky a region wide
> 10 Is opened round him; – hamlets, towers, and towns,
> And blue-topped hills, behold him from afar;
> In stately mien to sovereign Thames allied,
> Spreading his bosom under Kentish downs,
> With Commerce freighted or triumphant War.

(p. 699)

The *Essay upon Epitaphs* had already suggested the image of a river as the proper emblem for a consciousness that is able to contain origin and end into a single awareness.

> Origin and tendency are notions inseparably co-relative. Never did a Child stand by the side of a running Stream, pondering within himself what power was the feeder of the perpetual current, from what never-wearied sources the body of water was supplied, but he must have been inevitably propelled to follow this question by another: 'Towards what abyss is it in progress? what receptacle can contain the mighty influx?'

(p. 606)

In this poem, we have what seems at first sight like a progression, a continuous movement that flows 'in radiant progress' towards the triumphant ending:

> In stately mien to sovereign Thames allied,
> Spreading his bosom under Kentish downs,
> With Commerce freighted or triumphant War.

Equally convincing seems to be the movement that leads, in the poem, from the idyllic setting of 'flower-enamelled lands / And blooming thickets . . .' to the political, historically orientated language at the end. The progression from nature to history, from a rural to an urban world seems to be without conflict. We move from a relationship between the personified River Duddon and its pastoral banks, to a relationship that involves human creations such as 'hamlets, towers and towns', or human historical enterprises such as 'commerce and war'. And this gliding passage, similar to what is called in *The Prelude* 'love of nature leading to love of man' (title of 1850 Book VIII, cf. p. 395), appears as a liberation, an expansion that involves a gain in freedom. The river is no longer restricted 'by rocky bands' and now flows 'with unfettered sweep'. The order of nature seems to open up naturally into the order of history, thus allowing the same natural symbol, the river, to evoke the connection between both. The poem seems to summarize the 'growth of a mind' as espousing this movement, and to prove, by the success of its own satisfying completeness, that language can espouse poetically this very movement.

Some aspects of the language, however, prevent the full identification of the movement with natural process and put into question an interpretation of the river, which a subsequent poem in the same series addresses as 'my partner and my guide' ('Conclusion', 1, p. 699), as a truly natural entity. The beginning of the poem, for instance, casts a curious spell over the subsequent progression. It describes what the river no longer is in such forceful and suggestive language that we are certainly not allowed to forget what the river *has been* by the time we encounter it in its expanded form. The opening line, for example, cannot cease to haunt us, and no matter how strongly the italicized *now* (in '*now* expands') takes us to the present, so much has been told us so effectively about what came before that we can only seize upon this present in the perspective of its past and its future. The past is described as successive motions of falling and lingering. The dizziness of the Winander Boy poem and of the childhood scenes of *The Prelude* is certainly present in the image of the river 'hurled precipitous from steep to steep', which introduces, from the start, a powerful motion that dominates the entire poem, and that the various counterforces, including the initial *not*, are

unable to stem. For the idyllic stage that follows, among flowers and
blooming thickets, is a mere lingering, a temporary respite in a process
that is one of steady descent and dissolution. The implications of this
movement become clearer still when the radiant progress is said to be
'. . . tow'rd the Deep / Where mightiest rivers into powerless sleep /
Sink, and forget their nature.' This description of the sea is certainly far
removed from the image of a pantheistic unity with nature that one
might have expected. It is presented instead as a loss of self, the loss of
the *name* that designates the river and allows it to take on the dignity of
an autonomous subject. The diction of the passage, with the antithetical
balance of 'mightiest' and 'powerless', is all the stronger since the
apparent strategy of the poem does not seem to demand this kind of
emphasis. It makes the forgetting of one's nature that is here mentioned
into a movement that runs counter to the original progression; this
progression, which first seemed to lead from nature to history while
remaining under the dominant sway of nature, now becomes a
movement away from nature towards pure nothingness. One is
reminded of a similar loss of name in the Lucy Gray poems where death
makes her into an anonymous entity.

> Roll'd round in earth's diurnal course
> With rocks and stones and trees!
> ('A slumber did my spirit seal', 7–8, p. 165)

Similarly, the River Duddon is first lost into a larger entity, the Thames,
which in turn will lose itself in still larger anonymity. There is no cycle
here by means of which we are brought back to the source and reunited
with it by natural means. No prospect of natural rebirth is held out, and
the historical achievement at the end seems caught in the same general
movement of decay.

Nevertheless, the poem can overcome the feeling of dejection that this
irrevocable fall might suggest; it ends on a statement of assertion that is
not ironic. Not altogether unlike the uncertain heaven in 'The Winander
Boy' that was steadied in reflection, the fall here is not prevented, but
made tolerable this time by the assertion of historical achievement. There
seems to be an assertion of permanence, of a duration in what seems to
be an irrevocable waste, a falling away into sheer nothingness. It is based
on a certain form of hope, on the affirmation of a possible future, all of
which made it possible for man to pursue an enterprise that seems
doomed from the start, to have a history in spite of a death which
Wordsworth never allows us to forget.

In this poem, the possibility of restoration is linked to the manner in
which the two temporalities are structurally interrelated within the text.
If taken by itself, the progression towards history would be pure

delusion, a misleading myth based on the wrong kind of forgetting, an evasion of the knowledge of mortality. The countertheme of loss of self into death that appears in the first and second quatrain introduces a temporality that is more originary, more authentic than the other, but without reducing it to mere error. Rather, it creates a point of view which has gone beyond the historical world of which we catch a glimpse at the end of the poem, but which can look back upon this world and see it within its own, relative greatness, as a world that does not escape from mutability but asserts itself within the knowledge of its own transience. We have a temporal structure that is not too different from what we found in 'The Winander Boy'. Instead of looking back upon childhood, upon an earlier stage of consciousness that anticipates its future undoing, we here look back on a historical consciousness that existed prior to the truly temporal consciousness represented by the river. This historical stage is named at the end of the poem, but this end is superseded by the authentic endpoint named in line 5. We see it therefore, with the poet, as destined to this same end. Like the boy experiencing the foreknowledge of his death, history awakens in us a true sense of our temporality, by allowing for the interplay between achievement and dissolution, self-assertion and self-loss, on which the poem is built. History, like childhood, is what allows recollection to originate in a truly temporal perspective, not as a memory of a unity that never existed, but as the awareness, the remembrance of a precarious condition of falling that has never ceased to prevail.[14]

Hence, in the concluding sonnet of the same cycle, the emphasis on the italicized word *backward* in

> For, *backward*, Duddon! as I cast my eyes,
> I see what was, and is, and will abide.
>
> ('Conclusion', 3–4, p. 699)

As a mere assertion of the permanence of nature, the poem would be simply pious and in bad faith, for we know that as soon as we think of the river as analogous to a self, as a consciousness worthy of engaging our own, that it only reveals a constant loss of self. Considered as a partner and a guide, it has indeed 'past away' (line 2) and never ceases to do so. This is the Function it fulfills in the line, 'The Form remains, the Function never dies', in which the Form corresponding to this function is the trajectory of a persistent fall. The entire poignancy of the two sonnets is founded on the common bond between the I of the poem and its emblematic counterpart in the Duddon, which makes the river into something more than mere nature. Instead of merely letting ourselves be carried by it, we are able to move backwards, against the current of the movement.[15] This backward motion does not exist in nature but is the

privilege of the faculty of mind that Wordsworth calls the imagination;
asserting the possibility of reflection in the face of the most radical
dissolution, personal or historical. The imagination engenders hope and
future, not in the form of historical progress, nor in the form of an
immortal life after death that would make human history unimportant,
but as the persistent, future possibility of a retrospective reflection on its
own decay. The 1850 version of *The Prelude* makes this clearest when it
defines the imagination as being, at the same time, a sense of irreparable
loss linked with the assertion of a persistent consciousness:

> I was lost
> Halted without an effort to break through;
> But to my conscious soul I now can say –
> 'I recognise thy glory.'

> (1850 Prelude, VI, 596–99)

The restoring power, in Wordsworth, does not reside in nature, or in
history, or in a continuous progression from one to the other, but in the
persistent power of mind and language after nature and history have
failed. One wonders what category of being can sustain the mind in this
knowledge and give it the future that makes imagination dwell, in the
later version of *The Prelude*, with 'something evermore about to be' (VI,
608).

This may be the moment at which a return to Hartman's book is
helpful. Like all attentive readers of Wordsworth, he reaches a point at
which the nature of this restorative power has to be defined as the main
assertive power in Wordsworth's poetry. And the understanding he has
of Wordsworth's own mind allows him to give a very full and
penetrating description of the complexities involved. He has noticed,
more clearly than most other interpreters, that the imagination in
Wordsworth is independent of nature and that it leads him to write a
language, at his best moments, that is entirely unrelated to the exterior
stimuli of the senses. He has also noticed that there is a kind of
existential danger connected with this autonomy, and that when
Wordsworth speaks about the *daring* of his imagery in the 1815 Preface,
this risk involves more than mere experimentation with words. Hartman
refers to this danger as an apocalyptic temptation, in his words, 'a strong
desire to cast out nature and to achieve an unmediated contact with the
principle of things' (p. x). Carried by the imagination, Wordsworth
would at certain privileged moments come close to such visionary power,
although he reaches it without supernatural intervention and always in a
gradual and gentle way. Still, in the climactic passages of *The Prelude*, and
in the main poems generally, the evidence of a moving beyond nature is
unmistakable. What characterizes Wordsworth, according to Hartman,

and sets him apart from Milton, for instance, and also from Blake, is that the apocalyptic moment is not sustained, that it is experienced as too damaging to the natural order of things to be tolerated. Out of reverence not out of fear, Wordsworth feels the need to hide from sight the vision he has glimpsed for a moment; he has to do so, if his poetry is to continue its progression. And he finds the strength for this avoidance of apocalyptic abandon in nature itself – a nature that has been darkened and deepened by this very insight, and that has to some extent incorporated the power of imagination. But it has naturalized it, reunited it with a source that remains in the natural world. 'The energy of imagination enters into a natural cycle though apart from it' (p. 69), writes Hartman. The return to a natural image at the end of the famous passage on Imagination in Book VI of *The Prelude* 'renews the connection between the waters above and the waters below, between heaven and earth. Towards this marriage of heaven and earth the poet proceeds despite apocalypse. He is the matchmaker, his song the spousal verse' (p. 69). The road apparently beyond and away from nature in fact never ceased to be a natural road, albeit nature in a negative form, the *via naturaliter negativa*.

We cannot follow him in speaking of an apocalyptic temptation in Wordsworth. The passages that Hartman singles out as apocalyptic never suggest a movement towards an unmediated contact with a divine principle. The imagination (in Book VI, 371–2) is said to be 'like an unfather'd vapour' (527) and is, as such, entirely cut off from ultimate origins; it gives sight of 'the invisible world' (536), but the invisibility refers to the mental inward nature of this world as opposed to the world of the senses; it reveals to us that our home is 'with infinity' (538–9), but within the language of the passage this infinity is clearly to be understood in a temporal sense as the futurity of 'something evermore about to be' (542). The heightening of pitch is not the result of 'unmediated vision' but of another mediation, in which the consciousness does not relate itself any longer to nature but to a temporal entity. This entity could, with proper qualifications, be called history, and it is indeed in connection with historical events (the French Revolution) that the apostrophe to Imagination comes to be written. But if we call this history, then we must be careful to understand that it is the kind of history that appeared at the end of the Duddon sonnet, the retrospective recording of man's failure to overcome the power of time. Morally, it is indeed a sentiment directed towards other men rather than towards nature, and, as such, imagination is at the root of Wordsworth's theme of human love. But the bond between men is not one of common enterprise, or of a common belonging to nature: it is much rather the recognition of a common temporal predicament that finds its expression in the individual and historical destinies that strike the poet as exemplary. Examples abound, from 'The Ruined Cottage' to 'Resolution and Independence', and in the various time-eroded figures that appear through *The Prelude*. The common denominator that they share is not nature but time, as it unfolds its power in these individual and collective histories.

Nor can we follow Hartman in his assertion of the ultimately regenerative power of nature. His argument returns to passages like the passage on Imagination in Book VI of *The Prelude* in which, according to him, after having shown the 'conscious soul' as independent, Wordsworth has to return to a natural image. The soul is said to be

> Strong in herself and in beatitude
> That hides her, like the mighty flood of Nile
> Poured from her fount of Abyssinian clouds
> To fertilize the whole Egyptian plain . . .
>
> (1850 Prelude, VI, 613–16; Hartman, p. 69)

Perhaps enough has been said about the River Duddon to suggest that Wordsworth's rivers are not to be equated with natural entities. We don't even have to point to the further distancing from nature suggested by the exotic reference to an entity richer in mythological and literary than in natural assocations; the abyss in 'Abyssinian' maintains the source far beyond our reach, at a dizzying distance from ordinary perception and certainly not in 'any mountain-valley where poetry is made' (p. 69), as Hartman would have it. The fertile plain at the end occupies the same position that the historical world occupies in the last lines of the Duddon sonnet, and is thus not a symbol of regeneration. Hartman reads the 'hiding' as naturally beneficial, as the protective act of nature that makes possible a fertile continuation of the poem and of life, in contrast to the 'unfathered vapour' that rejects the source in a supernatural realm. The hiding rather refers to the invisibility, the inwardness, the depth of a temporal consciousness that, when it reaches this level, can rejoice in the truth of its own insight and find thoughts 'too deep for tears'. If rivers are, for Wordsworth, privileged emblems for the awareness of our mortal nature, in contrast to the natural unity of echoes and correspondences, then the use of an allegorical river at this point can hardly be the sign of a renewed bond with nature.

Hartman speaks of the need for Wordsworth 'to respect the natural (which includes the temporal) order' if this poetry is to continue 'as narrative' (p. 46). The equation of natural with temporal seems to us to go against Wordsworth's most essential affirmation. He could well be characterized as the romantic poet in which the separation of time from nature is expressed with the greatest thematic clarity. The narrative order, in the short as well as in the longer poems, is no longer[16] linear;

the natural movement of his rivers has to be reversed as well as transcended if they are to remain usable as metaphors. A certain form of narrative nevertheless persists, but it will have to adopt a much more intricate temporal movement than that of the natural cycles. The power that maintains the imagination, which Hartman calls nature returning after it has been nearly annihilated by apocalyptic insight, is time. The key to an understanding of Wordsworth lies in the relationship between imagination and time, not in the relationship between imagination and nature.

A late poem of Wordsworth's that appears among the otherwise truly sterile sequence of the *Ecclesiastical Sonnets* can well be used as a concluding illustration. Like all other romantic poets, Wordsworth claims a privileged status for poetic language – a formula which was most legitimately put into question during our last session[17] as standing in need of closer explanation. In Wordsworth, the privileged status of language is linked with the power of imagination, a faculty that rates higher than the fancy, or than rhetorical modes such as imitation, which, unlike the imagination, are dependent on correspondence with the natural world and thus limited by it. The language of imagination is privileged in terms of truth; it serves no empirical purposes or desires other than the truth of its own assertion:

> The mind beneath such banners militant
> Thinks not of spoils or trophies, nor of aught
> That may assert its prowess, blest in thoughts
> That are its own perfection and reward
> Strong in itself . . .
>
> (1805 Prelude, VI, 543–7; p. 372)

This truth is not a truth about objects in nature but a truth about the self; imagination arises 'before the eye and progress of my Song' (526), in the process of self-discovery and as self-knowledge. A truth about a self is best described, not in terms of accuracy, but in terms of authenticity; true knowledge of a self is knowledge that understands the self as it really is. And since the self never exists in isolation, but always in relation to entities, since it is not a thing but the common center of a system of relationships or intents, an authentic understanding of a self means first of all a description of the entities towards which it relates, and of the order of priority that exists among these entities. For Wordsworth, the relationships towards time have a priority over relationships towards nature; one finds, in his work, a persistent deepening of self-insight represented as a movement that begins in a contact with nature, then grows beyond nature to become a contact with time. The contact, the relationship with time, is, however, always a negative one for us, for the relationship between the self and time is necessarily mediated by death; it is the experience of mortality that awakens within us a consciousness of time that is more than merely natural. This negativity is so powerful that no language could ever name time for what it is; time itself lies beyond language and beyond the reach of imagination. Wordsworth can only describe the outward movement of time's manifestation, and this outward movement is necessarily one of dissolution, the 'deathward progressing' of which Keats speaks in *The Fall of Hyperion*. To describe this movement of dissolution, as it is perceived in the privileged language of the imagination, is to describe it, not as an actual experience that would necessarily be as brusque and dizzying as a fall, but as the generalized statement of the truth of this experience in its universality. Dissolution thus becomes mutability, asserted as an *unfailing* law that governs the natural, personal, and historical existence of man. Thus to name mutability as a principle of order is to come as close as possible to naming the authentic temporal consciousness of the self. The late poem entitled 'Mutability' comes as close as possible to being a language that imagines what is, in essence, unimaginable:

Mutability

From low to high doth dissolution climb,
And sinks from high to low, along a scale
Of awful notes, whose concord shall not fail;
A musical but melancholy chime,
Which they can hear who meddle not with crime,
Nor avarice, nor over-anxious care.
Truth fails not; but her outward forms that bear
The longest date do melt like frosty rime,
That in the morning whitened hill and plain
And is no more; drop like the tower sublime
Of yesterday, which royally did wear
Its crown of weeds, but could not even sustain
Some casual shout that broke the silent air,
Or the unimaginable touch of Time.

(p. 780)

Notes

1. This essay is transcribed by Tom Keenan from a photocopy of the manuscript. It is the fourth in a series of six lectures on *Contemporary Criticism and the Problem of Romanticism* that de Man delivered as the Christian Gauss Seminar in Criticism at Princeton University in April and May 1967. The manuscript has been transcribed with almost no editing other than the addition of

bibliographical information and all footnotes, minor grammatical changes, and the correction of quoted texts and titles. A few of de Man's more interesting deletions have been restored in the footnotes. All emphases and all (parentheses) apart from line references are de Man's; square brackets mark added material. The passages from the 'second layer' of de Man's text quoted in notes 4, 9, 12, 13, 14 and 16 were transcribed by Andrzej Warminski. Other notes are by Tom Keenan.

2. De Man refers here to the previous lectures in his Gauss series.

3. References to Hartman's text throughout this essay follow the pagination of *Wordsworth's Poetry 1787–1814* (New Haven and London: Yale University Press, 1964).

4. The opening paragraphs seem to have been left out when de Man gave this lecture again (around 1971 or 1972). The new lecture began with some more informal remarks about what it means to read based on a version of the following notes:

reading
　not declaim it – pure dramatic, vocal presence
　not analyze it structurally – as in Ruwet
　　semantic, thematic element remains present in
　　Jakobson/Riffaterre
　but read, which means that the thematic element remains
　　taken into consideration

we look for the delicate area where the thematic, semantic field and the rhetorical structures begin to interfere with each other, begin to engage each other

they are not necessarily congruent, and it may be (it is, as a matter of fact, it is the case) that the thematic and the rhetorical structures are in conflict and that, in apparent complicity, they hide each other from sight

in truth, there are no poems that are not, at the limit, about this paradoxical and deceptive interplay between theme and figure; the thematization is always the thematization of an act of rhetorical deceit by which what seems to be a theme, a statement, a truth-referent, has substituted itself for a figure

I can't begin to prove this, but want to hint at what I mean by reading two Wordsworth poems

Wordsworth, because he is the anti-rhetorical, natural poet (i.e. thematic) *par excellence*, not only because he explicitly attacked the use of figure as *ornatus*, but also because the thematic seduction is particularly powerful, in its transparency and clarity – one gets very far very quickly by meditative participation

no one has reached the point where this question of Wordsworth's rhetoricity can begin to be asked, except Hartman.

5. *Wordsworth Poetry and Prose*, selected by W.M. Merchant (Cambridge: Harvard University Press (The Reynard Library, 1955), pp. 352–3). *1805 Prelude*, V. 389ff. Merchant prints only the 1805 edition of *The Prelude*. All quotations from Wordsworth and page references, unless otherwise noted, are from this edition (which de Man used) and will be included in the text.

6. 'Preface (1800)', in WORDSWORTH and COLERIDGE, *Lyrical Ballads* 1798, ed. W.J.B. Owen (London: Oxford University Press, 1967), p. 167. De Man quotes from a section Wordsworth added for the 1800 edition.

7. Quoted in *The Norton Anthology of English Literature*, gen. ed. M.H. Abrams (New York: Norton 1962), 2, p. 152 n5.

8. De Man's manuscript reads 'Death men'. Restoring portions crossed out in the manuscript, the sentence fragment reads: 'Death men, as we all know from Western movies, tell no tales, but the same is not true of Western romantic poetry, which knows that the only interesting tale is to be told by a man who'.

9. In the second version of the lecture, the final sentences of this paragraph seem to have been replaced by the following passage:

> It is always possible to anticipate one's own epitaph, even to give it the size of the entire Prelude, but never possible to be both the one who wrote it and the one who reads it in the proper setting, that is, confronting one's grave as an event of the past. The proleptic vision is based, as we saw in the poem, on a metaphorical substitution of a first person subject by a third person subject, 'the boy' for 'I'. In fact, this substitution is, of all substitutions, the one that is, thematically speaking, a radical impossibility: between the living and the dead self, no analogical resemblance or memory allows for any substitution whatever. The movement is only made possible by a linguistic sleight-of-hand in which the order of time is reversed, rotated around a pole called self (the grammatical subject [first and third persons] of the poem). The posterior events that are to occur to the first person, I, (usually death) are made into anterior events that have occurred to a third person, the boy. A pseudo-metaphorical and thematically inconceivable substitution of persons leads to a temporal reversal in which anteriority and posterity are inverted. The structural mechanics of metaphor (for, I repeat, the substitution of the dead he for the living I is thematically, literally, 'unimaginable' and the metaphor is not a metaphor since it has no proper meaning, no sens propre, but only a metaphorical structure within the sign and devoid of meaning) – the structural mechanics of metaphor lead to the metonymic reversal of past and present that rhetoricians call metalepsis. The prolepsis of the Winander boy, a thematic concept – for we all know that we can proleptically anticipate empirical events, but not our death which is not for us an empirical event – is in fact metalepsis, a leap outside thematic reality into the rhetorical fiction of the sign. This leap cannot be represented, nor can it be reflected upon from within the inwardness of a subject. The reassurance expressed in the poem when the 'uncertain' heaven is received in the lake or when the meditative surmise seems to promise the reflective time of the meditation is based on the rhetorical and not on thematic resources of language. It has no value as truth, only as figure. The poem does not reflect on death but on the rhetorical power of language that can make it seem as if we could anticipate the unimaginable.
>
> This would also be the point at which we are beginning to 'read' the poem, or to 'read' Wordsworth according to the definition I gave at the start, namely to reach the point where the thematic turns rhetorical and the rhetorical turns thematic, while revealing that their apparent complicity is in fact hiding rather than revealing meaning.

10. A crossed-out clause here reads: 'and with the understanding that what is here called immortality stands in fact for the anticipated experience of death'.

11. A sentence crossed out here reads: 'Being the father of man, the child stands closer to death than we do.'

12. In reworking this passage for the second version of the lecture, de Man wrote the word 'rhetorical' above the word 'temporal' here (without crossing out 'temporal') and then rewrote the opening sentence of the following paragraph to read: 'Another brief poem of Wordsworth's will give us another version of his rhetorical movement; it may also make [. . .]' But ultimately de Man seems to have replaced this passage by the interpolated passage quoted in note number 13.

13. In the second version, the final sentences of this paragraph (from 'Stripped of whatever remnants . . .') seem to have been replaced by the following transitional passage:

> The metaphor of the voyage, with its vast stellar and heliotropic movements of rising and setting suns and stars, here makes the link between life and death, origin and end and carries the burden of the promise. But this is precisely the metaphor that was 'deconstructed' in the Winander boy, in which this kind of analogism is lost from the start and never recovered; as is often, but not always the case, a poetic text like the Boy of Winander takes us closer to an actual 'reading' of the poet than discursive statements of philosophical convictions and opinions, especially when these statements are themselves heavily dependent on metaphor.
>
> Another brief poem by Wordsworth may make the movement we are trying to describe less abstract.

14. In the second version, the final sentences of this paragraph (beginning with 'We see it therefore . . .') seem to have been replaced by the following passage:

> Middle and end have been reversed by means of another metonymic figure in which history, contained within a larger dimension of time, becomes, in the poem, the container of a temporal movement that it claims to envelop, since it is present at the end of the text. But, again, as in the Boy of Winander, this metonymy of a content becoming a container, of an *'enveloppé'* becoming an *'enveloppant'*, is a rhetorical device that does not correspond to a thematic, literal reality. When Wordsworth chooses to name mutability for what it is, in one of his most suggestive poems, the Mutability sonnet from the Ecclesiastical Sonnets, no historical triumphs are mentioned but only decay. It would take us a great deal more time and effort than we have available tonight to reveal the de-constructive rhetoricity of the Mutability poem; though it could be done. It would take us closer to an actual reading of Wordsworth, for which these remarks are only introductory exercises.
>
> My entire exposition could be seen as a gloss on a sentence in Hartman's admirable book on Wordsworth in which he speaks of the need, for Wordsworth, 'to respect the natural (which includes the temporal) order' if his poetry is to continue 'as narrative'. The narrative (which is itself metonymic) depends indeed on making the natural, thematic order appear as the container, the *enveloppant*, of time rather than as its content; the narrative is metonymic not because it is narrative but because it depends on metonymic substitution from the start. I can therefore totally subscribe to Hartman's reading of Wordsworth's strategy. The only thing I might

(Note that in this interpolated passage de Man seems to be re-reading his own metaphor of 'enveloping' above (the more authentic temporality 'envelopes the other' in the fourth sentence of the paragraph), that is, is reading his own text rhetorically.)

15. The remainder of the sentence, crossed out here, reads: 'and thus to become aware of the persistence of the movement that can then be asserted as an eternal truth, almost regardless of its negative connotation'.

16. In the second version, the following passage was inserted (directly after the words 'no longer') to replace the rest of the sentence:

   a natural metaphor but a veiled metonymy. Wordsworth's most daring paradox, the claim to have named the most unnamable of experiences, 'the unimaginable touch of time', is still based on a metonymic figure that, skillfully and effectively, appears in the disguise of a natural metaphor. In this least rhetorical of poets in which time itself comes so close to being a theme, the theme or meaning turns out to be more than ever dependent on rhetoric.

17. A lecture on Hölderlin as read by Heidegger. It and this essay, together with the other Gauss Lectures by de Man, are included in *Romanticism and Contemporary Criticism: The Gauss Seminar and Other Papers*, E.S. Burt, K. Newmark, and A. Warminski, eds (Baltimore: Johns Hopkins University Press, 1992).

3 The Notion of Blockage in the Literature of the Sublime*

Neil Hertz

The mind 'blocked' in confronting a multiplicity or vastness too much to comprehend: such a moment seems to have become so inseparable from the idea of the sublime that asking why, and how, takes an imaginative effort. Neil Hertz makes that effort here, in a study that examines how sublime scenarios operate in theoretical and historiographical writing as well as in poetry. His essay shows, within a variety of texts, how the 'notion of blockage' (his characteristically casual but precise phrasing) functions to consolidate the idea of a self that is single, whole, and distinct from its representations.

Hertz's mode of procedure is as revealing as any results of his enquiry. He takes seriously the rhetorical structure not only of such a text as Wordsworth's 'London' (Book VII of *The Prelude*) but of a review of the year's work in nineteenth-century studies, for instance, which he enables us to recognize as 'a contemporary instance of the mathematical sublime', and to see just how its rhetorical gestures both enable and complicate its thematic statement. In Hertz's reading, a critical or theoretical text illuminates a poetic text not chiefly through what it says about it but in so far as it *does* the same thing, or some of the same things. In each of these passages – in *The Prelude* and in eighteenth- and twentieth-century theoretical or critical writing – the dominant version of the sublime serves to represent as an experience of a self what other aspects of the portrayal of the sublime suggest is rather a discontinuity or 'difficulty' intrinsic to a process, that of interpretation or reading. Hertz finds that Wordsworth's 'London' summons up this kind of 'difficulty' – of orientation or understanding in a world in which representation seems the motive and the

* Reprinted from Neil Hertz, *The End of the Line: Essays on Psychoanalysis and the Sublime* (New York: Columbia, 1985), pp. 40–60. This essay also appears in Geoffrey H. Hartman, ed., *Psychoanalysis and the Question of the Text* (Baltimore and London: Johns Hopkins University Press, 1978), pp. 62–85.

meaning, as well as the mechanism, of all activity. How to convey – as experience – that which is not the experience of a self: this may be said to be Hertz's central problem as well as his topic in *The End of the Line: Essays on Psychoanalysis and the Sublime*, of which this essay is the third chapter. The informal, spoken quality of his writing reflects this paradox, and goes along with a demystifying or de-idealizing stance toward cultural monuments. Hertz's writing is *criticism* of the sublime; it makes things speakable.

In this essay he suggests that the scenario of blockage is a way of restructuring as a clear confrontation the multiplying and attenuating of differences that takes place as one 'looks' or reads. Psychoanalytic interpretation of the sublime as replaying the resolution of the Oedipus complex (the ego's intense identification with the super-ego) does not so much account for the scenario of blockage, Hertz observes, as it restates it. Interpreting the sublime as an essentially Oedipal strategy is not so much an explanation as an enabling strategy.

In later chapters Hertz describes the complex configuration of what he calls the 'end-of-the-line' structure fully worked out in passages of Wordsworth, George Eliot and Flaubert and in the paintings of Courbet. *The End of the Line* gives an idea of what the rhetorical reading of Romantic and psychoanalytic texts can accomplish. It elucidates a figural structure fully elaborated in and central to Romantic texts and demonstrates that it determines a problematic central to realism. And, analysing various writings on revolutionary upheaval in France (in his penultimate chapter 'Medusa's Head: Male Hysteria under Political Pressure'), Hertz is able to argue that 'the same operations that can be found concentrated at end-of-the-line moments in works of art will turn up producing the acts and the actings-out of historical experience'.

There is, according to Kant, a sense of the sublime – he calls it the mathematical sublime – arising out of sheer cognitive exhaustion, the mind blocked not by the threat of an overwhelming force, but by the fear of losing count or of being reduced to nothing but counting – this and this and this – with no hope of bringing a long series or a vast scattering under some sort of conceptual unity. Kant describes a painful pause – 'a momentary checking of the vital powers' – followed by a compensatory positive movement, the mind's exultation in its own rational faculties, in its ability to think a totality that cannot be taken in through the senses.[1] In illustration, Kant alludes to 'the bewilderment or, as it were, perplexity which it is said seizes the spectator on his first entrance into St

Peter's at Rome',[2] but one needn't go to Rome to experience
bewilderment or perplexity. They are available in quantity much closer to
home. Professional explainers of literature have only to try to locate
themselves in the current intellectual scene, to try to determine what is to
be learned from the linguists or the philosophers or the psychoanalysts
or the political economists, in order to experience the requisite mental
overload, and possibly even that momentary checking of the vital
powers. It is difficult to speculate about literature just now without
sounding either more assured or more confused than one really feels. In
such circumstances, some remarks about the mathematical sublime, that
is, about one version of the play between confusion and assurance,
might prove useful. In particular, it may be useful to examine that
moment of blockage, the 'checking of the vital powers', to consider both
the role it played in eighteenth- and nineteenth-century accounts of the
sublime and the fascination it still seems to exert on contemporary
historians and theorists of literature.

I

Consider first some paragraphs from a recent issue of *Studies in English
Literature*; they express a scholar's fear that soon we shall all be
overwhelmed by the rising tide of academic publication. The genre of
this writing may be that of the omnibus review (Thomas McFarland is
here reporting on a year's worth of literary studies), but tonally and
thematically it can be grouped with the last lines of *The Dunciad*, with the
'Analytic of the Sublime', or with Wordsworth's dream of the Arab
bearing the emblems of culture just ahead of 'the fleet waters of a
drowning world'. First, the threat represented by the dimensions of the
problem:

> It is not simply that there is no one – such is the exponential
> accumulation of secondary discussion – who can any longer claim to be
> competent to provide specialist commentary on more than a decade or
> two . . . it is, more complexly, that the burgeoning contributions call
> into question the use and purpose of culture as such. Just as the
> enormous increase in human population threatens all the values of
> individuality so carefully inculcated by centuries of humanistic
> refinement, so too does the flood of publication threaten the very
> knowledge that publication purports to serve.[3]

Notice that the population explosion is not brought into the argument
literally, as yet another problem (one with a certain world-historical
urgency of its own), but figuratively, as a thrilling comparison, a current

topos of the mathematical sublime. We might suspect that other figures of scary proliferation may be at hand, and indeed they are:

What then will be the eventual disposition and use of most of these secondary studies? The answer seems clear: in due course their contents will be programmed into a computer, and, as time passes, will more and more be remembered by the computer and forgotten by men. And in a still further length of time, it will be possible not only to reproduce instantaneously any aspect of previous secondary work, but actually to produce new work simply by instructing the computer to make the necessary recombinations. The wheel will then have come full circle: computers will be writing for computers, and the test of meaningful publication will be to think and write in a way a computer could not.

Certain turns of phrase – the fine Johnsonian cadence of 'remembered by the computer and forgotten by men', for example – suggest that McFarland may have taken a mournful pleasure in working up this fragment of science fiction, but we may suspect that he's also quite serious: this is something more than a reviewer's ritual groan. In fact, the statement of the problem is accompanied by a rapid and pointed analysis of its causes. McFarland sees that the justification for much scholarly activity is itself a fiction; one pretends a work is 'needed' on, say, Shelley's life; in truth, as McFarland notes, 'the need goes the other way. The student needs the doctorate; then needs an academic position; then needs recognition and advancement'. Critical and scholarly writing proliferates as the energies of personal ambition are fed into an increasingly unwieldly and mindless institutional machine.

If one agrees with McFarland's analysis and shares his dismay, one reads on with certain ethical or political expectations, imagining that one is about to be told what ought to be done, or perhaps one is about to see something being done right then and there – the reviewer savagely but righteously clearing the field of at least a few unnecessary books. In fact, nothing of the sort develops. What follows this intense and, I assume, earnest indictment is a summary of nineteenth-century studies distinguished by its critical intelligence and knowledgeability but not in any other way out of the ordinary. It is written with a great deal of generosity and with no signs whatever that its writer is anything but content with his role: he has made a professional commitment to review these books and he is carrying it out in a professional fashion.

We seem to have come a long way from the mathematical sublime, but I believe we are still very much within its field of force. We have simply followed the reviewer to a point of blockage: he has written of the threat of being overwhelmed by too much writing, and it may not be possible to go beyond that – in writing. The appropriate corrective measures may still be taken elsewhere, and we can assume McFarland knows what they are: in his dealings with his students and colleagues, in the pressure he applies to publishers and to the makers of university, foundation, and government policy, he can still wield varying degrees of influence on the politics of literary scholarship. If he nevertheless sounds thwarted, it may not be chiefly because the dimensions of the political problem are out of proportion to his own practical force, but rather because he has run his sense of the problem to the point where he can glimpse another sort of incommensurability. That, at least, is what I gather from another paragraph in the review, one that may be read as a gesture beyond blockage, but that produces only a further occasion for bewilderment.

> The scholar, in Emerson's conception, is 'man thinking'. With the proliferation of secondary comment, he must necessarily become ever more something else: man reading. And yet, in a very real sense the whole aim of culture should be the integration of awareness – should be eventually to read less, not more. 'The constant influx of other people's ideas', writes Schopenhauer, 'must certainly stop and stifle our own, and indeed, in the long run paralyze the power of thought. . . . Therefore incessant reading and study positively ruin the mind. . . . Reading no longer anticipates thinking, but entirely takes its place.'

In the face of 'the proliferation of secondary comment' – plural, heterogeneous, dismaying – the reviewer posits an ideal, 'the integration of awareness', and the human, if abstract, embodiment of that ideal, the figure of 'man thinking'. But if McFarland would enjoin us, and himself, to read less, why has he gone on to cite Schopenhauer, when Schopenhauer is saying much the same thing that he has just thoughtfully set down himself? Why wasn't once enough, especially for someone who is insisting that enough is enough?

I don't think a serious answer to that question can be framed either in terms of personal psychology or in terms of institutional structures: those vocabularies of motivation have been left behind by the language of the paragraph. Its rhetorical heightening (its invocation of Emerson and Schopenhauer, the urgency we hear in phrases like 'in a very real sense'), its insistence that thinking is to be distinguished from reading just when, paradoxically, it is displaying what looks like an unavoidable contamination of the one by the other – all this suggests that the reviewer has led us, willy-nilly, into the region of the sublime. In a scenario characteristic of the sublime, an attempt to come to terms with plurality in the interest of an 'integration of awareness' has generated a curiously spare tableau: the mind blocked in confrontation with an unsettling and indeterminate play between two elements (here called 'man thinking' and 'man reading') that themselves resist integration. We can better understand the logic of this scenario if we turn back to some of its earlier manifestations.

II

The moment of blockage is a familiar one to readers of Wordsworth, who repeatedly represents himself as, in his phrasing, 'thwarted, baffled and rescued in his own despite',[4] checked in some activity – sometimes clearly perverse, sometimes apparently innocuous – then released into another order of experience or of discourse: the Simplon Pass episode and the encounter with the Blind Beggar are but two of the most memorable of such passages in *The Prelude*. If the experience seems to us both very Wordsworthian and perfectly natural, that may be in part a tribute to the persuasiveness of Wordsworth's poetry, in part a way of acknowledging how commonplace the scenario (if not the experience) had become by the end of the eighteenth century. Kant's 'Analytic of the Sublime' (1790) offers the most rigorous philosophical account, but the staging of blockage had been blocked out much earlier. Samuel Monk finds it already informing Addison's description of the imagination's pleasurable dealings with greatness, 'its aspiration to grasp the object, the preordained failure, and the consequent feeling of bafflement, and the sense of awe and wonder'.[5] 'Various men', Monk comments, 'were to use this pattern with varying significance, but it is essentially the sublime experience from Addison to Kant.' In fact, it was his noticing the continuity of this pattern that allowed Monk to organize his history of what he refers to as the 'chaos' of esthetic speculation in the eighteenth century. His book opens with a careful paraphrase of Kant because, as he says, 'it would be unwise to embark on the confused seas of English theories of the sublime without having some ideas as to where we are going';[6] it concludes with a long citation from the sixth book of *The Prelude* – the lines on the Simplon Pass – which Monk reads as the 'apotheosis' of the eighteenth-century sublime.

Because the task of the historian – the reduction to narrative order of a large, sometimes seemingly infinite mass of detail – resembles the play of apprehension and comprehension, of counting and organizing, associated with the mathematical sublime, it might be worth dwelling for a moment on Monk's introductory remarks about his history. 'Theories of beauty', he writes, 'are relatively trim and respectable; but in theories of the sublime one catches the century somewhat off its guard, sees it, as it were, without powder or pomatum, whalebone and patches'. What people are led to call 'chaos' sometimes strikes them as the confused seas on which they must embark; here, in a figure equally traditional, chaos is a woman out of Swift or Rowlandson, in disarray and *déshabillé*, slightly all over the place, not yet fit to be seen. There is a *soupçon* of blockage about this fondly misogynistic turn, but Monk's mind recuperates its powers and reestablishes its forward movement: 'Indeed, the chief problem has been the problem of organization. The necessity of imposing form of some sort has continually led to the danger of imposing a false or artificial form.' If raw heterogeneity – the world without whalebone and patches – is a danger, so is sheer willfully cosmetic unity, 'artificial form'; we are led to expect an image of synthesis or integration, and we are not disappointed: 'I have therefore grouped the theories together loosely under very general headings in an effort to indicate that there is a progress, slow and continuous, but that this progress is one of organic growth. . . . The direction of this growth is toward the subjectivism of Kant.'[7]

Monk's book was written over forty years ago, when historians of eighteenth-century literature and philosophy were not afraid of using the word 'preromanticism' or of picturing the century teleologically, as if it were *en route* to writers like Wordsworth or Kant, or to concepts like that of the Imagination. That mode of historical argument has been sufficiently challenged so that Monk's narrative may seem dated. Yet a recent theoretical study of the sublime, a splendidly intelligent book by Thomas Weiskel,[8] still finds its organizing figures in Kant and Wordsworth, and more particularly, in their accounts of the mind's movement, blockage, and release. Is the moment of blockage, then, simply a *fact* about the experience of the sublime, attested to by one after another eighteenth-century writer, available for the subsequent generalizing commentary of historians like Monk or literary theorists like Weiskel? I think not; rather, a look at the provenance of the notion of blockage will reveal a more interesting development.

Eighteenth-century writers do not use the word 'blockage'; they use verbs like 'baffle' and 'check' or nouns like 'astonishment' or 'difficulty'. Here, for example, is Hume on the reason we venerate 'the relicts of antiquity': 'The mind, elevated by the vastness of its object, is still farther elevated by the difficulty of the conception; and being oblig'd every moment to renew its efforts in the transition from one part of time to another, feels a more vigorous and sublime dispositon.'[9] 'Difficulty', Hume had just written, 'instead of extinguishing [the mind's] vigour and alacrity, has the contrary effect, of sustaining and increasing it.' Language such as this – and there is much similar talk throughout the century of the tonic effects of opposition or sheer recalcitrance – language such as this is easily enough assimilated to the pattern of motion and blockage, but it is worth noticing that it is not saying quite the same thing: here the mind is braced and roused but not absolutely (even if only for a moment) checked. This may sound trivial, a mere difference in degree, but such differences, between the absolute and the not-so-absolute, often take on philosophical and narrative importance. When Saul, on his way to Damascus, was thwarted, baffled, and rescued in his own despite, the Bible does not report that he merely faltered in his purpose, slumped to his hands and knees, then rose at the count of nine. The example can serve as a reminder that the metaphor of blockage draws much of its power from the literature of religious conversion, that is, from a literature that describes major experiential transformation, the mind not merely challenged and thereby invigorated but thoroughly 'turned round'.

As for the notion of difficulty, Angus Fletcher has shown that it too has a religious origin, although it is associated not with the act of conversion but with the more commonplace – and continuous – activity of interpreting the figurative language of Scripture, of working out the sense of what had come to be known as 'difficult ornament'. I quote from Fletcher's discussion in his book on allegory:

> 'Difficulty' implies here a calculated obscurity which elicits an interpretive response in the reader. The very obscurity is a source of pleasure, especially to the extent that the actual process of deciphering the exegetical content of a passage would be painfully arduous and uncertain. Obscurity stirs curiosity; the reader wants to tear the veil aside. 'The more they seem obscure through their use of figurative expressions', says Augustine, 'the more they give pleasure when they have been made clear.'[10]

The citation of Augustine can remind us that discussions of religious conversion and of biblical exegesis are not entirely irrelevant to one another, the intermediate notion, as Fletcher indicates, being that of an ascesis of reading:

> Augustine is pointing to a cosmic uncertainty embodied in much of Scripture, in response to which he can only advocate an interpretive frame of mind, which for him becomes the occasion of an *ascesis*. The mixture of pain and pleasure, an intellectual tension accompanying the hard work of exegetical labor, is nothing less than the cognitive aspect of the ambivalence which inheres in the contemplation of any sacred object. Whatever is *sacer* must cause the shiver of mingled delight and awe that constitutes our sense of 'difficulty'.

Augustinian ascesis organizes reading so that it becomes a movement, albeit with difficult steps, down the line toward a pleasure that is also a guarantee of the proximity of the sacred object. I think we can find an equivalent of that in the eighteenth century's absorption of the rhetorical concept of difficulty into the experiential notion of blockage. This process is contemporary with the progressive loss of interest in Longinus's treatise, or rather, with the selective appropriation of elements of his rhetoric as modes of extraliterary experience. The two processes would seem to go together, although in ways I have not yet made clear. The translation of 'difficulty' into 'blockage' and the submersion of the rhetorical sublime so that its figures function as a sort of experiential underwriting both seem like strategies designed to consolidate a reassuringly operative notion of the self. A telling paragraph from an eclectic mid-century theorist, Alexander Gerard, can provide us with an illustration of the strategy at work:

> We always contemplate objects and ideas with a disposition similar to their nature. When a large object is presented, the mind expands itself to the extent of that object, and is filled with one grand sensation, which totally possessing it, composes it into a solemn sedateness, and strikes it with deep silent wonder and admiration: it finds such a difficulty in spreading itself to the dimensions of its object, as enlivens and invigorates its frame: and having overcome the opposition which this occasions, it sometimes imagines itself present in every part of the scene which it contemplates; and from the sense of this immensity, feels a noble pride, and entertains a lofty conception of its own capacity.[11]

Notions of 'difficulty' and 'blockage' are loosely accommodated by this prose, which draws on Addison and Hume as well as on Longinus. The mind, seeking to match itself to its object, 'expands', and that 'enlivens' and 'invigorates' it; but when its capacity matches the extent of the object, the sense of containing the object, but also (with a hint of theological paradox) of being filled by it, possessed by it, blocks the mind's further movement and 'composes it into a solemn sedateness', 'strikes it with deep silent wonder'. The *activity* of the mind may be associated with an enlivening sense of difficulty, but the mind's *unity* is most strongly felt when it is 'filled with one grand sensation', a container practically indistinguishable from the one thing it contains; and it is precisely the mind's unity that is at stake in such discussions of the natural sublime. The 'integration of awareness' thus posited is achieved by a passage to the limit that carries the notion of difficulty to the point where it turns into absolute difficulty, a negative moment but nevertheless a reassuring one.

III

Earlier, in considering Samuel Monk's introductory remarks, I assumed an analogy between the scholar's imagining himself heroically coming to grips with a chaotic heap of historical matter and the situation of the hero of one of Kant's sublime scenarios, that of the mathematical sublime. I wish now to look a bit more closely at Kant's 'Analytic of the Sublime', this time in connection with the work of Thomas Weiskel. It is Weiskel's distinction to have seen that the poetic and philosophic language of the primary sublime texts could be made to resonate with two quite different twentieth-century idioms, that of psychoanalysis and that of the semiological writings of Saussure, Jakobson, and Barthes. Weiskel's fine responsiveness to poetry, along with the patience and lucidity with which he elaborates a complex argument, make his book a difficult one to excerpt or to summarize, but my own understanding of the sublime requires me to come to terms with at least some elements of it, to question it at certain points and to explore the ways it locates itself in relation to its material. I shall be chiefly concerned with his discussion of the mathematical sublime, more particularly still with his attempt to bring Kant within the explanatory range of Freudian metapsychology.

Partly to satisfy the internal necessities of the Critical Philosophy, partly in response to an observable difference in accounts of sublime experience, Kant divides his consideration of the sublime into two sections, depending on whether the feeling is generated by the mind's confrontation with a seemingly overwhelming natural force (this is the dynamical sublime, the sublime of waterfalls, hurricanes, earthquakes, and the like) or else by the disturbances of cognition I described in the first section of this essay. This latter is the sublime of magnitude, the mathematical sublime, and it is of this mode that Kant writes: 'For there is here a feeling of the inadequacy of [the] imagination for presenting the ideas of a whole, wherein the imagination reaches its maximum, and, in striving to surpass it, sinks back into itself, by which, however, a kind of emotional satisfaction is produced.'[12] This is, one senses, the intellectual's sublime (Weiskel calls it, appropriately, the reader's or hermeneutical sublime). Kant is seemingly evenhanded in his treatment of the two modes; he makes no attempt to subordinate the one to the other, but rather, he locates each in relation to the branching symmetries of his entire system. The mathematical sublime is associated with cognition and hence with the epistemological concerns of the *Critique of Pure Reason*; the dynamical sublime, because it confirms man's sense of his 'spiritual destination', is referred to what Kant calls the faculty of desire and hence to the ethical concerns of the second *Critique*. But here an important qualification is introduced: the mathematical sublime too, it develops, shares this link with the ethical. For, as Kant presents this drama of collapse and compensation, the 'emotional satisfaction' he finds there is taken to be an effect of the recognition that what the imagination has failed to bring into a unity (the infinite or the indefinitely plural) can nevertheless be *thought* as such, and that the agent of this thinking, the reason, must thus be a guarantor of man's 'supersensible destiny'. What is intriguing is that the drama seems to be available for two incompatible interpretations: we can think of it as the story of Ethics coming to the rescue in a situation of cognitive distress, or we can see that distress as slightly factitious, staged precisely in order to require the somewhat melodramatic arrival of Ethics. This is the sort of puzzle to which Weiskel addresses himself.

Weiskel's deliberate strategy is that of a translator. He would seek to understand the sublime by construing it, as he puts it, outside the presuppositions of idealism.[13] The drama of the imagination's collapse and reason's intervention, for example, looks as if it might allow itself to be restaged in modern dress and in a psychoanalytic vernacular. The delight in the mathematical sublime, Kant had written, is a feeling of 'imagination by its own act depriving itself of its freedom by receiving a final determination in accordance with a law other than that of its empirical employment'. 'In this way', Kant continues, 'it gains an extension and a power greater than that which it sacrifices. But the ground of this is concealed from it, and in its place it *feels* the sacrifice or deprivation to which it is subjected.' Weiskel cites the passage, then wonders at its motivational structure: why can't the imagination share the mind's pleasure in reason? Why this talk of sacrifice and concealment? There is further, he notices, a hint that the imagination has been, in a way, entrapped, led into this disaster by reason itself and for reason's own ends. 'The real motive or cause of the sublime', Weiskel suggests, 'is not efficient but teleological; we are ultimately referred not to the failure of empirical imagination but to reason's project in requiring this failure. The cause of the sublime is the *aggrandizement of reason at the expense of reality and the imaginative apprehension of reality*.'[14]

Readers of Freud should have no trouble predicting the general direction of Weiskel's argument: the Kantian sublime, in both its manifestations, becomes 'the very moment in which the mind turns within and performs its identification with reason. The sublime recapitulates and thereby reestablishes the Oedipus complex', with Kant's reason taking the role of the superego, that agency generated by an act of sublimation, 'an identification with the father taken as a model'.[15]

What one could not have foreseen is the turn Weiskel's argument takes at this point. Throughout his discussion of the mathematical sublime, he has had to come to terms with the question of excess; for the theme of magnitude, of that which resists conceptualization, was bound to raise the problem. Until now, to the extent that both the mathematical and the dynamical sublime could be rendered as affirmative of reason – that is, of the superego – it had been possible to think of excess in terms of Freud's discussion of excessive identification, of that supererogatory strength of investment that turns the super-ego into a harsher taskmaster than the father on whom it is modeled. But there may be other forms of excess associated with the mathematical sublime that are not so easily accounted for: is it possible that there is excess that cannot, in Jacques Derrida's phrase, be brought back home to the father? Weiskel takes up the question in a section that begins with what sounds like a scholar's twinge of conscience about his own sublime operations of mind: 'Have we not', he asks, 'arrived at [this] model by pressing one theory and suppressing a multitude of facts for which it cannot account?' This qualm, intensified by a further look at some of the lines from *The Prelude*, leads Weiskel to suspect that the 'anxiety of the sublime does not ultimately result from the pressure of the super-ego after all . . . that the Oedipus complex is not its deep structure'.[16] What follows is an intensely reasoned and difficult four pages, as Weiskel works to integrate this new discovery into the larger movement of his argument. This involves him in an exploration of the terrors and wishes of the pre-Oedipal phases, where he finally locates the motivating power of the mathematical sublime, then sees that as rejoining a secondary system that is recognizably Oedipal and more clearly manifested in the dynamical sublime. I quote his conclusion:

> We should not be surprised to find that the sublime movement is overdetermined in its effect on the mind. The excess which we have supposed to be the precipitating occasion, or 'trigger', directly prompts the secondary anxiety in the case of the dynamical sublime of terror. In the mathematical sublime, however, the traumatic phase exhibits a primary system on which the secondary (guilt) system is superimposed. This situation explains an odd but unmistakable fact of Kant's analytic. Whenever he is generalizing about both versions of the negative sublime, the (secondary) rhetoric of power dominates. It is not logically necessary that the reason's capacity for totality or infinity should be invariably construed as power degrading the sensible and rescuing man from 'humiliation' at the hands of nature. But though the sublime of magnitude does not originate in a power struggle, it almost instantaneously turns into one as the secondary Oedipal system takes over.[17]

If we step back a moment, it may now be possible to state, in a general and schematic fasion, just where the fascination of the mathematical sublime lies and what sort of problem it represents for the historian or the theorist. Weiskel's scrupulosity in raising the question of excess, in wishing not to suppress 'a multitude of facts' in the interest of establishing a theoretical model, parallels Samuel Monk's qualm lest he impose a 'false and artificial form' on a chaotic mass of material. We might even see in Weiskel's invocation of the (maternal) pre-Oedipal phases, in his interpretation of them as constituting the deep (hence primary) structure of the sublime and yet as still only a tributary of the Oedipal system into which it invariably flows, a more serious and argued version of Monk's joking about the woman not fit to be seen. The goal in each case is the Oedipal moment, that is, the goal is the sublime of conflict and structure. The scholar's *wish* is for the moment of blockage, when an indefinite and disarrayed sequence is resolved (at whatever sacrifice) into a one-to-one confrontation, when numerical excess can be converted into that supererogatory identification with the blocking agent that is the guarantor of the self's own integrity as an agent.

I suggested earlier that something similar could be seen at work during the eighteenth century, as the notion of difficulty or recalcitrance was transformed, through a passage to the limit, into the notion of absolute blockage. This too would seem to have been the result of a wish, for although the moment of blockage might have been rendered as one of utter self-loss, it was, even before its recuperation as sublime exaltation, a confirmation of the unitary status of the self. A passage to the limit may seem lurid, but it has its ethical and metaphysical uses.

IV

At the beginning of this essay I proposed some paragraphs written by the scholar Thomas McFarland as a contemporary instance of the mathematical sublime. There, I suggested, we could trace a scenario that eighteenth-century theorists would have found familiar: the progress of the mind as it sought to take in a dismaying plurality of objects. If we look back at McFarland's text now, we should be able to bring its movement into clearer focus.

The mind is set in motion by a threat, the 'exponential accumulation of secondary discussion', the 'flood of publication', a threat directed not at the exterior intellectual landscape but at the inner integrity of the mind itself, that is, at the integrity of the individual scholar's mind. No single reader can 'claim to be competent to provide specialist commentary on more than a decade or two', McFarland notes. And it is the ideal of a cultured – i.e., broadly competent – individual that McFarland would defend. Hence, McFarland makes no attempt to 'totalize' or 'integrate' the objects of his dismay, whatever that might mean in practice (perhaps a reorganization of literary scholarship along more efficient lines?). Setting such activity aside as impracticable and no doubt undesirable in any case, and therefore checked in its commerce with its objects, the scholar's mind, in Kant's phrase, 'sinks back into itself', not without 'a kind of emotional satisfaction': what is generated is a rhetoric of interior totalization, the plea for 'the integration of awareness' and its embodiment in the figure of 'man thinking'. But at this point a further difficulty arises: for the scholar to contemplate the Emersonian description of 'man thinking' is to be quite literally cast in the role of 'man reading'; or, more accurately, to discern that one's thinking and one's reading are, in the best of scholarly times (and when would that have been? before what Fall?), hard to disentangle. In response to this puzzling recognition the figure of Schopenhauer is called up. He appears as McFarland's double, reiterating his dismay, seconding his call for an integration of awareness in still more authoritative tones. But the presence of his words within quotation marks serves as one more reminder that 'other people's ideas' are as much the material of genuine thinking as they are a hindrance to it. Schopenhauer, we could say, is the name of that difficulty; he stands for the recurrent and commonplace difficulty of distinguishing thinking from reading, and he is conjured up here as an agent of sublime blockage, an eloquent voice at the end of the line.[18]

But why this thrust toward eloquence and confrontation? My discussion of the eighteenth-century sublime suggests one answer: that the self cannot simply think but must read the confirmation of its own integrity, which is only legible in a specular structure, a structure in which the self can perform that 'supererogatory identification with the blocking agent'. That, I believe, is what drives McFarland to summon up Schopenhauer from the grave, and it is the same energy that erodes the stability of that specular poise: the voice of Schopenhauer is replaced, in the next paragraph, by the fantasy of the computer. This grimly comic version is set in the future ('The wheel will then have come full circle; computers will be writing for computers') but it is an embodiment of a threat that has been present all along. The computer is the machine inside the ghost of Schopenhauer, the system of energies that links 'thinking' to 'reading' to 'remembering' to 'citing' to 'writing'. It serves here as a figure for what makes scholars run, when that process is felt to be most threatening to the integrity of the individual awareness, a threat from which even 'the strongest are not free'.

> Oh, blank confusion! true epitome
> Of what the mighty City is herself
> To thousands upon thousands of her sons,
> Living amid the same perpetual whirl
> Of trivial objects, melted and reduced
> To one identity, by differences
> That have no law, no meaning, and no end –
> Oppression, under which even highest minds
> Must labour, whence the strongest are not free.[19]

Bartholomew Fair, as it is imagined in the last lines of Book VII of *The Prelude*, was Wordsworth's computer, a city within the City, a scale model of urban mechanisms, designed to focus his fear:

> Tents and Booths
> Meanwhile, as if the whole were one vast mill
> Are vomiting, receiving on all sides,
> Men, Women, three-years Children, Babes in arms.

(VII, 718–21)

The lines on Bartholomew Fair repeat, in a condensed and phantasmagoric fashion, what had been the burden of the earlier accounts of London: the sometimes exhilarating, sometimes baffling proliferation, not merely of sights and sounds, objects and people, but of consciously chosen and exhibited modes of representation. Book VII is the book of spectacle, theatricality, oratory, advertising, and *ad hoc* showmanship, not just the book of crowds. A Whitmanesque passage from early in the book catches the mixture as well as providing an instance of Wordsworth's own narrative – or rather *non*-narrative – stance:

>   Rise up, thou monstrous ant-hill on the plain
> Of a too busy world! Before me flow,
> Thou endless stream of men and moving things!
> Thy every-day appearance, as it strikes –
> With wonder heightened, or sublimed with awe –
> On strangers, of all ages; the quick dance
> Of colours, lights and forms; the deafening din:
> The comers and the goers face to face,
> Face after face; the string of dazzling wares,
> Shop after shop, with symbols, blazoned names,
> And all the tradesman's honours overhead:
> Here, fronts of houses, like a title-page,
> With letters huge inscribed from top to toe,
> Stationed above the door, like guardian saints;
> There, allegoric shapes, female or male,
> Or physiognomies of real men,
> Land-warriors, kings, or admirals of the sea,
> Boyle, Shakespeare, Newton, or the attractive head
> Of some quack-doctor, famous in his day.

(VII, 149–67)

These lines, so full of detail, are not exactly narrative; they conjure more than they describe. And what they summon up is a different order of experience from what we think of as characteristically Wordsworthian. They resist the phenomenological reading that seems so appropriate elsewhere in *The Prelude*, a reading attuned to the nuanced interinvolvements of centrally Wordsworthian modes of experience – seeing and gazing, listening, remembering, feeling. Instead, they present a plethora of prefabricated items – tradesmen's signs, statuary – that are intended to be legible, not merely visible, and mix these in with sights and sounds, 'men and moving things', in rapid appositional sequence until everything comes to seem like reading matter ('Face after face; the string of dazzling wares, / Shop after shop, with symbols, blazoned names . . .').

As the book goes on, the prodigious energy Wordsworth experiences in London is more and more made to seem a function of the tradesmen's and showmen's and actors' wish to represent and of the populace's complementary hunger for spectacle: representation comes to seem like the very pulse of the machine. And in a startling moment, too strange to be simply satirical, the showman's crude inventiveness and the audience's will to believe are brought into touch with the developing opposition between what can be seen and what can be read. Wordsworth is describing a performance of 'Jack the Giant-killer' at Sadler's Wells:

> Lo!
> He dons his coat of darkness; on the stage
> Walks, and achieves his wonders, from the eye
> Of living Mortal covert, 'as the moon
> Hid in her vacant interlunar cave.'
> Delusion bold! and how can it be wrought?
> The garb he wears is black as death, the word
> 'Invisible' flames forth upon his chest.
>
> (VII, 280–7)

I have offered these citations and have been teasing out thematic strands as a way of suggesting the drift of Book VII toward a sublime encounter, the episode with the Blind Beggar, who occupies what we might call the 'Schopenhauer position' in the structure of the poem. Wordsworth himself has been drifting through the book, sometimes presenting his experience anecdotally, in the autobiographical past tense ('I saw . . .'; 'I viewed . . .') that we are accustomed to in *The Prelude*, more often presenting himself as poet-impresario of the great spectacle, in a generalized present tense ('I glance but at a few conspicuous marks, / Leaving a thousand others, that, in hall, / Court, theatre . . .'). Without forcing the poem, I think we can say that the difference between the subject of autobiographical experience and the poet-impresario is made to seem, in Book VII more than elsewhere in *The Prelude*, like the difference between seeing and reading. In London, more than in the country, everybody's experience is mediated by the semiotic intentions of others; in Book VII, more than anywhere else in *The Prelude*, the poet adopts the showman's stance. I believe it is the developing confusion of these two roles, the odd slackening of the tension between them, as much as the accumulating overload of urban detail, that precipitates the critical scene with the Blind Beggar. I cite the episode in its earlier version, which is less elegantly worded but at one point more revealing:

> How often in the overflowing Streets,
> Have I gone forward with the Crowd, and said
> Unto myself, the face of every one
> That passes by me is a mystery.
> Thus have I look'd, nor ceas'd to look, oppress'd
> By thoughts of what, and whither, when and how,
> Until the shapes before my eyes became
> A second-sight procession, such as glides
> Over still mountains, or appears in dreams;
> And all the ballast of familiar life,
> The present, and the past; hope, fear; all stays,
> All laws of acting, thinking, speaking man
> Went from me, neither knowing me, nor known.
>
> (1805 text, VII, 594–606)

The last four lines of this passage, eliminated when Wordsworth revised the poem, tell of a moment, a recurrent moment, of thoroughgoing self-loss – not the recuperable baffled self associated with scenarios of blockage, but a more radical flux and dispersion of the subject. The world is neither legible nor visible in the familiar way; faces, which had earlier been associated with signs, are there but they cannot be deciphered, while visible shapes have taken on a dreamlike lack of immediacy. This loss of 'ballast' is made to sound like the situation of 'blank confusion' at Bartholomew Fair, when objects become 'melted and reduced / To one identity, by differences / That have no law, no meaning, and no end': it is not that differences disappear, but that the possibility of interpreting them as significant differences vanishes. It may be, for instance, that seeing and reading are not that distinct, that as the possibility of interpreting differences diminishes, the possibility of distinguishing presentation from representation does too, and with it, the possibility of drawing a clear demarcation between the subject of autobiography and the poet-impresario. Some remarkable effects can be generated by crossing that line (the famous instance would be the rising up of Imagination in Book VI), but the line needs to be established in order to be vividly transgressed. These are the threats, this is the 'ferment silent

and sublime' (VIII, 572), that inhere in these lines, and I believe it is in
response to them that the Blind Beggar is brought into the poem:

> 'twas my chance
> Abruptly to be smitten with the view
> Of a Blind Beggar, who, with upright face,
> Stood propp'd against a Wall, upon his Chest
> Wearing a written paper, to explain
> The story of the Man, and who he was.
> My mind did at this spectacle turn round
> As with the might of waters, and it seem'd
> To me that in this Label was a type,
> Or emblem, of the utmost that we know,
> Both of ourselves and of the universe;
> And, on the shape of the unmoving man,
> His fixèd face and sightless eyes, I look'd
> As if admonish'd from another world.
>
> (1805 text, VII, 609–22)

In one sense, the Beggar simply allows Wordsworth to reiterate his sense
of bafflement. Earlier he had told himself 'the face of every one /
That passes by me is a mystery'; now he is faced with 'an emblem of the
utmost we can know'. And in the play between the Beggar's blank face
and the minimally informative text on his chest, the difference between
what Wordsworth can see and what he can read is hardly reestablished
in any plenitude: it is a fixed difference – the text won't float up and blur
into the lineaments of the Beggar's face – but it is still almost no
difference at all. However, it is precisely the fixity that is the point – a
point softened in the direction of a more intelligibly humane reading by
Wordsworth's decision to change 'His fixèd face' (1805) to 'His steadfast
face' (1850). The encounter with the Beggar triangulates the poet's self in
relation to his double, who is represented, for a moment as an emblem of
minimal difference fixed in relation to itself. The power of the emblem is
that it reestablishes boundaries between representer and represented
and, while minimizing the differences between them, keeps the poet-
impresario from tumbling into his text. I would suggest that this is the
common function of the moment of blockage in sublime scenarios.

Notes

1. Immanuel Kant, *Critique of Judgement*, trans. J.H. Bernard (New York: Hafner, 1966), p. 83.

2. Ibid., p. 91.

3. THOMAS MCFARLAND, 'Recent Studies in the Nineteenth Century', *Studies in English Literature* **16**, (1976): 693–4.

4. WILLIAM WORDSWORTH, *The Prose Works of William Wordsworth*, ed. W.J.B. Owen and Jane Worthington Smyser, 3 vols. (Oxford: Clarendon, 1975), 2: 355

5. SAMUEL MONK, *The Sublime: A Study of Critical Theories in Eighteenth-Century England* (1935; rpt., Ann Arbor: University of Michigan Press, 1960), p. 58.

6. Ibid., p. 6.

7. Ibid., pp. 3–4.

8. THOMAS WEISKEL, *The Romantic Sublime: Studies in the Structure and Psychology of Transcendence* (Baltimore: Johns Hopkins University Press, 1976), pp. 22–23.

9. DAVID HUME, *A Treatise of Human Nature*, ed. L.A. Selby-Bigge (Oxford: Clarendon, 1888), p. 436.

10. ANGUS FLETCHER, *Allegory: The Theory of a Symbolic Mode* (Ithaca: Cornell University Press, 1964), pp. 234–35.

11. ALEXANDER GERARD, *An Essay on Taste*, 2nd ed. (Edinburgh, 1764; rpt., New York: Garland, 1970), p. 12.

12. KANT, *Critique of Judgement*, p. 91.

13. WEISKEL *Romantic Sublime*, p. 21.

14. Ibid., p. 41.

15. Ibid., pp. 92 ff.

16. Ibid., pp. 99 ff.

17. Ibid., p. 106.

18. This may be the moment to acknowledge some other people's ideas. Henry Abelove pointed out to me the nice irony, no doubt conscious on McFarland's part, of his selecting Schopenhauer for this particular role. Schopenhauer is the occasion for a peculiarly devious development in Proust's essay 'On Reading.' (Originally published as the preface to Proust's translation of Ruskin's *Sesame and Lilies* in 1906, the essay has been reprinted, in a bilingual edition, ed. and trans. Jean Autret and William Burford (New York: Macmillan, 1971). On p. 51, Proust offers Schopenhauer as 'the image of a mind whose vitality bears lightly the most enormous reading'; on the next page, Schopenhauer is praised for having produced a book 'which implies in an author, along with the most reading, the most originality'; between these two accolades Proust quotes a series of fifteen or so passages, taken, he says, from one page of *The World as Will and Representation*, which he strings together so as to produce a rapid, abbreviated, reiterative, and finally comical parade of bits of Voltaire, Byron, Herodotus, Heraclitus (in Latin), Theognis (in Latin), and so on, down to Byron (again) and Balthazar Gracian. The effect is like that of riffling the pages of Curtius; the whole run-through is punctuated by Proust's repetition of 'etc.' as he cuts off one citation after another. Josué Harari has drawn my attention to a fine reading of this essay by Barbara Harlow in *MLN* **90**, (1975): 849–71.

19. WILLIAM WORDSWORTH, *The Prelude: 1799, 1805, 1850*, ed. Jonathan Wordsworth, M.H. Abrams, and Stephen Gill (New York: Norton, 1979). Henceforth, references to *The Prelude* will appear in the text; unless otherwise indicated, line numbers refer to the 1850 version of book VII.

4 Past Recognition: Narrative Origins in Wordsworth and Freud*

CATHY CARUTH

This essay is a chapter of Cathy Caruth's *Empirical Truths and Critical Fictions: Locke, Wordsworth, Kant and Freud*. An exemplary rhetorical reading, Caruth's essay demonstrates the complexity of the accounts of the self's origin given in texts of Freud and Wordsworth. (See Introduction.) A fundamental topic of the essay is the fact and figure of the death of the mother as a condition of the emergence of the 'poetic spirit' which *The Prelude* defines. Caruth's essay reveals the impossibility of bringing together under a single heading the diverse rhetorical functions and figural strategies that the theme of the mother's death involves. Spinning out the irreducible and incommensurable stories of the self's origin that Caruth calls 'the affective story' and 'the propping story' (which 'cannot exactly be considered *a* story', as she explains), *The Prelude* performs the work of mourning, a process which turns out to figure significantly in texts of Kant and Locke as well as Freud and Wordsworth. Caruth's readings turn our attention to the materiality of language – to 'aspects of language such as syntax or punctuation, which articulate "prior" to, or as the condition of the possibility of, meaningful discourse'. Because they simply 'remain' – remain irreducible to the literal or figural meaning of a passage – such aspects of language may prevent the work of mourning or of the internalization of meaning from coming to an end.

The word *ego* has a place in the discourse of Romantic literature, but to speak today of the 'Romantic ego', or to read Romantic texts in terms of other psychoanalytic concepts, is necessarily to juxtapose two different

* Reprinted from Cathy Caruth, *Empirical Truths and Critical Fictions: Locke, Wordsworth, Kant, Freud* (Baltimore and London: Johns Hopkins University Press, 1990), pp. 44–57, 147–51.

discourses: Romantic and psychoanalytic.[1] And this is also to suggest that our self-understanding, as articulated within psychoanalytic discourse, can be understood historically, in terms of the relation between psychoanalytic theory and the texts of an earlier period called Romanticism. The nature of this gesture – the representation of self-knowledge as a history of its evolving discourses – is not entirely clear, but it is nevertheless entirely appropriate, since it is precisely this configuration of self-knowledge, history, and discourse which many 'Romantic' texts explore. By reading these texts in a search for our past, therefore, we can learn more about this very attempt to recognize ourselves in them.

A similar gesture, although apparently inadvertent, is made by Jeffrey Mehlman in translating a passage from Freud's *Three Essays on Sexuality*. In the section explaining the sexual drive in terms of its origins in the nursing baby, Mehlman offers a new translation for the word *Anlehnung*, which designates the relation of the sexual drive to the instinct of hunger. In place of Strachey's 'anaclisis', Mehlman suggests the word 'propping.[2] The oddness of the word in this context recalls a striking use of it in Wordsworth's *Prelude*: after describing the origin of the poetic spirit in the baby at the breast, the poet refers to the mother as the 'prop' of the child's affections. Mehlman's translation calls our attention to a problem common to the narratives of personal history in both texts. Each explains the dynamics of a self which cannot be called empirical (the sexual drive or poetic spirit)[3] in terms of its origins in an empirically situated event, the physical relation of the mother and the nursing baby. But this produces, in each text, two different stories, one of which describes an intimate affective relation between the baby and the mother's body, and another which is less concerned with affect, and less clearly a matter of subject and object, and which refers instead to a propping or leaning activity. The possibility of understanding Freud's and Wordsworth's narratives of self-knowledge revolves around the problem of reading these two stories together.

The importance of emphasizing the role of discourse in this problem, as we have done by focusing on the word *ego* and on Mehlman's translation, is suggested by both Wordsworth's and Freud's texts. The Blessed Babe passage in *The Prelude* locates the origins of 'our first poetic spirit' in a 'being' whose history moves from 'mute dialogues with my mother's heart' to 'conjectures' that 'trace' this progress.[4] A 'poetic spirit' is a 'being' whose history is the mediation of two discourses, or who defines the difference between two discourses as its own history. The place of the empirical world in this history, and the distinction between the affective and propping stories in regard to it, bypass from the beginning any simple oppositions between language, self-knowledge, and the body, and concern rather differences in the configuration of these terms.

A similar framework is established in Freud's *Three Essays,* in which the patient's self-understanding is not strictly distinguishable from the language of the psychoanalytic interpretation. In describing the way psychoanalysis explains neurotic symptoms to certain patients, Freud says:

> With the help of their symptoms and other manifestations of their illness, [psychoanalysis] traces their unconscious thoughts and translates [übersetzt] them into conscious ones. In cases in which someone who has previously been healthy falls ill after an unhappy experience in love it is also possible to show with certainty that the mechanism of his illness consists in a turning-back of his libido onto those whom he preferred in his infancy.[5]

The word *translates* identifies the process of becoming conscious with the linguistic 'return' from a foreign language, the 'symptoms and other expressions' of the illness, to the mother tongue. These symptoms turn away from, or translate figuratively, the unconscious thoughts, which are thus conceived of as a 'literal' meaning distorted by neurosis. When the literal meaning is retrieved, however, it has become part of a history; the unconscious thoughts are always ultimately revealed to be *infantile* libidinal desires. The self recognizes itself, therefore, as a relation between unconscious and conscious thoughts, and narrates this relation as the history of the sexual drive. The movement described by this narrative, between the sexual drive and the narrative's own language of self-understanding, is made possible by repression, which makes the drive appear as symptoms that can be read like a language.

The formation of symptoms also governs normal development in Freud's 'affective' version of sexual origins. The development of sexuality in general involves the same negative activity of repression that operates in neurosis:

> At a time at which the first beginnings of sexual satisfaction are still linked with the taking of nourishment, the sexual instinct has a sexual object outside the infant's body in the shape of his mother's breast. It is only later that the instinct loses that object, just at the time, perhaps, when the child is able to form a total idea of the person to whom the organ that is giving satisfaction belongs. As a rule the sexual drive then becomes auto-erotic, and not until the period of latency has been passed through is the original relation restored. There are thus good reasons why a child sucking at his mother's breast has become the

prototype of every relation of love. The finding of an object is in fact a refinding of it.[6]

This narrative is structured very much like the interpretation of a neurosis: adult sexual relations are translated, like symptoms, into a history. The 'refinding' of the object in 'every relation of love' is in fact a displacement of the 'original relation', a substitution which functions figuratively much like a neurotic symptom. Similarly, while the loss of the mother's breast is not described as a repression, it is nonetheless suggestive of it, as if the connection of the breast with the mother made the breast taboo, and the substitution of other objects necessary. Repression, then, results in adult sexual objects serving as figurative substitutes for the mother's breast. This means, first of all, that repression makes all (adult) sexual relations symptomatic, and thus capable of being read and interpreted in a psychoanalytic narrative, which itself constitutes a moment of sexual development. It is repression which aligns the sexual drive with language; repression and psychoanalytic translation hold similar positions with regard to the drive, differentiated as before (symptoms) and after. Secondly, repression distorts a relation to a *physical* object; the breast is the empirical element that locates the origin of the drive. The figurative meaning of adult sexual objects depends on their substitution for the mother's real breast as their 'literal' meaning.

The other story that Freud tells about the origins of the drive offers an alternative to this model of sexuality as repression and substitution. It is uncertain if any negativity, corresponding to repression, is operative here: 'To begin with, sexual activity attaches itself to [props itself upon] functions serving the purpose of self-preservation and does not become independent of them until later . . . At its origin . . . it has as yet no sexual object.'[7] Harold Bloom, following Laplanche, notes an important difference in this story from the first: there is no original sexual object in the breast itself; the only real object is the breast as a source of milk.[8] We could put this another way: the empirical relation of baby and breast – instinct and physical object – is replaced by the relation of drive and instinct, a displacement that is not a substitution, but a 'propping'. It is propping that makes the breast sexual, but only in fantasy; if, in Bloom's words, the first relation is 'literal', sexuality is from the beginning figurative. The confusion of literal and figurative in the two stories, and the shifting status of repression, suggest that the principle that relates mind, body, and language may be difficult to determine.

We can further explore such configuration in Wordsworth in terms of the imaginative activity of poetry. The emphasis on imaginative transformation in *The Prelude* is part of a critical response to Hartleyan associationist psychology, a tradition out of which Freud's psychoanalytic theory, through the work of James Mill, also developed.[9] Freud's critique, centered on the concepts of drive and defense, is anticipated in the Wordsworthian dynamic of passion and memory. In Book IV of *The Prelude*, this dynamic operates through the figure of self-knowledge as a 'reflection' which is also a motion:

> As one who hangs down-bending from the side
> Of a slow-moving boat upon the breast
> Of a still water, solacing himself
> With such discoveries as his eye can make
> Beneath him in the bottom of the deeps,
> . . . now is crossed by gleam
> Of his own image, by a sunbeam now,
> And motions that are sent he knows not whence,
> Impediments that make his task more sweet;
> Such pleasant office have we long pursued
> Incumbent o'er the surface of past time.
>
> (1805, IV, 247–63)

Motion, here, is a figure of the continuity between past and present, a continuity upon which the similarity of physical reflection and memory depends. As the operation of a specifically poetic memory, furthermore, it is also the figure of figurative language, conceived of as the motion from one meaning to another. The words *hang*, *deeps*, and *gleam*, however – often associated in Wordsworth with imaginative figuration – suggest that these motions are not necessarily straightforward, and, indeed, we can read this as a critique of the Hartleyan kinetics in which natural motions caused and were continuous with cognitive and affective ones.[10] By reversing the direction of motion and making it originate in the observer, the passage replaces this simple kinetics with a more complex causality. The distorting function of the motion is thereby emphasized as the possibility of an affective gain, the 'solacing' and 'sweetness' of what otherwise might be a less rewarding 'task'. Motion thus also connotes its eighteenth-century meaning of 'movement' as e-motion, and the rhetoric of figurative substitution attains a persuasive dimension. In this scene, then, memory is a form of rhetorical self-persuasion, which could be said to reinterpret associationist doctrine (as it was developed after Locke by philosophers such as Hume and Hartley) in terms of the rhetorical tradition out of which it sprang.[11]

This complex, distorting act is not in the least inimical to self-knowledge, however, and indeed makes it possible. By means of this rhetorical activity, the mere 'eye' that looks into the water receives a whole 'image', or face in return: the motion from past to present is also a passage from eye to face, or a totalization of the self by means of metonymical substitution. The simultaneously distorting and supporting capacities of this substitution are exemplified in the naming of the surface upon which the boat moves as a 'breast', the supportiveness of which is both physical and affective. This also links the 'solace' of the memory to a very specific origin, which is both the empirical relation of baby and breast, and the moment in the poem in which the words 'breast' and 'eye' have a presumably 'literal' status. This is the Blessed Babe scene in Book II, quoted here in part:

> blest the babe
> Nursed in his mother's arms, the babe who sleeps
> Upon his mother's breast, who, when his soul
> Claims manifest kindred with an earthly soul,
> Doth gather passion from his mother's eye.

> (1805, II, 239–43)

This scene is also governed by the figure of passage, present here in the word *passion* as a sort of originary movement; and here, too, the breast supports an eye-to-eye relationship. Indeed, the phrase in Book IV 'crossed by his own image' describes the figurative structure of the two passages: the self-recognition of the poet is structured as a chiasmus, or crossing between past and present relations. If the relation of the poetic self to its past self, the babe, is like the relation of the babe to the mother, the continuity of the two is a crossing in which the babe becomes an object for itself (in poetic memory) and the eye of the mother is replaced by the figurative 'eye' of the poetic self (the movement of self-consciousness).[12] The displacement of the eye thus governs a dialectical movement which mediates between self-consciousness and figurative language, by making the discursive figure akin to a phenomenal 'image'.

This cognitive – affective gain is achieved, however, at the price of a negation: the breast supports the transition between passion and memory only in its absence. Shortly after the Blessed Babe passage, the movement of substitutions begins again with the mother's death:

> For now a trouble came into my mind
> From unknown causes: I was left alone
> Seeking the visible world, nor knowing why.
> The props of my affections were removed,
> And yet the building stood, as if sustained
> By its own spirit. All that I beheld
> Was dear to me, and from this cause it came
> That now to Nature's finer influxes
> My mind lay open – to that more exact
> And intimate communion which our hearts

Maintain with the minuter properties
Of objects which already are beloved.

(1805, II, 291–302)

The use of the word *influxes* – designating a moving inward – suggests
that this passage too engages an associationist doctrine of motion. The
critique of this doctrine involves an emphasis on the necessity of a
destructive moment in order for motion to begin: the movement that
leaves the mind open is first the 're-*moval*' of an impediment (the
mother). Substitution occurs as a transformation of this negation into a
positive gain: the 'props' of the mother are replaced by the 'properties' of
nature in an act of 'communion', the Christian connotations of which
suggest the turning of death into life, and the dead letter into the living
poetic figure. The association of this transformation with causality – the
disturbing 'unknown causes' which become a more positive 'this cause' –
also complicates the Hartleyan kinetics with the suggestion of a dynamic
element, named earlier as the 'gravitation and the filial bond' (II, 263) of
child and nature.

The phrase 'unknown causes', however, and the reference to a
'trouble', are somewhat obscure. It would seem that these causes are
something other than the mother's death, since that is, presumably,
known (and singular).[13] Yet perhaps we need not entirely rule out the
possibility that the unknown causes are related to the death as something
that is not known, or assimilable to cognition. This would suggest that
the lines pose an alternative to the model of loss as a known cause, an
alternative represented also by the peculiar pairing of the figure of
communion with that of 'props'. To describe the mother – or is it just her
body, the breasts? – as 'props', is to make of her support an artificial
structure, part of an edifice which the soul manipulates for its own
architectonic purposes. Props have no place in a dynamic of life and
death, but are rather part of a mechanical operation of placement and
removal. The mother becomes something like the joints of a skeletal
structure; the sustaining 'spirit' of this 'building', in spite of the later
'communion', does not seem to be a very holy ghost. The cognitive
uncertainty of the death is thus associated with a figurative uncertainty
in the language, in which the figure of communion is placed side by side
with a mechanical language of joining and propping, the latter having
the effect of disjoining the figure of the breast from the mother, and the
mother from nature. This disrupts the passage from maternal props to
natural properties, and even from the mother to what is proper to her,
leaving us with the unexpected figure of a mother with a prosthetic
breast.

The uncertainty of the 'unknown causes' is evident also in the passage
in Book IV in which knowledge is introduced in a negative mode. The

observer, as we recall, 'now is crossed by gleam / Of his own image, by a
sunbeam now, / And wavering motions sent he knows not whence.' The
perceptual certainty of the 'now, now' is echoed by a 'knows not' that
serves less as a sign of mere ignorance than a warning of a knowledge
not only unknowable but also better left unknown, an ominous 'no,
no'.[14] Indeed, in Book V, the figuration of this passage finds a 'literal'
repetition that is far less solacing than the scene with the mother. This is
the well-known episode of the drowned man, which is also a search for a
recognizable face, in a lake referred to again as a 'breast' (l. 440):

> some looked
> In passive expectation from the shore,
> While from a boat others hung o'er the deep,
> Sounding with grappling irons and long poles.
> At last the dead man . . . bolt upright
> Rose, with his ghastly face.
>
> (1805, V, 444–50)

A critical emphasis on motion, or passing, is once again apparent in the
contrast of 'passive' looking and the 'sounding' motions of those who
'hung o'er the deep'.[15] The image of a face is replaced here, however, by
a real dead face which, presumably, stops this motion. What is
disturbing is that the motion is *not* entirely stopped: the dead man 'rises'
as if by his own power, making his ghastly face rather ghostly. The
breast of water on which he floats serves in this case as a prop that
supports and makes the dead appear living: it propagates, so to speak,
the appearance of a living motion. This complicates the opposition of
motion and stillness as figurative and literal meaning, specifically in
relation to the knowledge of a death. Indeed, the propping function of
the water suggests that the 'props' of the mother have not, in fact, been
entirely removed, and that the 'unknowability' of their movement
concerns precisely this remaining. The remainder of the props in some
way disturbs the balance of literal and figurative meaning, and hence the
cognitive assimilation of loss.

This question is raised again in Books IV and VII, where props
reappear in connection with the other ghastly figures of the Discharged
Soldier 'propped' by a milestone and the Blind Beggar 'propped against a
wall'.[16] Both characters, like the drowned man, are associated with the
stopping of a movement, but in the place of a physical motion each of
them provides the story of his life. The peculiarity of this story, in the
case of the solider, is characterized by the 'indifference' with which he
tells it. While this indifference designates the emotional condition of
being 'unmoved', it also describes the process of storytelling, or
listening, as the subsumption of a series of articulated differences in the

appearance of a narrative 'movement'. In the later description of the
Blind Beggar, this peculiar relation of difference and indifference
becomes the disjunction between the 'sightless eyes' of the man and the
written paper on his chest – or breast – which he cannot read, and which
yet makes possible, for the poet, a story of his own.[17] The disturbance of
the literal–figurative relation seems to concern a shift to another relation,
between the articulation of differences in reading, and the meaningful
whole of the narrative movement.

The association of the breast with reading intimated by the scene of the
poet reading the paper on the beggar's chest suggests that the Blessed
Babe scene, considered in this context, might have something to tell us
about the 'remainder', which, associated with props, connects the
reading of narratives with the relation to the mother. The problem of
difference and indifference, furthermore, resituates this passage in terms
of the polemic against empirical philosophy which introduces it, and in
which a prop once again surfaces. The error attributed here (ll. 208ff.) to
philosophy – the confusion of things 'which we perceive' with things
'which we have made' – is not altogether unlike the activity of reading a
series of signs as a sign of life. The similarity of Wordsworth's polemic to
Locke's comments (in the *Conduct of the Understanding*) on distinction
('the perception of a difference that nature has placed in things') and
division ('making a division where there is yet none'), which associate
their confusion with the art of disrupting, also suggests that this error is
shared by philosophy and poetry, uniting science or empirical
philosophy, the 'prop of our infirmity', with the 'prop of our affections'.
Thus the Blessed Babe passage, while appearing to offer itself as an
alternative to the errors of mere philosophical quibbling, examines more
profoundly the conditions of its own narration, or the problem of
marking the difference between difference and indifference.[18]

Turning briefly, once again, to this passage, we see that the problem of
narrative 'distinction and division' rests, as might be expected, on the
figure of passage:

> Blessed the infant babe –
> For with my best conjectures I would trace
> The progress of our being – blest the babe
> Nursed in his mother's arms, the babe who sleeps
> Upon his mother's breast, who, when his soul
> Claims manifest kindred with an earthly soul,
> Doth gather passion from his mother's eye.
> Such feelings pass into his torpid life
> Like an awakening breeze, and hence his mind . . .
> Is prompt and watchful, eager to combine
> In one appearance all the elements

And parts of the same object, else detached
And loth to coalesce.

(1805, II, 237–50)

The movement from 'passions', to 'passing', to combining elements 'in one appearance' suggests that the substitution we earlier saw beginning with the mother's death in fact has its origins here. The negative side of 'passion' in its Christian connotations strengthens this suggestion. But what does it mean to situate this negativity in the relation with the living mother? If we read the figure of passion in relation to the 'communion' after the mother's death, we can perhaps understand passion as a sort of prefiguration of loss, a figure for the mortality of a soul that has entered the empirical world. But this does not account for the odd phrase 'gathers passion from his mother's eye'. However, an alteration in the 1850 version, and included in at least one edition of the 1805 version,[19] provides another link between these lines and the death passage, one which depends not on the figurative – or literal – meaning of the lines, but on a syntactical mark. This version adds an exclamation point after 'mother's eye' as well as at the end of the line describing the removal of the props.[20] If passion can be read as a function of life and death, the 'gathering' of passion is closer to the more arbitrary combining of two passages on the basis of a syntactical repetition. As opposed to the substitutive 'combining in one appearance', which works figuratively to assimilate visual perception to language, this 'gathering' is a throwing together (like the poet's 'con-jectures'), a bonding which, like a syntax, is not itself a function of meaning but rather the prop upon which meaning leans, and with which it is immediately confused. The repetiton of the exclamation point in these passages foregrounds those aspects of langauge, such as syntax and punctuation, which articulate 'prior' to, or as the condition of possibility of, meaningful discourse, and which remain to disturb the balance of syntax and semantics, literal and figurative meaning.[21]

This second story of the child at the breast, however, cannot exactly be considered *a* story the way the other can; for the prop is, from the beginning, double. The mother can be considered a prop in two ways: as an empirical body, a 'breast', she is the empirical element necessary for the beginning of a life story (just as, according to Kant, experience is necessary for, although not the origin of, conceptual activity). To this extent she is the prop of nature, the 'prop of our infirmity', perhaps. But to the extent that the mother's body is used, or manipulated, for articulating a story, that is, marked and read as the 'mother', it has become purely part of an articulated structure, the skeletal hinge of a syntactical chain. In so far as 'she' is the latter, or is the name given to the latter, the mother is no longer *present* in any empirical sense and can thus be said to be 'removed'; but since this articulation is, from the 'beginning', necessary for the relation of affection, the mother has to be a 'prop', and hence 'removed', in order to be accessible to experience in the first place. We might say that, as a prop, the mother is not experienced, but read; and while this is necessary for her to become a 'mother', or 'kin', to this extent she is also not a 'natural relation'.[22] If the scene of the poet reading the paper on the beggar's chest recalls the 'original' relation with the mother, it is only because in order to nurse *his mother's* breast the babe first has to read it.[23]

To speak of this activity in terms of 'propping' is, however, to have shifted into the realm of figuration, which then encompasses, if somewhat uncomfortably, other figures such as that of passion and communion. This shift, which allows for the totalizing movement of self-recognition, the 'combining in one appearance' that is described for example in Book IV, is marked by the word *eye*, which could be said to designate the confusion of reading and seeing, or to figure reading as something that is peculiar to the ocular sense organ. If we understand the two stories, of passion and of propping, in terms of the relation of figuration and articulation, we must recognize that this distinction can also be understood in terms of figuration itself, as assimilable to sense perception, and as unassimilable to it. This suggests that the mother, while designating an empirical beginning, can also be read as the figure of an 'origin' that cannot be located temporally or spatially and leaves its traces over and over again in syntactical remainders. Understanding this repetitive, 'originary' moment in terms of the relation of articulation and figuration, it might be possible to read certain histories of self-knowledge, such as those of Wordsworth and Freud, as the narrativization of a less *knowable* relation, which may even be disruptive to the narrative as such. We might think of this, for example in Freud, in terms of the relation of trace and symbol in the trauma theory, which could prove interesting in the understanding of Freud's theory of sexuality. It is not possible to elaborate at this point on the implications of this reading, but only to suggest it as a possible approach to the questions raised in the beginning of this chapter.

How this would affect the concept of repression is uncertain. How it affects the concept of death in *The Prelude* is evident in the reference to the babe's activity as 'mute dialogues with my mother's heart', which echoes the description, in Book V, of the poet standing 'mute' before the Boy of Winander's grave. To the extent that the poet reads the story of a life in the inscription on a gravestone, the babe has, with its first 'articulate prattle', already written the mother's epitaph on her body. But to read this is also for the babe to read its own birth certificate, the beginning of its self-knowledge as a historical being. It is our task, then, to follow in Freud's texts the traces of such a double movement, and perhaps also to hear in his frequent reference to the mother's role in emotional life Wordsworth's double eulogy, in *The Prelude*, for his mother:

> Early died
> My honoured mother, she who was the *heart*
> And *hinge* of all our learnings and our loves.

(1805, V, 256–8, italics added)

Notes

1. A somewhat shorter version of this chapter was originally presented at a panel of the 1984 MLA Convention entitled 'The Romantic Ego'. A highly sophisticated analysis of romantic authors through a psychoanalytic vocabulary can be found in THOMAS WEISKEL, *The Romantic Sublime: Studies in the Structure and Psychology of Transcendence* (Baltimore: Johns Hopkins University Press, 1976).

2. Jeffrey Mehlman, trans., *Life and Death in Psychoanalysis*, by JEAN LAPLANCHE (Baltimore: Johns Hopkins University Press, 1976), pp. 15 ff. Strictly speaking, Mehlman is translating Laplanche's translation of *Anlehnung* as *étayage*.

3. Freud distinguishes the sexual 'drive' from the physical 'instinct' of hunger in the *Three Essays*, referring to the former as a concept 'lying on the frontier between the mental and the physical.'

4. I refer here to the Blessed Babe passage proper as well as the passage following it in Book II of *The Prelude*. Quotations of this work in the essay are from Jonathan Wordsworth, M.H. Abrams, and Stephen Gill, eds., *The Prelude, 1799, 1805, 1850*, Norton Critical Edition (New York: Norton, 1979), with edition (1805 or 1850) and line numbers provided in the text. I have chosen to quote from the 1805 version (unless otherwise noted) because the alterations in the 1850 version of the Blessed Babe passage and the one immediately succeeding it eliminate interesting material. What they add, however, is also interesting, and is treated toward the end of the essay. See note 20 for a brief discussion of difficulties in determining certain details of the 1805 version.

5. SIGMUND FREUD, *Three Essays on Sexuality*, trans. James Strachey, *The Standard Edition of the Complete Psychological works of Sigmund Freud*, Vol. 7 (London: Hogarth Press, 1953), p. 228. Hereafter cited as SE 7. German text is supplied from the *Studienausgabe*, vol. 5 (Frankfurt am Main: Fischer Taschenbuch Verlag, 1982).

6. SE 7, p. 222.

7. SE 7, p. 182, with modifications in translation (in brackets) from *Life and Death in Psychoanalysis*, p. 18.

8. HAROLD BLOOM, 'Wrestling Sigmund: Three Paradigms for Poetic Originality',

in *The Breaking of the Vessels* (Chicago: University of Chicago Press, 1982), p. 69; cf. LAPLANCHE, *Life and Death in Psychoanalysis*, p. 22.

9. The connection with associationism is particularly clear in Freud's early work, *On Aphasia* (not included in the Standard Edition, but available in English translation as *On Aphasia: A Critical Study*, trans. E. Stengel (New York: International Universities Press, 1953).

10. See DAVID HARTLEY, *Observations on Man*, 2 vols., 1749. On motion in Wordsworth see MILTON WILSON, 'Bodies in Motion: Wordsworth's Myths of Natural Philosophy,' in Eleanor Cook et al., eds., *Centre and Labyrinth: Essays in Honour of Northrop Frye* (Toronto: University of Toronto Press, 1983).

11. The close relation between associationism and classical rhetoric is proposed by HAROLD BLOOM in 'Coda: Poetic Crossings', in his *Wallace Stevens: The Poems of Our Climate* (Ithaca: Cornell University Press, 1977), pp. 397–98. Other useful discussions of the use or interpretation of a classical rhetorical tradition and of the language of emotion are to be found in KLAUS DOCKHORN, 'Wordsworth und die rhetorische Tradition in England', in *Macht und Wirkung der Rhetorik: Vier Ansätze zur Ideengeschichte der Vormoderne* (Berlin: Verlag Gehlen, 1968), and JOSEPHINE MILES, *Wordsworth and the Vocabulary of Emotion* (Berkeley: University of California Press, 1942).

12. This could be written as follows:

$$\frac{\text{Poetic 'Eye'}}{\text{Babe}} \times \frac{\text{Babe}}{\text{Mother's eye}}$$

13. GEOFFREY HARTMAN notes the peculiarity of this passage and offers an interesting reading of it in 'A Touching Compulsion: Wordsworth and the Problem of Literary Representation', *Georgia Review*, **31** (1977).

14. Another pattern evoking a 'no no' is discussed by CYNTHIA CHASE in 'Accidents of Disfiguration: Limits to Literal and Rhetorical Reading in Book V of *The Prelude*', *Decomposing Figures: Rhetorical Readings in the Romantic Tradition* (Baltimore: Johns Hopkins University Press, 1986), pp. 25–6.

15. I quote from the 1850 version here because it develops some of the implicit figurative connections between passages in the 1805 version. This does not assume, however, that the versions can simply be exchanged for one another as if they were the same poem; see the discussion below on some of the differences between the versions.

   A helpful analysis of the relation between the boat passages in Books Four and Five is to be found in SUSAN WOLFSON, 'Wordsworth's Revisions of "The Drowned Man of Esthwaite"', *PMLA* **99** (October 1984).

16. See the passages beginning at (1805) IV. 400ff. and (1805) V. 595ff. The final appearance of props in *The Prelude* is to be found in the 'Vaudracour and Julia' episode in Book IX of the 1805 version only (ll. 453ff.). I have offered a reading of this episode in 'Unknown Causes: Poetic Effects', *Diacritics* (Winter 1987).

17. For a fine analysis of the Blind Man passage see GERALDINE FRIEDMAN, 'History in the Background of Wordsworth's Blind Beggar,' *ELH* **56** (Spring 1989).

18. LESLIE BRISMAN writes that the lines that end this passage 'conclude the strongest dismissal of hunting for nonmythic origins, and . . . introduce the

great myth of romantic origins'. I would add that the movement from one passage to the next also involves a complication of this difference. See his *Romantic Origins* (Ithaca: Cornell University Press, 1978), p. 303. It might also be of interest to consider the analysis of the relation between Locke and Hartley, or of the development of 'empiricism', made possible by Wordsworth's poem. (One could for example develop a reading of Locke, through Wordsworth's narrative of the mother and babe, which would pose a counterpoint to some of the later empiricist interpretations, or reductions, of Locke's work.)

19. The difference between an original version and an edition is not clear-cut in Wordsworth. Note 20 discusses this problem further.

20. De Selincourt's edition differs from the Norton Critical Edition in placing the exclamation points in the 1805 version as well as the 1850 version; it also makes some other changes in punctuation, and capitalizes *mother* and *babe* (see Ernest de Selincourt, ed., *The Prelude, or, Growth of a Poet's Mind*, new edition corrected by Stephen Gill (Oxford: Oxford University Press, 1970). Both are apparently following Manuscript A, but the editors of the Norton edition point out that punctuation and some capitalization in the 1805 manuscripts is 'editorial'. They also note, however, that 'punctuation in the manuscripts is so spasmodic that its absence tells us nothing. Wordsworth seems not to have believed that his poetry could be misread (for instance, asking Humphrey Davey, whom he had never met, to correct the punctuation of *Lyrical Ballads* 1800' (p. 511). This poses an interesting problem for reading the texts, since in order to decide which punctuation to choose, or to decide that any single punctuation can't be chosen, one has to shift attention from the story 'in' the text to the story 'of' the text, that is, the story of its manuscripts and their alterations. The exclamation points thus introduce in another way an element not entirely subordinated to the meaning of the narrative. Thus, also, the elimination of 'gather' in the 1850 version does not eliminate the general problem, since in order to tell the difference between 'Doth gather passion from his mother's eye' (1805) and 'Drinks in the feelings of his Mother's eye!' (1850) one has to tell the story of the manuscripts.

21. It should be emphasized that these 'conditions of possibility' are not *transcendental*, just as they are nonempirical; it is in the odd sense of nonempirical, nontranscendental conditions of possibility that syntax and punctuation disturb the 'affective' story. For a discussion of syntax and semantics in *The Prelude* see ANDRZEJ WARMINSKI, 'Missed Crossing: Wordsworth's Apocalypses,' *MLN* **99** (December 1984).

22. Paul de Man suggests a reading of the Blessed Babe passage which focuses on the 'claim' to 'manifest kindred', which, he points out, is verbal and thus 'not given in the nature of things.' See 'Wordsworth and the Victorians,' in PAUL DE MAN, *The Rhetoric of Romanticism* (New York: Columbia University Press, 1984), CYNTHIA CHASE's discussion of the de Man text in 'Giving a Face to a name', *Decomposing Figures*, and ANDRZEJ WARMINSKI, 'First Poetic Spirits', in *Diacritics* (Winter 1987).

23. Frances Ferguson suggests that the 'mute dialogues' are to be understood as carrying with them 'the constant affirmation of ocular and tangible proof'. My analysis suggests a re-reading of the ocular and tangible in terms of the nonperceptual conditions of possibility of meaning in the Blessed Babe passage. See FRANCES FERGUSON, *Wordsworth: Language as Counter-Spirit* (New

Haven: Yale University Press, 1977). RICHARD J. ONORATO, in *The Character of the Poet: Wordsworth in 'The Prelude'* (Princeton: Princeton University Press, 1971), proposes an interpretation similar to Ferguson's by reading the 'mute dialogues' as a 'metaphor' for the 'unlimited sensation and fantasy' of the prelinguistic infant in the presence of its mother. The interpretation of the passage in terms of a prelinguistic stage of infancy subordinates language to a nonverbal experience of the presence and absence of the mother, generally understanding language empirically as actual speaking and writing, which is derivative of, or inadequate to, a more fundamental 'passion'. Wordsworth's text, however, resists an empirical interpretation of language and suggests (1) that, if the narrative is interpreted as a history of development, the child is from the beginning 'reading' and (2) that the narrative is not limited to its reference to such a history, and that the 'gathering' of 'passion' and the 'removal' of the 'props' do not concern a physical mother and an experienced relation to her presence and absence.

5 'Splitting the Race of Man in Twain': Prostitution, Personification and *The Prelude**

MARY JACOBUS

What notions of language, of speaking and of writing, are involved in the writing of autobiography, and how and why are they gendered? These are the fundamental questions Mary Jacobus pursues in *Romanticism, Writing, and Sexual Difference: Essays on* The Prelude (1989). The chapter included here focuses on the peculiar vicissitudes of prosopopoeia or personification, the form of figurative language identified by Paul de Man (in *The Rhetoric of Romanticism*) with autobiography. Jacobus posits that both the self-difference involved in language or representation and sexual difference itself threaten the subject's illusion of integrity, and she traces the very diverse ways in which these threats are represented and displaced and made to stand for one another, in writings of Freud as well as in nineteenth-century texts. In this essay Jacobus makes us see the immense and complex effort that goes into the repression of sexual difference in Wordsworth's autobiographical poem.

In Book VII of *The Prelude*, the figure of the prostitute or fallen woman recurs insistently, because, Jacobus argues, she serves as 'an emblem of representation': a personification of the 'fall into language', and indeed into figurative language and prosopopoeia, involved not just in autobiography but in all representation. In Book VII, as in Milton's *Samson Agonistes*, figurative language in its seeming threat to the singleness and integrity of the self is cast as a woman – and cast out; the result is the figure of the outcast woman or prostitute. This is the logic of allegory and of dreams. It is an important achievement of this essay to bring to light the allegorical dimension of *The Prelude*. Jacobus succeeds in making us pay heed to both the linguistic and unconscious origins of the figure or fantasy of the fallen woman, and

* Reprinted from Mary Jacobus, *Romanticism, Writing, and Sexual Difference: Essays on 'The Prelude'* (Oxford: Clarendon Press, 1989), pp. 206–36.

to prostitutes' real existence in the Cambridge and London of Wordsworth's day. Her at once rhetorical and historicist reading makes for
compelling *feminist* criticism. Thus she determines: the division
between fallen and unfallen women summoned up in Wordsworth's
text is a defensive fantasy that works for men, but at the expense of
women, instituting a denigrated class.

Here Jacobus reads not only Wordsworth but the readers of *The
Prelude*, especially Thomas De Quincey. Her first book, *Tradition and
Experiment in Wordsworth's Lyrical Ballads (1798)* (1976) argued a thesis
not unrelated to her critical perspective, in this essay, on 'High
Romantic critical quests'. She argued there that readers of Wordsworth have found his poetry passionately interesting because they
identified with 'the self-defining process' which underlies it. The
present essay is first of all a challenge to the received idea that the
marriage of the mind and nature is the main plot of 'high Romanticism' (the phrase derives from Wordsworth's Prospectus to *The
Recluse*, ll. 816–24, naming as 'our high argument' the mutual fitting
of nature and mind). Literary history as the History of Ideas, Jacobus
suggests, is all unselfconsciously a story of masculine Mind and its
conquests or possessions. Her alternative is a history of persons and
personifications (for instance the Geoffrey Hartman of note 2), and of
words. Like Jerome Christensen's book on Byron, which he calls
'post-structuralist biography', Jacobus's writing dissolves the protective divisions between persons and texts.

'Every Jack will have his Jill.'[1] With what he calls 'This utopian and
'romantic' proverb', Geoffrey Hartman begins a gnomic essay 'On the
Theory of Romanticism'. An authorized gloss might run: 'Every
intellectual desire will finally find its scholastic fulfilment.'[2] The role of
Woman (Jill) is to put man (Jack) in possession of his desire. High
Romantic critical quests might be said to have been waylaid by this
enchanting and discriminatory plot (also know as 'Natural
Supernaturalism'); the metaphoric consummation or spousal union of
masculine mind and feminine nature haunts A.O. Lovejoy's Romantic
heirs, giving M.H. Abrams's shaping narrative its underlying form (that
of the History of Ideas) and lingering on in Hartman's 'romantic'
proverb.[3] As Gayatri Spivak has pointed out, the elision of sexual
difference, or occlusion of woman, is a by-product of the Romantic
master-plot.[4] Domesticated by her role in the Great (male) Tradition, Jill
settles down with Jack in Dove Cottage to raise their brood of Romantic
daughters; in the Romantic family, the only good daughter is a dutiful
one (Dora), or a dead one (Kate – 'Surprised by joy . . .').

I want to try to sketch a different Romantic plot, as well as an alternative profession for the Romantic daughter. What if the mind addressed its courtship, not to nature, but to the city (in Wordsworth's poetry, a city of dreadful art)? And what if the Romantic quester is accosted by a voice that speaks shamelessly, not from the world of the dead (*Siste viator*) but from the *demi-monde*? What if the long journey home were that of a prodigal daughter instead of the Romantic son and heir in Abrams's story? I have in mind the possibility of a prostituted and indiscriminate Romanticism, perhaps infected by the French disease. Hartman's essay asks us to make allowance 'for the seductive presence of romance motifs' in Romantic poetry, akin to the use of the *persona* in neo-classical and modern poetry.[5] My concern in this chapter is with the seductive presence of persons, or rather personifications, in Wordsworth's poetry, and with the turn towards Romance, or Spenserian allegory, which signals that seduction.[6] My argument will be not only that high Romanticism depends on the casting out of what defines its height – figurative language, and especially personification – but that the characteristic form of this figure is a Romantic woman. The fate of personification (the outcast of Romantic figuration) and of prostitution (the outcast of spousal verse) tells us how these rhetorical and figurative schemes are constituted and at what price. My example will be Mary of Buttermere in Book VII of *The Prelude*, and the girl prostitute, Ann of Oxford Street, from De Quincey's *Confessions of an English Opium-Eater*; my route will be digressive, accosted by the wandering forms of Romantic error (figured here as Milton's Spenserian allegory of Sin and Death), and I will conclude with a brief encounter with the economics of autobiography.

The Maid of Buttermere

On the face of it, sexual difference seems the most completely repressed aspect of *The Prelude*. Except for the Vaudracour and Julia episode, later excised, the theme of sexual desire is either banished to the realm of the pastoral or else thoroughly domesticated. Mary of Buttermere, to whose seduction Wordsworth alludes in Book VII, prompts the improbable pre-seduction fantasy that 'we were nursed . . . On the same mountains' (VII, 342–3) – risking Johnson's testy objection to Milton's similarly pastoral fiction in *Lycidas* ('For we were nursed upon the self-same hill', l. 23): we *know* they never drove afield together. In Book XI the same pre-Freudian view of the nursery crops up in connection with the virginal Mary Hutchinson, here named as 'Nature's inmate'; 'Even like this maid', Wordsworth insists, he loved nature ('nor lightly loved, / But fervently') without being enthralled by the later tyranny of the eye which he terms a 'degradation' (XI, 213, 223–6).[7] And, in Book XIII, Dorothy Wordsworth is invoked as 'Child of my parents, sister of my soul' (XIII, 211); here, as always in Romantic poetry, the motif of brother–sister love (whether overtly incestuous or not) swiftly assimilates sexual difference to narcissistic identity. No less than the maid and the wife, the sister simultaneously figures the repression of sexuality and the refusal of sexual difference. Women are all the same (as the young Wordsworth).

Romantic women routinely appear in *The Prelude* at moments when Wordsworth wants to emphasize the continuity of his mature poetic identity with an imaginary latency period, or undifferentiated sexuality, belonging to his Lake District boyhood. Far from being emblems of sexual difference, they function precisely as defences against it. Just as nature, at the opening of Book XI, interposes itself 'betwixt the heart of man / And the uneasy world – 'twixt man himself . . . and his own unquiet heart' (XI, 17–19),[8] so the purified and purifying figure of woman interposes itself healingly between man and his own unquiet, pre-existing, inner division. But there is one important exception. In Book VII of the *The Prelude*, what I will call the Maid of Buttermere sequence – beginning with an account of the Sadler's Wells melodrama, 'The Beauty of Buttermere', and ending approximately a hundred lines later with the words 'I quit this painful theme' – introduces a figure whose traumatic effect is to split 'the race of man / In twain' (VII, 426–7).[9] Like the beggars of London, the figure of the prostitute is almost synonymous with late eighteenth-century representations of the city. But Wordsworth's circuitous approach to the overwhelming visibility of prostitution at this period (in 1803, estimates put the number of London prostitutes between 50,000 and 70,000) suggests an internal obstacle to broaching 'this painful theme'.[10] His compulsively digressive returns to the same point of fixation – rather as Freud, in his essay on 'The Uncanny', relates his own involuntary return to the red light district of an unknown city – signal one effect of that traumatic 'splitting'; namely, repression. Or, as Blake puts it at just about the time of Wordsworth's first encounter with London, the Romantic family is blighted by the harlot's curse.

The most common literary form taken by the uncanny is doubling. Mary of Buttermere raises the spectre of a theatrical other, or dark interpretess, whose urban fall shadows her Lake District purity. Wordsworth's brief account of 'The Maid of Buttermere' as presented on the London stage in 1803,

how the spoiler came, 'a bold bad man'
To God unfaithful, children, wife, and home,
And wooed the artless daughter of the hills,

> And wedded her, in cruel mockery
> Of love and marriage bonds.
>
> (*Prelude*, VII, 323–7)[11]

introduces his 'memorial verse' on the bigamously unmarried mother, a
personal recollection of the real Mary Robinson as he and Coleridge had
met her during their walking tour of 1799 ('in her cottage-inn / Were
welcomed, and attended on by her', VII, 327–46). This tribute, he writes,
'Comes from the poet's heart, and is her due'; it makes amends for her
immodest stage career. But her image cannot be laid so easily, rising up
in the poet's path like an unexorcized ghost when he attempts to resume
his interrupted account of the London theatre:

> These last words uttered, to my argument
> I was returning, when – with sundry forms
> Mingled, that in the way which I must tread
> Before me stand – *thy image rose again*,
> Mary of Buttermere!
>
> (*Prelude*, VII, 347–51; my italics)

The unmarried mother comes athwart the poet like the 'unfathered
vapour' of imagination in Book VI, halting him in the time of writing
with the crisis of interpretative confusion which has been identified by
Weiskel and others with the Romantic Sublime.[12] Here, however, an
encounter with the 'unfathered' or unfathering Oedipal Sublime is
replaced by an unlaid female apparition who blocks further poetic
progress. The unsuccessful exorcism has to be repeated a second time in
the succeeding lines ('She lives in peace . . . Without contamination does
she live / In quietness . . . Happy are they both, / Mother and child!', VII,
351–4, 359–60) – but this time with an added sacrifice. Her new-born and
unfathered child sleeps in earth ('Fearless as a lamb') in order that Mary
may live on 'without contamination' as the Mary Magdalene of *The
Prelude*. The infant's burial tranquillizes her unquiet life, allowing her to
stand in for the purified, pre-sexual, Lake District poet (himself, one
might note, the parent of an 'unfathered' child). This hushing up of the
sexual drama is effected by making Mary no longer – or again not yet – a
mother, still emphatically the *Maid* of Buttermere.

But the matter of sexuality cannot be laid to rest quite so easily as the
babe. Or, someone, somewhere, is always getting laid. As if *The Prelude*
were a Spenserian narrative in which the moment of interpretive
difficulty produces an insistent doubling of allegorical persons, Duessa
splits off from Una. In this theatrical city, how are we to recognize the
difference between the Maid of Buttermere and a Sadler's Wells
prostitute, between a Romantic woman and a painted theatrical whore?

> foremost I am crossed
> Here by remembrance of two figures: one
> A rosy babe, who for a twelvemonth's space
> Perhaps had been of age to deal about
> Articulate prattle, child as beautiful
> As ever sate upon a mother's knee;
> The other was the parent of that babe –
> But on the mother's cheek the tints were false,
> A painted bloom.
>
> (*Prelude*, VII, 366–74)

In the semiotics of sexuality, 'painted bloom' is the sign of solicitation, and solicitation the sign of shamelessness; Sadler's Wells (like Drury Lane and Covent Garden, notoriously the haunt of prostitutes at the end of the eighteenth century) brings together anti-theatrical and sexual prejudices in one scene. But what about the rosy babe, who, we might note, differs in three important respects from Mary of Buttermere's dead, ungendered, new-born infant? He is alive, he is specified as male ('The lovely boy', VII, 396), and he is no longer 'infans' (i.e. he has been prattling for about a year). Not the mother ('scarcely at this time / Do I remember her', VII, 394–5) but this beautiful boy becomes the focus of Wordsworth's 'remembrance'. I want to emphasize the displacement from mother to child, since it will help to refine one common reading of the episode: namely, that it allows Wordsworth to depict himself as ultimately uncontaminated by the fall into writing or representation which London symbolizes in Book VII of *The Prelude*. And, once more, we should notice the disappearance of the mother during the decontamination process.

This mother-and-child pair, obviously parodic of the duo in the 'Blessed the infant babe' passage, implies a theory of pre-Oedipal relations previously unglimpsed in *The Prelude* – that of gathering dangerous passions from one's mother's eye; a theory, in fact, of maternal seduction. If the mother seduces, the child must be 'stopped' ('through some special privilege / *Stopped* at the growth he had', VII, 401–2; my italics), presumably lest he grow up gay as the result of a too-loving mother, like Freud's type of the homosexual artist, Leonardo da Vinci. Wordsworth fondly imagines the boy spared this fate, 'as if embalmed / By Nature',

> destined to live,
> To be, to have been, come, and go, a child
> And nothing more, no partner in the years

That bear us forward to distress and guilt,
Pain and abasement . . .

(Prelude, VII, 400–6)

We can glimpse here the shadow cast by an earlier family romance or incestuous primal scene. If the mother is Sin, accosting Wordsworth on his journey as she accosts Milton's Satan *en route* for chaos, then the final tendency of 'the years / That bear us forward' is not so much homosexuality as Death, Milton's name for Sin's incestuously conceived and incestuous son. Arrested development becomes the only alternative. This arrest or stoppage, it hardly needs pointing out, not only precludes growing up as distressed and guilty as the rest of us; it precludes the growth of a poet.

Like the Winander Boy in Book V, the embalmed child is arrested in a moment of indeterminacy, a pause that suspends him between mimic hootings or 'articulate prattle' on the one hand, and on the other the silent writing or reading of his own epitaph which Wordsworth characteristically undertakes at such self-reflexive moments.[13] Here a structure of address sketches the temporal relations between the two pairs (Mary of Buttermere with her nameless infant, and the painted woman with her rosy boy), installing Wordsworth himself in loving commiseration with his own future:

he perhaps,
Mary, may now have lived till he could look
With envy on *thy* nameless babe that sleeps
Beside the mountain chapel undisturbed.

(Prelude, VII, 409–12; my italics)

In these lines the poet in the time of writing addresses a purified Mary (the Mary of his Lake District past), just as the unembalmed, unstopped city boy might look with envy (*invidia*) on her nameless babe – a babe imagined as not only immune to time (euphemistically asleep), but immune to the division which besets all subjects, especially what has come to be known as the subject in language; hence, a babe immune to sexual division.[14] The unstopped boy occupies the same position as the guilty, autobiographically split Wordsworth who is also subject to growth; but his fall has been displaced on to the forgotten mother. The reason why the mother is scarcely remembered 'at this time' is that she has been cast out – in the Kristevan terms which I will elaborate later, 'abjected' – so that Wordsworth can throw in his lot with the 'embalmed' and separate self figured by the beautiful boy. In order to save the boy, Wordsworth has to get rid of the mother.

It is not surprising, then, that the residual form taken by the mother is that of the prostitute. Cast out, she becomes (by a neat symbolic reversal) an outcast. As if possessed by its own internal momentum, the sequence digresses yet again from its theatrical context, this time to invoke the earlier journey when Wordsworth, *en route* from the Lake District to Cambridge in 1787, first heard and saw a cursing prostitute,

> for the first time in my life did hear
> The voice of woman utter blasphemy –
> Saw woman as she is to open shame
> Abandoned, and the pride of public vice.
>
> (*Prelude*, VII, 417–20)

The Prelude represents the effect – or affect – as 'immense', a permanent and founding split in the autobiographical subject that is simultaneously trauma and repression:

> Full surely from the bottom of my heart
> I shuddered; but the pain was almost lost,
> Absorbed and buried in the immensity
> Of the effect: a barrier seemed at once
> Thrown in, that from humanity divorced
> The human form, splitting the race of man
> In twain, yet leaving the same outward shape.
>
> (*Prelude*, VII, 421–7)

A pain 'absorbed . . . in the immensity / Of the effect' sounds remarkably like the pain of castration anxiety before naked female sexuality as Freud describes it – in his account, a pain buried by the immense effects of fetishism. Even as sexual difference is recognized, it is denied or disavowed by means of a defensive 'splitting' (what might be termed the both / and defence).[15] The barrier permits a 'divorce' which paradoxically allows the subject not to confront difference structured as division or as equally unacceptable alternatives (the either/or trauma). Characteristically, the fetishist clings to a representation associated with the last moment before his sight of the apparently castrated mother. Here that representation is 'the human form', or rather, 'man' – the ostensibly undifferentiated (male) body which serves as the measure of Romantic humanism while serving also to deny sexual difference.

Splitting becomes the means to defend an imaginary bodily integrity, warding off castration anxiety by means of the fantasy of organic wholeness with which Romantic humanism is invested, whether its subject is man or simply his imagination. In the context of Book VII of *The Prelude*, the book of representations, the painted or fallen woman becomes an emblem of representation itself, allowing Wordsworth to cling to the (here perilously sustained) fiction of a self that is not the subject of, or in, representation (and hence inevitably split). 'The overthrow / Of her soul's beauty' (VII, 432–3) – we might note that Wordsworth's soul is regularly feminized in *The Prelude* – is the ostensible trade-off for Wordsworth's immunity to division; but the female body is the actual price paid, since the overthrow of the prostitute's soul means the throwing over of her body. In other words, the passage allows us to see how the fetishistic compromise works for men (splitting keeps them whole), but only, and contradictorily, at the expense of women (splitting creates the division fallen / unfallen, and thus institutes a denigrated class). Once this compromise between incompatible ideas has been effected, Wordsworth can move on from the 'Distress of mind [that] ensued upon this sight' (VII, 428) to a more manageable 'milder sadness'. 'In truth', he writes, 'The sorrow of the passion *stopped* me here' (VII, 434–5; my italics). This stoppage is so effective that Wordsworth can finally 'quit this painful theme' (VII, 436) – shut his eyes to division – and return to his account of the London stage. 'Stopped' is the same word used of the beautiful boy's arrest ('through some special privilege / Stopped at the growth he had', VII, 401–2). It halts Wordsworth by returning him in fantasy to the moment before the distressing and anxiety-inducing sight of sexual difference. We should also notice that Wordsworth's insistence on the child being father to the man (the *post hoc ergo propter hoc* recipe for embalming infants) allows him to adopt the myth of nature as Romantic Mother without ever confronting maternal desire, whether the mother's for and in him, or his own for the mother. To call sexual difference the most completely repressed aspect of *The Prelude* amounts to saying that it is put a stop to, whether by the fiction of Natural Supernaturalism, or by systematic domestication, or, as here in Book VII, by being cast out in the figure of the prostitute.

Sexual difference and 'my single self'

At this point, a digression by way of Wordsworth's Cambridge education permits an alternative approach to the question of sexual difference. I want to propose Milton as the obvious candidate for homo-erotic influence on, or in, *The Prelude*. Wordsworth represents Cambridge as an extension of his imaginary Lake District latency period ('Hushed meanwhile / Was the under-soul, locked up in such a calm . . .', III, 539–40). Full term becomes a 'deep vacation', or period of prolonged unisex play with former alumni who were later destined for literature ('The nurslings of the Muses', III, 473); Wordsworth calls sweet Spenser (the Muses' erstwhile 'Page of State', III, 280) his brother, and in imagination bounds along in the footsteps of a stripling Milton – 'A boy,

no better, with his rosy cheeks / Angelical' (III, 291–2). Successfully
embalmed, the rosy babe of Book VII might have turned into this rosy-
cheeked cherub, with his 'conscious step of purity and pride' (III, 293).
There were, of course, possibiliites for what *The Prelude* calls 'dissolute
pleasure' (III, 535) in late eighteenth-century Cambridge as well as in
London – possibilities only glimpsed in Christopher Wordsworth's *Social
Life at the English Universities in the Eighteenth Century* (1874),[16] but
surfacing in Coleridge's confused nightmare of 'a university Harlot' ('out
rushes a university Harlot, who insists on my going with her . . . The
Harlot in white with her open Bosom certainly was the Cambridge Girl
[Sal Hall]').[17] Wordsworth's desires, however, seem to have been as
sublimated as those of 'the Lady of Christ's', or, rather, they seem to
have taken the form of that Miltonic strength-in-singleness embodied by
the 'blind poet, who, in his later day / Stood almost single, uttering
odious truth' (III, 284–5). (One such odious truth, we might recall, was
Milton's advocacy of divorce when spousal union failed or when, as in
Paradise Lost, woman fell.)

Wordsworthian desire for singleness is figured in his Book III account
of Cambridge by the wish to be a uniquely favoured or 'chosen' son: 'my
single self', Wordsworth recalls, was 'bred up in Nature's lap, was even /
As a spoiled child' (III, 356–9). Associated at the outset with the
autobiographical theme of *The Prelude* ('A theme / Single and of
determined bounds', I, 668–9), the term 'single' becomes synonymous
with inner life or 'what passed within me', and with the interiority
privileged by spiritual autobiography ('Not of outward things . . . –
words, signs, / Symbols or actions – but of my own heart / Have I been
speaking', III, 174–7). This secret, silent breathing-place of
'incommunicable powers' ('far hidden from the reach of words', III, 185)
abuts on the point of embattled solitude where the blind Milton 'Stood
almost single, uttering odious truth' (III, 285). The assertion that 'Points
have we all of us within our souls / Where all stand single' (III, 186–7) is
an affirmation of the Miltonic strength which lies both in silence and in
unpopular utterance, or utterance that falls on deaf ears. (The fallen
woman, by contrast, announces herself all too loudly by 'utter[ing]
blasphemy', as if all female public utterance was an obscenity and should
be hushed up.) The *locus classicus* for the depiction of a fall from and
recovery of this singling, God-given, and above all masculine strength-in-
silence is *Samson Agonistes*, which Romantic poets, including
Wordsworth, tended to read as Milton's spiritual autobiography.
Wordsworth's allusions to *Samson Agonistes* in Book VII have been
exhaustively and fruitfully studied in *Prelude* criticism.[18] But with the
assistance of a recent essay by Jim Swan, 'Difference and Silence: John
Milton and the Question of Gender', I want to sketch an alternative
reading of the relations between the two, one potentially able to

illuminate the relation between masculine creativity, silence, and sexual difference. Since, as Swan emphasizes, Milton is above all the poet who 'bestowed on us a vision of solitary male creativity that dominated English literary culture for centuries',[19] Samson's 'case' as chosen son may be especially instructive for the case of Wordsworth, the spoiled brat of *The Prelude*.

Close readers of Book VII will recall that Wordsworth quotes *Samson Agonistes* four lines before the start of the Maid of Buttermere sequence, in the motley company of Jack the Giant-killer, whose coat of darkness hides him 'safe as is the moon / "Hid in her vacant interlunar cave"' (VII, 306–7). Although the quotation is facetious, it is far from innocent. The thematic link between the London stage and the Maid of Buttermere lies, presumably, in the implicit contrast between the shameless immodesty of the theatre and the modest trust of the maid.[20] In a 'Delusion bold' like that of John Hatfield's audacious seduction of Mary, the actor wears the word 'INVISIBLE' on his chest. Read for its rhetorical rather than thematic bearing on *The Prelude*, *Samson Agonistes* might be thought of as confronting Wordsworth (like the Blind London Beggar's label elsewhere in Book VII) with 'the utmost that we know' – with the limits of poetic possibility or the (im)possibility of meaning; that is, with a de Manian view of poetry's privative muting of language or voice (a privation figured as blindness in Milton's poem).[21] Equally, *Samson Agonistes* might be read as figuring the sublimity of Miltonic blindness; here the issue is not so much privation as legibility. Wordsworth's eyes are 'smitten with the view' of the blind beggar, echoing Samson's boast that his blind strength 'with amaze shall strike all who behold' (*Samson Agonistes*, l. 1645), as if obliterating the spectacle of urban chaos. When Samson assaults the pillars 'As with the force of winds and waters pent' (l. 1647), the sublime convulsion washes into *The Prelude*, making Wordsworth's mind 'turn round / As with the might of waters' (VII, 616–17). Just as Samson's terminal violence could be read as a consoling fiction of performative language (like his glorious deeds, which 'though mute, spoke loud the doer') in the face of Milton's actual powerlessness to gain a hearing, so the Beggar (in this reading) serves the defensive function of substituting reading for unreadability. The (bare) legibility of 'The story of the man, and who he was' takes the place of 'an unmanageable sight' (VII, 615, 709), much as Wordsworth substitutes the autobiography of a discrete, single self for 'differences / That have no law, no meaning, and no end' (VII, 704–5).[22] Read not as Milton's autobiography but as a reading of autobiography itself, *Samson Agonistes* is an indispensable subtext for reading Book VII of *The Prelude*.

But what of sexual difference? Swan is alone in pointing out that Samson's blindness results specifically from his seduction – from succumbing to a femininity that is figured as speech. It is this emphasis which I want to pursue in relation to Book VII of *The Prelude*. Samson's self-betrayal, writes Swan, is of 'a silence which is also a secret – or rather, *the* secret of the self'; his fall 'implies that the encounter with sexual difference is somehow connected with the transformation of silence into speech'.[23] Swan's reading of *Samson Agonistes* goes something like this: the repeated references to Samson's secret are a displacement of Milton's own anxiety about prying into, and blasphemously publishing, sacred truths (Marvell's ironic encomium on *Paradise Lost*, Swan notes, specifically compares Milton to Samson, ruining the temple 'to revenge his sight'). Samson's crime is also publication: 'I God's counsel have not kept, his holy secret / Presumptuously have published' (ll. 497–8). Once Samson betrays the secret of his strength (which is silence), he suffers a fall into language, becoming effeminate, like Dalila, who overwhelms him with words – the talking woman, as usual, serving as a misogynist trope. By his own account, Samson 'for a word, a tear . . . divulged the secret gift of God / To a deceitful woman' and 'vanquished with a peal of words (O weakness!) / Gave up my fort of silence to a woman' (ll. 200–2, 235–6). But even before his enslavement by the Philistines, he declares, 'foul effeminacy held [him] yoked / Her bond-slave' (ll. 410–11). When Dalila tells Samson during their ritual exchange of ex-marital accusations and counter-accusations, 'To what I did thou show'dst me first the way', Samson concedes her point: 'I led the way; bitter reproach, but true' (ll. 781, 823). It is not just that *Samson Agonistes* equates orality and sexual intercourse as sources of infection by treacherous femininity; rather, Samson is seen by himself as already self-betrayed, feminized by an internal weakness. As he puts it, 'I to myself was false ere thou to me' (l. 824).

Swan's essay casts the problem of masculine psychosexual identity in Chodorowian terms. In this scheme, the child's first identification is with the mother. Whereas, 'in maturity, women look back to an origin of identity with one who is the same . . . men look back to an identity with one who is different'. In order to distinguish themselves from the mother, men, 'more than women, will feel compelled to assert an identity separate and distinct from others' – compelled, that is, by their original self-division to make a stronger, more insistent assertion of distinct and separate identity. There is thus a fundamental asymmetry in the way men and women experience their assumption of (gender) identity.[24] In *Samson Agonistes*, Swan argues, Milton represents individuality both as nostalgia for primal unity with the mother prior to being singled out (as neither / nor), and as the agonistic separation or division (either / or) that comes later. The boy-child's sense of not being fully separate from the mother, yet not at one with her either, structures Samson's struggle 'to reassert his identity as the one man singled out by God for heroic action'.[25] Sexual difference becomes a figure for, or displacement of, issues involving 'strong' or 'single' masculine poetic identity because the terms 'masculine' and 'feminine' – even though an arbitrary set of markers – allow for the assertion of a fixed difference (either/or). By contrast, the temporally prior neither/nor structure of undifferentiated wholeness can only be represented as the muteness and absence of the maternal moon, hid in her vacant interlunar cave, or, alternatively, as Samson's lost secret of silence – the secret that is his divinely appointed rather than self-published strength.[26]

Thus, Swan argues, the arrival of a woman on the scene demands that Milton/Samson assume a single, distinct identity figured conveniently in terms of gender identity, or strong manhood. For Swan, one might add, Renaissance representations of woman have less to do with the relation between unity and division (Una and Duessa) than with the problem of representing 'the double and divided *subject*, who suffers a fall into language'.[27] I want, however, to suggest a slightly different way of formulating questions relating to the subject and to language. Following Chodorow, Swan apparently assumes both that boys somehow always will be boys, and that the constitution of identity differs for boys and girls (girls 'naturally' identify with their mothers, while boys undergo an identity crisis). The question of identification is naturalized and elided with the process by which the constitution of gender identity takes place; the radical separation involved in the constitution of gender identity for *all* subjects is therefore played down. Kristeva's theory of the emergence of the pre-Oedipal subject has the advantage (in this instance at any rate) of avoiding the assumptions implicit in the Chodorowian paradigm. That is, Kristeva neither begs the psychoanalytic question of the constitution of the (for Chodorow, already) gendered subject, nor does she distinguish between the process which constitutes masculine and feminine subjects in terms of an inevitable same-sex identification (feminine) vs. different sex origin (masculine). One reason for this difference in emphasis lies in the fact that while Kristeva may seem to favour the pre-Oedipal, it is a pre-Oedipal structured from the outset by a third term, the father. A Kristevan account of the pre-Oedipal also reveals, as Swan's does not, why the process demands not only differentiation, but a maternal scapegoat.

Kristeva posits the earliest emergence of the pre-Oedipal subject in terms of an archaic, always present split, the minute gap existing between the mother and infant (not yet a subject in the full sense) on which depends the process she calls 'abjection'. This split Kristeva sees as demarcating an archaic paternal space, or imaginary father. Collusively, the child comes to identify, not with the mother, but with this gap or *vide* – even if it is only the mother's imaginary desire for something other than her child (Lacan would call it the phallus). The emergent, not-yet-subject is constituted by the primal narcissism of identification with the mother's images, with the Imaginary, or the Other (the place of the imaginary father); by means of this narcissistic crisis, it becomes a subject of and in signification – in Lacanian terms, the subject is enabled finally to take up a position, via the Imaginary, in the Symbolic realm. A necessary by-product of the process of abjection is the 'abjecting' of the mother, or of what symbolically blurs the boundaries of the emergent, still archaic self, threatening to collapse it back into an indifferentiated maternal origin.[28] How would this scheme work in Milton's *Samson Agonistes* and Wordsworth's *Prelude*? If language in *Samson Agonistes* is what assaults the boundaries of single self ('my fort of silence'), then words themselves – which, as we have seen, are associated with weakness and with the talking woman – must be cast out; we might note in passing that by the end of the poem non-verbal noise has been appropriated for the strong man. Samson's final identification, then, is not with the pre-Oedipal silence and absence of the moon (with what can be imagined as a pre-linguistic era preceding the Symbolic or paternal realm, the mother's cave-like *chora*); it is with the archaic space of the paternal Logos, or sun – with God the Father, whose originating divine act (his Word) provides the ground for Samson's and Milton's fantasy of speaking deeds or the language of presence ('deeds which spoke loud the doer'). The presence of God in Samson's act is what makes the actor able to declare himself without loss of strength.

It is in this sense only – a sense predicated on the myth of an originating but unuttered or unutterable paternal Word – that we would be justified in alluding to a 'fall into language'. Positing such a fall involves entering into Samson's and Milton's interpretive collusion, their fantasy of language as feminine, enfeebled by its divorce from the power and presence of God. *Samson Agonistes* pits feminine chatter or weakness against language as performance, which is either the secret of Samson's silence or the thunderous utterance of his strength. If, in Book VII of *The Prelude*, London means nothing less than the necessity of becoming a subject of, and in, signification – a process which involves both producing and being produced by the split between sign and thing, or the temporal and significatory difference between words and what they name – then the bandage for that wound of problematic identification-in-and-as-division is Wordsworth's 'abjection' of the city itself. Located as the source of the production and reproduction of signs, the city is like a woman whose soul has been overthrown, or a man who has been feminized by publishing his secret. By associating London with the blasphemy (words out of place, just as dirt may be called matter out of place), 'painted bloom', and 'open shame' of the prostitute, Wordsworth taints the city with the ambiguity which threatens the constitution of the (masculine) single self, while purifying his own utterance. Besides throwing light on the question of poetic identity, and on the constitution of the signifying subject (the growth of the poet), Kristeva's theory of abjection thus helps to explain the function of the prostitute in Book VII of *The Prelude*, and in particular to clarify her relation to the city as simultaneously a representation and a casting out of the fallenness of poetry or language itself.

Later in Book VII, 'The feeble salutation from the voice / Of some unhappy woman' (VII, 639–40) haunts an imaginary emptying out and silencing of the London scene during a night-piece whose effect, like that of Wordsworth's 'Sonnet Composed Upon Westminster Bridge', is to assimilate the city to natural archetypes; or rather, to impose on it the arrested sleep of death. In Milton's allegory, Death is the child of Sin, born incestuously of a difference that is insufficiently different, and giving birth to the error of endlessly multiplying repetition which forever returns to its origin in the womb of the mother. By making the solitary woman accost him – by arresting her, so to speak, as solitary women on the streets of eighteenth-century London were regularly arrested for loitering with intent – Wordsworth casts out the dangerous possibility of being himself mistaken for a nocturnal loiterer, or fallen woman. He too, after all, was the product of a late eighteenth-century sociological drift from country to city that turned him (like Poor Susan) into a Lake District outcast from his father's house. But Wordsworth also makes the prostitute prefigure all that is soul-destroying about the 'unmanageable sight' of the city, for which Bartholomew Fair is the culminating type, with its blank confusion and unnatural, man-made ('Promethean') freaks. Casting out woman as prostitute, the form that 'split[s] the human race / In twain' protects Wordsworth himself from division by projecting the split as sexually differentiated; two voices are there – the voice of the fallen (woman) and the voice of the chosen (son). The gap or 'barrier' created by Wordsworth's first sight of a prostitute effects a saving 'divorce' between his soul and the body of representation; between Wordsworthian poetic identity and the figures or signs that constitute him as a poet. Or, to put it another way, prostitution in *The Prelude* screens the process by which the Romantic poet separates himself from the natural unity he purports to espouse, in order to permit an illicit intercourse with the painted bloom of Sin and the self-spawning reproductive capacities of Death. In this version of the Miltonic allegory, for Sin read 'figurative language', and for Death read 'writing', or the unnatural multiplication of signs figured by and in the city.[29]

Autobiography and the prodigal daughter

De Quincey's *Confessions of an English Opium-Eater* opens with an apology to the reader 'for breaking through that delicate and honourable reserve, which, for the most part, restrains us from the public exposure of our own errors and infirmities'. English feelings, De Quincey continues, are revolted by the spectacle 'of a human being obtruding on our notice his moral ulcers or scars, and tearing away that "decent drapery"' by which they should be concealed.[30] Consequently, most English confessions proceed from those whose status is socially ambiguous or deviant – from 'demireps, adventurers, or swindlers'. This is not the case, he observes, in French literature, where decent and self-respecting citizens may perform 'acts of gratuitous self-humiliation' that are confined in England to the criminal classes. Autobiography is the French disease, the immodest exhibition of moral ulcers which taints literature with 'the spurious and defective sensibility of the French', i.e. the feminine and demi-reputable sensibility of a Jean-Jacques Rousseau. De Quincey identifies confession not only with the 'demirep' or prostitute, but with the effeminate foreignness that infects his own 'English' confessions from within, much as femininity (the weakness of self-betrayal or self-publication) infects Samson. Or, as de Man puts it apropos of Rousseau, excuses are catching; there can never be enough of them to keep up with the infection of rhetorical effects.[31] Autobiography, in a word, is sick, and of itself.

De Quincey's self-advertised 'guilt and misery' are terms commonly applied to the fallen woman ('Let other pens dwell on guilt and misery', Jane Austen begins the last chapter of *Mansfield Park*, alluding there to the fall of Maria Rushworth). In the *Confessions*, the sister-double with whom De Quincey can never be reunited except in opium visions or death is the fifteen-year-old prostitute, Ann of Oxford Street. Hers are the extenuating circumstances which Mary Wollstonecraft had pleaded in *A Vindication of The Rights of Woman* (1791): 'many innocent girls . . . are, as it may emphatically be termed, *ruined* before they know the difference between virtue and vice . . . prostitution becomes [their] only refuge'.[32] Ruined before she knows (the) difference, Ann stands in for the young De Quincey, who traces his route to opium addiction back to his own weeks as a starving and destitute adolescent street-walker. 'Being myself at that time of necessity a peripatetic, or a walker of the streets', he recalls, 'I naturally fell in more frequently with those female peripatetics who are technically called Street walkers.' Ann's peripatetic wanderings – a harlot's progress or quest of error – images the deviance of De Quincey's later addiction. But the metaphor of the prostitute's wandering toward dissolution and death ('the central darkness of a London brothel, or . . . the darkness of the grave'),[33] stands for more than opium addiction. Ann's wanderings on the London streets and De Quincey's never-ending quest for her become a metaphor for his own attempt to recover the past through memory. The retrospective and confessional movement of autobiography is De Quincey's primary addiction, which is also the compulsion of autobiography to repeat.

By some oversight, De Quincey has either never enquired or forgotten Ann's surname, and he calls his inability to trace her his 'heaviest affliction'. Like his opium habit, his quest for Ann in the labyrinthine streets of London can never attain its imaginary goal, reunion with a lost self; though 'perhaps even within a few feet of each other' they are divided by a 'a barrier . . . amounting in the end to a separation for eternity!'[34] Eternal separation severs empirical being-in-the-world from purgatorial being-in-the-text. This is the writerly fate to which De Quincey is perpetually condemned. In his dealings with the money-lenders, for instance, he finds it difficult to establish his credit-worthiness – his credibility – until he produces letters addressed to him as proof of his identity: 'It was strange to me', writes De Quincey, 'to find my own self, *materialiter* considered . . . accused, or at least suspected, of counterfeiting my own self, *formaliter* considered.' Here De Quincey, alert to his own legal usage, is '(to use a forensic word) *soliciting*' (his italics).[35] He solicits money on the basis of his name and his patrimony; Ann solicits money on the basis of her body, but – a significant difference – at the price of losing her paternal name ('It is a general practice . . . with girls of humble rank in her unhappy condition . . . to style themselves . . . simply by their Christian names, *Mary, Jane, Frances,* &c.').[36] By commodifying her sexuality (entering the oldest profession), she also loses the means to purchase a new surname in exchange for an old one; the marriage market – the realm of 'social' (re)production – is barred to her as a fallen woman. Ann becomes the non-exchangeable outcast of patriarchal economics by selling herself; De Quincey commodifies his identity by pawning it to the brokers. Both enter the capitalist and mercantile system symbolized by the city at the price of alienation from their fantasized origins (the Romantic family) and loss of imaginary unity between 'material' self (body) and 'formal' self (name of the father); hence De Quincey's initial, self-confessed identification with 'demireps, adventurers, or swindlers'.

The crime to which the subject-in-writing must confess is the one that debars her or him from natural identity or guaranteed wholeness; what she or he has for sale is signs, or a signature. The loss of integrity between body and name, or this splitting of imaginary self-identity, might also be seen as a metaphor for authorship. As Catherine Gallagher has argued apropos of George Eliot, both prostitution and usury – another form of unnatural reproduction – come increasingly to be identified with authorship in the nineteenth century; during the Victorian period, she writes, 'The activities of authoring, of procuring illegitimate income, and of alienating one's self through prostitution seem particularly associated with one another.'[37] Late eighteenth- and early nineteenth-century changes in the legal and economic status of the author – the emergence of copyright law, the growth of a popular readership, increasing dependence on the market-place – brought the legally commodified text into being, along with the modern notion of authorship (*'formaliter* considered', in De Quincey's phrase). In a displaced fashion, De Quincey's financial dealings with the money-lender figure the self-sale by the commodifier of a 'confessional' autobiography whose very saleability requires the guarantee of authenticity, or legal identity. This may, indeed, be the reason why De Quincey prefers to think of Ann 'as one long since laid in the grave . . . of a Magdalen; taken away, before injuries and cruelty had blotted out and transfigured her ingenuous nature'.[38] Like the beautiful boy embalmed in *The Prelude*, she is laid in her grave in order to save the author from a fate worse than death, that of the fallen writer – self-sold, self-divided, and self-seduced into the error of confessional, demi-reputable autobiography.

De Quincey's *Confessions* end with a vision of his reunion with Ann in the tranquillity of a Judaean Easter Sunday. The religious landscape of this culminating vision merges the garden of resurrection with the Lake District landscape that is now De Quincey's home. Wordsworth's Poor Susan looks longingly northward to 'a single small cottage, a nest like a dove's', to which she is urged 'Poor outcast! return' ('to receive thee once more / The house of thy Father will open its door', ll. 17–18).[39] In De Quincey's *Confessions*, Oxford Street – the scene of his wanderings with Ann – is both the scene of his first opium purchase and the road to the north which leads to the Lake District, to Dove Cottage, and to Wordsworth:

> oftentimes on moonlight nights . . . my consolation was . . . to gaze from Oxford-street up every avenue in succession . . . for *that*, said I, travelling with my eyes up the long vistas . . . '*that* is the road to the North', and therefore to [Grasmere], and if I had the wings of a dove, *that* way I would fly for comfort.[40]

Ann's place at his side is later taken by Peggy Simpson, the Lake District girl whom De Quincey seduced but married, and whom at the time of writing – significantly, he has had to return to the city in order to meet his obligations to the *London Magazine* – he imagines 'sitting alone in the same valley, and mistress of that very house [Dove Cottage] to which my heart turned in its blindness, nineteen years ago'. What he calls 'the impotent wishes of childhood' surface again in the refrain-like motif of his desire for an always distant, always lost maternal comfort: 'Oh, that I had the wings of a dove . . . and *that* way I would fly for comfort.'[41] In De Quincey's version of the long journey homeward, the present can only repeat the fixations of the past. His demonic parody of Wordsworthian domesticity turns Dove Cottage itself into the scene of the *Oresteia*, with Dorothy Wordsworth's part taken by Peggy-as-Electra, witness to the furious pains of opium which now possess him. The wages of sin are the deaths of infant children, orchestrated by sighs of farewell 'such as the caves of hell sighed when the incestuous mother uttered the abhorred name of death'.[42] In De Quincey's incestuous family romance, it goes without saying, these sibling deaths are desired (as perhaps even Kate Wordsworth's death was desired) so that the mother may be more certainly and uniquely possessed.

Signs of absence or 'everlasting farewells!' signal the central darkness or lack at the core of being. Facelessness – the sign of lost identity – figures the dispersal of self as an undifferentiated London crowd. Like Wordsworth in Book VII of *The Prelude*, unable to read the faces of the city streets ('The face of every one / That passes by me is a mystery', VII, 597–8), or violently confronted by the minimal characters of a blind man's label, De Quincey experiences the autobiographical text itself as a lawless, meaningless multiplication of difference – as textuality without a face. Hence his attempt to anchor the wanderings of self-loss by fixing identity on the (ever-to-be) recovered face of Ann: 'I suppose that, in the literal and unrhetorical use of the word *myriad*, I may say that on my different visits to London, I have looked into many, many myriads of female faces, in the hope of meeting her.'[43] 'The tyranny of the human face' – a legacy of this obsessive self-reading – becomes one of the pains of opium as De Quincey's addiction enters its demonic phase. The infinitely agitated characters of the addictive sublime ('the sea appeared paved with innumerable faces, upturned to the heavens: faces, imploring, wrathful, despairing, surged upwards by thousands, by myriads, by generations, by centuries')[44] represent death by self-multiplication, or death by signs. Ann's face never surfaces from the apocalyptic flood to render De Quincey's identity 'literal and unrhetorical' (that is, non-figurative) with the illusion of a stabilizing, specular reflection.

This fixing of an illusory or 'literal' identity was to be Wordsworth's function, as De Quincey describes it in his *Recollections of the Lakes and the Lake Poets*. The long-delayed meeting with Wordsworth at Dove Cottage in 1807 brings De Quincey 'face to face' with 'that man whom, of all the men from the beginning of time, [he] most fervently desired to see', and their confrontation is the autobiographical climax of his essay on Wordsworth.[45] The meeting is momentous not only because it signifies the return of the prodigal to the house of his father, but because it permits a powerful, specular, assertion of identity. De Quincey believes that his resemblance to Wordsworth lies in the singular defect they share, 'namely . . . a peculiar embarrassment and penury of words'. This singular defect is swiftly redefined as a distinction, 'a most distinguished talent "pour le silence"'.[46] Hard up for words, De Quincey needs a literary identity card; he finds it not only in his resemblance to Wordsworth, but in the filial relationship which permits his return to the bosom of the Romantic family. The question of resemblance turns out to be crucial to De Quincey in a number of ways. His memoir is curiously, disproportionately concerned not so much with their shared defect of silence, but with Wordsworth's defective physique ('it impressed a spectator with a sense of absolute meanness, more especially when viewed from behind, and not counteracted by his countenance'). Not Wordsworth's physique but Wordsworth's face ('one which would have made amends for greater defects of figure')[47] becomes the talisman of his greatness and, by extension, the guarantee or reflection of De Quincey's own identity – as if 'face' could be detached from 'figure' to become an emblem of poetic greatness, or rather, a figure for it, like the head of a poet fronting his Poetical Works.

Wordsworth's face, De Quincey asserts, is a national face, that of an Englishman (long rather than round). No one could mistake him for a round-faced Frenchman; the defect of *his* sensibility is strength-in-silence, not Rousseau's confession of feminine weakness. Forehead, eyes, nose, mouth (especially mouth) – the catalogue builds up an identikit portrait. But the portrait is not, as it turns out, of Wordsworth. Milton's is the poetic face or front, De Quincey insists, which resembles Wordsworth's even more closely than the Carruthers portrait of 1817.[48] Richardson's laurel-crowned engraving, the frontispiece to De Quincey's long-sought edition of *Paradise Lost*, confronts him with a shock of recognition which he ventriloquizes by a dramatic rehearsal of Richardson's anecdote about Milton's last surviving daughter, who, when she saw the Richardson portrait, 'burst out into a rapture of passionate recognition; exclaiming – "This is my father! this is my dear father!"'.[49] In Wordsworth's face, De Quincey finds himself as prodigal daughter; it was, after all, the poet's infant daughter, Kate, with whom De Quincey most deeply identified, and it was Kate's premature death which unleashed his mourning for the original self-loss prefigured in the childhood death of his sister Elizabeth, and repeated over and over in the face of the lost girl prostitute, Ann.

If De Quincey re-enters the literary fold (symbolized by the Romantic family at Dove Cottage) in the guise of Milton's daughter, what are the implications for his literary relations to Wordsworth? As a dutiful daughter rather than a dead one, De Quincey becomes the amanuensis who gives Wordsworth his eyes – or (since blindness is an image of privation) the voice, symbol of poetic presence, that issues from such a poet's face. Domesticating the great poet as 'a household image', like

Shakespeare, De Quincey memorializes Wordsworth in the prime of his powers by restoring to the portrait (as close readers of Shakespeare's portraits have also attempted) the empirical existence of the man: 'Commensurate with the interest in the poetry will be a secondary interest in the poet – in his personal appearance, and his habits of life, *so far as they can be supposed at all dependent upon his intellectual characteristics*.'[50] When De Quincey asks, in Westmorland fashion, ' "what-like" was Wordsworth?' his answer is, tautologically: Wordsworth resembles his life as told in *The Prelude*; that is, it exhibits 'a most remarkable (almost a providential) arrangement of circumstances, all tending to one result' – namely, the writing of his poetry. Everything in Wordsworth's life tends to make him 'Wordsworth', the poet of the autobiographical *Prelude*. The providential dispensation allows for the convergence of the life and the poetry, insisting on the identity of Wordsworth the man and his representative autobiographical text. Some of this naturalized poetic identity inevitably rubs off on De Quincey too, personifying the biographer (a chosen daughter) as *The Prelude* personifies the autobiographical poet ('I was a chosen son', III, 82), and underwriting his own claims to literary distinction.

We might ask what further function this providential scheme serves and how it is connected with the person – the persona – of Wordsworth. Wordsworth's London in Book VII of *The Prelude* is a gigantic shopping centre. With its 'string of dazzling wares, / Shop after shop', its 'symbols, blazoned names, / And all the tradesman's honours overhead', and its 'fronts of houses, like a title-page / With letters huge inscribed from top to toe' (VII, 173–7), the city becomes a symbol of the eighteenth-century consumer revolution. One visible aspect of this revolution was advertising, which often took the allegorical form of life-size statues, 'physiognomies', busts, or portraits – 'allegoric shapes, female or male . . . physiognomies of real men . . . Boyle, Shakespear, Newton . . . the attractive head / Of some quack-doctor, famous in his day' (VII, 179–83). Elsewhere in *The Prelude*, Wordsworth uses the word 'front' to refer to his own poem ('On the front / Of this whole song is written . . .', VI, 669–70). In poetic or highly rhetorical usage, 'front' means forehead, and, by extension, the whole face as expressive of character. Elsewhere in Book VII, 'Advertisements of giant size . . . Press forward in all colours on the sight',

> These, bold in conscious merit – lower down,
> That, fronted with a most imposing word,
> Is peradventure one in masquerade.

> (*Prelude*, VII, 210–14)

This most imposing word, according to MS X, was 'inviting' (compare the masquerading word, 'INVISIBLE', on the actor's chest).[52] Counterfeiting identity ('masquerade') and soliciting money, perhaps under false pretences, advertising takes its place alongside the 'inviting' masquerades of the eighteenth-century leisure industry associated with Ranelagh and Vauxhall Gardens. Just as public places, and especially crowd-activities such as masquerades and theatres, were also the scene of prostitution, so advertising had notoriously become the language of euphemistic 'invitation' by the end of the eighteenth century (indeed, 'advertisements of an indelicate or immoral tendency' were the object of contemporary denunciation).[53] If a blind London beggar touting his own story is the other face of the adman or conman, the blind London poet (Milton) is the other face of the impecunious Grub Street hack whose financial solicitations placed him in the same relation to the commodification of texts as the prostitute stood in relation to the commercialization of leisure and the commodification of sex.

This textual commodification is the socio-economic reality of writing which the providential scheme in Wordsworth's poetry, and especially his legacy from Calvert, serves to screen. For De Quincey, whose own hand-to-mouth existence as a journalist made him the outcast or prostitute of contemporary letters, Wordsworth's pastoral seclusion would have had redemptive connotations; not for nothing does his saving vision of Ann take place at Easter. Yet not even Wordsworth is entirely immune to the fall figured by De Quincey's addictive autobiography. For all its refusal of the city and its strategic relocation of poetry in the north, *The Prelude* too is a piece of effrontery or self-advertisement – an invitation to enter into an illicit reading relationship with a man named Wordsworth. Rhetorically speaking, 'Wordsworth' is a personification, like the 'allegoric shapes, female or male, / Or physiognomies of real men' in the London streets. Personification is well known to be the most devalued figure in late eighteenth-century and Romantic critical discourses about poetic diction. 'I wish to keep my Reader in the company of flesh and blood', writes Wordsworth in the 1800 'Preface' to *Lyrical Ballads*, eschewing 'personification of abstract ideas'.[54] As Steven Knapp has argued persuasively in *Personification and The Sublime*, critical ambivalence towards allegorical personification is symptomatic of a wider Romantic ambivalence about figurative language.[55] Significantly, in their notes to Wordsworth's remarks on personification in the 1800 'Preface', the editors of Wordsworth's *Prose Works* refer the reader to one of the 'interludes' in the third edition of Darwin's *The Loves of the Plants* (1791). 'The Muses are young ladies, and we wish to see them dressed', writes Darwin, introducing sexual difference into art as if by analogy with vegetable reproduction.[56] Not only must poetry be decently clothed, however, but personification itself is only allowed into poetry if properly 'dressed', that is, it must be veiled or invisible, rather than shamelessly painted or nakedly displayed. Darwin's preferred example of personification in action, therefore, is the modestly silent 'person' (a woman, naturally) of Shakespeare's 'concealment' in *Twelfth Night*: 'She never told her love . . . concealment, like a worm i' th' bud . . .'.[57] If to declare one's love is tantamount to a sexual invitation, or even a harlot's curse, then to fail to conceal the presence of personification is to cease to be a respectable poet.

In their notes to the 'Preface' of 1800, the editors of the *Prose Works* go on to footnote Hugh Blair's *Lectures on Rhetoric and Belles Lettres* (1783) – the source of many of Wordsworth's central poetic arguments in the 'Preface' – for his views on prosopopoeia. The rhetorical figure associated by de Man specifically with autobiography, prosopopoeia is for Blair the highest form of personification, 'when inanimate objects are introduced . . . as speaking to us, or hearing and listening when we address ourselves to them'.[58] Prosopopoeia gives voice to the face of Wordsworth, inviting us to identify the autobiographical front of *The Prelude* – its masquerade of identity – with the figure of the poet. Figuratively speaking, it masquerades as a self that is 'literal and unrhetorical', concealing the representational and economic structures which produce such a person. That these structures should involve reference to an allegorical fall which is itself a privileged example of the fall into allegory gives special resonance to the Maid of Buttermere sequence and the accompanying figure of the prostitute in Book VII of *The Prelude*. In the eighteenth-century debate over the propriety of figurative language, Milton's allegory of Sin and Death – as Knapp has argued – provided the test case.[59] Johnson's criticism of the introduction of figures into the literal narrative of Satan's journey ('Sin is indeed the mother of Death . . . but when they stop the journey of Satan, a journey described as real . . . the allegory is broken . . . to this there was no temptation, but the author's opinion of its beauty') makes the Puritan Milton the most notorious victim of seduction by Spenserian romance, or 'beauty'.[60] When the painted woman and her beautiful boy rise up in Wordsworth's path, what they figure is the seduction of figuration itself, along with the error of romance (the romance of error). Like the beautiful boy, Romanticism is saved for the History of Ideas or the history of consciousness – for the high Romanticism of Lovejoy and Abrams, or for what Hartman calls a 'viable *poetic* form of enlightenment (or post-enlightenment) thought'[61] – only if it can be 'stopped' before the castrating encounter with Sin or sexual difference. The prostitute who 'split[s] the race of man / In twain' figures the concealed shame of Romantic personification, outcast in *The Prelude* as the seductively feminine face of the autobiographical persona in an age of textual and sexual commodification.

Notes

1. G. HARTMAN, *The Fate of Reading and Other Essays* (Chicago and London: University of Chicago Press, 1975), 277.

2. Personal communication.

3. See M.H. ABRAMS, *Natural Supernaturalism* (New York: Norton, 1971).

4. G. SPIVAK, 'Sex and History in *The Prelude* (1805): Books Nine to Thirteen', *Texas Studies in Literature and Language*, **23** (1981): 336.

5. HARTMAN, *The Fate of Reading*, pp. 277–8.

6. I am indebted to STEVEN KNAPP, *Personification and the Sublime: Milton to Coleridge* (Cambridge, Mass., and London: Harvard University Press, 1985), for suggesting the relation between allegorical romance and Romantic attitudes to personification.

7. These lines belonged originally to drafts connected with 'Nutting', where 'Nature's inmate' presumably referred to Dorothy. See *The Prelude*, ed. de Selincourt, rev. Darbishire, p. 612.

8. *Prelude* XI, 17–19 also belonged originally to drafts connected with 'Nutting'; see ibid., 610.

9. See also L. KRAMER, 'Gender and Sexuality in *The Prelude*: The Question of Book Seven', *ELH*, **54** (1987): 619–37, for a detailed psychoanalytic reading of the Maid of Buttermere episode in relation to Wordsworth's larger repression of the theme of sexuality, and to related issues of representation figured in Book VII by the city; I am grateful to Professor Kramer for the opportunity to read his essay while working on my own.

10. See A. PARREAUX, *Daily Life in England in the Reign of George III* (London, 1966), pp. 122–8, 134–40. For a fuller account of prostitution in eighteenth-century London, see F. HENRIQUES, *Prostitution and Society* (3 vols.; London, 1963), II, 143–91. During the 18th century, London was said to have twice as many prostitutes as Paris; in 1789, the West End alone contained an estimated 30,000 prostitutes (see ibid. p. 144). For literary representations of the prostitute, see also J.B. RADNER, 'The Youthful Harlot's Curse: The Prostitute as Symbol of the City in Eighteenth-Century English Literature', *Eighteenth Century Life*, **2** (1976): 59–63.

11. As Kenneth R. Johnston writes, pointing out the anachronism whereby Wordsworth introduces a play which he not only did not see in the 1790s but may not in fact have seen later, 'Wordsworth's oddly self-implicating account of *The Beauty of Buttermere*' seems to block his narrative and thematic progress as well: see *Wordsworth and The Recluse*, pp. 160–3. For Mary Robinson, see also D.H. REIMAN, 'The Beauty of Buttermere as Fact and Romantic Symbol', *Criticism*, **26** (1984): 139–70.

12. See e.g. WEISKEL, *The Romantic Sublime* (Baltimore: Johns Hopkins University Press, 1976) pp. 173–5, 200–4.

13. See HERTZ, *The End of the Line* (New York: Columbia University Press, 1985), pp. 218–19, for what he calls 'structures of minimal difference' in relation to the Winander Boy episode.

14. The term *invidia* is Lacan's, as elaborated by R. YOUNG, 'The Eye and Progress

of his Song: A Lacanian Reading of *The Prelude'*, *Oxford Literary Review*, **3** (1979): 78–98; for the connection between this passage and the 'Blessed the Infant Babe' passage in Book II, see especially pp. 89–90.

15. See S. FREUD, 'Fetishism' (1927): 'what happened [in the case of the fetishist] . . . was that the boy refused to take cognizance of the fact of his having perceived that a woman does not possess a penis. . . . It is not true that, after the child has made his observation of the woman, he has preserved unaltered his belief that women have a phallus. He has retained that belief, but he has also given it up. In the conflict between the weight of the unwelcome perception and the force of his counter-wish, a compromise has been reached . . .', *The Complete Psychological Works of Sigmund Freud*, trans. and ed. J. Strachey, XXI, pp. 153–4.

16. See e.g. CHRISTOPHER WORDSWORTH on university 'Toasts' at Cambridge and Oxford, in *Social Life at the English Universities in the Eighteenth Century* (Cambridge: Cambridge University Press, 1874), pp. 363, 367–73, 397. 'Toasts' (like 'Beauties') were often the daughters of university tradesmen rather than open prostitutes; while Christopher Wordsworth documents the drinking habits of eighteenth-century undergraduates, he represses the question of sexuality outside imprudently contracted marriages. For prostitution at Oxford – a well-established problem for the university authorities in the mid-nineteenth century – see A.J. ENGEL, ' "Immoral Intentions": The University of Oxford and the Problem of Prostitution, 1827–1914', *Victorian Studies*, **3** (1979): 79–107.

17. *The Notebooks of Samuel Taylor Coleridge*, ed. K. Coburn (3 vols; London, 1957–73), I. 1726.

18. See e.g. C. CHASE, 'The Ring of Gyges and the Coat of Darkness: Reading Rousseau with Wordsworth', *Decomposing Figures: Rhetorical Readings in the Romantic Tradition* (Baltimore: Johns Hopkins University Press, 1986), pp. 32–64.

19. J. SWAN, 'Difference and Silence: John Milton and the Question of Gender', in S.N. Garner, C. Kahane, and M. Sprengnether (eds), *The (M)other Tongue: Essays in Feminist Psychoanalytic Interpretation* (Ithaca, NY, and London: Cornell University Press, 1985), p. 144.

20. 'Faith must needs be coy', *Prelude*, VII, 308.

21. See Cynthia Chase's reading in *Decomposing Figures*, pp. 58–62.

22. Cf. Neil Hertz's reading for the discrimination between seeing and reading: 'The encounter with the Beggar triangulates the poet's self in relation to his double, who is represented . . . as an emblem of minimal difference fixed in relation to itself. The power of the emblem is that it reestablishes boundaries between representor and represented and . . . keeps the poet-impresario from tumbling into his text', *The End of the Line*, p. 60.

23. Garner, Kahane and Sprengnether (eds), *The (M)other Tongue*, p. 144.

24. Ibid., p. 160. Cf. also ibid., p. 160 n. for Chodorow's formulation of the problem of gender identity: 'Underlying, or built into, core male gender identity is an early, nonverbal, unconscious, almost somatic sense of femaleness that continually . . . challenges and undermines the sense of maleness', N. CHODOROW, 'Feminism and Difference: Gender, Relation, and Difference in Psychoanalytic Perspective', *Socialist Review*, **46** (1979): 63.

25. Garner, Kahane, and Sprengnether (eds), *The (M)other Tongue*, p. 158.

26. Swan at this point is brought to question Chodorow's object-relations-derived account by way of Juliet Mitchell's more Lacanian position. His own footnoted formulation runs as follows: 'At the primitive, originative core of identity is not femaleness or maleness but an undifferentiated wholeness that is neither. Most discussions of this issue that are based entirely on object relations theory tend to view the beginning of gender as both/and, both masculine *and* feminine. But that comes later as a reading of difference back upon a moment that is *neither/nor*', ibid., p. 162n.

27. Ibid., p. 168.

28. For Julia Kristeva's theory of maternal 'abjection', see *Powers of Horror: An Essay on Abjection*, trans. L.S. Roudiez (New York: Columbia University Press, 1982), especially pp. 1–18, 32–55 *passim*, and the further elaboration in 'Freud and Love: Treatment and its Discontents' (originally published as 'L'abjet d'amour'), *The Kristeva Reader*, ed. T. Moi (Oxford: Basil Blackwell, 1986), 238–71. See also Neil Hertz's brief but helpful discussion in *The End of the Line*, pp. 231–3.

29. As Catherine Gallagher has pointed out, prostitution is a common metaphor for 'one of the ancient models of linguistic production: the unnatural multiplication of interchangeable signs; see 'George Eliot and *Daniel Deronda*: The Prostitute and the Jewish Question', in R.B. Yeazell (ed.), *Sex, Politics, and Science in the Nineteenth-Century Novel. Selected Papers from the English Institute* (Baltimore: Johns Hopkins University Press, 1986), p. 41.

30. De Quincey, *Confessions of an English Opium-Eater*, ed. Lindop (Oxford: Oxford University Press, 1985), p. 1.

31. See P. de Man, 'Excuses (*Confessions*)', *Allegories of Reading: Figural Language in Rousseau, Nietzsche, Rilke, and Proust* (New Haven: Yale University Press, 1979), pp. 278–301.

32. M. Wollstonecraft, *A Vindication of the Rights of Woman*, ed. M. Kramnick (Harmondsworth: Penguin, 1975), p. 165.

33. *Confessions of an English Opium-Eater*, pp. 20, 22.

34. Ibid., p. 34.

35. Ibid., pp. 25, 23.

36. Ibid., p. 27.

37. Gallagher in Yeazell (ed.), *Sex, Politics, and Science in the Nineteenth-Century Novel*, p. 43.

38. *Confessions of an English Opium-Eater*, p. 34.

39. As Lamb observed mischievously,

> The last verse of Susan . . . threw a kind of dubeity upon Susan's moral conduct. Susan is a maid servant. I see her trundling her mop and contemplating the whirling phenomenon thro' blurred optics; but to term her a poor outcast seems as much as to say that poor Susan was no better than she should be, which I trust was not what you meant to express. (*The Letters of Charles and Mary Anne Lamb*, ed. Marrs, III, p. 147)

For an interesting argument relating to Poor Susan and her outcast status, see P.J. Manning, 'Placing Poor Susan: Wordsworth and the New Historicism',

SiR, **25** (1986): 351–69. See also D. Simpson, 'What Bothered Charles Lamb About Poor Susan?', *SEL*, **26** (1986): 589–612.

40. *Confessions of an English Opium-Eater*, p. 35.

41. Ibid., pp. 36–7.

42. Ibid., p. 77.

43. Ibid., p. 34.

44. Ibid., p. 72.

45. *Recollections of the Lakes and the Lake Poets*, ed. D. Wright (Harmondsworth: Penguin, 1970) p. 127.

46. Ibid., p. 124.

47. Ibid., pp. 136, 137.

48. See F. Blanshard, *Portraits of Wordsworth* (Ithaca, NY: Cornell University Press, 1959), plate 5 and pp. 53–9.

49. *Recollections of the Lakes and the Lake Poets*, ed. Wright, p. 140.

50. Ibid., pp. 144–5.

51. Ibid., pp. 134, 148.

52. 'That, peradventure, one in masquerade / Inviting is the leading word . . .' (MS X): *The Prelude*, ed. de Selincourt, rev. Darbishire, p. 232 app. crit.

53. See e.g. N. McKendrick, 'George Packwood and the Commercialization of Shaving: The Art of Eighteenth-Century Advertising or "The Way to Get Money and be Happy"', in N. McKendrick, J. Brewer and J.H. Plumb (eds), *The Birth of a Consumer Society: The Commercialization of Eighteenth-Century England* (Bloomington, 1982), pp. 146–94, especially p. 151 n. For the association of public parks and gardens such as Ranelagh and Vauxhall with prostitution, see Henriques, *Prostitution and Society*, II, p. 159.

54. *Prose Works*, I, p. 130.

55. See *Personification and the Sublime*, pp. 1–7, and, for Wordsworth and personification, pp. 98–129 *passim*.

56. See *Prose Works*, I, p. 172 n. and E. Darwin, *The Botanic Garden: Part II, The Loves of the Plants* (Lichfield, 1789), p. 43.

57. Ibid., p. 44: '. . . the person of Concealment is very indistinct, and therefore does not compel us to attend to its improbability, in the following beautiful lines of Shakespeare: "She never told her love; / But let Concealment, like a worm i' th' bud, / Feed on her damask cheek."'

58. See *Prose Works*, I. p. 173 n., and cf. de Man, *The Rhetoric of Romanticism* (New York: Columbia University Press, 1984), pp. 67–82.

59. See *Personification and the Sublime*, pp. 51–65, for the eighteenth-century debate over Milton's Sin and Death.

60. S. Johnson, *Lives of the English Poets*, ed. G. Birkbeck Hill (3 vols); Oxford, 1905), I, pp. 185–6; see *Personification and the Sublime*, pp. 62–3.

61. Hartman, *The Fate of Reading*, p. 277.

6 Literary Gentlemen and Lovely Ladies: The Debate on the Character of *Christabel**

KAREN SWANN

What was so disturbing or exasperating to contemporary readers about Coleridge's *Christabel*, which Wordsworth struck from *Lyrical Ballads* (1800) and reviewers berated for the 'degeneracy' it revealed in its author? Christabel's embrace by the mysteriously disfigured Geraldine may explain why critics attacked the poem as licentious, but what does it mean that contemporary discussion of *Christabel* panned its author as like a woman, as effeminate and hysterical – like his heroine who 'cannot tell' what ails her?

In two essays, the second of which is included here, Karen Swann shows that Coleridge's readers thereby play out the central cultural fantasy and defence that his poem holds up to view: that of a possessed female body, unable to control its own speech. The fantasy functions to localize, and domesticate, anxieties not only about sexuality and gender but about representation – about the subject's autonomy in relation to cultural forms, and about what Swann's first essay calls 'the enigma of form'. 'Female bodies "naturally" seem to figure an ungraspable truth', Swann writes: 'that form, habitually viewed as the arbitrary, contingent vessel of more enduring meanings, is yet the source and determinant of all meanings, whether the subject's or the world's' ('*Christabel*: The Wandering Mother and the Enigma of Form', *Studies in Romanticism*, 23, Winter 1984: 544). Mary Jacobus traces in Wordsworth and Milton the fantasy that language is feminine. Karen Swann traces in Coleridge and his critics the feminization of form.

The disturbing fact, for instance, that we need to know the genre of a text to know how to take it – and that knowing its genre also means acknowledging its conventionality, and so also destabilizes its meaning – like other such anxieties about the extent to which one

---

* Reprinted from *English Literary History*, **52** (spring 1985): 397-418.

controls one's experience of making meaning, is handled by Coleridge's contemporaries through the framing of an opposition: 'an opposition between authentic, contained "manly" speech and "feminine" bodies – the utterly conventional yet licentiously imaginative female characters, readers, and genres of the circulating libraries' (*ibid.*, p. 535). The reception of 'Christabel' shows readers' wish to differentiate what they are doing from passive repetitive absorption of cultural materials, and shows the repetitiveness of that very attempt. Again and again, both 'in' Coleridge's poem and around it, 'a feminine body comes to represent a threat to the wishfully autonomous self' (*ibid.*, p. 551).

Swann's reading brings out an impressive critical power and sense of humour in Coleridge's poem. His subject emerges as 'the relation between cultural processes and (fantasized) feminine erotic experience' – or 'literature's *fantastic appeal*' (my italics). Swann's own language plays out the blurring of boundaries on which she comments, between literature, its commentary, and 'real life'. The richness of her argument partly comes from her extraordinarily canny reading of how Coleridge can be seen to project himself into various figures in a scene. Her subject, however, is as she says 'cultural fantasy' or 'the projects of culture', not the defences of an individual author or reader. Swann's work is thoroughly informed by psychoanalysis, especially in the way she conveys the playfulness and desire as well as the defensiveness of the moves that construct a masculine self. That literary insight also supports her feminist perception of the less than inevitable or 'natural' status of the family romance or the Oedipus complex – the, rather, at once political and gratuitous nature of masculine fantasy.

Often when Coleridge discusses *Christabel*, his poem becomes a lady whose character needs protecting or explaining. In April 1803, writing to Sara Coleridge from London, he boasts of Sotheby's interest in the poem:

> To day I dine again with Sotheby. He ha[s] informed me, that ten gentlemen, who have met me at his House, desired him to solicit me to finish the Christabel, & to permit them to publish it for me/they engaged that it should be in paper, printing, & decorations the most magnificent Thing that had hitherto appeared. – Of course, I declined it. The lovely Lady shan't come to that pass – Many times rather would I have it printed at Soulby's on the true Ballad Paper – .[1]

Refusing Sotheby and the ten gentlemen, Coleridge stands on his literary principles: a ballad is a popular form, and it would be politically and aesthetically inappropriate to publish one in a guinea volume. But with a shift symptomatic of his and his critics' writing on *Christabel*, he frames the genre question in the poem's own terms, playfully casting its *literary* character as a *feminine* character. Posing as a Baron-like protector of maiden innocence, he asserts that his *Christabel* shall not become a Geraldine, making up in 'magnificence' for what she has lost in honest virtue.

The Baron is not the only role Coleridge plays here. His soliciting 'ten gentlemen' recall Geraldine's 'five ruffians', the anonymous and plural abductors who eventually deposit her under Christabel's tree. Like the story Geraldine tells to Christabel, Coleridge's tale is itself a solicitation, an attempt to convince Sara that this latest flight from home has yielded professional if not financial returns. He simply plays his enchantress as a flirt – a heartless flirt, one might add, noticing the way he flaunts his power to attract monied gentlemen. He leads Sara to hope for his capitulation, then drops her flat with his protest that a lady's good character cannot be bought; he charms her with a glimpse of a world from which she is exluded – a world where gentlemen make deals and dine together, and where *he* is attractive because he possesses a certain 'lovely Lady'. Despite what he tells his wife about the lady's good character and his own honorable intentions, Coleridge is toying here with the unstable, charming character of *Christabel*.

This essay addresses the question of *Christabel's* generic status. Coleridge's letter to Sara Coleridge might seem at best a negative example of how to go about such an inquiry: defining the proper literary form of his poem, Coleridge quite improperly comes under the sway of its fictional content, conflating the poem with its 'lovely Lady', and incorporating that feminine character into the dramas of real life. This negative example, however, is also a good example of his and his contemporaries' habitual ways of writing about *Christabel*. When the poem was finally published in 1816, its reviewers attacked it on literary grounds, declaring it an improper *kind* of poem. Their terms, however, had more to do with gender than genre: the lady, they declared, was immodest and improper, and its author, not simply 'unmanly', but an 'enchanted virgin', a 'witch', and an 'old nurse'.

My analysis of the debate of *Christabel's* character will dwell on the poem's peripheries. The first two sections of this essay explore Coleridge's references to his poem's disturbingly ambiguous status and his reviewers' scandalized responses to the poem. I propose that men of letters reacted hysterically to *Christabel* because they saw the fantastic exchanges of Geraldine and Christabel as dramatizing a range of problematically invested literary relations, including those between writers and other writers, and among authors, readers, and books. By feminizing the problem, critical discourse on *Christabel* both played out and displaced the excessive charges of these literary relations: it cast impropriety as *generic* impurity, and then identified this impurity with dangerously attractive feminine forms – the licentious body of Geraldine, and more generally, of the poem *Christabel*. The final sections of the essay argue that the feminization of the terms of the debate on *Christabel* repeats, in an exemplary way, a strategy habitually adopted by high culture when defending its privileges. *Christabel* can be located in the context of Coleridge's writings on a variety of ghostly exchanges between observers or readers and representations. Coleridge's thinking about perception suggests that what is at stake in these exchanges is the identity and autonomy of the subject in relation to cultural forms; a footnote to the *Biographia Literaria* on circulating library fare indicates that it is ladies' literature – the derogated genres of romantic fiction – which conventionally represents this threat in the discourse of literary gentlemen. *Christabel's* connections with Gothic romance account for the conventionality of the critics' responses to the poem; its exposure of their hysterical defences accounts for its exemplary power among Coleridge's poems of the supernatural.

I

Perhaps Coleridge's only uncontroversial definition of *Christabel's* literary character is in Chapter 14 of the *Biographia Literaria*, where he classifies the poem with others whose 'incidents and agents were to be, in part at least, supernatural'.[2] But his intention here is to lay old controversies to rest, and his emphases are on harmony – disquietingly so. According to him, the idea of the *Lyrical Ballads* presented itself to two minds working as one – mutually possessed minds, if we care to edge his description toward the concerns of *Christabel*: 'The thought suggested itself (to which of us I do not recollect) that a series of poems might be composed of two sorts.' Describing his and Wordsworth's respective tasks, Coleridge implies that the difference between the two collaborators hardly amounts to more than an accident of light or shade: his poems were to give a 'semblance of truth' to supernatural incidents, while Wordsworth's would 'give the charm of novelty to things of every day' and thus 'excite a feeling analogous to the supernatural'. 'With this view', he continues, 'I wrote "The Ancient Mariner", and was preparing among other poems, "The Dark Ladie", and the "Christabel", in which I should have more nearly realized my ideal, than I had done in my first attempt.' If in the end his poems came to seem like 'heterogeneous' material, the reasons were purely circumstantial: 'But Mr Wordsworth's industry had proved

143

so much more successful . . . that my compositions, instead of forming a balance, appeared rather an interpolation of heterogeneous matter' (*BL*, 2, p. 6).

Several chapters later, though, Coleridge hedges on *Christabel's* character and charges the poem with introducing discord into his life. Although professing surprise that a work which 'pretended to be nothing more than a common Faery Tale' should have excited such 'disproportionate' responses, he himself clearly attaches 'disproportionate' significance to *Christabel*. His account of the 'literary men' who '[took] liberties' with it before it went on 'common sale' but failed to defend it in 1816 identifies that date as a major divide: whereas in the past '[he] did not know or believe that [he] had an enemy in the world', now he must reproach himself 'for being too often disposed to ask, – Have I one friend?' (*BL*, 2, pp. 210–11). Pointing to the date of *Christabel's* publication as a great rupture in his life, Coleridge plays a role he had created more than sixteen years before – the Baron, betrayed into solitude by 'whispering tongues [that] poison truth'.

Actually, from the very beginning Coleridge had difficulty keeping *Christabel* in proportion – or rather, he was always happy to exaggerate its proportions. Already by 1799 he was casting it as controversial, disruptive of generic categories and collaborative efforts alike. *Christabel* would be an 'improper opening poem' for that year's *Annual Register*, he explains to Southey:

> My reason is – it cannot be expected to please all / Those who dislike it will deem it extravagant Ravings, & go on thro' the rest of the Collection with the feeling of Disgust – & it is not impossible that were it liked by any, it would still not harmonize with the *real-life* Poems that follow.
>
> (*CL*, 1, p. 545)

Whatever *Christabel's* character here, it is emphatically *not* the decorous, modest character of a 'true ballad', nor the 'common' character of a 'Faery Tale', nor yet the character of a poem of the supernatural, if the latter is meant to 'balance' with the poems of real life.

This hyperbolic account of the poem's reception is of course more indicative of Coleridge's extravagance than *Christabel's* – he is amusing Southey at the expense of an overnice reading public, and lightening with bluster a tacit admission that *Christabel* will not be ready in time for the *Annual Register*. His remarks were prophetic, however, not only of the poem's reception in 1816, but also, of Wordsworth's response to it in 1800, when after the second edition of the *Lyrical Ballads* had already gone to press he decided to pull *Christabel* from the volume.[3] The *Biographia* account of the great collaborative project suppresses

Christabel's role in its disintegration – *Christabel* was the poem that made Wordsworth realize that the poetry of real life and the poetry of the supernatural do not 'balance'. Explaining his decision to Longman & Rees, Wordsworth emphasizes the 'impropriety' of including a poem that does not harmonize with the others: 'A Poem of Mr Coleridge's was to have concluded the Volumes; but upon mature deliberation, I found that the Style of this Poem was so discordant from my own that it could not be printed along with my poems with any propriety' (quoted in *CL*, 1, p. 643). His words fulfill Coleridge's predictions of 1799, and contradict the *Biographia's* explanation of Coleridge's 'heterogeneity' – *quality*, not quantity, makes his work discordant.

Wordsworth's tone – his defensive or exasperated emphases on '*mature* deliberation', '*so* discordant', '*any* propriety' – hints at personal as well as literary differences between the two men; perhaps 1800, not 1816, was the year that *Christabel* was instrumental in sundering friendships. In contrast, Coleridge's account of the same event tempers personal discord. It also produces some strange, Christabellian effects. Writing to Josiah Wedgewood shortly after the decision, Coleridge seems to parrot Wordsworth's accusation of 'discordancy': *Christabel* was 'discordant in its character' with the *Lyrical Ballads*, he explains. At the same time, he bestows a character of generosity on his friend and vicarious praise on himself by passing on Wordsworth's extravagant appreciation of the poem's excellencies: 'My poem grew so long & in Wordsworth's opinion so impressive, that he rejected it from his volume as disproportionate both in size & merit' – sentiments so discordant with Wordsworth's letter to Longman that we suspect Wordsworth of speaking them under compulsion, or Coleridge of putting words into his friend's mouth (*CL*, 1, p. 643).

Although Coleridge's claims about his poem generally address its literary improprieties, a measure of its extravagance would seem to be its capacity to disrupt the boundaries between literature, commentary, and real life. Asserting *Christabel's* problematic literary status, Coleridge conflates the poem with the extravagant, ambiguous Geraldine, the character *in* the poem who excites desire and disgust, and introduces discord into apparently harmonious circles; describing the poem's origin in a collaborative endeavor and its receptions in 1800 and 1816, he produces muted versions of *Christabel's* story of an uncanny exchange and a friendship 'rent asunder', and recreates, in the register of his own telling, the slippages of identity that mark the exchanges of Geraldine and Christabel. Reading Coleridge's accounts of *Christabel*, we begin to feel that all the characters involved – the 'literary gentlemen' through whom he ventriloquizes his fluctuating, extravagant responses to his poem, the poem he employs as a go-between in his extravagant relations with other gentlemen, and the figure of the author, who appears by turns as the Baron and an enchantress – acquire the curious status of Geraldine, a figure from fantasy or dream who intrudes into daytime existence.[4]

Like all uncanny effects, Coleridge's apparent possession by *Christabel* is a motivated and gainful loss of control, allowing him to perform, domesticate, and manipulate the charged relations of his literary life. His strategy is most overtly one of domestication, of course, when he casts his poem as a woman – as a 'lovely Lady' whose character must be defended, as the 'other woman' in his sparring with Sara Coleridge, or as a doubtful character with whom gentlemen 'take liberties'. The lady becomes the locus of rhetorical and erotic play, when, disarmingly, Coleridge figures his lapses of authorial control as capitulations to extravagant femininity, or renders the exchanges of poems among literary gentlemen as the movements of a scandalous woman from man to man. *Christabel* circulates licentiously, captivating readers and tainting its author with its femininity. Flaunting his poem's impropriety, but coyly withholding it from 'common sale', he presents himself as both master and possessor of its charms.

Even Coleridge's more hysterical performances with *Christabel* figure and control the operations of fantasy in literary life. In an oddly explicit accession to the poem's femininity he becomes its mother, in 1801 producing the second part of *Christabel* with 'labor-pangs' in competition with Sara's delivery of Derwent: announcing the double event in a letter to James Tobin, he relegates his wife's labors to a postcript (*CL*, 1, p. 623). Later, writing to De Quincey, he associates his poem's publication, its 'embodiment in verse', with birth and death: *Christabel* 'fell almost dead-born from the Press' (*CL*, 5, p. 162).[5] When he holds it in 'suspended animation', however, it has the virulent life of fantasy.[6] Repossessing the poem after Wordsworth rejected it in 1800, Coleridge enacted a possession as lurid and extreme as the enchantments of *Christabel* – an illness he dramatizes in numerous letters to his friends as a hysterical pregnancy. It began with a symbolic castration, inflamed eyes and boils on the scrotum;[7] the next '9 dreary months' or more he passed with 'giddy head, sick stomach, & swoln knees', his left knee at one point '"*pregnant* with agony" as Mr Dodsley says in one of his poems' (*CL*, 2, pp. 745, 748). During one of his 'confinements', he reports, 'one ugly Sickeness has followed another, fast as phantoms before a vapourish Woman' (*CL*, 2, pp. 729, 725).[8] Flirting now with actual madness, but still performing the woman for an audience of gentlemen, he figures his strange entanglement with literature as the apparent duplicity of the female body when it is pregnant with child or with the vaporish conception of the 'wandering mother' or womb. Inhabiting him as an alien, internal body, his poem constitutes him as a female hysteric who cannot 'tell', but can only enact the intrusion of fantasy into real life.

II

Christabel engaged the fantasy lives of more than a narrow circle of literary gentlemen. In 1799, Coleridge imagined his apparently 'extravagant Ravings' exciting the equally extravagant response of 'Disgust', which he predicted would cling to the reader even after he had finished reading the poem. Urging Coleridge to publish the poem in 1815, Byron attests to its excessive, clinging 'hold': '[the poem's details] took a hold on my imagination which I never shall wish to shake off' (quoted in *CL*, 4, p. 601). When the poem came out the next year the critics described it as 'ravings', hysterically assessing poem and author in a Christabellian vocabulary of dream and possession.[9] Frequently they attribute its strange, singular character to its author's wild confounding of genres, styles, and intentions. *Scourge*, for example, criticizes the poem's blending of 'passages of exquisite harmony' with 'miserable doggrel'; in a similar vein, the *Augustan Review* complains that 'there are many fine things [in the poem] which cannot be extracted, being closely connected with the grossest absurdities' (*RR*, 2, p. 866, 1, p. 36). But the vocabulary of poetic decorum easily becomes the vocabulary of sexual, and particularly feminine, decorum: when *Christabel's* reviewers protest that 'poetry itself must show some modesty', or criticize the poem for merely 'affecting' simplicity, they capitalize on that play (*RR*, 1, pp. 229–40). Like Coleridge, they hint that *Christabel's* extravagances are more than rhetorical, and have a peculiarly feminine character.

Moreover, just as in Coleridge's imagined scenes, the extravagant, sexual character of *Christabel* proves to be contagious. In the hands of the critics, the author's poetic license becomes more-than-poetic 'licentiousness': 'In diction, in numbers, in thought, . . . Mr Coleridge's licentiousness out-Herod's Herod', the *Champion* protests, while *Farrago* claims that 'on no occasion has Mr Coleridge appeared in so degraded and degenerate a light as in the present publication' (*RR*, 1, p.269, 2, p. 546). Coleridge's breaches of decorum are not simply 'unmanly', they feminize him: his 'epithets of endearment, instead of breathing the accents of manly tenderness, are those of the nurse', charges *Scourge*; according to others, he tells an 'old woman's story', and is himself acting the part of an 'enchanted virgin' or a 'witch' (*RR*, 2, p. 866, 1, p. 214, 1, p. 373, 2, p. 531). Reading *Christabel* would seem to draw one into a charmed circle where all the participants have the taint of affected, licentious femininity. Even the poem's real-life readers are feminine, according to the *AntiJacobin* reviewer. Professing bewilderment at the poem's success despite the universally scathing reviews, he concludes that the ladies must be responsible: 'for what woman of fashion would not purchase a book recommended by Lord Byron' (*RR*, 1, p. 23).

If, pursuing *Christabel's* character, we ask the critics why *Christabel* became the poem they loved to hate, we might choose William Hazlitt's review in the *Examiner* as our focus; one of the earliest, it set the tone for subsequent notices. From the very first lines of his essay, Hazlitt adopts a strategy of diminishment against *Christabel* and its author. The review begins with some biting comments on the 'mastiff bitch', regularly cited by critics as an example of the poem's 'doggrel'. Appealing to 'gentlemen' to share his contempt for her impotence ('Is she a sort of Cerberus to fright away the critics? But – gentlemen, she is toothless!'), he reduces the poem's impropriety to toothless naughtiness, its author to a buffoon (*RR*, 2, pp. 530–1). Then, still on the subject of Coleridge's caprice, he makes a spectacle of withered femininity for a second time. Quoting the scene of Geraldine's undressing, he pauses to supply a missing line:

> The manuscript runs thus, or nearly thus: –
> 'Behold her bosom and half her side –
> *Hideous, deformed, and pale of hue.'*
> This line is necessary to make common sense of the first and second part. 'It is the keystone that makes up the arch.' For that reason Mr Coleridge left it out. Now this is a greater physiological curiosity than even the fragment of *Kubla Khan*.

The 'sight to dream of, not to tell' ought simply to be *told*, Hazlitt protests, deploring 'Mr Coleridge''s power play while trumping him with a line from his own manuscript. The reviewer's quarrel with the author is rendered as a battle for control of Geraldine: the author conceals her bosom from view, and the critic unveils it again. As when he made sport of the 'mastiff bitch', Hazlitt implicates poem and author in the fate of the impotent female, reducing the former's obscurity to a transparent mystery, and the latter's motives to a 'physiological curiosity', a deformity like Geraldine's.

So far, Hazlitt's tactics have been similar, not just to those he imputes to *his* 'Mr Coleridge', but also to those Coleridge adopts when he uses the poem's feminine subject to domesticate its impropriety, and then employs the poem as a third character in his relations with other literary gentlemen. In the last paragraph of the review, however, *Christabel* threatens to escape its bounds. Here, Hazlitt's description of *Christabel's* hold on the reader's mind recalls Byron's approbation of the 'hold' he 'never shall wish to shake off':

> In parts of *Christabel* there is a great deal of beauty, both of thought, imagery, and versification; but the effect of the general story is dim, obscure, and visionary. It is more like a dream than a reality. The mind, in reading it, is spell-bound. The sorceress seems to act without

power – *Christabel* to yield without resistance. The faculties are thrown into a state of metaphysical suspense and theoretical imbecility.

Hazlitt implies that interpretive mastery involves locating a source of power and meaning in the text. *This* poem, however, is obscure in its treatment of volition, depicting sorceress and victim in mysterious communion. Disclosing a radical complicity between actor and yielder, good and evil, the exchanges between Christabel and Geraldine confound the logical and moral categories the reader attempts to bring to bear on the poem, throwing his faculties into a state of 'metaphysical suspense and theoretical imbecility'. Thwarted in his effort to interpret, he becomes 'bound' passively to imitate the relation between Christabel and Geraldine in his own relation to the story.

Continuing his final remarks about *Christabel*, though, Hazlitt rescues this hypothetical reader from impotence by providing him with a dual focus of moral outrage – an unnamed, unsavory content, 'something disgusting at the bottom of the subject', and a willful author at the bottom of it all:

> The poet, like the witch in *Spenser*, is evidently
>   'Busied about some wicked gin.' –
> But we do not foresee what he will make of it. There is something disgusting at the bottom of his subject, which is but ill glossed over by a veil of Della Cruscan sentiment and fine writing – like moonbeams playing on a charnel-house, or flowers strewed on a dead body. Mr Coleridge's style is essentially superficial, pretty, ornamental, and he has forced it into the service of a story which is petrific.

Many readers of this review, including Coleridge himself, have speculated that Hazlitt has 'something' specific in mind here – something he *could* tell, but won't. Rumor has identified him as the source of a scandalous report that Coleridge intended to unmask Geraldine as Christabel's male lover.[10] But significantly, at this point Hazlitt does not band with other 'gentlemen' to deride the poem's impropriety as sophomoric naughtiness, nor does he simply identify Geraldine's deformity as the suppressed 'key-stone' of the poem. Rather, bursting into rhetorical flower at just the moment he purports to descry 'something . . . at the bottom' of *Christabel*, he gives the impression that there is more to the poem than is in his or Coleridge's power to declare. In this Gothic scenario, Geraldine's body is not the 'keystone' to the poem's obscurity, but a figure of the problem: Hazlitt displaces her character onto both poet and poem, metaphorizing the former as a 'witch', and the latter as a veiled, horrific site. 'Something' which cannot be figured is 'disgusting' or 'petrific' 'at the bottom' of that site, in the poem's nether regions – 'something' which ought to be well hidden, but is only 'ill glossed over'. Hazlitt's rhetoric suggests that he is now seeing the poem, not as a woman who has been or could be had, but as a potent figure of castration, a Medusa. His 'scandalous' rumor, then, is a subterfuge masking the *real* scandal of *Christabel* – that Geraldine is a woman.

But Hazlitt, who put down these clues, may have prepared a trap. Certainly, the movement of the whole paragraph suggests that this melodramatic scene of a horrific, buried 'something' is a feint. For it follows an acknowledgment that there is *nothing* 'at the bottom' of *Christabel* – no single source of power or significance: 'The sorceress seems to act without power; *Christabel* to yield without resistance.' This 'nothing' is not the lack psychoanalysis allots to women, but a strange overdetermination which creates disturbances in the register of metaphysics as well as sexuality. Hazlitt suggests that the obscure and compelling logic of *Christabel*, effecting displacements of identity and power which reveal the affinity of apparent opposites, is the logic of dream or fantasy; that the danger of this 'dim, obscure, and visionary' poem is that it threatens to hold the reader as if it were his *own* dream or fantasy. He holds this imagined experience of complete surrender to *Christabel* within bounds, however, by almost immediately transforming the poem's unsettling, uncentered power into a disgusting 'something' obscurely visible behind a veil of language and sentiment, thus reducing to its sexual content power he has just described as having philosophical as well as erotic dimensions: he contains this power in the 'bottom' and invites us to declare it female. Although it suggests that *Christabel* is potent and horrific, Hazlitt's melodrama, which associates the poem with a derided genre (the Gothic) and gender (the feminine), actually reduces it as fully as did his play with the 'mastiff bitch'.[11]

Like Coleridge, Hazlitt cannot or will not 'tell' what is enchanting or distressing about *Christabel*. Instead he objectifies the poem as a feminine body, in a move which allows him to disentangle matters of intellect from matters of desire to some extent; admitting the pull of, and stridently defending himself against, this body, he charges his writing with the libidinal possibilities he has contained. *Christabel* has subterfuges of its own, however. In a sense it is the poem which contains its critics, whose two responses to it – a spellbound accession to play and a petrified and petrifying refusal of exchange – are figured in the text. When Hazlitt asserts manly judgment against a feminized author and poem at the close of his essay, he only substitutes one form of impotency for another, shedding the role of a mute, enthralled Christabel to become the Baron, whose world is a 'world of death'.[12]

Turning now to Coleridge's writing on perception, on circulating library literature, and on the poetry of the supernatural, we see him exploring, in a range of situations, how individuals and culture produce 'bodies' – hallucinated 'realities', but also literary genres, bodies of literature. *Christabel* figures the responses it elicits because in the poetry of the supernatural, Coleridge is dramatizing and manipulating a conventional or 'bound' relation between certain kinds of figures and certain kinds of responses; particularly, he is examining the way certain bodies conventionally function to objectify a problematic response to representation.

III

'Disgust' is the response Coleridge and his reviewers most frequently attached to *Christabel*. When at the end of his review Hazlitt attempts to shake off the poem's hold, he locates 'something digusting' – something like a body or a corpse – under its decorative surface. His gesture is dismissive: the disgusting body is elsewhere. During the years 1799–1801 Coleridge was already predicting that his poem would inspire 'disgust', but the investigations would have prompted him to insist on the complicity of mind and body, and self and elsewhere, in disgusted response. 'Define Disgust in philosophical Language – . – Is it not, speaking as a materialist, always a stomach-sensation conjoined with an idea?' he asks, and answers, Humphry Davy in January of 1800: the object of disgust is 'always' an already-internalized 'idea' (*CL*, 1, p. 557). Just a day later, writing to Thomas Wedgewood about a similar sensation, he implies an even more thorough entanglement of physiological and ideational entities and processes in certain responses: 'Life were so flat a thing without Enthusiasm – that if for a moment it leave me, I have a sort of stomach-sensation attached to all my Thoughts, like those which succeed to the pleasurable operation of a dose of Opium' (*CL*, 1, p. 558). In this description of the conjoined response, Coleridge's analogy to the 'dose' implies that even a terminological distinction between 'sensation' and 'idea' may distort: perhaps the very 'sensation' of difference between mind and body is one stage in a self-perpetuating economy of desire. 'Disgust' is not the mind's critical pronouncement on a body (although it may masquerade as such), but a symptom of the subject's mourning or revulsion for the lost, mutual pleasures of mind and body.

Two notebook entries, also from the *Christabel* period, allow us to link the complex response Coleridge was pursuing to a category, or genre, of representation. In one, Coleridge describes yet another 'unpleasant sensation' – this time, a response to the confusion of physical bodies and ideational elements in an observed scene:

> Objects, namely, Fire, Hobs, and Kettle, at the first Look shone
> apparently upon the green Shrubs opposite to the Parlour, but in a few
> seconds acquired *Ideal* Distance, & tho' there were of course no objects
> to compare that Distance by, the Shrubbery limiting the view, yet it
> appeared *indefinitely* behind the Shrubbery – I found in looking an
> unpleasant sensation, occasioned as I apprehend from the distinctness
> of the Shrubbery, and the distinct shadowyness of the Images.
>
> (*N*, p. 894)

Here, in a different context, is the difficulty of locating 'something . . . at
the bottom' – and the 'unpleasantness', too, for Coleridge's sensation
would seem to be occasioned by an idle attempt to do just that. When he
first looks out the parlor window he perceives a variety of 'Objects'
existing relatively in the same space: images from the room in which he
sits shine 'upon' the shrubs outside. But 'in a few seconds', prompted by
what he knows – that 'Images' are the immaterial derivatives of real
objects – he sorts real things from images, locating the latter in 'Ideal'
space: they seem '*indefinitely* behind' the shrubbery. Thus he comes to
identify two mutually exclusive perceptual fields in a single field of view;
furthermore, his separation of material and 'Ideal' elements according to
what he knows about representation contradicts what he sees, two
'distinctnesses', and other knowledge he possesses: the objects he has
placed indefinitely behind the shrubs outside are actually *inside* the room.
Paradoxically, then, the very speculative activity that attempted to grasp
the scene leads to the vertiginous play of objects and representations,
inside and outside, and even of perception, speculation, and sensation.
For as Coleridge's attempts to grasp the scene result in its oscillation
between warring interpretive possibilities, the scene itself comes to
represent a queasy 'sensation': he seems, first to 'find' his bodily
'sensation', and then to 'apprehend' his understanding, outside of him.

This experience is something like reading *Christabel*, judging from its
reader's accounts and our knowledge of what it is about – *Christabel's*
readers become caught up in the interactions of a 'real' lady and a
possibly more fantastic lady, and they seem to 'find' their own
spellbound or disgusted reactions to this exchange figured in the poem.
The second notebook entry we will consider, related to the first and to
Christabel by its attention to a 'ghost' image, suggests why some people
might find such an experience distressing enough to want to ward it off:
'Ghost of a mountain – the forms seizing my Body as I passed & became
realities – I, a Ghost, till I had reconquered my Substance' (*N*, p. 523).

Like *N*, p. 894, *N*, p. 523 describes a confrontation between the 'real' –
here, 'my Body' – and an optical projection; once again, the scene's
power, now rendered as mortal, is a redounding effect of speculative
operations idly performed by the subject. He identifies the image of the

mountain as a 'ghost' or 'form', apportioning it to the category of immaterial, ideal representations, and opposing it to (his own) body or substance. But the 'ghost of a mountain', an image projected onto mist by the sun, is a 'real' optical phenomenon. Working from the logic of the narrated event, we could propose that the observer's apprehension of the ghost's autonomy effects a crossing of the terms he has used to secure his relation to the scene: the 'ghost' preempts or 'seizes' body, while the 'I' becomes derivative, a 'ghost'. This crossing is not a simple reversal. At once a projection and an invested 'form', but detached, apparently deriving neither from an empirical ground nor from the subject, the 'ghost' become 'reality' acquires the status of a hallucination. 'Seizing . . . Body' – snatching away body from the subject but also, introjecting its body into '*my* Body' – it effects a split between 'my Body' and 'I'. Simultaneously displaced and colonized by fantasy, the 'I' is seized with an intuition that identity is derivative, a 'ghost' of the body.

These two notebook entries share a structure and an effect: both conjoin physical bodies and optical or material images, and in each, a scene provokes speculative operations which finally betray the observer into a possessing, destabilizing reading of his own activity.

Together, these two entries allow us to construct a category or genre of problematic representations – of representations which disrupt the very idea of category by exposing the arbitrariness of the fundamental categories of 'inside' and 'outside', 'self' and 'world'. For in these two encounters, the spectator apprehends that the physical shell of the body is no guarantee of the subject's autonomy and difference; and that representations – scenes, images, and ideas, including, perhaps, the 'ideas' of body, substance, reality – are in some sense material and primary, constitutive of subjects and objects. Finally, subject, representation, and the specular configuration that embodies their difference are all revealed to him as the same *kind* of structure, invested constructions of the real, or fantasies – 'sensation[s] conjoined with . . . Idea[s]', or, in Freud's terms, 'fiction[s] cathected with affect'.[13]

Christabel, which figures the responses it provokes, would seem to be related to this genre of representations. But of course it is more conventionally placed in the class 'literature'. Within *this* class, *Christabel* and the problematic representations we have just been discussing are related, at least by Coleridgean association, to the family or gender of genres which represent conventionality in nineteenth-century critical discourse. For, tellingly, when Coleridge describes the experiences of bookworms in a long, whimsical, and self-revealing footnote to the *Biographia Literaria*, he relies on a figure from optics, the *camera obscura*, to illustrate how circulating library literature takes over, not so much life, as fantasy life:

For as to the devotees of the circulating libraries, I dare not
compliment their *pass-time*, or rather *kill-time*, with the name of *reading*.
Call it rather a sort of beggarly day-dreaming, during which the mind
of the dreamer furnishes for itself nothing but laziness, and a little
mawkish sensibility; while the whole *materiel* [*sic*] and imagery of the
dose is supplied *ab extra* by a sort of mental *camera obscura*
manufactured at the printing office, which *pro tempore* fixes, reflects,
and transmits the moving phantasms of one man's delirium, so as to
people the barrenness of a hundred other brains afflicted with the
same trance or suspension of all common sense and all definite
purpose.

(*BL*, 1, p. 34)

There are only shades in this underworld – a literary subculture,
confined by Coleridge to a note 'at the bottom' of the *Biographia's*
legitimate matter. Here, through the mediation of a 'sort of mental *camera
obscura*', a delirious brain 'people[s] the barrenness' of brains as ghostly
as its own with representations, in a travesty of authentic literary
experience. The *camera obscura* mass-produces fantasy life for consumers
who receive it, not because it sounds depths of communal experience,
but because they are too ennervated even to supply the purely
conventional details of their own daydreams.

The *camera* comes between minds which mirror each other: author and
public share the same afflictions, 'trances or suspensions of all common
sense and all definite purpose' – aimlessness coupled with vague
expectancy, 'mawkish sensibility' lacking material and imagery on which
to fasten. This last is supplied *ab extra*, being simply the materiality of the
printed book, or more fundamentally, of its systems of narrative codes
and signs. These effect the translation of trancelike or suspended mental
states into the plots and characters of circulating library literature – into
the 'sensationalist' 'ghost' stories of Gothic romance and into the
literature of 'sensibility', tales of 'suspense' whose stock characters
languish, wander without 'definite purpose', mysteriously fall into
trances and can't stop repeating themselves. Like the parlor window of
N, p. 894 and the mist of *N*, p. 523, a true *camera obscura* effaces its own
materiality, producing an apparently ungrounded image – an uncannily
material, non-derivative representation. Coleridge's analogy attributes to
bad books a like capacity both to conceal the means of production and to
betray the materiality of the objectified product. In the charmed circle he
constructs, readers find their minds 'peopled' with apparently
unmediated representations of their own mental lives, with their
phantasms made uncannily 'material'.

Even as he deplores the '*kill-time*' of novel reading, the literary man of
the *Biographia Literaria* participates in the play of mirrors he describes. As

the footnote continues he goes on to include the activity he 'dares not' call 'reading' within 'that comprehensive class characterized by the power of reconciling the two contrary yet co-existing propensities of human nature, namely, indulgence of sloth, and hatred of vacancy', and then launches into an extensive catalogue of species belonging to the same genus: 'gaming, swinging, or swaying on a chair or gate; spitting over a bridge; smoking; snuff-taking: . . . &c&c&c'. '&c&c&c': could attacks on bad literature by literary men be numbered among the mildly pleasurable, wanton, marginal, and thoroughly conventional activities comprising the genus 'kill-time'? Coleridge's prose hints at certain affinities between men of letters and circulating library devotees. It, too, might seem to have been produced in response to the combined pressures of 'indulgence of sloth and hatred of vacancy': his taste runs to excess and repetition, even to the baroque – he jingles and alliterates, multiplies clauses and subspecies, and overreaches what is generally considered decorous in sentence and footnote length. And through much of the note he seems under the spell of a metaphorical and 'mental' *camera obscura* – the only 'material' image in his long and wayward account of a captivating and aimless pleasure.

The writer's peculiarly complicitous engagement with this scene prompts us to consider the figure of the *camera obscura* as the *Biographia Literaria's* fantastic projection or 'ghost'. It is intended to illustrate the subject of fantasy life, 'a sort of beggarly day-dreaming', and thus could be thought of as being thematically opposed to the 'real' matter of the *Biographia*. The text at the top of the page is a narrative of time lived, of intellectual under-takings actively pursued along lines endorsed by culture; the note below depicts time killed or suspended in activities having no significance or returns for the self. But of course the 'real' life of the *Biographia* is the life of the mind, particularly as it has been lived through books, rather than any palpably material 'reality', and despite the author's protests, the scene at the bottom of the page represents both a species and a construction of the genus 'reading', rather than its opposite. Judging from these very protests, the scene is a construction – an objectification – of something fantastic or uncanny in this literary man's interest in literature.[14]

Indeed, this attack on mass culture strikes us as self-revelatory – a mock exorcism of a peculiarly Coleridgean spook. It seems to have a direct and obvious relation, for example, to a life which we know was exceptionally and self-destructively given over to addictive kill-times. A 'library cormorant' whose appetite for romance was particularly keen, Coleridge may have constructed this scene of rapt absorption in order to reject it extravagantly, dramatizing in the relation of speaker to scene how the memory of the 'pleasurable operation of a dose' might acquire the negative, morally charged affect of distaste or disgust. Alternatively, the footnote can be read as an oblique acknowledgement that there is something fantastic about the *Biographia Literaria's* relation to the received ideas of a 'legitimate' cultural tradition – evident in its author's obvious anxiety about questions of originality and priority, and, more bizarrely, in his apparent incapacity or refusal to recognize boundaries between his writing and that of others.

But although this note may strike us as characteristic of Coleridge's writing at its most distinctive or eccentric, his derogatory representation of ladies' literature also 'fixes, reflects, and transmits' once more a moving fantasy of his day. In yet another coincidence of the individual (and in this case, highly personalized) and the received, Coleridge's manner of speaking about popular literature engages and burlesques a polemic against the vitiation of culture by tainted literary forms carried on by his contemporaries, and, before them, by Burke and Johnson. By the common consensus of literary men, popular literature, including circulating library fare, is set over and against authentic intellectual activity as its travesty. It is aligned with the mechanical reproduction of conventions and the proliferation of commodities, and with the falsely or unnaturally inspirational 'dose' which circulates a taint of diseased sexuality through a body of increasingly dependent and emasculated consumers, most of whom were of course female to begin with. Apparently confirmed by a market of 'real' products and consumers, this happily and indignantly excoriated representation of mass culture is at the same time high culture's ghostly representation of its own processes, a depiction of the transmission of knowledge as the circulation of fantastically invested materials.[15]

IV

The language of Coleridge's footnote circulates around *Christabel*. The second part of the poem was conceived after a 'dose' that peopled 'barrenness' according to its author, who then imagines it as infinitely reproducible ('I would rather have written Ruth, and Nature's Lady than a million such poems', he confesses to Davy after *Christabel* was rejected from the *Lyrical Ballads* [*CL*, 1, pp. 643, 632]); he isn't sure how to classify *Christabel* but knows to exclude it from the category of 'real-life' poems, a genus whose boundaries he suggests it has the capacity to disturb. Its readers responded to it with hysterical attacks of the sort burlesqued in Coleridge's note. Almost all of them connected the poem's disturbing character to its licentious femininity, one even going so far as to suggest it appeals only to the devotees of Lord Byron. To suggest that these terms and postures are conventional does not answer the question of why *Christabel* excited the response it did, but perhaps helps to explain the coincidence between Coleridge's perception of the poem and the way it was received: he must have suspected that *Christabel* would be regarded as belonging to a tainted category of literary endeavor.

Christabel, then, is not just a ghost story, but also the 'ghost' of literature: men of letters perceive it as belonging to a body of literary products which figure the possibility that books are fantastic representations exercising a dangerous attraction for the subject. We should not imagine that the typical man of letter's relation to this category of goods is straightforwardly defensive, however. For the scenario of the *camera obscura* translates the energy of systems that drive the subject into libidinal energy, which circulates back to 'one man', and, eventually, to the man of letters and the body of his text. The scene encysts a state of pleasurable indeterminacy, where representations transmit 'doses' of fantasy from devotee to languid devotee, whose 'hundred [feminine] brains' are loosely but gratifyingly oriented toward the potentate who 'peoples [their] barrenness'. The speaker closes off this circle from 'time' and his literary life, and then by his self-ironic admission of his complicity in it charges his own discourse with libidinal possibility: this is not 'real' literature, and yet literature and literary men are always flirting with the dangerous and heady attractions of fantasy. And surely, both Hazlitt and Coleridge seem at their most seductively interesting to the critic when by hysterically charged attack or coy self-betrayal they reveal their attraction to a charmed circle, whether that represented by Christabel in the arms of Geraldine, or that of the circulating library.

Modulated just a little, Coleridge's attack on lending library culture becomes the famous account of his role in the *Lyrical Ballads*, an experiment he is anxious to legitimize in the *Biographia Literaria*:

> [M]y endeavors should be directed to persons and characters supernatural, or at least romantic; yet so as to transfer from our inward nature a human interest and a semblance of truth sufficient to procure for these shadows of imagination that willing suspension of disbelief for the moment, which constitutes poetic faith.
>
> (*BL*, 2, p.5)

The terms he used earlier to protest the devotees' absorption are here employed to describe the ideal reader's generosity: if successful, he will procure 'for the moment' ('pro tempore') the reader's 'suspension of disbelief' (a 'suspension of all common sense') for his 'shadows of the imagination' ('phantasms'). But as a formerly excluded experience of books is admitted to the genus 'reading', a new category, actual madness, is produced as a figure of that which is at once other than literature and literature's internal possibilities and limit. If readers are deluded by the 'shadows' of his poetry, Coleridge implies, it may be because in real life they have actually confounded shadow and substance and come under the spell of hallucinated realities: 'And real in *this* sense [supernatural incidents] have been to every human being who, from whatever source of delusion, has at any time believed himself under supernatural agency.' 'For a moment' the reader of supernatural poetry may touch the perimeters of madness. The experience is not limited to one genre; even Wordsworth, Coleridge's writer of real-life poems, 'for short spaces of time' plays with shadows, as any good poet might. Describing the figure of the poet in the 1802 preface to the *Lyrical Ballads*, Wordsworth suggests he must be something of a madman – and something of a Christabel: 'Nay, for short spaces of time perhaps, [the poet might] let himself slip into an entire delusion, and even confound and identify his own feelings with [those of his characters].'[16]

In moments of imaginative generosity, of voluntary relinquishments of self to fictions, writers and readers flirt with the possibility of going too far – of losing their 'Substance' to a 'ghost', of 'letting themselves slip' into delusions which could become difficult to escape, of acceding to 'holds' they might 'never – wish to shake off'. In these moments the subject touches a perpetually bracketed, continually displaced representation of literature's fantastic appeal, a 'moving phantasm' of Coleridge's discourse and a discourse about literature in which he participates.

Coleridge's poems of the supernatural illustrate mental states, including states where the mind comes under the sway of a hallucinated 'reality'. When 'for the moment' a reader of these poems suspends disbelief and gives himself over to representations, he touches madness – doubling, in his own relation to fiction, the very condition the poem dramatizes. But although *all* the poems of the supernatural are intended to produce this effect in the reader, it is *Christabel* which most alarms its public. Coleridge's account in the *camera obscura* footnote of the circulating library devotees casts the pleasure one takes in certain kinds of books as a feminine pleasure: the implicit message is that to read is to behave like a woman, an axiom the man of culture might find both alarming and alluring to contemplate. I would propose that Coleridge explores the relation between cultural processes and (fantasized) feminine erotic experience in *Christabel*, a poem which dramatizes hysteria, conventionally figured as the flights of a 'wandering mother', which alienates female subjects from their own speech. To 'tell' the story of *Christabel*, a narrator or narrators – we cannot tell if we hear one voice or two – resurrect the ghosts of genres as apparently disparate as Spenserian romance and pulp fiction; they reenact and tumble into the exchanges of Christabel and Geraldine, and suggest that the subject's

relation to cultural forms is hysterical.[17] It may be a measure of the
poem's success that many of its contemporary readers responded to it
like hysterics who 'cannot tell' what ails them – who could only repeat its
effects in the manner of Byron, Scott, and a host of other imitators and
parodists of the poem, or, like Hazlitt, resist its effect by hysterical
defense.

Notes

1. *Collected Letters of Samuel Taylor Coleridge*, ed. Earl Leslie Griggs (Oxford:
    Clarendon Press, 1956–71) 2, p. 941 (hereafter cited as *CL*).

2. *Biographia Literaria*, ed. J. Shawcross (Oxford: Oxford University Press, 1907) 2,
    p.5 (herafter cited as *BL*).

3. This episode is discussed by MARILYN KATZ in 'Early Dissent Between
    Wordsworth and Coleridge: Preface Deletion of October, 1800', and by JAMES
    KISSANE in '"Michael", "Christabel", and the *Lyrical Ballads* of 1800.' Both
    articles appear in *The Wordsworth Circle*, 9: 1 (1978).

4. My reading of *Christabel's* capacity to disturb and to influence Coleridge's
    literary relationships is indebted to REEVE PARKER's essay, '"O could you hear
    his voice!" Wordsworth, Coleridge, and Ventriloquism', in *Romanticism and
    Language*, ed. Arden Reed (Ithaca: Cornell University Press, 1984).

5. In 1801, Coleridge was also thinking of the poem's 'birth' as a death: he
    marked *Christabel's* and Derwent's simultaneous appearance with a spate of
    notebook entries about dead or dying children which have interesting
    connections with his post-partum feelings about *Christabel* as well as with his
    sickly child: in one, he recalls a local woman's expression of relief at parting
    with a 'little Babe one had had 9 months in one's arms'; in another, he quotes
    from the *Star* a description of a drowned infant, 'a spectacle &c' whose 'flesh
    was more yielding to the touch than is either necessary or agreeable to
    describe' – a 'sight to dream of, not to tell' (*The Notebooks of Samuel Taylor
    Coleridge*, ed. Kathleen Coburn, New York: Bollingen Series: Pantheon Books,
    1957–73, 1; pp. 814, 809; hereafter cited as *N*).

6. Coleridge's descriptions of his relation to the poem come from the preface to
    Christabel:

    > Since the latter date [1800], my poetic powers have been, till very lately, in a
    > state of suspended animation. But as, in my first conception of the tale, I
    > had the whole present to my mind, with the wholeness no less than the
    > loveliness, of a vision; I trust that I shall yet be able to embody in verse the
    > three parts yet to come.

    In Coleridge's account it is the author's 'powers', not the poem, which have
    existed 'in a state of suspended animation'; but my shift is, if not excused, at
    least precedented by his own.

7. See, for example, Coleridge's letter to Davy, 11 January 1801 (*CL*, 2,
    pp. 662–3).

8. See also *CL*, 2, pp. 731–2, 735–6, 739. For a more extended discussion of this

period and these letters see JEROME CHRISTENSEN, *Coleridge's Blessed Machine of Language* (Ithaca: Cornell University Press, 1981), 76–81. Christensen focuses on the grandiose philosophical claims that appear in the letters I have been quoting, relating them to attempts, described in the *Notebooks*, to derive knowledge and perception from infantile experience of the mother.

9. Variously, they liken it to 'a strange fantasy', 'a nightmare', a 'symptom' of madness, and the 'ravings of insanity'. These reviews are all printed in *The Romantics Reviewed*, edited, with introductions, by Donald H. Reiman (New York: Garland, 1972). I have just quoted from 1, p. 239, 2, p. 470, and 1, p. 36 (hereafter cited as *RR*).

10. For Coleridge's speculations, see *CL*, 4, pp. 917–18. This rumor found its boldest public expression in a parody printed in 1818, which took up the story of *Christabel* nine months after Geraldine's first visit, with the heroine in the advanced stages of pregnancy (*Christabel*, by 'Morgan O'Doherty', published in *Blackwood's Edinburgh Magazine*, 5, April – September 1819: 286–91).

11. This strategy – of reducing the poem to *just* a Gothic tale of terror – repeats tactics conventionally used on the Gothic itself. In 'The Character in the Veil: Imagery of the Surface in the Gothic Novel' (*PMLA*, 96, 1981: 255–70), Eve Kosofsky Sedgwick describes a prevalent critical tendency to read the Gothic as a literature of 'depth and the depths', and argues that this reading is blind to the Gothic novel's thematic insistence on surfaces as 'quasi-linguistic' carriers of sexuality: to see the Gothic in terms of a convention of surfaces and depths is to repress the possibility that (one's own) identity and responses are conventional. Coleridge's and Hazlitt's readings of *Christabel* suggest that one moment – itself highly conventionalized – in this repressive strategy is an imagined accession to the logic of contaminative linguistic experiences; the glimpse of this threat to the self's autonomy becomes a pretext for a hyping-up of an attack on the (supremely conventional) literature of buried things.

12. Like the Baron, who in a moment of confusion imagines separating 'souls / From the bodies and forms of men', and like Perseus, Hazlitt takes cutting measures to reassert the implicitly hierarchical categories of thought that allow one to 'tell': he dissevers surface from 'bottom', decoration from content, and life and play from death and stasis. Then, almost as if to acknowledge his affinity with Sir Leoline, as a coda to his review of *Christabel* he attaches lines which he calls 'the one genuine burst of humanity' in the poem, lines he claims show what the author can do when 'no dream oppresses him, no spell binds him'. The passage he has in mind describes the ruined friendship of Roland de Vaux and the Baron. I excerpt what I suspect moves him most:

> They stood aloof, the scars remaining
> Like cliffs which had been rent asunder;
> A dreary sea now flows between,
> But neither heat nor frost nor thunder
> Shall wholly do away, I wean,
> The marks of that which once had been.

My selection is not arbitrary. Not only Hazlitt, but virtually every contemporary reviewer of *Christabel*, no matter what his opinion of the poem as a whole, cites these 'manly' lines with approval. It almost seems to be a conspiracy of gentlemen – to find, in a poem which describes a mysterious contract between two women, so much to admire in these lines about manly friendship unambiguously 'rent asunder'.

13. Freud's formulation is quoted by JEAN LAPLANCHE and J.B. PONTALIS in their essay, 'Fantasy and the Origins of Sexuality', which appears in the *International Journal of Psycho-Analysis*, 49 (1968): 1–18. My own understanding and use of the term 'fantasy' is indebted to this work.

14. Indeed, part of the joke is that what is at the top of this particular page differs very little from what is at the bottom. Coleridge is describing how the continual perusal of periodical literature has weakened the memory of the reading public. It is *this* public from which the devotees have been excluded.

15. In 'Concepts of Convention and Models of Critical Discourse' (*NLH*, 13, 1982: 31–52), Laurence Manley proposes that conventions have a 'quasi-objective status' for the people who share them, a formulation that would seem to bear on my suggestion that the 'genre' of ladies' literature has the status of a cultural fantasy in Coleridge's day.

16. *Lyrical Ballads 1798*, ed. W.J.B. Owen (Oxford: Oxford University Press, 1969), p. 166.

17. I discuss the poem more thoroughly in my essay '*Christabel*: The Wandering Mother and the Enigma of Form', *Studies in Romanticism*, **23** (winter 1984).

7 Bearing Demons: *Frankenstein* and the Circumvention of Maternity*

Margaret Homans

Margaret Homans's *Bearing the Word: Language and Female Experience in Nineteenth-Century Women's Writing* (1986) makes a strong case for an important tenet of feminist criticism: works by women reflect the fact that women necessarily accede differently than men to the position of author, within a culture in which the thinking subject is implicitly assumed to be a man. How does a woman produce a literary work in a tradition in which women are associated with nature or with the literal (or conversely, with rhetorical ornament and the duplicity of figures of speech)? Homans shows that women writers address this problem in the plots and figures of their texts and thereby expose the unquestioned assumptions about language and gender that make up, she suggests, the underlying myth of Western thought.

The central fiction of *Frankenstein* is the artificial production of a human being. Homans reads it as a telling portrayal of a masculine fantasy, that of doing without the mother and the physical embodiment that the relation to her implies. For Homans the fiction reflects Mary Shelley's experience of being the target of such a fantasy, rather than that of sharing it. Other feminist readings have followed Mary Shelley's lead in referring to the novel in her preface as 'my hideous progeny' and have identified Frankenstein's creation of the monster with Shelley's creation of her book, her self-creation as an author – taking the novel as an autobiography of its own writing. (See Barbara Johnson, 'My Monster, My Self', in her *A World of Difference*, Baltimore: Johns Hopkins University Press, 1987; and Mary Poovey, cited in Homans's note 1.) Unlike such a reading, Homans's interpretation

---

* Reprinted from Margaret Homans, *Bearing the Word. Language and Female Experience in Nineteenth-Century Women's Writing* (Chicago and London: University of Chicago Press, 1986), pp. 100–119.

keeps the writer from falling into her text. (Such falls are not, of course, a special proclivity of female authors, but follow from the self-referential aspect of literary texts.) Homans sees in Mary Shelley's novel the definitive transformation of her experiences as a woman, in the deliberate miming and framing of a narcissistic masculine discourse. In offering us a Mary Shelley with whom we could willingly identify (a survivor, a canny writer), *different* from her fictional narrators, Homans reads critically in the important sense that she works against the novel's allure: she offers a counterweight to its most dizzying effect – the way its first-person narratives draw us into identifying with both the monster and his creator. That such a response remains possible suggests perhaps the fact that women as well as men learn to identify with the masculine position Homans describes. It reflects, too, the power of the autobiographical effect so characteristic of Romantic literature (the positions of reader and imaginary author mutually defining one another).

Married to one romantic poet and living near another, Mary Shelley at the time she was writing *Frankenstein* experienced with great intensity the self-contradictory demand that daughters embody both the mother whose death makes language possible by making it necessary and the figurative substitutes for that mother who constitute the prototype of the signifying chain. At the same time, as a mother herself, she experienced with far greater intensity than did any of the authors considered so far a proto-Victorian ideology of motherhood, as Mary Poovey has shown.[1] This experience leads Shelley both to figure her writing as mothering and to bear or transmit the words of her husband.[2] Thus Shelley not only practices the daughter's obligatory and voluntary identification with the literal, as do Dorothy Wordsworth and Charlotte and Emily Brontë, but she also shares with George Eliot and Elizabeth Gaskell (and again with Charlotte Brontë) their concern with writing as literalization, as a form of mothering. It is to Shelley's handling of these contradictory demands, and to her criticism of their effect on women's writing, that my reading of *Frankenstein* will turn.

Frankenstein portrays the situation of women obliged to play the role of the literal in a culture that devalues it. In this sense, the novel is simultaneously about the death and obviation of the mother and about the son's quest for a substitute object of desire. The novel criticizes the self-contradictory male requirement that that substitute at once embody and not embody (because all embodiment is a reminder of the mother's powerful and forbidden body) the object of desire. The horror of the demon that Frankenstein creates is that it is the literalization of its creator's desire for an object, a desire that never really seeks its own fulfillment.

Many readers of *Frankenstein* have noted both that the demon's creation amounts to an elaborate circumvention of normal heterosexual procreation – Frankenstein does by himself with great difficulty what a heterosexual couple can do quite easily – and that each actual mother dies very rapidly upon being introduced as a character in the novel.[3] Frankenstein's own history is full of the deaths of mothers. His mother was discovered, as a poverty-stricken orphan, by Frankenstein's father. Frankenstein's adoptive sister and later fiancée, Elizabeth, was likewise discovered as an orphan, in poverty, by Frankenstein's parents.[4] Elizabeth catches scarlet fever, and her adoptive mother, nursing her, catches it herself and dies of it. On her deathbed, the mother hopes for the marriage of Elizabeth and Frankenstein and tells Elizabeth, 'You must supply my place to my younger children' (Chapter 3). Like Shelley herself, Elizabeth is the death of her mother and becomes a substitute for her. Justine, a young girl taken in by the Frankenstein family as a beloved servant, is said to cause the death of her mother; and Justine herself, acting as foster mother to Frankenstein's little brother, William, is executed for his murder. There are many mothers in the Frankenstein circle, and all die notable deaths.

The significance of the apparently necessary destruction of the mother first emerges in Frankenstein's account of his preparations for creating the demon, and it is confirmed soon after the demon comes to life. Of his early passion for science, Frankenstein says, 'I was . . . deeply smitten with the thirst for knowledge' (Chapter 2). Shelley confirms the Oedipal suggestion here when she writes that it is despite his father's prohibition that the young boy devours the archaic books on natural philosophy that first raise his ambitions to discover the secret of life. His mother dies just as Frankenstein is preparing to go to the University of Ingolstadt, and if his postponed trip there is thus motivated by her death, what he finds at the university becomes a substitute for her: modern scientists, he is told, 'penetrate into the recesses of nature and show how she works in her hiding-places' (Chapter 3). Frankenstein's double, Walton, the polar explorer who rescues him and records his story, likewise searches for what sound like sexual secrets, also in violation of a paternal prohibition. Seeking to 'satiate [his] ardent curiosity', Walton hopes to find the 'wondrous power which attracts the needle' (letter 1). Frankenstein, having become 'capable of bestowing animation upon lifeless matter', feels that to arrive 'at once at the summit of my desires was the most gratifying consummation of my toils'. And his work to create the demon adds to this sense of an oedipal violation of Mother Nature: dabbling 'among the unhallowed damps of the grave', he 'disturbed, with profane fingers, the tremendous secrets of the human frame' (Chapter 4). This

violation is necrophiliac. The mother he rapes is dead; his researches into
her secrets, to usurp her powers, require that she be dead.[5]

Frankenstein describes his violation of nature in other ways that recall
what William Wordsworth's poetry reveals when read in conjunction
with Dorothy Wordsworth's journals. Of the period during which he is
working on the demon, Frankenstein writes,

> The summer months passed while I was thus engaged, heart and soul,
> in one pursuit. It was a most beautiful season; never did the fields
> bestow a more plentiful harvest or the vines yield a more luxuriant
> vintage, but my eyes were insensible to the charms of nature . . .
> Winter, spring, and summer passed away during my labours; but I did
> not watch the blossom or the expanding leaves – sights which before
> always yielded me supreme delight – so deeply was I engrossed in my
> occupation.
>
> (Chapter 4)

Ignoring the bounteous offering nature makes of itself and substituting
for it his own construction of life, what we, following Thomas Weiskel,
might call his own reading of nature, Frankenstein here resembles
William Wordsworth, reluctantly and ambivalently allowing himself to
read nature, to impose on nature apocalyptic patterns of meaning that
destroy it. Dorothy Wordsworth herself makes an appearance in the text
of *Frankenstein*, if indirectly, and her presence encodes a shared women's
critique of the romantic reading of nature. Much later in the novel,
Frankenstein compares his friend Clerval to the former self William
Wordsworth depicts in 'Tintern Abbey', a self that he has outgrown but
that his sister remains. Shelley quotes (with one major alteration) the
lines beginning, 'The sounding cataract / Haunted him like a passion'
and ending with the assertion that the colors and forms of natural objects
(rock, mountain, etc.) were

> a feeling, and a love,
> That had no need of a remoter charm,
> By thought supplied, or any interest
> Unborrow'd from the eye.[6]

If Clerval is like Dorothy, then Frankenstein is like William, regrettably
destroying nature by imposing his reading on it.

When, assembled from the corpse of nature, the demon has been
brought to life and Frankenstein has recognized – oddly only now that it
is alive – how hideous it is, Frankenstein falls into an exhausted sleep
and dreams the following dream:

I thought I saw Elizabeth, in the bloom of health, walking in the streets of Ingolstadt. Delighted and surprised, I embraced her, but as I imprinted the first kiss on her lips, they became livid with the hue of death; her features appeared to change, and I thought that I held the corpse of my dead mother in my arms; a shroud enveloped her form, and I saw the grave-worms crawling in the folds of the flannel. I started from my sleep with horror.

(Chapter 5)

He wakes to see the demon looking at him, hideous, but clearly loving. The dream suggests that to bring the demon to life is equivalent to killing Elizabeth, and that Elizabeth dead is equivalent to his mother dead. Elizabeth may have been the death of the mother, but now that she has replaced her, she too is vulnerable to whatever destroys mothers.[7] And, indeed, the dream is prophetic: the demon will much later kill Elizabeth, just as the demon's creation has required both the death of Frankenstein's own mother and the death and violation of Mother Nature. To bring a composite corpse to life is to circumvent the normal channels of procreation; the demon's 'birth' violates the normal relations of family, especially the normal sexual relation of husband and wife. Victor has gone to great lengths to produce a child without Elizabeth's assistance, and in the dream's language, to circumvent her, to make her unnecessary, is to kill her, and to kill mothers altogether.

Frankenstein's creation, then, depends on and then perpetuates the death of the mother and of motherhood. The demon's final, and greatest, crime is in fact its murder of Elizabeth, which is, however, only the logical extension of its existence as the reification of Frankenstein's desire to escape the mother. The demon is, to borrow a phrase from Shelley's *Alastor*, 'the spirit of' Frankenstein's 'solitude'. Its greatest complaint to Frankenstein is of its own solitude, its isolation from humanity, and it promises that if Frankenstein will make it a mate, 'one as hideous as myself. . . . I shall become a thing of whose existence everyone will be ignorant' (Chapter 17). That is, no longer solitary, the demon will virtually cease to exist, for its existence is synonymous with its solitude. But, on the grounds that 'a race of devils would be propagated upon the earth', Frankenstein destroys the female demon he is in the process of creating, thus destroying yet another potential mother, and the demon promises, 'I shall be with you on your wedding-night' (Chapter 20). If the demon is the form taken by Frankenstein's flight from the mother, then it is impossible that the demon should itself find an embodied substitute for the mother, and it will prevent Frankenstein from finding one too.

The demon's promise to be present at the wedding night suggests that there is something monstrous about Frankenstein's sexuality. A solipsist's sexuality is monstrous because his desire is for his own envisionings rather than for somebody else, some other body. The demon appears where Frankenstein's wife should be, and its murder of her suggests not so much revenge as jealousy. The demon's murder of that last remaining potential mother makes explicit the sequel to the obviation of the mother, the male quest for substitutes for the mother, the quest that is never intended to be fulfilled. Elizabeth suggests in a letter to Frankenstein that his reluctance to marry may stem from his love for someone else, someone met, perhaps, in his travels or during his long stay in Ingolstadt. 'Do you not love another?' she asks (Chapter 22). This is in fact the case, for the demon, the creation of Frankenstein's imagination, resembles in many ways the romantic object of desire, the beloved invented to replace, in a less threatening form, the powerful mother who must be killed.[8] This imagined being would be an image of the self, because it is for the sake of the ego that the mother is rejected in the first place. Created right after the death of the mother to be, as Victor says, 'a being like myself' (Chapter 4), the demon may be Adam, created in God's image. Indeed, this is what the demon thinks when it tells Frankenstein, 'I ought to be thy Adam, but I am rather the fallen angel' (Chapter 10). But it is also possible, as Gilbert and Gubar suggest, that the demon is Eve, created from Adam's imagination.[9]

When the demon takes shelter in the French cottager's shed, it looks, repeating Milton's Eve's first act upon coming to life, into the mirror of a 'clear pool' and is terrified at its own reflection: 'I started back' (Chapter 12). Here is the relevant passage from Milton, from Eve's narration in Book 4 of her memory of the first moments of her creation.[10] Hearing the 'murmuring sound / Of waters issu'd from a Cave and spread / Into a liquid Plain', Eve looks

> into the clear
> Smooth Lake, that to me seem'd another Sky.
> As I bent down to look, just opposite,
> A Shape within the wat'ry gleam appear'd
> Bending to look on me, I started back,
> It started back, but pleas'd I soon return'd . . .
>
> (4, 453–63)

But the disembodied voice instructs her, 'What there thou seest fair Creature is thyself' (l. 468), and tells her to follow and learn to prefer him 'whose image thou art' (ll. 471–2). Christine Froula argues that the fiction of Eve's creation by a paternal God out of the flesh of Adam values the maternal and appropriates it for the aggrandizement of masculine creativity.[11] Frankenstein revises this paradigm for artistic creation: he does not so much appropriate the maternal as bypass it, to demonstrate

167

the unnecessariness of natural motherhood and, indeed, of women. Froula points out that in this 'scene of canonical instruction', Eve is required to turn away from herself to embrace her new identity, not as a self, but as the image of someone else.[12] Created to the specifications of Adam's desire, we later learn – 'Thy likeness, thy fit help, thy other self, / Thy wish, exactly to thy heart's desire' (8, 450–1) – Eve is, like Frankenstein's demon, the product of imaginative desire. Milton appropriates the maternal by excluding any actual mother from the scene of creation. Eve is the form that Adam's desire takes once actual motherhood has been eliminated; and in much the same way, the demon is the form taken by Frankenstein's desire once his mother and Elizabeth as mother have been circumvented. These new creations in the image of the self are substitutes for the powerful creating mother and place creation under the control of the son.

That the demon is, like Eve, the creation of a son's imaginative desire is confirmed by another allusion. The novel was written when Percy Shelley had completed, of all his major works besides *Queen Mab*, only *Alastor*, the archetypal poem of the doomed romantic quest, and it is to this poem that Mary Shelley alludes.[13] Just before Frankenstein receives Elizabeth's letter, just after being acquitted of the murder of his friend Clerval, Frankenstein tells us, 'I saw around me nothing but a dense and frightful darkness, penetrated by no light but the glimmer of two eyes that glared upon me' (Chapter 21). This is a direct allusion to a passage in *Alastor* in which the hero, who has quested in vain after an ideal female image of his own creation, sees

> two eyes,
> Two starry eyes, hung in the gloom of thought,
> And seemed with their serene and azure smiles
> To beckon him.

(ll. 489–92)

In *Alastor*, these eyes belong to the phantom maiden, the 'fleeting shade' whom the hero pursues to his death, a beloved who is constructed out of the poet's own visionary narcissism. The girl he dreams and pursues has a voice 'like the voice of his own soul / Heard in the calm of thought' (ll. 153–4), and like him, she is 'Herself a poet' (l. 161). In the novel, the starry eyes become glimmering, glaring eyes, alternately the eyes of the dead Clerval and the 'watery, clouded eyes of the monster, as I first saw them in my chamber at Ingolstadt' (Chapter 21). This conflation of the eyes of the poet's beloved with the eyes of the demon suggests, even more surely than the allusion to Eve, that the demon is the form, not only of Frankenstein's solipsism, of his need to obviate the mother, but also of the narcissism that constitutes the safety of the ego for whose

sake the mother is denied. The monster is still the object of
Frankenstein's desire when Elizabeth writes to him, just as its creation
was the object of his initial quest.[14] It is this monster of narcissism, that
intervenes on the wedding night, substituting Frankenstein's desire for
his own imagining for the consummation of his marriage, just as the
visionary maiden in *Alastor* takes the place both of the dead Mother
Nature of the poet's prologue and of the real maiden the hero meets,
attracts, and rejects in the course of his quest.

That the demon is a revision of Eve, of emanations, and of the object of
romantic desire, is confirmed by its female attributes. Its very bodiliness,
its identification with matter, associates it with traditional concepts of
femaleness. Further, the impossibility of Frankenstein giving it a female
demon, an object of its own desire, aligns the demon with women, who
are forbidden to have their own desires. But if the demon is really a
feminine object of desire, why is it a he? I would suggest that this
constitutes part of Shelley's exposure of the male romantic economy that
would substitute for real and therefore powerful female others a being
imagined on the model of the male poet's own self. By making the
demon masculine, Shelley suggests that romantic desire seeks to do
away, not only with the mother, but also with all females so as to live
finally in a world of mirrors that reflect a comforting illusion of the male
self's independent wholeness. It is worth noting that just as
Frankenstein's desire is for a male demon, Walton too yearns, not for a
bride, but for 'the company of a man who could sympathize with me,
whose eyes would reply to mine' (letter 2).[15]

It may seem peculiar to describe the demon as the object of
Frankenstein's romantic desire, since he spends most of the novel
suffering from the demon's crimes. Yet in addition to the allusions to Eve
and the 'fleeting shade' in *Alastor* that suggest this, it is clear that while
Frankenstein is in the process of creating the demon, he loves it and
desires it; the knowledge that makes possible its creation is the
'consummation' of his 'toils'. It is only when the demon becomes
animated that Frankenstein abruptly discovers his loathing for his
creation. Even though the demon looks at its creator with what appears
to be love, Frankenstein's response to it is unequivocal loathing. Why
had he never noticed before the hideousness of its shape and features?
No adequate account is given, nor could be, for as we shall see, this is
what most mystifies and horrifies Shelley about her own situation.
Frankenstein confesses, 'I had desired it with an ardour that far exceeded
moderation; but now that I had finished, the beauty of the dream
vanished, and breathless horror and disgust filled my heart' (Chapter 5).
The romantic quest is always doomed, for it secretly resists its own
fulfillment: although the hero of *Alastor* quests for his dream maiden and
dies of not finding her, his encounter with the Indian maid makes it clear

that embodiment is itself an obstacle to desire, or more precisely, its termination. Frankenstein's desire for his creation lasts only so long as that creation remains uncreated, the substitution for the too-powerful mother of a figure issuing from his imagination and therefore under his control.

To return to the terms with which we began in Chapter 1, we might say that the predicament of Frankenstein, as of the hero of *Alastor* is that of the son in Lacan's revision of the Freudian Oedipal crisis. In flight from the body of the mother forbidden by the father, a maternal body that he sees as dead in his urgency to escape it and to enter a paternal order constituted of its distance from the mother, the son seeks figurations that will at once make restitution for the mother and confirm her death and absence by substituting for her figures that are under his control. Fundamentally, the son cannot wish for these figurative substitutes to be embodied, for any *body* is too reminiscent of the mother and is no longer under the son's control, as the demon's excessive strength demonstrates; the value of these figurations is that they remain figurations. In just this way, romantic desire does not desire to be fulfilled, and yet, because it seems both to itself and to others to want to be embodied, the romantic quester as son is often confronted with a body he seems to want but does not.[16] Thus Frankenstein thinks he wants to create the demon, but when he has succeeded, he discovers that what he really enjoyed was the process leading up to the creation, the seemingly endless chain of signifiers that constitute his true, if unrecognized, desire.

Looking at *Alastor* through *Frankenstein*'s reading of it, then, we see that the novel is the story of a hypothetical case: what if the hero of *Alastor* actually got what he thinks he wants? What if desire were embodied, contrary to the poet's deepest wishes? That Shelley writes such a case suggests that this was her own predicament. In real life, Percy Shelley pursued her as the poet and hero of *Alastor* pursue ghosts and as Frankenstein pursues the secrets of the grave. That he courted the adolescent Mary Godwin at the grave of her mother, whose writing he admired, already suggests that the daughter was for him a figure for the safely dead mother, a younger and less powerfully creative version of her. Yet when he got this substitute, he began to tire of her, as he makes quite explicit in *Epipsychidion*, where he is not embarrassed to describe his life in terms of an interminable quest for an imaginary woman. Mary starts out in that poem as one 'who seemed / As like the glorious shape which I had dreamed' (ll. 277–8) but soon becomes 'that Moon' with 'pale and waning lips' (l. 309). The poet does not seem to notice that each time an embodiment of the ideal turns out to be unsatisfactory, it is not because she is the wrong woman, but because the very fact of embodiment inevitably spoils the vision. Emily, the final term in the poem's sequence of women, remains ideal only because she has not yet been possessed, and indeed at the end of the poem, the poet disintegrates and disembodies her, perhaps to save himself from yet one more disappointment. Shelley was for herself never anything but embodied, but for Percy Shelley it seems to have been a grave disappointment to discover her substantiality, and therefore her inadequacy for fulfilling his visionary requirements. *Frankenstein* is the story of what it feels like to be the undesired embodiment of romantic imaginative desire. The demon, rejected merely for being a body, suffers in something of the way that Shelley must have felt herself to suffer under the conflicting demands of romantic desire: on the one hand, that she must embody the goal of Percy's quest, and on the other, his rejection of that embodiment.

Later in the novel, when the demon describes to Frankenstein its discovery and reading of the 'journal of the four months that preceded my creation', the discrepancy between Percy's conflicting demands is brought to the fore. The demon notes that the journal records 'the whole detail of that series of disgusting circumstances' that resulted in 'my accursed origin', and that 'the minutest description of my odious and loathsome person is given, in language which painted your own horrors and rendered mine indelible' (Chapter 15). This summary suggests that while Frankenstein was writing the journal during the period leading up to the demon's vivification, he was fully aware of his creature's hideousness. Yet Frankenstein, in his own account of the same period, specifically says that it was only when 'I had finished, the beauty of the dream vanished, and breathless horror and disgust filled my heart' (Chapter 5). If Frankenstein is right about his feelings here, why should his journal be full of 'language which painted [his] horrors'? Or, if the account in the journal is correct, if Frankenstein was aware from the start of his creature's 'odious and loathsome person', why does he tell Walton that the demon appeared hideous to him only upon its awakening? If the text of this journal is, like *Alastor*, the record of a romantic quest for an object of desire, then the novel is presenting us with two conflicting readings of the poem – Frankenstein's or Percy's and the demon's or Shelley's – confirming our sense that Shelley reading *Alastor* finds in it the story of Percy's failure to find in her the object of his desire, or the story of his desire not to find the object of his desire, not to find that she is the object.

A famous anecdote about the Shelleys from a few days after the beginning of the ghost story contest in which *Frankenstein* originated lends support to this impression of Shelley's experience. Byron was reciting some lines from Coleridge's *Christabel* about Geraldine, who is, like the demon, a composite body, half young and beautiful, half (in the version Byron recited) 'hideous, deformed, and pale of hue'. Percy 'suddenly shrieking and putting his hands to his head, ran out of the room with a candle'. Brought to his senses, he told Byron and Polidori that 'he was looking at Mrs Shelley' while Byron was repeating Coleridge's lines, 'and suddenly thought of a woman he had heard of who had eyes instead of nipples'.[17] If disembodied eyes are, in *Alastor*, what are so alluring to the hero about his beloved, eyes in place of nipples may have been Percy's hallucination of the horror of having those ideal eyes reembodied in the form of his real lover. This is an embodiment that furthermore calls attention to its failure to be sufficiently different from the mother, whose nipples are for the baby so important a feature. An actual woman, who is herself a mother, does not fit the ideal of disembodied femininity, and the vision of combining real and ideal is a monster. Mary's sense of herself viewed as a collection of incongruent body parts – breasts terminating in eyes – might have found expression in the demon, whose undesirable corporeality is expressed as its being composed likewise of ill-fitting parts. *Paradise Lost*, *Alastor*, and other texts in this tradition compel women readers to wish to embody, as Eve does, imaginary ideals, to be glad of this role in masculine life; and yet at the same time, they warn women readers that they will suffer for such embodiment.

It requires only a transposing of terms to suggest the relevance of this reading of *Frankenstein* to the myth of language we traced in chapter 1 in its form as the romantic quest. The demon is about the ambivalent response of a woman reader to some of our culture's most compelling statements of woman's place in the myth. That the mother must vanish and be replaced by never quite embodied figures for her is equivalent to the vanishing of the referent (along with that time with the mother when the referent had not vanished) to be replaced by language as figuration that never quite touches its objects. Women's role is to be that silent or lost referent, the literal whose absence makes figuration possible. To be also the figurative substitute for that lost referent is, Shelley shows, impossible, for women are constantly reminded that they are the mother's (loathed, loved) body, and in any case, 'being' is incompatible with being a figure. The literal provokes horror in the male poet, or scientist, even while he demands that women literalize his vision.

That Shelley knew she was writing a criticism, not only of women's self-contradictory role in androcentric ontology, but also of the gendered myth of language that is part of that ontology, is suggested by the appearance of a series of images of writing at the very end of the novel. Once again, the demon is the object of Frankenstein's quest, pursued now in hate rather than in love. Frankenstein is preternaturally motivated in his quest by an energy of desire that recalls his passion when first creating the demon, and that his present quest depends on the killing of animals recalls his first quest's dependence on dead bodies. Frankenstein believes that 'a spirit of good' follows and directs his steps:

'Sometimes, when nature, overcome by hunger, sank under the exhaustion, a repast was prepared for me in the desert that restored and inspirited me. . . .I will not doubt that it was set there by the spirits that I had invoked to aid me' (Chapter 24). He says this, however, directly after pointing out that the demon sometimes helped him. Fearing 'that if I lost all trace of him I should despair and die, [he] left some mark to guide me', and Frankenstein also notes that the demon would frequently leave 'marks in writing on the barks of the trees or cut in stone that guided me and instigated my fury'. One of these messages includes the information, 'You will find near this place, if you follow not too tardily, a dead hare; eat and be refreshed.' Frankenstein, it would seem, deliberately misinterprets the demon's guidance and provisions for him as belonging instead to a spirit of good: his interpretation of the demon's marks and words is so figurative as to be opposite to what they really say. The demon, all body, writes appropriately on the body of nature messages that refer, if to objects at a distance, at least at not a very great distance ('you will find near this place . . .'). Frankenstein, however, reads as figuratively as possible, putting as great a distance as possible between what he actually reads and what he interprets. His reading furthermore puts a distance between himself and the object of his quest, which he still cannot desire to attain; figurative reading would extend indefinitely the pleasure of the quest itself by forever putting off the moment of capture. Just at the moment when Frankenstein thinks he is about to reach the demon, the demon is transformed from a 'mark', as if a mark on a page, into a 'form', and Frankenstein seeks to reverse this transformation. One of Frankenstein's sled dogs has died of exhaustion, delaying him; 'suddenly my eye caught a dark speck upon the dusky plain'; he utters 'a wild cry of ecstasy' upon 'distinguish[ing] a sledge and the distorted proportions of a well-known form within' (Chapter 24). Frankenstein's response, however, is to take an hour's rest: his real aim, which he does not admit, is to keep the demon at the distance where he remains a 'dark speck', a mark on the white page of the snow, his signification forever deferred.[18]

At the same time that *Frankenstein* is about a woman writer's response to the ambiguous imperative her culture imposes upon her, it is also possible that the novel concerns a woman writer's anxieties about bearing children, about generating bodies that, as we have seen with reference to *Jane Eyre* and *Wuthering Heights*, would have the power to displace or kill the parent. Ellen Moers first opened up a feminist line of inquiry into the novel by suggesting that it is a 'birth myth', that the horror of the demon is Shelley's horror, not only at her own depressing experience of childbirth, but also at her knowledge of the disastrous consequences of giving birth (or of pregnancy itself) for many women in her vicinity.[19] The list is by now familiar to Shelley's readers. First, Mary Wollstonecraft died eleven days after she gave birth to Mary; then, during the time of the writing of the novel, Fanny Imlay, Mary's half-sister, drowned herself in October 1816 when she learned that she was her mother's illegitimate child by Gilbert Imlay; Harriet Shelley was pregnant by another man when she drowned herself in the Serpentine in December 1816; and Claire Clairmont, the daughter of the second Mrs Godwin, was, scandalously, pregnant by Byron, much to the embarrassment of the Shelleys, with whom she lived.[20] Illegitimate pregnancy, that is, a pregnancy over which the woman has particularly little control, brings either death to the mother in childbirth (Wollstonecraft) or shame, making visible what ought to have remained out of sight, the scene of conception (Claire), a shame that can itself result in the death of both mother (Harriet Shelley) and child (Fanny).

At the time of the conception of the novel, Mary Godwin had herself borne two illegitimate children: the first, an unnamed girl, died four days later, in March 1815; the second was five months old. In December 1816, when Harriet Shelley died and Shelley had finished Chapter 4 of the novel, she was pregnant again. With but a single parent, the demon in her novel is the world's most monstrously illegitimate child, and this illegitimate child causes the death of that parent as well as of the principle of motherhood, as we have seen. Read in connection with the history of disastrous illegitimacies, the novel's logic would seem to be this: to give birth to an illegitimate child is monstrous, for it is the inexorable life of these babies, especially those of Mary Wollstonecraft and of Harriet Shelley, that destroys the life of the mother. Subsequently, as Marc Rubenstein argues, the guilty daughter pays for the destruction of her own mother in a fantasy of being destroyed by her own child.[21]

In the Brontës' novels, childbirth is structurally equivalent to (and indeed also often situated in) the coming true of dreams, which has, like childbirth, an ironic relation to the original conception. Shelley's 1831 Introduction to her novel makes a comparable equation of giving birth, the realization of a dream, and writing. As many readers have pointed out, this introduction to her revised version of the novel identifies the novel itself with the demon, and both with a child.[22] She tells of being asked every morning if she had thought of a story, as if a story, like a baby, were necessarily to be conceived in the privacy of the night. And at the close of the introduction she writes, 'I bid my hideous progeny go forth and prosper', and she refers to the novel in the next sentence as 'the offspring of happy days'. The genesis of the novel, furthermore, is in a dream that she transcribes, a dream moreover that is about the coming true of a dream. One night, she says, after listening to conversation about the reanimation of corpses, 'Night waned upon this talk. . . . When I placed my head on my pillow I did not sleep, nor could I be said to think. My imagination, unbidden, possessed and guided me.' Then follows her account of the famous dream of 'the pale student of unhallowed arts kneeling beside the thing he had put together', the 'hideous phantasm of a man' stirring 'with an uneasy, half-vital motion', and the 'artist' sleeping and waking to behold 'the horrid thing . . . looking on him with yellow, watery, but speculative eyes'. Waking in horror from her dream, she at first tries 'to think of something else', but then realizes that she has the answer to her need for a ghost story: ' "What terrified me will terrify others; and I need only describe the spectre which had haunted my midnight pillow." . . . I began that day with the words, "It was on a dreary night of November", making only a transcript of the grim terrors of my waking dream.' Making a transcript of a dream – that is, turning an idea into the 'machinery of a story' – a dream that is about the transformation of a 'phantasm' into a real body, is equivalent here to conceiving a child.

Despite Ellen Moers's delineation of the resemblance of the demon to the apprehensions a mother might have about a baby, it is the introduction that supplies the most explicit evidence for identifying demon and book with a child. Mary Poovey has demonstrated that this introduction has a significantly different ideological cast from the original version of the novel (or even from the revised novel). Written in 1831, fourteen years after the novel itself and following the death of Percy Shelley (as well as the deaths of both the children who were alive or expected in 1816–17), the introduction takes pains to distance itself from the novel, and it aims to bring the writing of the novel further within the fold of the conventional domestic life Shelley retrospectively substitutes for the radically disruptive life she in fact led.[23] Referring obliquely to her elopement with Percy and its effect on her adolescent habit of inventing stories, for example, she writes, 'After this my life became busier, and reality stood in place of fiction.' Echoed later by Robert Southey's remark to Charlotte Brontë, that 'literature cannot be the business of a woman's life', Shelley's busyness refers largely to her responsibilities as a mother and wife. When she describes her endeavor to write a ghost story she repeats this term for family responsibility: 'I busied myself *to think of a story.*' This echo suggests that her busyness with story writing is somehow congruent with, not in conflict with, her 'busier' life as a wife and mother. It makes the novel, 'so very hideous an idea', seem somehow part of the busy life of a matron. It is this effort, to domesticate her hideous idea, that may be at the bottom of her characterizing it as a 'hideous progeny'.

Thus the novel may be about the horror associated with motherhood, yet this reading seems unduly influenced by the superimpositions of the introduction, and furthermore it ignores the novel's most prominent feature, that the demon is not a child born of woman but the creation of a man.[24] Most succinctly put, the novel is about the collision between androcentric and gynocentric theories of creation, a collision that results in the denigration of maternal childbearing through its circumvention by male creation. The novel presents Mary Shelley's response to the expectation, manifested in such poems as *Alastor* or *Paradise Lost*, that women embody and yet not embody male fantasies. At the same time, it expresses a woman's knowledge of the irrefutable independence of the body, both her own and those of the children that she produces, from projective male fantasy. While a masculine being – God, Adam, Percy Shelley, Frankenstein – may imagine that his creation of an imaginary being may remain under the control of his desires, Mary Shelley knows otherwise, both through her experience as mistress and wife of Percy and through her experience of childbirth. Shelley's particular history shows irrefutably that children, even pregnancies, do not remain under the control of those who conceive them.

Keats writes that 'the Imagination may be compared to Adam's dream – he awoke and found it truth.'[25] In *Paradise Lost*, narrating his recollection of Eve's creation, Adam describes how he fell into a special sleep – 'Mine eyes he clos'd, but op'n left the Cell / Of Fancy my internal sight' (8, 460–1) – then watched, 'though sleeping', as God formed a creature,

> Manlike, but different sex, so lovely fair,
> That what seem'd fair in all the World, seem'd now
> Mean, or in her summ'd up.

(8, 471–3)

This is 'Adam's dream'. But what of 'he awoke and found it truth'? Adam wakes, 'To find her, or for ever to deplore / Her loss' (8, 479–80), and then, 'behold[s] her, not far off, / Such as I saw her in my dream' (ll. 481–2), yet what Keats represses is that the matching of reality to dream is not so neat as these lines suggest.[26] Eve comes to Adam, not of her own accord, but 'led by her Heav'nly Maker' (8, 485), and as soon as he catches sight of her, Adam sees Eve turn away from him, an action he ascribes to modesty (and thus endeavors to assimilate to his dream of her) but that Eve, in Book 4, has already said stemmed from her preference for her image in the water. Though designed by God for Adam 'exactly to thy heart's desire' (8, 451), Eve once created has a mind and will of her own, and this independence is so horrifying to the male imagination that the Fall is ascribed to it.

It is neither the visionary male imagination alone that Mary Shelley protests, then, nor childbirth itself, but the circumvention of the maternal creation of new beings by the narcissistic creations of male desire. While Keats can gloss over the discrepancy between Adam's dream and its fulfillment, Shelley cannot. As Frankenstein is on the verge of completing the female demon, it is for her resemblance to Eve that he destroys her. Just as Adam says of Eve, 'seeing me, she turn'd' (8, 507), Frankenstein fears the female demon's turning from the demon toward a more attractive image: 'She also might turn with disgust from him to the superior beauty of man' (Chapter 20). Also like Eve, who disobeys a prohibition agreed upon between Adam and God before her creation, she 'might refuse to comply with a compact made before her creation', the demon's promise to leave Europe. Frankenstein typifies the way in which the biological creation of necessarily imperfect yet independent beings has always been made to seem, within an androcentric economy, monstrous and alarming. Although Mary Wollstonecraft would in any case have died of puerperal fever after Mary's birth, her earlier pregnancy with Fanny and the pregnancies of Harriet Shelley, Claire Clairmont, and Mary Godwin would have done no harm had they not been labeled 'illegitimate' by a society that places a premium on the ownership by a man of his wife's body and children. The novel criticizes, not childbirth itself, but the male horror of independent embodiment.

At the site of the collision between motherhood and romantic projection another form of literalization appears as well. While it is important how Shelley reads texts such as *Alastor* and *Paradise Lost*, it is also important to consider, perhaps more simply, that her novel reads them. Like the Brontës' novels, whose gothic embodiments of subjective states, realizations of dreams, and literalized figures all literalize romantic projection, Shelley's novel literalizes romantic imagination, but with a different effect and to a different end. Shelley criticizes these texts by enacting them, and because enactment or embodiment is both the desire and the fear of such texts, the mode of her criticism matters. Just as the heroes of these poems seem to seek, but do not seek, embodiments of their visionary desires, these poetic texts seem to seek embodiment in 'the machinery of a story'. For in the ideology of post-romantic culture, it is part of a woman's duty to transcribe and give form to men's words, just as it is her duty to give form to their desire, or birth to their seed, no matter how ambivalently men may view the results of such projects. In the same passage in the introduction to the novel in which Shelley makes the analogy between the book and a child, between the conception of a story and the conception of a baby, and between these things and the coming true of a dream, she also identifies all these projects with the transcription of important men's words. Drawing on the ideology of maternity as the process of passing on a male idea, Shelley describes her book-child as the literalization of two poets' words:

Many and long were the conversations between Lord Byron and Shelley to which I was a devout but nearly silent listener. During one

177

of these, various philosophical doctrines were discussed, and among
others the nature of the principle of life, and whether there was any
probability of its ever being discovered and communicated. . . .
Perhaps a corpse would be reanimated; galvanism had given token of
such things: perhaps the component parts of a creature might be
manufactured, brought together, and endued with vital warmth.

Directly following this passage appears her account of going to bed and
vividly dreaming of the 'student of unhallowed arts' and the 'hideous
phantasm', the dream of which she says she made 'only a transcript' in
transferring it into the central scene of her novel, the dream that equates
the conception of a book with the conception of a child.

Commentators on the novel have in the past taken Shelley at her word
here, believing, if not in her story of transcribing a dream, then certainly
in her fiction of transcribing men's words.[27] Mario Praz, for example,
writes, 'All Mrs Shelley did was to provide a passive reflection of some of
the wild fantasies which, as it were, hung in the air about her.'[28] Harold
Bloom suggests that 'what makes *Frankenstein* an important book' despite
its 'clumsiness' is 'that it contains one of the most vivid versions we have
of the Romantic mythology of the self, one that resembles Blake's *Book of
Urizen*, Shelley's *Prometheus Unbound*, and Byron's *Manfred*, among other
works'.[29] It is part of the subtlety of her strategy to disguise her criticism
of such works as a passive transcription, to appear to be a docile wife and
'devout listener' to the conversations of important men. Indeed, central
to her critical method is the practice of acting out docilely what these
men tell her they want from her, to show them the consequences of their
desires. She removes herself beyond reproach for 'putting [her]self
forward', by formulating her critique as a devout transcription, a 'passive
reflection', a 'version' that 'resembles'. She inserts this authorial role into
her novel in the form of a fictive M.S., Walton's sister, Margaret Saville,
to whom his letters containing Frankenstein's story are sent and who
silently records and transmits them to the reader.

Now that we have assembled the parts of Shelley's introductory
account of the novel's genesis, we can see that she equates childbearing
with the bearing of men's words. Writing a transcript of a dream that
was in turn merely the transcript of a conversation is also giving birth to
a hideous progeny conceived in the night. The conversation between
Byron and Shelley probably represents Shelley's and Byron's poetry, the
words, for example, of *Alastor* that she literalizes in her novel. That the
notion of motherhood as the passive transcription of men's words is at
work here is underscored by the allusion this idea makes to the Christ
story. 'Perhaps a corpse would be reanimated' refers initially, not to
science's power, but to that occasion, a myth but surely still a powerful
one even in this den of atheists, when a corpse was reanimated, which is

in turn an allusion to the virgin birth. Like the creations of Adam and Eve, which excluded the maternal, Christ's birth bypassed the normal channels of procreation. It is this figure, whose birth is also the literalization of a masculine God's Word, who serves as the distant prototype for the reanimation of corpses. And within the fiction, the demon too is the literalization of a word, an idea, Frankenstein's theory given physical form. As Joyce Carol Oates remarks, the demon 'is a monster-son born of Man exclusively, a parody of the Word or Idea made Flesh'.[30] The book-baby literalizes Shelley's and Byron's words, the words of their conversation as figures for Shelley's words in *Alastor*, just as the demon-baby literalizes Frankenstein's inseminating words. Christ literalizes God's Word through the medium of a woman, Mary, who passively transmits Word into flesh without being touched by it. Literalizations again take place through the medium of a more recent Mary, who passively transcribes (or who seems to), who adds nothing but 'the platitude of prose' and 'the machinery of a story' to the words of her more illustrious male companions who for their own writing prefer 'the music of the most melodious verse'. And yet, as we will see again with Eliot's *The Mill on the Floss*, it is precisely the adding of this 'machinery', which would seem only to facilitate the transmission of the ideas and figures of poetry into the more approachable form of a story, that subverts and reverses what it appears so passively to serve.

Notes

1. MARY POOVEY, *The Proper Lady and the Woman Writer* (Chicago: University of Chicago Press, 1984), pp. 114–42. Hereafter I will refer to Mary Shelley as Shelley (except where her unmarried name is necessary for clarity) and to her husband as Percy.

2. SANDRA GILBERT and SUSAN GUBAR's reading of the novel focuses on its 'apparently docile submission to male myths' and identifies it specifically as 'a fictionalized rendition of the meaning of *Paradise Lost* to women' (*The Madwoman in the Attic* (New Haven: Yale University Press, 1979), pp. 219, 221). Although my interest in Shelley as a reader of prior, masculine texts, as well as some of my specific points about the novel's reading of Milton, overlaps with theirs, I am putting these concerns to uses different from theirs.

3. For example, ROBERT KIELY writes that Frankenstein 'seeks to combine the role of both parents in one, to eliminate the need for the woman in the creative act, to make sex unnecessary' (*The Romantic Novel in England* (Cambridge: Harvard University Press, 1972), p. 164), MARC RUBENSTEIN remarks on 'the series of motherless family romances which form the substance of Frankenstein's past' ('"My Accursed Origin": The Search for the Mother in *Frankenstein*', *Studies in Romanticism*, **15** (1976): 177). The general argument of his psychoanalytic reading of the novel is that the novel represents Shelley's quest for her own dead mother. U.C. Knoepflmacher, in the course of arguing that the novel

presents a daughter's rage at her parents, mentions 'the novel's attack on a male usurpation of the role of mother' ('Thoughts on the Aggression of Daughters', in *The Endurance of Frankenstein*, eds George Levine and U. C. Knoepflmacher (Berkeley: University of California Press, 1979), p. 105). MARY JACOBUS writes that 'the exclusion of woman from creation symbolically "kills" the mother' ('Is There a Woman in This Text?' *New Literary History*, **14** (1982): 131). Barbara Johnson suggests that the novel focuses on 'eliminations of the mother' as well as on 'the fear of somehow effecting the death of one's own parents' ('My Monster/My Self', *Diacritics*, **12** (1982): 9). Christine Froula's argument about the maternal in Milton, although it focuses on the author's appropriation of the maternal for masculine creativity (as differentiated from its circumvention or elimination), helped to stimulate my thinking. See FROULA, 'When Eve Reads Milton', *Critical Inquiry*, **10** (1983): 321–47.

4. I am following, in this reading, the 1831 revised text of the novel; in the 1818 version, Elizabeth is Frankenstein's cousin. All quotations from the novel will be from the Signet edition (Mary Shelley, *Frankenstein, Or The Modern Prometheus* (New York: NAL, 1965)), which prints the text of 1831. Future references will be cited in the text by chapter number or by letter number for the letters that precede the chapter sequence. See also James Reiger's edition of the 1818 version, with revisions of 1823 and 1831 (Chicago: University of Chicago Press, 1982).

5. RUBENSTEIN notes the sexual nature of Walton's quest, as well as the maternal associations of those aspects of nature on which Frankenstein carries out his research ('My Accursed Origin', pp. 174–5, 177). KIELY notes the necrophilia of the passage from *Alastor*'s invocation to Mother Nature and suggests its similarity to Frankenstein's 'penetrating the recesses of nature' (*The Romantic Novel*, pp. 162–3).

6. Quoted p. 149; Frankenstein quotes lines 76–83 of the poem, altering the original 'haunted *me* like a passion' to fit a third person.

7. In the context of arguing that the novel critiques the bourgeois family, Kate Ellis shows that Frankenstein's mother passes on to Elizabeth her 'view of the female role as one of constant, self-sacrificing devotion to others', and she suggests that 'Elizabeth's early death, like her adopted mother's, was a logical outgrowth of the female ideal she sought to embody' ('Monsters in the Garden: Mary Shelley and the Bourgeois Family', in *The Endurance of Frankenstein*, p. 131). My argument would explain why what created this 'female ideal' also determined the interchangeability of mother and daughter.

8. HAROLD BLOOM suggests the resemblance between the demon and Blake's emanations or Shelley's epipsyche, in his afterword to the Signet edition of the novel, p. 215. The essay is reprinted in *Ringers in the Tower* (Chicago: University of Chicago Press, 1971), pp. 119–29. PETER BROOKS makes a similar point when he writes, 'fulfillment with Elizabeth would mark Frankenstein's achievement of a full signified in his life, accession to plenitude of being – which would leave no place in creation for his daemonic projection, the Monster' ('Godlike Science/Unhallowed Arts: Language and Monstrosity in *Frankenstein*', *New Literary History*, **9** (1978): 599). ELLIS also suggests, though for different reasons, that the demon is a representative for Elizabeth ('Monsters in the Garden', p. 136). JACOBUS writes that Frankenstein 'exchang[es] a woman for a monster', and she discusses Frankenstein's preference for imagined over actual beings ('Is There a Woman in This Text?' p. 131).

9. GILBERT and GUBAR suggest first that 'the part of Eve *is* all the parts' and then discuss at length the demon's resemblance to Eve (*The Madwoman*, pp. 230, 235–44). However, in describing this resemblance, they focus primarily on the patriarchal rejection of women's bodies as deformed and monstrous, as well as on Eve's motherlessness, but not, as I do here, on Eve as Adam's imaginative projection. Joyce Carol Oates also suggests the demon's resemblance to Eve, also using the scene I am about to discuss, in 'Frankenstein's Fallen Angel', *Critical Inquiry*, **10** (1984): 547.

10. Quotations from *Paradise Lost* are from *Complete Poems and Major Prose of John Milton*, ed. Merritt Hughes (Indianapolis: Bobbs-Merrill, 1957), and are cited in the text by book and line numbers. Other critics have noted Shelley's allusion to this Miltonic scene; see, for example, Brooks, 'Godlike Science', p. 595.

11. Froula writes, 'Through the dream of the rib Adam both enacts a parody of birth and gains possession of the womb by claiming credit for woman herself'. Milton, she goes on to argue, reenacts Adam's solution to his 'womb envy' by analogously repressing female power in his account of the origin of his poem: 'The male Logos called upon to articulate the cosmos against an abyss of female silence overcomes the anxieties generated by the tension between visible maternity and invisible paternity by appropriating female power to itself in a parody of parthenogenesis' ('When Eve Reads Milton', pp. 332, 338; and see passim pp. 326–40).

12. Ibid., pp. 326–28.

13. All quotations from Shelley's verse are from the Reiman and Powers edition of his works.

14. Gilbert and Gubar also discuss narcissistic love in the novel, although with reference only to the potentially incestuous relation between Frankenstein and Elizabeth, not with reference to the demon (*The Madwoman*, p. 229). My reading would suggest that Frankenstein's relation to Elizabeth is far less narcissistic than his relation to the demon; in his descriptions of Elizabeth, he focuses on her difference from him, which is what I believe makes her like the mother and therefore theatening.

15. Jaya Mehta pointed out to me the significance of this aspect of Walton, in a seminar paper at Yale in 1984.

16. Kiely discusses 'the sheer concreteness' of the demon, though his concern is with the mismatching between ideal and real in the novel (*The Romantic Novel*, p. 161).

17. *The Diary of Dr John William Polidori*, ed. W.M. Rossetti (London: Elkin Matthews, 1911), pp. 128–29, entry for 18 June 1816. Cited also by Rubenstein, who reads it as as story about 'maternal reproach' and connects it with Frankenstein's dream of his dead mother ('My Accursed Origin', pp. 184–85). I am grateful to Marina Leslie for her discussion of this episode in a seminar paper at Yale in 1984.

18. Peter Brooks's essay on *Frankenstein* also connects the plot of desire with the plot of language in the novel, but to a somewhat different effect. Brooks argues that the demon's acquisition of the 'godlike science' of language places him within the symbolic order. Trapped at first, like any baby, within the specular order of the imaginary, the demon is first judged only by its looks; it is only when it masters the art of rhetoric that the monster gains sympathy.

But, Brooks continues, despite the promise that the symbolic seems to hold, the monster's failure to find an object of love removes its life from the signifying 'chain' of human interconnectedness and makes of it instead a 'miserable series', in which one signifier refers always to another with 'no point of arrest'. Thus Brooks sees the monster as a dark and exaggerated version of all life within the symbolic, where desire is never satisfied and where there is no transcendental signified. Although I agree with much of what Brooks writes, I would argue that in its materiality and its failure to acquire an object of desire, the demon enters the symbolic primarily as the (dreaded) referent, not as signifier. The negative picture of the demon's materiality is a product of its female place in the symbolic, and not of any lingering in the realm of the imaginary (which Brooks, with other readers of Lacan, views as tragic). I would also argue that the novel presents, not a vision of the condition of human signification, but a targeted criticism of those in whose interests the symbolic order constitutes itself in the ways that it does.

19. ELLEN MOERS, *Literary Women* (New York: Doubleday, 1977), p. 140.

20. Ibid., pp. 145–47.

21. This is the general tendency of Rubenstein's argument, carrying the material Moers presents into a psychoanalytic frame.

22. See RUBENSTEIN, 'My Accursed Origin', pp. 168, 178–81; POOVEY, *The Proper Lady*, pp. 138–42.

23. One of the central tenets of Poovey's argument concerns Shelley's endeavor in her 1831 revisions to make the novel more conservative, more in keeping with a proto-Victorian ideology of the family (see *The Proper Lady*, pp. 133–42). Poovey argues, however, that both versions of the novel oppose romantic egotism's assault on the family.

24. Gilbert and Gubar assert as part of their argument that everyone in the novel is Eve that 'Frankenstein has a baby' and that as a consequence he becomes female (*The Madwoman*, p. 232). I would argue, to the contrary, that Frankenstein's production of a new life is pointedly masculine, that it matters to the book that he is a man circumventing childbirth, not a woman giving birth.

25. Letter of 22 November 1817 to Benjamin Bailey, in *Letters of John Keats*, ed. Robert Gittings (London: Oxford University Press, 1970), p. 37.

26. I am indebted to Suzanne Raitt for her discussion of this point in a seminar at Yale in 1984.

27. Rubenstein also argues that Shelley deliberately created the impression that she merely recorded Percy and Byron's conversation as part of a project to make her creativity seem as passive and maternal as possible. He discusses at length the analogy she sets up between conceiving a child and conceiving a book, and he specifically suggests that the men's words in conversation are like men's role in procreation, which was, in the early nineteenth century, thought to involve the man actively and the woman only passively: 'She is trying to draw for us a picture of her imagination as a passive womb, inseminated by those titans of romantic poetry' ('My Accursed Origin', p. 181). I would agree with everything Rubenstein says, although I am using this idea for a somewhat different purpose: he is using it to show how the novel is about Shelley's effort to make restitution for her dead mother.

28. MARIO PRAZ, *The Romantic Agony*, trans. Angus Davidson (London: Oxford University Press, 1933), p. 114. Cited by Moers and also by Rubenstein in support of his argument discussed in note 27 above.

29. Harold Bloom, 'Afterword', *Frankenstein*, p. 215. It is worth noting that *Frankenstein* preceded *Prometheus Unbound* and was of course written in ignorance of the *Book of Urizen*.

30. Oates, 'Frankenstein's Fallen Angel', p. 552.

8 Introduction to *Keats's Life of Allegory**

MARJORIE LEVINSON

The introductory chapter of Levinson's book on Keats lays out her interpretation of his style and the peculiar history of its reception (vilified more than praised in his lifetime, canonized since, but also tellingly identified with the experience of 'embarrassment'). She sees both Keats's style and his reception as responses to his position as an aspirant to the middle class. Coveting the cultural 'heritage' rather than able to take it for granted (like Wordsworth or Byron), Keats writes poetry that reflects a desire for style as such and displays the effort of its accomplishment. His poetry thus plays out and makes visible 'the identity-problems of the middle class', which had paradoxically to find its identity in being always in the process of 'arriving' or 'making it'. Levinson's account of these complex relationships mines contemporary critical reactions to Keats for ways to bring together into the same argument the 'style' of a class and the 'style' of works of poetry. She finds an important one in Byron's epithet 'a sort of mental masturbation', since, as she argues, the fantasy of combining fulfillment and anticipation that masturbation involves is a fantasy that Keats's poetry evokes through its diction and images and that the middle class has recourse to for its self-definition.

Working within a Marxist tradition, Levinson looks on Keats's poetry as the aesthetic 'solution' to an ideological 'problem' (if not as the ideological solution to an economic one); as she writes, 'my Keats is a reconstruction of the problem . . . from the style of the solution . . . the system of wishes and resistances that had to exist in order to explain a poetry of this kind'. In this respect her models are Frederic Jameson and Jean-Paul Sartre (in his book on Flaubert). The further chapters of the book treat Keats's romances (*The Eve of St Agnes, La*

---

* Reprinted from Majorie Levinson, *Keats's Life of Allegory* (Oxford: Basil Blackwell, 1988), pp. 1–28, 36–7.

Belle Dame Sans Merci, Endymion, Hyperion and *The Fall of Hyperion, Lamia*), a deliberate choice (she explains) of poems that do not represent or thematize the polarities that define aesthetic pleasure (like the odes), so much as enigmatically enact it, making us wonder what is their point. Whereas Levinson's introductory chapter reflects on Keats's style and its reception, the other chapters interpret the poems' plots and imagery, and demonstrate that Keats's romances ultimately comment on their own implication in the modes of production and exchange (of commodities) that they portray and resist. Such a summary does little to indicate, though, the resources Levinson finds in her pleasure in Keats's and her own language.

The true cause of Mr Keats's failure is, not the want of talent, but the misdirection of it . . . [T]here is a sickliness about his productions, which shews there is a mischief at the core. He has with singular . . . correctness described his own case in the preface to Endymion [*sic*]: 'The imagination of a boy', he says, 'is healthy, and the *mature* imagination of a man is healthy; but there is a space of life between, in which the soul is in a ferment, the character undecided, the way of life uncertain, the ambition thick-sighted: thence proceeds mawkishness.' The diagnosis of the complaint is well laid down; his is a diseased state of feeling arising from the want of a sufficient and worthy object of hope and enterprise, and of the regulating principle of religion.

(Josiah Conder, *Eclectic Review*, September 1820)

He outhunted Hunt in a species of emasculated pruriency, that . . . looks as if it were the product of some imaginative Eunuch's muse within the melancholy inspiration of the Haram.

(*Blackwood's Magazine*, January 1826)

There is a cool pleasure in the very sound of the word vale. The English word is of the happiest chance. . . .It is a sort of Delphic Abstraction – a beautiful thing made more beautiful by being reflected and put in a mist.

(Keats, marginal note on *Paradise Lost*, I, 321)

[Keats] says he does not want ladies to read his poetry: that he writes for men. . . .

(Richard Woodhouse to John Taylor, letter, 20 September 1819)

The argument

There's no need, I think, to defend the statement that our commitment to a canonical Keats runs deep. Anyone who has thought critically about Keats in the past five years must appreciate the difference between the Keats commentary and the kinds of inquiries conducted on the poems of the other Romantics. This business of a canonical Keats is not a matter of explicitly idealizing or redemptive readings.[1] I'm talking about the assumptions that organize our practical understanding of the relations between Keats's life and writing and the social context in which they both materialized.

Keats, like Shakespeare, is a name for the figure of the capable poet. The best Keats criticism (Lionel Trilling, John Bayley, Christopher Ricks), and the smartest (the Harvard Keatsians), mark out the canonical extremes and define a range of problems, many of which are addressed in this study.[2] These greatly disparate critiques, sketched toward the end of this chapter, are both founded on a single premise, one which opposes *tout court* the governing thesis of the contemporary criticism of Keats's poetry. We all agree to know the man and his writing by their eminent authenticity: Bayley's 'Gemeine', Ricks's 'unmisgiving' imagination, Eliot's epistolary *idiot savant*, Vendler's true craftsman. In order to produce this knowledge, we put what the contemporary reviews called Keats's 'vulgarity' under the sign of psychic, social, and textual unselfconsciousness: roughly, the sign of sensuous sincerity. Further, by the providential tale of intellectual, moral, and artisanal development we find coded in Keats's letters, we put the vulgarity which cannot be so sublimed in the early verse and show its gradual sea-change into the rich, inclusive seriousness that distinguishes the great poetry. Thus do we rescue Keats's deep meanings from his alluring surfaces, his poetic identity from his poetical identifications. By and large, we read the poetry as a sweet solution to a bitter life: a resolution of the actual contradictions. The writing is not, we say, an escape from the real but a constructive operation performed upon it so as to bring out its Truth, which is also a new and deeply human Beauty. We describe, in short, a transformation of experience by knowledge and by the aesthetic practice which that knowledge promotes. The word that best describes this critical plot is romance: a march from alienation to identity. The governing figure of this narrative is the Coleridgean or Romantic symbol and its rhetorical device the oxymoron: irreducibly syncretic ideas. The hero of our critical history is a profoundly associated sensibility and his gift to us is the exemplary humanism of his life and art.

Trilling, Bayley and Ricks have discriminated a stylistic 'badness' that occurs throughout Keats's poetry: a certain remove whereby Keats signifies his *interest* in his representations and, we might add, in his own expressiveness. In so doing, these critics approximate the response of Keats's contemporaries, analyzed below. However, by emphasizing the psychic investment rather than the social remove which prompts it (and, by focusing mimetic and rhetorical rather than subjective disorders), Bayley and Ricks bring Keats's discursive alienations into the dominant romance.[3] Following these powerful writers, we read Keats's lapses from the good taste of innocent, object-related representation and transparent subjectivity as a determined consent to his own voluptuous inwardness *and* to the self-conscious recoil. By this willed abandon, Keats transcends both enthrallments, thereby releasing the reader into a more generous (in today's parlance, 'intersubjective') relational mode. In other words, those critics who acknowledge the stylistic vulgarity of Keats's writing put it in the redeemable field of creaturely instinct and defense, and not in the really unsettling category of externality, materiality, and ambitious reflexiveness. When Keats nods, we say, it is because he *dares* to nod ('swoon', 'sink', or 'cease'), not because he tries too hard.

The early reviews tell a different story. The most casual survey of this commentary (1817–35) reveals a response so violent and sustained, so promiscuous in its blending of social, sexual, and stylistic critique, and so sharply opposed to mainstream modern commentary as to imply a determinate insight on the part of Keats's contemporaries and a determined oversight on the part of his belated admirers. While we're all familiar with *Blackwood's* Cockney School attack (Lockhart's rebuke of Keats's literary presumption – 'so back to the shop Mr John, back to "plasters, pills, and ointment boxes . . ."'), we have not attended very closely to the sexual invective, and not at all to the relation between those two discourses. Time and again, the poetry is labelled 'profligate', 'puerile', 'unclean', 'disgusting', 'recklessly luxuriant and wasteful', 'unhealthy', 'abstracted', and 'insane'.[4] More specifically, it is graphed as a stylistically self-indulgent verse: prolix, repetitive, metrically and lexically licentious, overwrought. The diatribes culminate in the epithet 'nonsense'.

We have always related the savaging of the early poetry to the anomaly of Keats's social position and to the literary blunders which follow from that fact: generally, problems of diction, rhetoric, and subject matter, all of them reducible to the avoidable (and, finally, avoided) misfortune of Keats's coterie. Because we situate these blunders at a certain level and within a very contained biographical field, and because we isolate them from the beauties of the so-called great poetry, we have not understood the deeper insult of Keats's writing, that which explains the intensity and displacements of the early response and the equal but opposite distortions of the twentieth-century view.

From the distance of today, one can detect in those vituperative catalogues a governing discursive and even cognitive model. Keats's poetry was characterized as a species of masturbatory exhibitionism, an offensiveness further associated with the self-fashioning gestures of the petty bourgeoisie.[5] The erotic opprobrium pinpoints the self-consciousness of the verse: its autotelic reflection on its own fine phrases, phrases stylistically objectified as acquired, and therefore *mis*acquired property. The sexual language of the reviews was, of course, an expedient way to isolate Keats, but it is also a telling index to the social and existential project outlined by Keats's style. In his overwrought inscriptions of canonical models, the early readers sensed the violence of Keats's raids upon that empowering system: a violence driven by the strongest desire for an authorial manner and means, and for the social legitimacy felt to go with it. In the alienated reflexiveness of Keats's poetry, the critics read the signature of a certain kind of life, itself the sign of a new social phenomenon. Byron's famous epithet for the style of the Cockney writers, 'shabby genteel', puts the matter plainly.

> The grand distinction of the under forms of the new school of poets is their *vulgarity*. By this I do not mean that they are *coarse*, but 'shabby-genteel', as it is termed. A man may be *coarse* and yet not *vulgar*, and the reverse. . . .It is in their *finery* that the new under school are *most* vulgar, and they may be known by this at once; as what we called at Harrow 'a Sunday blood' might be easily distinguished from a gentleman. . . . In the present case, I speak of writing, not of persons.
> (Extract from letter to John Murray, 25 March 1821)

If we were not already convinced of Byron's ear for social nuance, we would only have to recall Keats's confession, 'I look upon fine Phrases like a Lover.'

Like our own criticism, the early reviews read in Keats's poetry 'a life of Allegory', but the meaning they develop by that allegory lies in the realm of social production, not aesthetics, metaphysics, or humanistic psychology. To those early readers, 'Keats' was the allegory of a man belonging to a certain class and aspiring, as that entire class was felt to do, to another: a man with particular but typical ambitions and with particular but typical ways of realizing them. A world of difference separates this hermeneutic from the 'poignantly allegorical life', an adventure in soul-making, which has become today's John Keats.[6] By respecting the social-sexual compounding evidenced by those reviews, we recover the sense of danger underlying our formalist and rhetorical readings of Keats's middling states: his adolescence, his literariness, his stylistic suspensions, his pronounced reflexiveness. We focus Keats's position – sandwiched between the Truth of the working class and the Beauty of the leisure class – not as a healthy both/and but as the monstrous neither/nor constructed in the reviews. We see that the problem of Keats's early poetry is not its regressive escapism (its instincts, so to speak), but its stylistic project: a social-ego enterprise. The deep contemporary insult of Keats's poetry, and its deep appeal (and long opacity) for the modern reader, is its idealized enactment of the conflicts and solutions which defined the middle class at a certain point in its development and which still to some extent obtain. We remember that Keats's style can delineate that station so powerfully because of his marginal, longing relation to the legitimate bourgeoisie (and its literary examplars) of his day. In emulating the condition of the accomplished middle class (the phrase is itself an oxymoron), Keats isolated the constitutive contradictions of that class. The final fetish in Keats's poetry is precisely that stationing tension.

By the stylistic contradictions of his verse, Keats produces a writing which is aggressively *literary* and therefore not just 'not Literature' but, in effect, *anti*-Literature: a parody. We will see that Keats's most successful poems are those most elaborately estranged from their own materials and procedures and thus from both a writerly and readerly subjectivity. The poetic I describe, following the lead of Keats's contemporaries, is the opposite of 'unmisgiving'.[7] The triumph of the great poetry is not its capacious, virile, humane authenticity but its subversion of those authoritarian values, effects which it could not in any case, and for the strongest social reasons, realize. This is the triumph of the double-negative. The awfulness of the early work, by contrast, is explained as an expression of the *single*, or suffered negative: a nondynamic reflection of Keats's multiple estrangements and of the longing they inspired. The accomplished poetry may be considered the negative knowledge of Keats's actual life: the production of his freedom by the figured negation of his given being, natural and social. To say this is not to consecrate Keats a precocious post-modernist, only to take seriously the social facts and meanings embedded in his representations and in the contemporary reception. It is to see in 'the continuous manner in which the whole is elaborated' a parodic reproduction of the social restrictions that marked Keats as *wanting*: unequipped, ineffectual, and deeply fraudulent.[8]

Keats did not accomplish by this greatly overdetermined stratagem the goodness he craved: that plenitude of being he worshipped in the great canonical models and which he images in Autumn's breeding passiveness. What he did produce by what Shelley called 'the bad sort of style' was a truly *negative* capability. I call this power 'virtual' to bring out its parodic relation to authorized forms of power, 'virtuoso' to suggest its professional, technically preoccupied character, and 'virtuous' by reference to its imposed and contrived limitations. In the celebrated poise of Keats's poetry, we read the effect of the impossible project set him by his interests and circumstances: to become by (mis)acquiring; to become by his writing at once authorized (properly derivative) and authorial (original); to turn his suffered objectivity into a sign of his self-estranged psyche, and to wield that sign as a shield and an ornament.

The life

The facts of Keats's life are too familiar to bear recounting here. I refer the reader to Aileen Ward's unsurpassed biography and to the important work of Walter Jackson Bate and Robert Gittings.[9] Below, I elaborate those aspects of the story that bear directly on Keats's stylistic development.

To observe that Keats's circumstances put him at a severe remove from the canon is to remark not only his educational deficits but his lack of those skills prerequisite to a transparent mode of appropriation: guiltless on the one side, imperceptible on the other. He knew some French and Latin, little Italian, no Greek. His Homer was Chapman, his Dante was Cary, his Provençal ballads translations in an edition of Chaucer, his Boccaccio Englished. Keats's art education was largely by engravings and, occasionally, reproductions. His absorption of the accessible English writers was greatly constrained by his ignorance of the originals upon which they drew and by his nonsystematic self-education. To say all this is to observe Keats's literally corrupt relation to the languages of poetry: his means of production.

We might also consider a more mundanely mechanical aspect of Keats's composition. Throughout his life, Keats felt compelled *physically* to escape his hard, London reality in order to write. A great deal of the poetry was conceived or composed at a number of modest, middle-class and, as it were, publicly designated resorts: Margate, Shanklin (the Isle of Wight), Burford Bridge (Surrey). Keats could afford only the leanest accommodations, of course, and often he adjourned to these spots alone and off-season. When even these small excursions were not possible, Keats sought his escape on Hampstead Heath, in the British Institution, or in a friend's well-furnished living room. In short, the graciously comformable bowers and dells enjoyed by Wordsworth and Coleridge were no more available to Keats than were the glory and grandeur of Greece and Rome, Byron's and Shelley's enabling resorts.

'Romantic retirement' gains a whole new dimension with Keats. Imagine the solitude of a young man in a seaside rooming house in April, a borrowed picture of Shakespeare his only companion: a man with nothing to do for a set period of time but write the pastoral epic which would, literally, *make* him. Compare this withdrawal to the seclusion of a writer musing in his garden, deserted by his wife and literary friends of an afternoon; or to the isolation of two English aristocrats, recognized poets both, galloping along the Lido and relishing their escape from the cant of high society and from its official voices. Better yet, imagine a conversation poem, a social verse, or a lyrical ballad by Keats; project from Keats's pen a sublimely inspired ode on the order of Shelley's 'Mont Blanc', or a *Defence of Poetry*, or a pamphlet on the Convention of Cintra. The experiment should point up the problematic nature for Keats of those elementary and, in the period, normative literary effects: authority, authenticity, and ease.

Apropos that last and deeply Romantic effect, ease, we recall that Keats hadn't the luxury for a 'wise passiveness'. His early detection of his disease, Tom's condition, the time constraints imposed by his medical training, his assumption of a responsibility for his sister, his haste to make a name so he could marry Fanny: all these familiar facts precluded the meditative quiescence which enabled in the other Romantics a rhetoric of surpassing naturalness.[10] Wordsworth's compositional program was simply not an option for a man who could not wait upon memory's slow digestive processes. Nor could Keats draw upon his everyday life, a monotonous struggle to get by and get ahead, for the interest, surprise, and suggestiveness which Byron and Shelley found in their large circumstances. Keats's necessary writing trips were hasty and purposive; the work of this simulated leisure was the production of pleasure, precondition for the rich, selfless, and suspended literary exercise which was Keats's dream of art. The result of these sad, self-vexing outings is a poetry evincing the paradoxes by which it is made. A poetry too happy by far, too full by half. When Shelley disdainfully rejected Keats's advice, 'load every rift with ore', he knew what he was about. He registered the class implications of Keats's plenitude, and knew that he, for one, did not have to plump his poems to the core.

Before we can begin re-reading Keats, we must really imagine what we know. We must see very clearly, as John Bayley saw, that Keats was a man whose almost complete lack of control over the social code kept him from living his life. He could not write his poetry in the manner he required, marry the woman he loved, claim his inheritance, hold his family together, or assist his friends. He could not, in short, seize any of the appurtenances of manhood. Keats was as helplessly and ignominiously a 'boy' poet as Chatterton, and Byron's 'Mankin' was a viciously knowing insult.

The range of paradoxes which Byron and his contemporaries observed in Keats's poetry is ultimately referrable to the fact that it was not given to Keats, a poet in Shelley's 'general sense', to be a poet in the most pedestrian, professional, 'restricted' sense. Keats had to make for himself a life (the training at Guy's; then, getting by on his allowance; finally, when the money ran out, the projected career of ship's surgeon), while writing a poetry that was, structurally, a denial of that life.[11] At no time did Keats make any money from his writing. (One wonders *how*, exactly,

Keats applied the title of 'poet' to himself. How did he introduce himself
in ordinary social interactions?) The oddly abstract materialism of the
poetry – its over-investment in its signs – takes on a new look when we
remember both Keats's remove from his representational manner and
means, and also his want of those real things that help people live their
lives. Is it any wonder that the poetry produced by this man should be so
autotelic, autoerotic, so fetishistic and so stuck? Should it surprise us to
find that his dearest fantasy – a picture of somebody reading, a window
on the one side, a goldfish bowl on the other – takes the form of a
multiply framed, *trompe-l'oeil* still life? 'Find the subject', we might call it;
or, what is the same thing, 'Find the frame'.

Keats's poetry was at once a tactical activity, or an escape route from
an actual life, and a final construction: the concrete imaginary to that
apparitional actual. What was, initially, a substitute *for* a grim life became
for Keats a substitute life: a real life of substitute things – simulacra –
which, though they do not nourish, neither do they waste. At the very
end of his career, Keats began, I believe, to position this parodic solution
as part of the problem. 'Lamia' is Keats's attempt to frame the
problematic of his life and writing and thus to set it aside.

It is crucial to see, as Bayley saw, that the deep desire in Keats's poetry
is not for aesthetic things or languages *per se* (that is, Byron's 'finery'),
but for the social code inscribed in them, a code which was, to Keats, a
human transformational grammar. Indeed, all Keats's meditations on art
and identity (typically, plasticity), should be related to his abiding desire,
to live. The real perversion of Keats's poetry is not its display of its
cultural fetishes but its preoccupation with the system felt to organize
those talismanic properties. Keats could have had all the urns, Psyches,
nightingales, Spenserianisms, Miltonisms, Claudes, and Poussins he
wanted; he was not, however, permitted possession of the social
grammar inscribed in that aesthetic array, and this was just what Keats
was after.

We illuminate Keats's legitimacy problem by way of the originality
anxiety that seems to have beset most of the Romantic and what used to
be called pre-Romantic poets. The past only lies like a weight on the
brain of those who inherit it. Or rather, the past imposes a special *kind* of
burden on those individual talents who feel themselves disinherited by
the Tradition, and, thus, excluded from the dialectic of old and new,
identity and difference. Wordsworth's celebrated defense of his poetical
innovations – 'every author, as far as he is great and at the same time
original, has had the task of *creating* the taste by which he is to be
enjoyed' – must be understood as the statement of a man so assured of
his entitlement that he can trust his originality to be received as
intelligible and valuable. (That Wordsworth's confidence was not always
confirmed is not the issue here.) Keats, by contrast, could not begin to

invent an original voice without first and *throughout* establishing his legitimacy: roughly, his derivativeness.

Chatterton, the poet with whom Keats felt the strongest affinities, developed a most economical solution to this problem. By his perfect reproduction of 'the medieval', Chatterton not only established that epochal concept as a normative style, thereby sanctioning his persona, Rowley, and that figure's verse; he produced as well and dialectically, *for the knowing reader*, the originality of the entire *oeuvre* (viz. poems, charts, maps, coins). We find considerable puzzlement among Chatterton's detractors, and ingenuity on the part of his defenders, regarding the anomaly of a writer who would seem to have preferred the inferior reputation of translator-editor to the glory of proper poetic genius: that is originality.[12]

Keats sidestepped Chatterton's final solution. By the self-signifying *imperfection* of his canonical reproductions (a parodic return upon his own derivativeness), Keats drew upon the licensing primacy of the code even as his *representation* of that total form changed the nature of its authority. The pronounced badness of Keats's writing figures the mythic goodness of the canon and, by figuring, at once exalts and delimits it. Thus did Keats plot for himself a scene of writing. By the double unnaturalness of his style, Keats projects the authority of an *anti*-nature, stable by virtue of its continuous self-revolutionizing and secured by its contradictions. Let me offer as a critical instance a reading of 'Chapman's Homer'.

On First Looking into Chapman's Homer

Much have I travelled [travell'd] in the realms of gold,
  And *many goodly* states and kingdoms seen;
   Round *many* western islands have I been
Which bards in fealty to Apollo hold.
Oft of one wide expanse had I been told
  That deep-browed [brow'd] Homer ruled as his demesne;
   Yet did I never breathe its pure serene
Till I heard Chapman speak out loud and bold.[:]
Then felt I like some watcher of the skies
  When a new planet swims into his ken;
Or like stout Cortez when with eagle eyes
  He stared [star'd] at the Pacific, – and all his men
Looked [Look'd] at each other with a wild surmise –
  Silent, upon a peak in Darien.

I have accented several words in the first three lines by way of amplifying the tone of Keats's address. Even if we were ignorant of Keats's social disadvantages, this fulsome claim to literary ease would give us pause. The very act of assertion, as well as its histrionically commanding and archly literary style, undermine the premise of natural authority and erudition. The contemporary reader might have observed as well some internal contradictions; not only *is* Homer the Golden Age, but not to 'have' Greek and not to have encountered Homer by the age of twenty-three is to make one's claim to any portion of the literary empire suspect (Keats's acquaintance with Pope's translation is suppressed by the sonnet). Keats effectively assumes the role of the literary adventurer (with the commercial nuance of that word) as opposed to the mythic explorer: Odysseus, Cortés, Balboa. More concretely, he advertises his corrupt access to the literary system and to those social institutions which inscribe that system systematically in the hearts and minds of young men. To read Homer in translation and after having read Spenser, Coleridge, Cary, and whoever else is included in Keats's travelogue, is to read Homer badly (in a heterodox and alienated way), and to subvert the system which installs Homer in a particular and originary place. Moreover, to 'look into' Chapman's Homer is to confess – in this case, *profess* – one's fetishistic relation to the great Original. Keats does not *read* even the translation. To 'look into' a book is to absorb it idiosyncratically at best, which is to say, with casual or conscious opportunism. Similarity, the substitution of 'breathe' for the expected 'read' in line 7 marks the rejection of a sanctioned mode of literary acquisition. To 'breathe' a text is to take it in, take from it and let it out, somewhat the worse for wear. It is, more critically, to miscategorize the object and in such a way as to proclaim one's intimacy with it. Both the claim and the title of Keats's sonnet are, in a word, vulgar.

One is reminded of Valéry's appraisal of museum pleasure: 'For anyone who is close to works of art, they are no more objects of delight than his own breathing'.[13] Keats, we observe, rejoices in his respiration and goes so far as to fetishize the very air he admits. I single out the phrase 'pure serene' not only because it is structurally foregrounded but because it reproduces in miniature the method – the working contradiction – of the sonnet. What Keats 'breathes' is, of course, anything but pure and Homeric (since he reads in translation and perversely with respect to canon protocol), and the phrase formally exposes that fact. We cannot help but see that 'pure serene', a primary reification, further calls attention to itself as a fine phrase, that Keats clearly looks upon as a lover. Not only is the phrase a Miltonic construction, but more recent usage would have characterized it as a sort of translator-ese. One thinks of Pope's 'vast profound' and indeed, of Cary's own 'pure serene', a description of Dante's ether (1814). Coleridge uses the phrase in his 'Hymn before Sunrise in the Vale of Chamouni' (1802). Keats's reproduction of the phrase designates both his access to the literary system and his mode of access – that of translator to Original.

In effect, he intentionalizes the alienation he suffers by his social deficits. By signifying the restriction, he converts it into restraint: 'might half-slumbering on its own right arm'. Let me note here that the translation of an adjective into a noun, while etymologically justifiable, transforms Homer's pure and therefore insensible atmosphere – his aura – into a palpable particular: a detached literary style and a self-reflexive one at that. What figures in Homer as a natural and epochal expressiveness is in Keats, and first, a represented object. Only by performing that office does the Homeric value assume for Keats an expressive function.

The thing to remark is the way Keats produces the virtues of his alienated access to the canon. The consummate image of the poem – that which accounts for its overall effect of 'energetic . . . calmness' – is, obviously, that of Cortés/Balboa 'star[ing] at the Pacific' while 'all his men/Looked [Look'd] at each other with a wild surmise – /Silent, upon a peak in Darien'. Cortés, we notice, is a 'stout' and staring fellow: a solid citizen. 'Stout' means, of course, 'stout-hearted', but in the context, where Cortés's direct stare at the object of his desire is juxtaposed against the 'surmise' of his men (and the alliteration reinforces these visual connections), one feels the energy of the men and the stuck or frozen state of their leader. By their surmise – a liminal, semi-detached state – the men are 'wild', a word which in the Romantic idiom means 'free'. We clearly see that the relation of the men to that (etymologically) literal 'pure serene', the Pacific, is indirect and perverse. Who in that situation would avert his gaze?

Claude Finney has reminded us that according to Keats's sources, Balboa's men were forbidden the prospect until their leader had had his full gaze.[14] We can see that the social discrepancy vividly sketched by Keats's original gets translated in the sonnet into an existential and self-imposed difference, and one that inverts the given power ratio by rendering the men, not the master, free and vital. One does not, I think, go too far in associating Keats with those capably disenfranchised men.

It is the stillness and strangeness of the men – their peculiar *durée* – which stations Keats's sonnet, all the gregarious exploration metaphors notwithstanding. Homer enters the poem as the Pacific enters the sensibilities of Cortés's men: through Chapman's/Cortés's more direct possession of/by the object of desire. Odysseus's extrovert energy animates Keats's sonnet but, again, perversely. In the Keatsian space, that energy turns self-reflexive, reminding us perhaps of Tennyson's 'Ulysses'. The poem looks at itself as the men look at each other. The virtue of both looks is their impropriety; what they refuse by that gesture is the Gorgon stare, the direct embrace of and by the authorizing Original. Keats's poem 'speak[s] out loud and bold' by not speaking 'out' at all. We finish the sonnet, which seems to be predicated on such a simple *donnée*, and we wonder where we have travelled. What happened

to Homer, and to Keats for that matter? Why does Keats interpose
between himself and his ostensible subject Chapman, Cary, Coleridge,
Gilbert, Robertson, Herschel, Balboa, Cortés, and Cortés's men? Why
does Keats leave us with his off-center cameo, an image of turbulent
stasis among the extras of the cast when what we expect is a 'yonder lie
the Azores' flourish by the principal? What *is* this poem? By the
conventions it sets, it should strike us as a graceful display of literary
inspiration and gratitude. But it seems other, and otherwise. How do we
explain the real power of its slant rhyme?

Let me recall Hunt's comment on the sonnet: 'prematurely masculine'.
By emphasizing the adverb for a change, we begin to see that Keats's
unnatural (illicit) assumption of power, signified by the 'poetical' octet,
does not *qualify* the 'masculinity' of the sestet, it constitutes it. The direct
and natural compression of the sestet is the stylistic effect of the
displayed disentitlement that is the functional representation of the
opening eight lines. The pivot which constructs this before-and-after
dynamic (the coordinates for a range of ratios: imitation–genuine,
protest–power, struggle–ease) is, of course, the experience of reading
Chapman. The experience takes place, significantly, in the breach
between the two movements of the sonnet. Rather than imitate
Chapman, Keats reproduces Chapman's necessarily parodic (that is,
Elizabethan) inscription of Homer. The queerness of Chapman's 'mighty
line, loud-and-bold' version is rewritten in Keats's own parodic
Elizabethan*ism*, and, through the queerness of the Cortés/Balboa image.
It is the self-reflexive, fetishistic inscription of the canon – the display of
bad access and misappropriation – that emancipates Keats's words.
Keats's sonnet breaks free of Homer and Chapman by mis-giving both.
By the English he puts on Homer's serenity (he reifies it) and on
Chapman's 'masculine' extrovert energy, Keats produces the perpetual
imminence which is the hero of his sonnet. In the Keatsian idiom, we
could call that imminence or suspension a 'stationing', with an ear for the
full social resonance of Keats's aesthetic word.[15]

The instance of this poem would suggest that Keats's relation to the
Tradition is better conceived as dialogic (Bakhtin) than dialectic (Bloom).[16]
The poetry does not clear a space for itself by a phallic agon; it opens
itself to the Tradition, defining itself as a theater wherein such contests
may be eternally and inconclusively staged.[17] The authority of this poetry
consists in its detachment from the styles or voices it entertains. By this
detachment, these styles become *signatures*: not audible voices but
visible, material *signs* of canonical voices. These signs – like all such
marks, inauthentic and incomplete – are *not*, ultimately, mastered by the
master-of-ceremonies. And because they remain external to authorial
consciousness, theirs is the empowering virtue of the supplement. In

these magic supplements, 'Things semi-real', lies the terrific charm of Keats's poetry.

The contained badness of 'Chapman's Homer' constitutes its goodness, which is to say, its rhetorical force. The paradox hinges, naturally, on the word 'contained'. When Keats is great, it is because he *signifies* his alienation from his *materia poetica*, a fact that modern criticism and textual studies have suppressed.[18] This alienation – inevitable, given Keats's education, class, and opportunities – was highly expedient. By it, Keats could possess the 'stuff of creativity' without becoming possessed by it. By 'stuff', I do not mean Bloom's primary, inspirational matter but the means and techne for exercises in literary production. Keats's poetry, inspired by translations, engravings, reproductions, schoolroom mythologies, and Tassie's gems, delivers itself through these double and triple reproductions as the 'true, the blushful Hippocrene'. That phrase describes, ironically, *precisely* a substitute truth. Again, Byron understood these things; 'You know my opinion of *that second-hand* school of poetry.'

Discussion

The early commentary has more to teach us. Byron's vivid epithets – 'a Bedlam vision', a 'sad abortive attempt at all things, "signifying nothing"' – suggest that the masturbation trope was a most economical way of designating the poetry nonsense: not bad Literature but *non*-Literature. In practical terms, it would seem that the association of Keats's poetry with masturbation was a way to isolate Keats without agonizing him.

We make sense of this tactic in two ways. First, the commonplace alignment of masturbation with madness suggests that whereas homosexuality was part of the normative heterosexual configuration – either a standard deviation or binary Other – masturbation was outside the curve: the age's $\frac{1}{0}$, 'signifying nothing'.[19] This speculation is consistent with the class affronts (revelations of practical and ideological projects) leveled by Keats's poetry and explored below. Second, while 'nonsense' attacks always suppress unwanted sense, this particular noncognition additionally implies a response to the subjective irreality of Keats's self-reflexive poetry. 'Frigging [one's] *Imagination*' is one thing; frigging an imagination tenanted by other minds is another and a double-perversity. ('Frig' means 'to chafe or rub', 'to agitate the limbs' (*OED*), and most commonly, of course, to copulate. The *'Imagination'* to which Byron refers is, thus, a male and female property; or, Keats was accused of masturbating/fucking a Nothing.) Byron's contempt for Keats's fetishistic relation to his acquired literary languages – borrowed 'finery' – masks a fearful insight into the subjective vacancy of Keats's writing. The

'Bedlam' association registers Keats's want of a propriety subject-form: a voice distinct from the entertained canonical echoes and offering itself as a point, however 'bad', of readerly identification and authorial control. In Keats's poetry, the diverse cultural languages which we call the Tradition are both the means and the *manner* of representation, both object and subject. The 'self' upon which the verse reflects is, precisely, 'not-self': a fetishized, random collection of canonical signatures. One can see that this bad imitation of that earnest Romantic exercise, self-reflection, was, in effect, a burlesque. Keats's operations objectified the naturalness (originality, autonomy, and candor) of all writerly origins, putting those transparencies at risk. Even Byron, that determinedly mad bad man, was threatened; Byronic irony, no matter how inclusive, is always recuperated by the biographical subject-form coded in all the poems. Keats's poetry is differently, but no *more* masturbatory than Wordsworth's or Byron's, the largest, most virile poets of the age. We could say that Keats offended his generation so deeply by practicing one of its dominant modes of literary production while showing his hand. The sexual slander developed in the reviews registers Keats's relation to the Tradition, understood as a limited-access code with powerful social functions, and the class contradictions which that relation stylistically defined. At the same time, the critique displaces those contradictions to the sphere of private life and pathology: a safety zone. Thus was a serious, or materially designing sensuousness converted into a grave sensual disease.

A juxtaposition of two professional responses to Keats's poetry gives us a practical purchase on the meaning of Keats's style. Wordsworth and Byron agreed on very little; their consensus on Keats argues their glimpse of that in his poetry which challenged a common interest or which exposed a contradiction at the center of both their very different practices.

Wordsworth's brisk dismissal of Keats's 'Hymn to Pan' – 'a Very pretty piece of Paganism' – concisely maps the manifold of impressions I've been describing. By 'pretty', with its resonance to 'fancy' (Imagination's weak sister), and its evocation of the ingenious, the trivial, the overcultivated *and* infantile, Wordsworth suggests both the mechanical elegance of Keats's writing and its servility to an imperfectly discriminating appetite. The adjective describes a taste at once immature and effete, under- and over-refined, and in both cases unhealthy: an appetite for 'dainties' or for 'luxuries', baby-food or caviar.[20] Wordsworth's disgust is the revulsion of a plain-eating, water-drinking man for a connoisseur of pulpy strawberries and claret. It is the contempt of a man who *transcends* class – an *essential* man addressing his peers in a language as limpid and restorative as mountain streams – for a man to whom class is a fetish, and whose language, impure and overcharged, must spoil the taste and the constitution of his readers. Putting the critique on the side of production, and with an ear to that 'Paganism', we might describe Wordsworth's Keats as a purveyor of substitute pleasures: real signs that provide lacks and differences.

Wordsworth's 'piece', while it describes, of course, the formal self-containment of the Hymn within *Endymion*, also marks out the thingness, partiality, and externality of Keats's attempt at an archetypal discourse of presence.[21] The word suggests the *essentially* extraneous character of Keats's writing, if we can allow that solecism for a moment. Wordsworth is out to imply the sheer factitiousness of the verse, an interested representation of what is already for Keats a received idea or, following Wordsworth, a 'poeticism': 'the Pagan'. Wordsworth's 'ism' is his way of naming this double fetish. The singsong alliteration of the phrase, an imitative tactic, contrastively conjures the austere, holistic, deeply qualitative hedonism which is Wordsworth's Pagan: 'the pleasure which there is in life itself'. The conceptual resonance amplifies the ontological corruptness of Keats's partial, purposive, and mechanical self-pleasuring. In a phrase (Wordsworth's), Keats's is a poetry of 'outrageous stimulation'; we might say, the pleasure of the ornament.

By the memorable epithets Byron coined for Keats and his poetry ('a sort of mental masturbation – frigging his *Imagination*', 'Johnny Keats's *piss-a-bed* poetry', 'the drivelling idiotism of the Mankin', 'dirty little blackguard Keates', 'Self-polluter of the human mind'), Byron crystallized the sexual associations diffused throughout the more modulated responses. A more interesting phrase, however, is Byron's 'shabby genteel', quoted above, an expression which seems to emerge from a different perceptual field. In context, the phrase identifies Keats's vulgarity less with his motives (cheap thrills; supplemental delights), than with his methods. Specifically, Byron censures Keats's display of his literary entitlement. 'It is in their *finery* that the new under school are *most* vulgar . . . I speak of writing, not of persons.' Byron's 'finery', like Wordsworth's 'Paganism', designates those elements in the poetry which are perceptible *as* styles ('ery', 'ism'), because imperfectly appropriated, heaped heterogeneously together, and reflected on by an 'author' who is but the alter ego to those styles. 'I don't mean he is *indecent*, but viciously soliciting his own ideas into a state, which is neither poetry nor any thing else but a Bedlam vision . . .' By his three-way equation, linking self-reflection, masturbation, and middle-class acquisition and display, Byron clarifies the broad social offensiveness of Keats's poetry.

Byron is repelled by Keats's psychic fane first, because it is filled with false things: not human qualities or even authorial properties, but *props*, or material signs of literary reality. Worse, everything acquired by the Keatsian consciousness, no matter how 'good' originally, gets falsified within that precinct. Fine becomes 'finery', cultivation becomes Culture, whole and living speech is rendered a quotation, and everything is as an artifact in an overwrought cabinet: framed, spotlighted, exhibited as possessions that are also signs *of* possession.[22] Keats's 'solicitation' of his ideas was manifest because practiced *on* false-consciousness, and 'vicious' because tending to *falsify* (that is, reify) some privileged *forms* of consciousness. Keats's canonical 'abstractions' (the word recurs obsessively in the reviews) effectively exposed the canon as a construct, as authoritarian, and as subject to violation. This is to say, Keats's scavenging replaced the authority of Authority, a natural and internal quality, with that of a more literal, original author-ity: with the figure of the literary entrepreneur. No poetic style could have been more abhorrent to the respectively private and public transparencies of Wordsworth and Byron, or rather, to the class subject forms projected by those good manners.

Keats's strangely alienated reflexiveness carried, I believe, an even stronger social charge than the one I've just identified. We get at this meaning by setting Keats's methods against the Wordsworthian model, which we read as an exemplary Romantic form, and by glossing that comparison with another of Byron's colorful commentaries. The governing antinomy here is not legitimacy/orginality but pleasure/work.

Wordsworth's poetry, like so much of Keats's, typically represents its coming *into* being as its reason *for* being, and also its chief delight. What distinguishes the Wordsworthian from the Keatsian method are its defenses against a mechanically divisive – analytic, one might say – reception. The devices of Wordsworth's poetry fend off a reading which would dissociate the verbal means from authorial and rhetorical ends, and, thus, set 'poet' against both 'human being' and reader, writing against speaking and reading. Wordsworth discourages this kind of attention first, by figuring the poem's formal materialization as a generically idealized human process: a development independent of authorial design and direction. Wordsworth's narrators loudly proclaim their passivity; and, their unselfconsciousness invites us to identify narrator with poet. By these techniques, the work's semiotic center of gravity gets displaced to the reader, a postulated activity center. The narrator's encounter with an object, memory, or event is the condition of a narration which claims to be nothing but a self-accounting, offered to the reader as a humanizing opportunity. 'It is no tale; but, should you think, / Perhaps a tale you'll make it' ('Simon Lee'). One is meant to translate this disclaimer as follows: this *is* a tale, a tale of telling, but like all discourse, it is also a contract, a 'Thing semi-real'. To actualize the form, the reader must take it 'kindly', or according to the usage of *essential* humankind. Any suggestion of distinct and divisive purposiveness – 'particular', *interested*, or class-specific self-consciousness – is neutralized by the textual gesture toward, if not a communicative, then a shared existential and social circuit. Wordsworth's pleasure becomes *our* delight when we cast off our minute particulars and make ourselves him; thus, of course, do we also discover the *essential* being within our historical being.

The framing devices of Keats's poetry do not, like Wordsworth's preemptive techniques, usher us into the poem, they frame us out. Think of the 'Ode on a Grecian Urn'. The final, bracketed epigram – formally, a parody of Wordsworth's closing, intersubjective immediacies – puts the entire poem and all its apparently human and authorial anguish in aesthetic space: museum space, to be precise. The triumph of this ode is its transformation of poetry into scripture, sound into silence, relief (the Truth of fantasy) into Relief (an art of surfaces: Beauty). 'End-stopped feel' is as good a phrase as any to describe the alienating closure of Keats's poetry.[23]

Moreover, Keats's poems tend rather to distinguish than to identify narrator (or lyric 'I') and writer. Rarely do we hear his verse as the utterance of an unmediated human voice. Even in so magical, so historically *sincere* a poem as 'La Belle Dame', one must remember that an anonymous working brain is continuously engendering and overhearing the reciprocally exclusive languages of the balladeer and 'knight-at-arms', low and high languages that can only engage within the artificial space of a sentimental ballad.[24] Keats, like Wordsworth, teases us out of thought by making his method of representation his representational *object* in the sense of 'purpose'. The difference is that by fetishizing this purpose, Keats makes of it an 'object' in the material sense and a 'subject' in the philosophic sense. With these transformations, self-reflexiveness crystallizes as a mode of production with determinate social meanings and purposes, some of them having no immediacy for the reader, others possessed of the most threatening and, thus, rejected immediacy. Keats's double alienation, from the textual interior and from his audience, outlines the contradictions which make the work, contradictions invisibilized by subject-related writing and object-related sex. Keats's pleasure stands revealed as work.

Again, consider the phenomenology of the Wordsworthian narration. The poet effortlessly reaps his memory of its rich and naturally integrated meanings. Indeed, by emphasizing both the strain of those lives which are often the originals of his mnemonic experience and the wise unconsciousness which fashions the inner verse, *and*, by arousing his readers to the challenge of their high and arduous calling, Wordsworth underscores the pure pleasure which is the poet's special gift: his character, even. The poet

is a man speaking to men: a man, it is true, endued with more lively
sensibility, more enthusiasm and tenderness, who has a greater
knowledge of human nature, and a more comprehensive soul . . . a
man pleased with his own passions and volitions, and who rejoices
more than other men in the spirit of life that is in him; delighting to
contemplate similar volitions and passions as manifested in the goings-
on of the Universe, and habitually impelled to create them where he
does not find them.

(Preface to *Lyrical Ballads*, 1802)

By contrast, Keats's careful inventories of his overdecorated psychic
interiors are at once pointless and busy, giving us something very like an
inversion or parody of Wordsworth's wise passiveness. Keats's authorial
exercise seems unrelated to the reader's imagined enjoyment, and to any
of the more familiar forms of expressive gratification. The early readers,
who recognized in Keats's ease a *display* of ease, experienced the verse as
entirely dis-eased. Again, it is Byron who clarifies the social
offensiveness of the Keatsian difference.

Here is the strange little fable Byron produced for the purpose of
characterizing Keats's poetry.

The *Edinburgh* praises Jack Keats or Ketch, or whatever his names are:
why, his is the *Onanism* of Poetry – something like the pleasure an
Italian fiddler extracted out of being suspended daily by a Street
Walker in Drury Lane. This went on for some weeks: at last the Girl
went to get a pint of Gin – met another, chatted too long, and Cornelli
was *hanged outright before she returned*. She like is the trash they praise,
and such will be the end of the *outstretched* poesy of this miserable Self-
polluter of the human mind.

(Extract from letter to John Murray, 4 November 1820)

We recall that during the Regency, as before, 'Jack Ketch' was an
appellation for the common hangman, and, that the name and character
were strongly associated with the puppet-play of Punchinello (*OED*).
With this double-dangling as his starting point, Byron goes on to explore,
as it were, the social and sexual nuances of the resonance attaching to
Keats's name. The fiction he unfolds describes a particularly laborious
form of masturbation, *le coup de corde*, a trick that requires the technical
assistance, here, of a prostitute. The 'Italian fiddler's' busy contrivance is
emphasized by his partner's fecklessness, and the comedy of the story
(literally, a 'hoist by one's own petard' narrative) involves the exposure
of a work–pleasure ratio where we least expect to find it, at the center of
an autoerotic activity. (The joke is perhaps more pointed yet; Byron
involves a distinctly lower-class character in a perversion associated with

aristocratic refinement, *ennui,* and unselfconsciousness – dare we say, *hauteur.* Presumably, one's valet would not leave one hanging. Byron's aspiring fiddler is punished for his violation of *social,* not sexual proprieties.) Byron's *'outstretched',* a comment on the ambitiousness, elaboration and sexual tension of Keats's poetry, says it all. So does this extract from an 1820 review appearing in the *London Magazine and Monthly Critical and Dramatic Review*: 'he says nothing like other men, and appears always on the stretch for words to shew his thoughts are of a different texture from all other writers'. The reviewer recommends to the clever but overwrought lad, suffering from a sort of literary priapism, some country air, a change of diet, and an introduction to 'the *retreat* at York', a private madhouse.

What Byron is driving at is the contradiction which organizes both masturbation and the reproductive habits of the middle class. Below, I propose that the dream or the concept of masturbation is one of conscious unconsciousness: 'the feel of not to feel it', or, as in the Nightingale Ode, sensible numbness. (Here again, we detect a debased because reified version of that Wordsworthian paradigm, 'wise passiveness'.) Inasmuch as one is both worker and pleasurer, giver and receiver, subject and object in masturbation, the act should produce a rare psychic consolidation. However, both the technical groundplot (a part of the body is fetishized and overworked), and the absence of a distracting other to absorb the purposiveness of the activity and naturalize the techne, install with unusual force the divided psyche, which must know itself busy for luxury.

No one cared, of course, about Keats's exposure of the contradiction which informs masturbation. What did concern Wordsworth and Byron was the poetry's exposure of the relation between 'working brain' and the 'spontaneous overflow' or 'rattling on exactly as I talk' of Romantic poetry: that is, Keats's demystification of a prestigious idea of literary production. In the case of Wordsworth, we might call this method 'natural selection': a darkling deliberation effected by memory and emerging as a spontaneous, strictly processual value. Byron's worldliness, the counterpart to Wordsworth's naturalism, establishes authorial purpose within a psyche so profoundly socialized (so *inherited,* one might say), and *accomplishes* those purposes through audience reciprocities so exact, that calculation has no place to surface. Both protocols are commonplaces of Romantic criticism. Less obvious, perhaps, is the fact that while these myths of production negate what the poets conceived as the age's dominant *material* productive mode, the mechanical, they also *rehearse* a mode of social and ideological production.

In order to constitute its structural betweenness (a neither-nor, 'Nothing' state), an 'existence', the middle class had to expose the historicity of value, clearing the ground as it were for its own violation of inherited and naturalized values. At the same time, and so as to sanction this originality and safeguard its middling position, threatened on the lower front by imitation, and the upper by assimilation, the class in the middle had to represent its own, invented values as either ahistorical or as history's telos. The trick was to look valuably and essentially ambitious – history's coming class – and also eternal: a class dreamed by Adam, who awoke and found it real. One logical solution to this stylistic problem (we will see it in Keats) was the phenomenology of the *nunc stans,* or the look of an *eternally coming* class, in motion/in place forever. The display of ease, a contradiction in terms, was another device for converting nothingness into prolific tension. By its self-identification as a profitably consuming class, the bourgeoisie imitated the *ontologically* productive condition of the aristocracy. At the same time, the rhetorical orientation of this mimesis, as well as its fetishism (the effect of its semiotic interests), marked it as an ambitious gesture: literally, as *wanting.* The power of this mark, a negative originality, was, of course, its determined negativity. A class that is *self*-violating makes itself inviolable. That which has no center cannot be seized; what has no character cannot be defamed, and what is always and by definition moving is not easily removed.

I am describing a 'bad' solution to an ideological bind: on the one hand, the middle-class commitment to a program of social mobility (Keats's 'camelion poet': an ethic of becoming, or, less Romantically, a work ethic), and on the other, its longing for the authority connected with the generative passivity, stable identity, and 'quiet being' which was an influential fantasy of the leisure class. Keats, we shall see, motivates the contradiction in the style of the middle class but, because this was not 'naturally' *his* solution, and because it was, for him, greatly polyvalent, that style gets reified. Keats works at his pleasure and stations himself by that oxymoron. Wordsworth, as we saw, tends to suppress that conflictual figure which is no less the agency of his art than of Keats's. Wordsworth's genius is to operate a kind of double-standard. Even as he identifies poet (for him, *speaker*) with reader–listener as both essential men, he splits apart production and consumption into respectively passive and active moments. The poet easily overflows with his own pre(*consciously*)meditated verse. The reader, however, is forbidden the spontaneous, inward delight which is the poet's prerequisite and prerogative. Indeed, the reader cannot emulate that noble ease without degrading it and himself, becoming but a seeker after 'the pleasure of Frontiniac or sherry'. Wordsworth's readers are instructed to *work* at their meanings, to 'find' tales in the things which the poet effortlessly makes available to them. By contrast, Keats's ambitiously masturbatory poetry correctly positions the work–pleasure contradiction in the act of production. Is it any wonder that Byron, a poet who reaped such profits by producing himself as an aristocrat for the delectation of the middle class, and Wordsworth, who did well enough by his 'habits of meditation', should have been so shaken by Keats?

Masturbation may be conceived as a fantasy of pleasure without the death of perfect gratification: or, meaning/value without the loss of reflexive consciousness *or* the object. The fantasized masturbatory experience is one of energy *and* luxury; giving and receiving; high (cerebral) and low (genital); infinite metamorphosis contemplated by a center of consciousness keen to enjoy that lability. Ideally, or in imagination, masturbation establishes a psychic wholeness which *knows itself* to be dialectically contingent. Thus is it also vitally, *capably in*complete.[25] The defensive virtue of masturbation, understood as a fantasy *of* (in place of/in addition to) proper sex, is its protection against the drive which, correctly enacted, must obliterate the consciousness which would *own* that pure pleasure, that death. 'Now more than ever seems it rich to die, / To cease upon the midnight with no pain. . . .Still wouldst thou sing, and I have ears in vain – / To thy high requiem become a sod.' Masturbation – the part for / in addition to the whole, the fantasy for / plus the actual, the oblique for / with the direct, the sign for / alongside the thing – is a holding action: a way of holding on to a holding off. The formula could be recast in temporal terms. Masturbation, that unnaturally hasty act, dreams of a 'slow time': a duration which neither wastes nor realizes, at once history's negation and its fulfillment. 'Deathwards progressing / To no death was that visage.' (Or, for a categorical association, 'purposiveness without purpose', Kant's definition of aesthetic experience.) Many of our fondest moments in Keats's poetry describe this condition: 'Their lips touched [touch'd] not, but had not bade adieu.' (The very time signature of 'To Autumn' is a code for this kind of *durée*, it is also the subject and object of this *undying* poem.) Many describe a fantasy wherein the sign (let us say, the Tradition: an empowering reproductive apparatus), and the thing (John Keats, an author-original) are simultaneous but distinct: a metonymic dream, or a fantasy of *being*, put under erasure by *having* and, thus, violated, idealized, effectuated, and *possessed*. Another way to frame this fantasy is as an instant(iation) wherein Beauty (the sign of legitimacy: the signifying possession) and Truth (the natural, unspeaking attribute) do not antithesize or succeed one another, neither do they coalesce. They exist, rather, side by side: parallel, mutually delimiting total systems, value *and* 'existences', Symbolic *and* Imaginary zones. In class terms, a logical category, all these couplings describe a conjunction of *having*, a function of distance, difference, and loss, and *being*, the form of presence, identity, and plenitude. In class terms, a *social* category, this conjunction describes a proprietary style and function. Nowhere is this coincidence so clearly and economically expressed as in Keats's typically ambiguous 'of' locutions, where the preposition is used both partitively (or genitively), and descriptively (for example, 'bride of quietness': belonging to quietness [having], and characterized by quietness [being]).

I have been describing a masturbation fantasy: the *concept* shadowed forth by Keats's strong practice. The special offensiveness of Keats's very early writing arises from its *incomplete* perverseness: its failure, thus, to realize that concept. (Byron's qualification, 'I don't mean he is *indecent* . . .', should be taken as part of the criticism; regarding the sexuality of Keats's writing, more *would* have been less.) The early poetry is bad in the commonplace colloquial sense: accidentally or passively imperfect. What vitiates it is the innocence of its self-consciousness, the intimacy of wish and word.

The poetry we call great is that which *signifies* – indeed, fetishizes – its alienation from its representational objects and subjects, and, thus, from its audience. This poetry is a discourse whose self-possession is a function of its profound structural *dis*possession; its pleasure is its knowledge of a 'wished away'/unavailable workaday world. 'Pleasant pain', 'a drowsy numbness pains/My sense', 'ditties of no tone', 'unheard' melodies. Each of these phrases, fetishized negations, captures the (il)logic of Keats's masturbatory exercise and of its social objective: a state of being at once 'first, and last, and midst, and without end' – a fair definition, that, of a state of nullity.

Finally, 'Lamia' evinces a badness that indicates a new scene of writing. Keats's bold plot in this last romance is to analyze materially and conceptually his own mode of literary production. The romance undoes itself even as it unfolds, and there is no interest in recuperating this deconstruction at another level. Neither are the contradictions motivated in the manner of the canonically central romances. 'Lamia' is the closest thing we have in the Romantic repertoire to a scientific poem.

I have already talked about the special and disturbing self-reflexiveness of Keats's poetry, one that brings out the difference between the subject and its internalized models, not their identity. To 'overhear' Keats's poetry is to hear nothing *but* intonation, to feel nothing but style and its meaningfulness. The effect is explained, of course, by the problematic nature of Keats's subjectivity, which we would call 'authorial' if Keats had had any other kind, and if that were not exactly his problem. Throughout this book, I try to show the terribly *dynamic* character of Keats's inner representations of those particular 'outsides' we call 'audience': both 'the public' (an idea of the present), and the People, philosophically characterized (the Tradition, a past and future thing). To read Wordsworth or Byron is to feel that the style is accessory to the subject or content of the writing. To read Keats is to focus the 'aboutness' of the verse as the vehicle for a stylistic design.

This impression of interestedness is just what we usually mean when we say that a poem is 'rhetorical'. Yet with Keats we are treating of something we can't really call rhetoric at all. While his poetry 'elaborates reciprocities at all registers', the elaboration is definitely laborious: more in the way of primary production than reflection. Moreover, where the textual labor does develop reciprocities already in place, these are not, typically, *audience* reciprocities – not, that is, engagements with institutionally mediated forms – but reciprocities with the structures and relations of production. If we are willing to give up the security of the graduated exegesis – an inductive or deductive advance from level to level until such time as the text – context distinction, which one had dissolved, reappears – we may begin to feel the shocking directness of Keats's engagement with the profoundest orders of determination. In that we have so deeply and for so long identified with Keats – so taken his subject-form for our own – it would seem that we can only start seeing him *clearly in the idea of him* by an act of self-estrangement. We must try to make ourselves anomalous subjects – 'bad' critics – in order to read Keats properly, even while remembering that this metamorphosis is also an effect of such a reading.

Notes

1. ALAN BEWELL's essay 'The Political Implication of Keats's Classicist Aesthetics' (*Studies in Romanticism*, **25** (Summer 1986): 220–9) represents the beginning of a departure from the critical norm for Keats studies. Bewell's sensitivity to the special political discourse of the writer situated by the *polis* on its *under*side or *between* its categorical positions, intimates a criticism beyond the margins of formalist, thematic, biographical, and metaphysical inquiry as these have developed in Romanticist scholarship over the past thirty years, *and also*, beyond the 'new historicism'. This last observation is part of an argument about the new historicism in Romantic studies (see LEVINSON, 'The New Historicism: Back to the Future', in Levinson et al., *Rethinking Historicism* (Oxford: Blackwell, 1989).

2. WALTER JACKSON BATE, *John Keats* (Cambridge, Mass.: Harvard University Press, 1963); JOHN BAYLEY, 'Keats and Reality', *Proceedings of the British Academy* (1962): 91–125; DOUGLAS BUSH, *John Keats* (New York: 1966); DAVID PERKINS, *The Quest for Permanence* (Cambridge, Mass.: Harvard University Press, 1959); CHRISTOPHER RICKS, *Keats and Embarrassment* (Oxford: Clarendon Press, 1974); LIONEL TRILLING, 'The Fate of Pleasure' in *Beyond Culture* (London: Secker and Warburg, 1955); HELEN VENDLER, *The Odes of John Keats* (Cambridge, Mass.: Harvard University Press, 1983); EARL WASSERMAN, *The Finer Tone* (Baltimore, Md: Johns Hopkins University Press, 1953).

3. John Bayley shrewdly divines that Keats's badness *is* his goodness. Had Bayley pushed his *aperçu* a little further, he would have come up against the

meanings shadowed forth by the contemporary criticism. He would, perhaps, have associated the vulgarity of Keats's poetry with the situation, activities, and interests of the burgeoning middle class. As it is, Bayley's interpretative construct neatly registers this association by negation. 'Das Gemeine' – a postulate of healthy, earthy, Elizabethan (that is, sociologically and physically nonstratified) consciousness – is the mirror image of the nineteenth-century Keats, or of a poetry experienced as sick, pretentious, horribly contemporary, and thoroughly mannered. To the early readers, Keats's poetry was the expression of a 'folk' degraded by a bad eminence: the petty bourgeoisie.

4. All excerpts from contemporary notices are drawn from DONALD REIMAN, *The Romantics Reviewed: Contemporary Reviews of British Romantic Writers* (New York: Garland Publishing, 1972), C, I, 91–3; C, I, 95; C, I, 330–3; C, I, 339; C, I, 344–5; C, I, 385; C, I, I, 423–4; C, II, 470; C, II, 479; C, II, 531; C, II, 587–90; C, II, 614; C, II, 768–9; C, II, 807–8; C, II, 824–5; C, II, 829–30; and from G.M. Matthews (ed.), *Keats, The Critical Heritage* (London: Routledge & Kegan Paul, 1971), pp. 35, 129–31, 150, 208–10, 248, 251. Censored Byron material checked against LESLIE MARCHAND, *Byron's Letters and Journals*, vol. 7, 1820 (Cambridge, Mass.: Belknap Press, 1977), p. 217 (from letter to John Murray, 4 November 1820; Matthews lists it as 4 September).

5. The association of masturbation with the individualism and materialism of the early middle class is something of an established literary theme. Swift's Master Bates, the physician to whom Gulliver is apprenticed, teaches his student more than a middle-class trade, he teaches him the principles of acquisition and display (in Gulliver's case, anthropological), which constitute the middle class as an *ideological* phenomenon over and above its economic being.

6. The much-quoted phrase 'poignantly allegorical life' is Bate's allusion to Keats's own observation that Shakespeare led 'a life of Allegory' (*Letters of John Keats*, ed. Robert Gittings, Oxford: Oxford University Press, 1970; 1979, p. 218).

7. 'Unmisgiving' is Ricks's class term, taken from Keats, for the social, psychic, and rhetorical generosity of the poetry.

8. FREDRIC JAMESON, *Sartre: The Origins of a Style* (New York: Columbia University Press, 1961; 1984), p. vii.
   In the course of my current research, I've discovered two books, both marvels of textual and theoretical exposition, that coincide closely with my reading of Keats's strategic defenses against, as well as his longing for, social and canonical majority. I refer to LOUIS RENZA's *'A White Heron' and the Question of Minor Literature* (Madison, Wisconsin: University of Wisconsin Press, 1984), pp. 11–129; and DAVID LLOYD's *Nationalism and Minor Literature: James Clarence Mangan and the Emergence of Irish Cultural Nationalism* (Berkeley,: University of California Press, 1987), pp. 19–26. I thank Renza for refreshing my memory of LESLIE BRISMAN's *Romantic Origins* (Ithaca: Cornell University Press, 1978): specifically, Brisman's derivation of George Darley's originality from his 'posture of weakness'.

9. AILEEN WARD, *John Keats, the Making of a Poet* (New York: Viking, 1963); W.J. BATE, *John Keats*, R.GITTINGS, *John Keats* (London: Heinemann, 1968). All source information from CLAUDE FINNEY, *The Evolution of Keats' Poetry*, 2 vols (New York: Russell & Russell, 1963); GEORGE RIDLEY, *Keats's Craftsmanship* (Oxford: Clarendon Press, 1933); IAN JACK, *Keats and the Mirror of Art* (Oxford:

Clarendon Press, 1967); MIRIAM ALLOTT, *The Poems of John Keats* (London and New York: Longman and Norton, 1970; 1972).

10. See GEORG LUKÁCS, *History and Class Consciousness*, trans. R.Livingstone (Cambridge, Mass.: MIT Press, 1971), pp. 164–72. See also FREDRIC JAMESON, *Marxism and Form, Twentieth-Century Dialectical Theories of Literature* (Princeton, NJ: Princeton University Press, 1971), on the worker's negative privilege: the lack of that leisure needed to 'intuit [the outside world] in the middle-class sense'. By the adjective 'middle-class' Jameson means the static and contemplative immediacy required by industrial capitalism's productive structures and relations.

11. Apropos Keats's medical training, see AILEEN WARD, *John Keats, the Making of a Poet*, pp. 23–4.

12. MARJORIE LEVINSON, *The Romantic Fragment Poem* (Chapel Hill, NC: University of North Carolina Press, 1986), pp. 41–3, 239–40.

13. Quoted in THEODOR ADORNO, *Prisms*, trans. Weber and Weber (Cambridge, Mass.: MIT Press, 1967; 1983). The essay from which that quotation derives, 'Valery Proust Museum', deeply informs my discussion.

14. FINNEY, *The Evolution of Keats' Poetry*, vol. 1, p. 126: 'When, with infinite toil, they had climbed up the greater part of that steep ascent, Balboa commanded his men to halt, and advanced alone to the summit, that he might be the first who should enjoy a spectacle which he had so long desired.' From ROBERTSON's *History of America*.

15. In his notes on Milton, Keats comments on 'what may be called his stationing or statuary. He is not content with simple description, he must station . . .', quoted in JACK, *Keats and the Mirror of Art*, p. 142.

16. To the extent that the inner voices in Keats's poetry tend to be maintained as signs, and also as signs of otherness, the 'we' experience central to Vološinov's dialogic analysis is missing. Keats's dialogism conforms more to the Bakhtinian model.

17. Allusions to the indeterminacy of Keats's gender (for example, 'Mankin', 'effeminate', 'boyish') should be taken as responses to Keats's mode of literary production or to the androgyny thereby implied. Keats's discourse 'mans' itself by a self-consciously autotelic receptivity, at once 'unmanning' the Tradition and, paradoxically, feminizing itself as well. Indeed, we might illuminate some of the more mysterious female figures in Keats's poetry by identifying them with the code or languages at once feared and desired by Keats: a phallic order. Aileen Ward's compelling defense of Fanny Brawne – her insistence that Keats loved Fanny precisely for the unpoetical distinctness of her character – is not contradicted by Keats's fascination with women like Isabella Jones: protean women who seemed, in addition, capable of transforming others, and, by liberating them from themselves, freeing them from their self-consciousness as well. Keats could love Fanny; he could *use* the Isabella Joneses of his life. What I'm suggesting is a loose association in Keats's poetry binding the phallic fetish-woman and the social code which Keats sought indirectly and defensively to embrace.

18. JEROME MCGANN, 'Keats and the Historical Method in Literary Criticism', *MLN*, **91** (1979): 988–1032. McGann's discussion of the textual history of 'La

Belle Dame' and of the Paolo and Francesca sonnet is an invaluable lesson in the ideological uses of textual scholarship.

19. See Tristram Engelhardt, Jr, 'The Disease of Masturbation: Values and the Concept of Disease', in *Bulletin of the History of Medicine*, **48** (1974): 234–48; Engelhardt, 'Ideology and Etiology', *Journal of Medicine and Philosophy*, I (1976): 256–68; Michel Foucault, *The History of Sexuality, An Introduction*, vol. 1, trans. R. Hurley (New York: Random House, 1978).

   Louis Crompton's fine study, *Byron and Greek Love* (Berkeley: University of California Press, 1985), has opened our eyes to the homophobia of the early nineteenth century. The special ignominy I confer upon 'the masturbator' is not meant to contest or in any way qualify Crompton's representation. I am only elaborating the lesson we first learned from the Romantics. Namely, that Satan is always God's product, structural complement, and support system; that which *threatens* divinity because it reveals the *machina* in the *deus* is either not named, or it is named as a non-phenomenon. Not evil, but monstrous.

20. 'Pretty' implies an imitation of 'nice', in the sense of 'exact' or 'appropriate'. 'Pretty' misses the mark, however, erring on the side of deficiency or excess, precisely because it imitates a fetishized Idea of the middle. Hence, perhaps, the adverbial usage: for example, 'pretty good', 'pretty warm'.

   Apropos what Shelley called Keats's 'false taste' – its resonance for Wordsworth – here is Hunt's synopsis of Wordsworth's famous Preface (from Notes on *The Feast of the Poets*, 1814): 'the taste of society has become so vitiated and so accustomed to gross stimulants . . . as to require the counteraction of some simpler and more primitive food, which should restore to readers their true tone of enjoyment, and enable them to relish once more the beauties of simplicity and nature' (pp. 90, 91).

21. Wordsworth's critique of Macpherson runs along the same lines (see Essay, Supplementary to the Preface, 1815). Wordsworth does not attack Macpherson's hoax *per se*; in the Essay, he is careful to indicate his awareness of the doubtful authenticity of Percy's *Reliques*, and also his great admiration for that anthology. What he condemns in the Fingal collection is its fraudulent expressiveness. Macpherson's failure to feel his subject, and thus to communicate in a quick and quickening manner, is for Wordsworth the intolerable flaw.

22. This discussion is informed throughout by Jean Baudrillard, *For a Critique of the Political Economy of the Sign*, trans. C. Levin (St Louis: Telos Press, 1981); *The Mirror of Production*, trans. M. Poster (St Louis: Telos Press, 1975); and *Simulations*, trans. Foss, Patton, and Beitchman (New York: Semiotext(e), 1983).

23. John Jones, *John Keats's Dream of Truth* (New York: Barnes and Noble, 1969), p. 111. For the context of my phrase 'museum space' see Philip Fisher, 'A Museum with One Work Inside: Keats and the Finality of Art', *Keats–Shelley Journal*, **33** (1984): 85–102.

24. Aileen Ward writes of 'La Belle Dame': 'One hesitates to press this poem for any meaning beyond itself, for it is poetry of a kind that, as Keats said of his favourite passage in Shakespeare, "One's very breath while leaning over these pages is held for fear of blowing these lines away"' (*The Making of a Poet*, p. 273).

25. To recast the model in a familiar philosophic idiom, one may conceive the dream or the concept of masturbation along the lines of self-enriching alienation.

9 Byron's *Sardanapalus* and the Triumph of Liberalism*

JEROME CHRISTENSEN

This essay on a play about Sardanapalus, an 'Oriental despot' whose violent end was a favourite theme of European painting and literature, shows the complexity of determining a work's historical status, of interpreting its relations with other contemporary discourses and – taking the word in the widest sense – its politics. Christensen begins by re-envisioning as an anomaly what might seem natural or unsurprising: references in all sorts of contexts to despots and despotism, during the period of the consolidation of liberalism in Britain. How do such allusions play into that historical development, and what do they reveal about it? Christensen observes that 'despotism' persists not only as a reference to what is ostensibly liberalism's other, as a bad and anachronistic form of government that has been or must be relegated to the past, but also as a model, a compelling idea of how power functions. Byron's *Sardanapalus* provides an explanation of why. Byron's despot's 'sway' lies in his being 'roused' to swaying: being swayed by the image of his own sovereignty held up to him as in a mirror by his Greek concubine, Myrrha. This is precisely the dynamics of consumerism's sway, the actual basis of the rule of liberalism, according to Christensen's analysis.

Christensen draws upon psychoanalytic concepts developed by Jacques Lacan – the *mirror stage* and the *Imaginary* – that designate the primordial role in the psyche's development of identification with a mirror image. As Jean Laplanche and J.B. Pontalis write in *The Language of Psycho-Analysis*:

> The infant perceives in the image of its counter-part – or in its own mirror image – a form (*Gestalt*) in which it anticipates a bodily unity which it still objectively lacks (whence its 'jubilation'): in other

---

* This essay appears for the first time in this volume.

words, it identifies with this image. This primordial experience is basic to the imaginary nature of the ego, which is constituted right from the start as an 'ideal ego' . . .'

The subject constituted in this way is – like Sardanapalus – 'swayed to battle': 'in so far as the intersubjective relationship bears the mark of the mirror phase, it is an imaginary, dual relationship inevitably characterized by an aggressive tension in which the ego is constituted as another and the other as an *alter ego*'. The love beween Sardanapalus and his Greek slave epitomizes the 'Myrrha-stage' (Christensen's pun), along lines that reveal how the paradoxical logic of specular or mirroring relationships is played out to the full in the relations between commodity and consumer. The despot or the consumer exerts his sway in so far as he is swayed by an idealizing image of himself held out by the object of consumption.

Hence the unusual density of Christensen's writing, which in much of this essay simultaneously sums up a psychical and a social and political situation. The first part of the essay places Byron's drama alongside contemporary readers' responses and a major work of early liberal ideology, Benjamin Constant's *The Spirit of Conquest and Usurpation in European Civilization*. Byron's drama manifests, against the thesis of Constant, the persistence of 'the despotic aim' – not simply that alluded to in Constant's title, but an aim involved in both politics and writing, at odds with the logic of representation: an aim or wish to maintain the distinction between a representation and an original having sovereign power to 'impress'; or the wish to have the entity or action and 'its' representation or image exactly coincide, presenting a perfect *illustration*. Those wishes, Christensen suggests, are involved in liberalism's attempted replacement of politics by sheer economics ('political economy') as well as in Byron's drama. Consumer society requires, for instance, a 'command economy': in which the picturing or fantasizing of an object constitutes its value and its power to command a price.

Christensen's writing makes words tell (and not only those of Byron's text). The final turn in his argument concerns their peculiar irreducibility or untranslatability, as he analyses a passage in which a bit of language in a speech by Sardanapalus – a bit of English: the single letter's difference between *king* and *kine* – sticks out, defacing the otherwise perfect picture or illustration that Byron's virtuoso closet drama provides. The anachronism makes Byron's Oriental despot impossible to swallow, and *Sardanapalus* ultimately not an object for consumption.

Christensen's argument establishes the mutual implication of seemingly distinct realms and problems: politics, the agency of the ego, economics, sex and literary representation. Some of his mediations or equations may be more compellingly laid out than others (does his argument have enough of a purchase, so to speak, for instance, on Friedrich Schlegel's concepts of 'romantic poetry' and 'reflection'?), but all of them imply further lines of thought worthy of exploration or elaboration.

This essay is a chapter of *Lord Byron's Strength: Romantic Writing and Commercial Society* (1992). A distinctive political stance emerges through Christensen's readings and his feel for why Romantic writing matters; examining how that happens is one of the interests of this work.

Inducements must then be found to rouse them from that idleness; motives to awaken their industry and habituate them to regular labour.

(Jane Marcet, *Conversations on Political Economy*)

It is the story of the feminine in the present tense, in a culture that produces everything, makes everything speak, everything babble, everything climax.

(Jean Baudrillard, *Seduction*)

The despotic aim

In *The Theory of Moral Sentiments* Adam Smith gives this sketch of the British gentleman:

[H]e acts upon the most indifferent occasions, with that freedom and elevation which the thought [that he is always noticed] naturally inspires. His air, his manner, his deportment, all mark that elegant and graceful sense of his own superiority, which those who are born to inferior stations can hardly ever arrive at: these are the arts by which he proposes to make mankind more easily submit to his authority, and to govern their inclinations, according to his own pleasure: and in this he is seldom disappointed. These arts, supported by rank and preeminence, are, upon ordinary occasions, sufficient to govern the world.[1]

Smith's gentleman has the negligent grace natural to those born to rule. In the Europe of the 1820s, after the cataclysms of the French Revolution and Napoleon's imperial adventure, however, the category 'born to rule' has come to have less self-evident grounding in the order of things. In Lord Byron's time – post-Waterloo, post-Peterloo – at the hour tolled by *Sardanapalus*, the notion of an 'indifferent' occasion has become an endangered fiction. This is the hour of rebellion actual and threatened. For those gentlemen whose right to rule has been confected over the abyss of their illegitimacy the difference between fact and portent has become merely nominal.

Literary rules are similarly imperilled. Consider the warning that the political reformer John Cam Hobhouse delivered to his friend in response to the publication of the first two cantos of *Don Juan* in 1819:

> If the world shall imagine that taking advantage of your great command of all readers you are resolved to make them admire a style intolerable in less powerful writers, you will find in a short time that a rebellion will be excited, and with some pretext, against your supremacy: and though you may recover yourself it will be only with another effort in your original manner.[2]

Extrapolating domestic resistance exponentially, Hobhouse warns of a popular rebellion against Byron's imperious ascendancy. Hobhouse sounds a note of emergency that was to become something of a commonplace in responses to Byron, shared by parties all along the political spectrum.[3] In his otherwise laudatory review of *Childe Harold IV*, John Wilson, who is to Reaction as Hobhouse is to Reform, takes up the theme and predicts an uprising of the coming generation:

> It is even probable, that they may perversely withhold a portion of just admiration and delight from him who was once the undisputed sovereign of the soul, and that they may show their surprise at the subjection of their predecessors beneath the tyrannical despotism of genius, by scorning themselves to bow before its power, or acknowledge its legitimacy.[4]

According to Wilson's analysis, the manifestation of genius is an expression of sovereignty; and the trouble of Byron's genius is the trouble of a sovereignty turned despotic. With the integration of poetry into 'the literary lower empire' established in the wake of Napoleon's ruin, criticism has become a kind of political science.

In *The Spirit of Conquest and Usurpation and Their Relation to European Civilization* (1813), one of the founding documents of nineteenth-century liberalism, Benjamin Constant offered an espcially influential model for the application of a traditional political vocabulary – largely Montesquieu's – to the novel circumstances of nineteenth-century Europe. Constant identified modern despotism as the usurpation of civil society by a state which had become 'the instrument of a single man'.[5] I say 'modern' despotism because Constant's liberalism cannot think itself except in terms of modernity, of a 'today' that has triumphed over with the mystifications of the past, specifically those illusions that had been cynically revived and hypocritically exploited by Napoleon Bonaparte. Writing in Hanover, during the final days of 1813, when, as his editor observes, 'Napoleon's power seemed on the point of collapse', Constant could confidently declare that

> any government that wished today to goad a European people to war and conquest would commit a gross and disastrous anachronism. It would labour to impose upon that nation an impulse contrary to nature. Since none of the motives that induced the men of past ages to brave so many dangers and to endure so many exertions remain for the men of our own day, it would have to offer them motives compatible with the present state of civilization. It would have to stimulate them to combat by means of that same desire for pleasure that, left to itself, could only dispose them to peace.[6]

Because Napoleon is a throwback to the days when men were roused by the slogans of a 'sterile glory', his ambition never had a future: it was the hope of an inveterate gambler and a ruthless day-dreamer – one who imagined himself a king and lived as a king only until 'nature' reasserted itself. For Constant 'nature' is a historical agent that conducts civilization out of history; its emergence coincides with the triumphant instauration of an enlightened epoch of peaceful commercial exchange which abrogates the need for further revolutionary convulsions and military conflict. At one level of the liberal argument, breaking the Napoleonic grip and restoring the partition between the state and civil society entails little more than inducing the burghers of Europe soberly to reset their clocks with an eye to the passage of the sun and awaiting nature's restoration of the balance. Thus Constant orientalizes Napoleon's career, representing it as a regressive detour from the westering progress of enlightenment: 'Since he could not bring ignorance and barbarism to the heart of Europe, he took some Europeans to Africa, to see if he could succeed in forming them in barbarism and ignorance; and then, to maintain his authority, he worked to make Europe go backwards.'[7] For Constant, who learned from Montesquieu, as for Marx, who learned from both, Asiatic despotism stagnates in the wings of history as the very type of anachronism.[8]

According to Constant's rendering of the modern chronotope, despotism should have vanished from the earth with the confinement of Napoleon on Elba. The evidence is otherwise. There is, of course, the Hundred Days. Like Scott and Byron, Constant underestimated Bonaparte's resilience.[9] But there is, as Hobhouse and Wilson illustrate, also a remarkable persistence of the *language* of despotism, an oriental residue that, dissociated from the alibi of the Napoleonic career, remarks on a critical lack of synchrony between liberal theory and liberal practice. The discrepancy is most glaring in the United Kingdom that the Anglophiliac Constant took as his pattern for the European future; it reflects the failure of liberal economics to break with the political forms of the past.[10] As we shall see, Lord Byron's baroque recourse to Diodorus Siculus for an Asiatic hero on which to build a classical drama is symptomatic of the widespread reoccupation of a superseded and disreputable political vocabulary by the most advanced economic system in the world.

Lord Byron's Preface sets the scene for his manoeuvre by advertising his contempt for contemporary English dramatic practice and announcing his resolution to return to those 'unities' which in a better day were 'the law of literature throughout the world'. Characteristically, however, Byron immediately softens his authoritarian manner. 'The writer', he modestly remarks, 'is far from conceiving that any thing he can adduce by personal precept or example can at all approach his regular, or even irregular predecessors'; the writer is, as he says, 'merely giving a reason'. This 'gift' should be appraised in light of Byron's dedicatory address to 'the Illustrious Goethe', who, he adds, 'has created the literature of his own country, and illustrated that of Europe'. Goethe may genially illustrate the literature of Europe, but *Sardanapalus* has a more ambiguous design; it is offered as reason, or as precept, or as exemplification of the 'law of literature'. The Preface's vacillation may indicate that Byron knows as well as anyone that there is no longer a universal law of literature; he may adhere to this sterile standard because, in exiled remoteness from the audience that has sustained him (he was holed up in Ravenna at the time), he doubts his continued capacity to persuade others to believe his poetry has the strength to rule regardless of the variable moods of its audience. Like the character Sardanapalus, who at a crucial juncture of the rebellion against his regime elects to display himself outside his fortified palace, the Preface appears outside the drama to persuade that its authority is based on grounds manifestly beyond deliberation or debate. Risky business. Even so, the exact relations between Goethean 'illustration' and Byronic 'precept', and 'example' are left hanging. Perhaps we might adduce the precept that *Sardanapalus* is meant both to illustrate and to apply the force of examples.

From despotic politics to economic despotism

The political crisis of *Sardanapalus* – how to preserve the regime – is imagined as a rhetorical problem: how to induce other people to do what you want. Sardanapalus conceives of that problem romantically: he wishes only to wish for others to want to do something in order to have them do it. A prisoner of the very reflexivity that defines his sovereignty, before he can move others the despot/child/poet must come to imagine how he could be moved to want something from others; therefore, he must be moved to put himself in the position of another. Salamenes, the emperor's martial brother-in-law, bluntly declares his strategy right off: 'He must be roused' (1, 9). Sardanapalus has been *corrupted* from martial activity into the effeminate enjoyment of luxury. Practical-minded, Hobhousian, the trustworthy brother-in-law aims to recall the degraded Sardanapalus to his 'original manner'. Although Salamenes gives his reasons, the prevailing state of emergency subordinates moral reasons 'why' to the rhetorical challenge 'how'. Salamenes, the stoic soldier, Myrrha, the Greek concubine, Zarina, the discarded wife – all characters in the play reduce to stratagems for arousing Sardanapalus by methods austere or gentle (indeed, all reasons for arousal are interventions designed to arouse). And if the problem is how to arouse a degraded and sated monarch, the answer, we soon learn, is by means of his Myrrha. Mildly chastized by Sardanapalus for being 'too prompt to sacrifice [her] thoughts for others', Myrrha answers, 'I have no happiness / Save in beholding thine; yet – ' 'Yet! What YET?' (ll. 73–4) Sardanapalus replies. Not stopping for an answer, he hastens to add that Myrrha's 'sweet will' is the only barrier between them. Despots are hard to please: criticized for being too prompt to sacrifice, Myrrha is then charged with wilfulness when she qualifies her love. Clearly Sardanapalus does not conceive of himself as belonging to that category labelled 'others'. Myrrha's 'yet' remarks on a fault-line of contingency threading the relations between master and slave, but the alacrity with which Sardanapalus trumps her qualification, shows how the flaw in her happiness (as if she could have a happiness not designed for her by the law of the despot) is instantaneously translated into a flaw in his: an imperative symmetry will inexorably drive out the contingent query or quibble in the name of a more perfect reflection, a higher unity.

Sardanapalus, then, is roused from a state of passivity to action, but for him action is itself reflection, merely mirroring – what Myrrha calls 'civic popular love, *self*-love, / Which means that men are kept in awe and law, / Yet not oppress'd' (I, 537–9). The 'other' for whom Myrrha sacrifices her thought is, it turns out, Sardanapalus after all – not the Sardanapalus of the harem but that *ideal* Sardanapalus who, having become as kingly as his state, would be a self worthy of his own love. Ethical applications to a despot may be futile, but Sardanapalus can be lured to sacrifice his thoughts for that Myrrhad image of himself, that example of him, offered by his slave. Myrrha's precept 'For he who loves another loves himself, / Even for that other's sake' (I, 533), is the mildest of all possible forms of constraint on Sardanapalus' behaviour; it urges him to an action that is nothing more than the improvement of his reflection. In a perversion of the psychological dynamics on which Constant aims to found a liberal comity, Sardanapalus is lured to combat by a self-love which should dispose him to repose. Yet how could Sardanapalus resist? Who would not love himself for the sake of his mirror?

Self-entrapped, Sardanapalus becomes the image of his Myrrha's desire. The key exchange is this, which occurs in Act III, just after Sardanapalus has refused the helm of battle:

Sfero	Sire, the meanest
	Soldier goes not forth thus exposed to battle.
	All men will recognise you – for the storm
	Has ceased, and the moon breaks forth in her
	brightness.
Sardanapalus	I go forth to be recognised, and thus
	Shall be so sooner. Now – my spear! I'm arm'd.
	[*In going stops short and turns to* SFERO.]
	Sfero – I had forgotten – bring the mirror.
Sfero	The mirror, sire?
Sardanapalus	Yes, sir, of polish'd brass,
	Brought from the spoils of India – but be speedy.
	[*Exit* SFERO]
Sardanapalus	Myrrha retire unto a place of safety.
	Why went you not forth with the other damsels?
Myrrha	Because my place is here.
	(3, 139–50

Sfero returns with the mirror. Sardanapalus admires his reflection and then pivots:

Sardanapalus	Myrrha, embrace me; – yet once more – once more –
	Love me, whate'er betide. My chiefest glory
	Shall be to make me worthier of your love.

Sardanapalus is induced to action in the anticipation of a return to his Myrrha – a figure equal to her image of him.

As Constant warned, to be so induced is also to be traduced. During the first heady days after the Fall of the Bastille, Thomas Paine jocularly reported to Edmund Burke a Jacobin street etymology that twinned 'Iscariot' and 'aristocrat'.[11] In his drama Lord Byron works out the implications of the connection for his king of love, who, in returning to what he takes to be his 'original manner' – the manner of the line of

Nimrod and Semiramis – is called to be his own Judas and betrays himself by a kiss:

> Sardanapalus   My Myrrha: [*He kisses her.*]
>   Kiss me. Now let them take my realm and life!
>   (4, 521–2)

Whatever obscure pleasure the oriental despot once took offstage, in his pavilion on the brink of the Euphrates, he now finds an occidental pleasure in the lucid representation of himself. The misrecognition of the other as mirror is part and parcel of the misrecognition of his lordly self as being that which corresponds to the image that the other reflects. Like the Bonaparte of *Childe Harold III*, Sardanapalus is swayed by that example of the sovereign self with which he would sway; the condition of defending his sovereignty is to image it and lovingly to subject himself to an always virtual or speculative identity. Entering on the Myrrha-stage* of his career, Sardanapalus becomes *Sardanapalus*, a 'sort of *ignis fatuus*' to the theatre-going public (*Don Juan*, 11, 214).

Constant promoted the liberal society he found in place in England as a model for modern Europe. Having overcome the forces of barbarism, the victorious Western sovereignties could claim the right to a future in which commerce would succeed to war. 'War and commerce', Constant writes, 'are only two different means to achieve the same end, that of possessing what is desired. . . . [Commerce] is an attempt to obtain by mutual agreement what one can no longer hope to obtain through violence.'[12] Something approaching Constant's perception is implicit in Sardanapalus' retort to the unfavourable comparison drawn between his reign and the Napoleonic militarism of his predecessor Semiramis: 'I sway them', he counters, 'she but subdued them' (I, 192). Conquering is the easy part. The maintenance of hegemony calls for subtlety of a higher order. Yet if in his professions Sardanapalus plausibly mimics Constant, *Sardanapalus* nonetheless dramatizes the Constantine truth that a despot's liberal professions do not count, for despotism must resort to force to retain its power. The transition from symbolic swaying to physical subduing in the play is smooth and evidently inexorable, largely because in its seeming swaying it is already seamed: Sardanapalus is swayed to battle by a mirrored image that subdues him into an identification with his framed likeness.

---

* See remarks in Headnote on the *mirror stage*. A good discussion of this concept's uses and significance is Fredric Jameson, 'Imaginary and Symbolic in Lacan: Marxism, Psychoanalytic Criticism, and the Problem of the Subject', in Shoshana Felman (ed.) *Literature and Psychoanalysis. The Question of Reading: Other-wise, Yale French Studies*, **55–6** (1978): 338–95, especially pp. 353–61.

This swing from swaying to subduing follows a logic of representation that troubles both Sardanapalus the despot and *Sardanapalus* the play. Sardanapalus' troubles begin in Act I, when, in response to Salamenes' appeal that he be trusted to stifle the incipient anti-dynastic conspiracy, the emperor relinquishes to him his royal signet, thereby making what, in a letter objecting to the staging of his plays, Byron called a 'cursed attempt at representation'.[13] Once Sardanapalus has loaned his signet to Salamenes, he has constituted him as a representative and has transformed the basis of power in Assyria: henceforth the possession and display of that stereotype will be more decisive than a claim to birthright or than any other dynastic mystery. Approval of Sardanapalus' impulse lies behind the effort of the sympathetic reviewer for the *Examiner* to save *Sardanapalus* for the cause of reform by denying that Sardanapalus is truly a despot. Instead the reviewer perceives a fledgling liberal monarch who deserves credit for his good intentions: 'In a word, the license which he takes he grants to his subjects, and would have them, with himself, glide on with love and revelry to the tomb' (*RR* B, 3, p. 1013). Unfortunately, Sardanapalus was better at communicating his intentions to the *Examiner* than to his own subjects, obstinate in rebellion despite their lord's liberality.[14] The transfer of the signet does not have the effect of universally granting the licence of luxury; instead it becomes the sign that licence cannot be so universalized. It does so for two reasons. First, to grant a licence presumes a sovereign and reserved right *to* grant. Hence Sardanapalus has every power but the power *fully* to license licence. Politically, that qualification is momentous, for at the limit of despotic giving emerges the potential for democratic taking. Second, if the authoritarian ruler is restricted in his ability to grant freedom, so is he constrained in his effort to sway. Although the signet is used to allow the exercise of despotic power at a distance, it is a risibly limited extension of power, little more than a doubling, since there can be one and only one signet. The signet may be a representation of the despot, but its sign value is authorized by its approximation of despotic self-display. Even employing the signet, the despot can only show 'himself' at two places at once; he cannot display his authority to each and every subject at one time and in one place. And it is at the boundaries of the scene of self-display (the wall of the city, the outlying provinces) where the unsubdued emerge and conflict ensues. Sardanapalus' reliance on the signet as on his myrrahed image shows the limits of the technology by which despotism aims to sway.

But if licence cannot be universalized neither can authority be reclaimed. When Sardanapalus, having recovered his ring, eventually appears before his people to redeem his power by quelling that murmur he could not prevent, he appears as himself a representative or, in the words of the Preface, an *example* of that despotic authority for which ·

every act of exemplification potentially triggers a state of emergency. Self-display anywhere, it would appear, is as threatening to despotic hegemony as is the inability to appear everywhere. In this baroque rendition of the plight of absolute power, any representation, however prudent, that the despot makes irreversibly fractures the foundation of despotic power, which subsists (theoretically? fantastically?) only in the dazzlingly inapparent, scandalously personal body of the despot.

Although *Sardanapalus'* rendition of the susceptibility of enlightened self-interest to recruitment in the project of despotic consolidation suggests an ironic turn on Constant's optimism (the lesson learned earlier by Voltaire and later by Don Juan at the court of Catherine, that every enlightened despot remains a despot at heart), the play turns back on itself (and here is where we feel romantic irony rushing in where *philosophes* fear to tread) by dramatizing the futility of such martial measures: such actions, however politic, entail a representational gesture. That gesture is cursed because it will in time (in the time that westering representation introduces into the stagnant prehistory that is Asia) destroy the myth of a unique inviolability which grounds despotic power. And this is true whether the power is that which Sardanapalus, tyrant, exercised over Assyria or that which Lord Byron, author, claimed over his so-called closet dramas, which were, one after the other, staged in the West End despite his objections. As we shall see, the end of the play, which spectacularly stages the dissolution of the despot and all that belongs to him in a consuming fire, exploits the metaphorical possibilities of closure to identify the final triumph of Sardanapalus over all that stuff by which he has been represented with the triumph of *Sardanapalus* over all the examples of itself that will ever be staged.

But – and this is where the play breaks with Constant – the play's ironic critique of Asiatic despotism entails only the abandonment of the oriental technology of swaying and subduing, not the despotic aim. Indeed, the foregrounding of that aim is one of the most prominent features of the cultural phenomenon called Byronism. Reviewing *Childe Harold IV* for the *Edinburgh Review*, John Wilson, for example, remarked that all of Byron's 'heroes' were 'stamped with the leaden signet of despotism'. Wilson's image aptly characterizes the way the scarred brows of the heroes of *The Giaour* and *The Corsair* are imagined irresistibly to sway the fascinated watcher; and Wilson implies that the poet's rendering of such scenes inscribes a certain wish that he might have similarly irresistible power to imprint feeling on his readers.

If pathological, such an ambition is hardly peculiar to Lord Byron. Indeed, it was the predominant trait of that tragic theatre which in Edmund Burke's account, as well as others, most signally distinguished Great Britain from all other nations.[15] The mark of the primitiveness of the political culture of Assyria in comparison to the United Kingdom is simply that Assyria is a theatre stage without a theatre. Remarking on the compelling intimacy of theatrical experience, John Wilson, always sensitive to the social implications of art, comments that the

> tenderest tones of acted tragedy reach our hearts with a feeling as if that inmost soul which they disclose revealed itself to us alone. The audience of a theatre forms a sublime unity to the actor; but each person sees and feels with the same incommunicated intensity, as if all passed only before his own gifted sight.

(RR B, 2, p. 895)

Yet if the ideological protocol of the British theatre shows a decided advance on Assyrian methods, the limitations of the theatre state in Assyria nonetheless antithetically expose the intrinsic shortcomings of stage representation as an effective instrument of hegemony maintenance. Nineteenth-century Britain no longer has a *Globe*, no single orb in which the populace can be gathered to be swayed by the despotic image of their subjection. *Sardanapalus'* critique of theatrical representation is hand-in-glove with political economy's assault on the realm of the political as dangerously contingent: located on the edge of the districts devoted to finance, the theatre contributes nothing either practically or symbolically to the grand project of capital formation; although all hearts may by a lucky stroke of genius be gathered into a sublime unity, as Laurence Sterne's Yorick discovered in Paris, in the theatre bodies noble and vulgar rub and jostle; friction occurs and with friction a democratic turbulence that threatens the fluid equilibrium designed by the English Constitution and executed by the commercial economy. From the perspective of a liberal-minded Englishman in the first decades of the nineteenth century the rebellious populace of Nineveh is a theatre audience run amok, recalling the riot over ticket prices at the reopening of Covent Garden in 1809, itself anticipative of the rebellion over the price of corn at Peterloo in 1819. Under the sign of technology, which supposedly allows objective discrimination between the efficient and the wasteful, the modern and the anachronistic, the play seeks to proscribe politics 'itself', understood as a zone of unprescribed give and take, assertion and resistance, as a domain with frontiers where the future may appear and the past lurks unsubdued, a conflictual practice which is, in truth, never simply 'itself'.[16]

The eighteenth-century background

The eighteenth-century British discourse of despotism cut across the party spectrum. As J.G.A. Pocock has shown, country ideology associated republican virtue with aristocratic ownership and occupancy of the land, each aristocratic holding separate from every other and each at a bracing distance from the oppressive presence of king and court.[17] Republican politics was a sometime thing: having civic virtue meant exercising it only as the occasion warranted; and the aptness of the occasion was determined by local considerations and personal connections. From the point of view of the capital, these multiple *loci* of independent power presented an implicit challenge to the legitimacy of central authority, to the reliable conduct of commerce in the inland market and, indeed, to the great and glorious compromise of 1688 on which the Union itself was based; they represented the constant possibility of local broils or, worse, networks of Jacobite conspirators. The taming of the aristocracy by the centralized apparatus of the monarchical state meant overcoming the local political advantage that the nobility commanded by virtue of their proximity to the populace and their control of the militia. In the eighteenth century the distance between king and subject was closed not by Elizabethan royal progresses or the ceremonial transport of the signet from place to place but by dispersing agents and distributing the signs of central authority (the posting of standing armies, of course, but also Ralph Allen's rationalization of the mail, improvements in roads, dissemination of the fashion doll, broadcasting of periodical essays on manners, regular assizes), thereby mediating the traditional relations between one countryman and another by means of the currency of the capital and subjecting formerly autonomous citizens to a control that, to the republican imagination, could only appear despotic if it was to appear in any recognizable shape at all.

This despot, however, was not the absolutist terror of Whig ideology – James II *redivivus* – but was instead the notional shadow or personification of the compromise formation which was in fact and in theory mixed government under the Hanovers. Specifically, the eighteenth-century variant of the despot responded far less to an actual individual threat (even the incursion of the Pretender in 1745 functioned primarily to allow the ventilation of internal pressure) than it responded to the conspicuously fictional status of the monarch within the commercialist system. We can call that fiction pre-capitalist insofar as it answered the failure on the part of even such sophisticated theorists as David Hume and Adam Smith to realize fully the place and function of capital within modern society. We can call that fiction pre-Romantic insofar as its volatility would later be mitigated by the Romantic meditation on the necessity of fictions to stabilize national and individual identity that was inaugurated by Edmund Burke's *Reflections on the Revolution in France*. The idea of the despot, therefore, articulated the insistence of an equivocal, ungrounded *political* agency that was, like each George, I–IV, both the residue of an absolutist past and the place-saver for a capitalist future.

The same republican discourse of virtuous resistance to the forces of corruption and arbitrary power that was the ideological resort of aristocrats unable or unwilling to accommodate themselves to regulation by the capital was wielded by emergent professionals and marginal tenants who were intimidated by locally powerful aristocrats. Although those lords of the land may have considered themselves to be exemplars of republican virtue resisting Hanoverian exactions, they could be and were portrayed as behaving in their neighbourhoods with the licence of oriental despots. Godwin's *Caleb Williams* and Goldsmith's *The Vicar of Wakefield* exemplify this gentrified despotism in the depredations of Tyrrell and the caprices of Mr Thornhill respectively. Godwin and Goldsmith turn republican ideology on its head, exploiting country ideology to mount an attack on its traditional exponents, the country squires themselves. They do so not from a nostalgia for the ancient constitution of things but as part of a revaluation of social being, which drastically discounts the merit of individual political activity in favour of a providential economy which (no surprise here) only the novel can adequately represent. Goldsmith is especially pertinent because his criticism of republican shibboleths – laid out by the Vicar in his declamation to the masquerading butler (*The Vicar of Wakefield*, Chapter 19) – implicitly offers the novel as a more efficient vehicle for inducement to identify with a remote and impersonal monarchic power than an established clergy (to which the Vicar ever more marginally belonged), genre painting (which the Vicar's improvident family vainly commissioned), or travelling stage companies (in which the Vicar's prodigal son had thriftlessly enlisted). *Caleb* and *The Vicar* herald a new dispensation in which authoritarian sloppiness would be remedied through the elaboration of a sophisticated technology of metaphoric identification. That technology is a kind of book called the realist novel which persuasively presents an image of the everyday as the modest yet infinitely elastic recuperation of the failed ambitions of earlier representational regimes. And no matter how multivalent and articulated that image becomes, under the dispensation of the political economy of the novel, it will be regarded as if projected from an authorial/ monarchical centre.

Godwin and Goldsmith would have given quite different and divergent accounts of their interests. Nuances aside, however, Godwin and Goldsmith – professional writers scrambling for a living in an embryonic and unforgiving literary market – contributed to the late eighteenth-century constitution of interest rather than either domination or obligation as the key to explain social behaviour. They contributed to a decisive shift from political and ethical to economic modes of explanation, from theatrical and rhetorical to novelistic modes of social control.

The political economy of sex

Sardanapalus, swaying between the closet and the stage, hyperbolically both dramatizes and redescribes the shift from the political to the economic. Thus far we have examined that shift in terms of a fault inherent in the representation of the despot that plunges him into an allegorical enactment of the inevitable futility of political action. But no matter how subjective it is, the play is not a soliloquy. Sardanapalus represents himself in part because representations are made to him. Consider the sovereign not as actor (author or producer) but as one who is acted upon (spectator or consumer). Initially, the play posits as the apparent alternative to decisive political action a thriftless life of sybaritic and secluded revelry. Salamenes and Myrrha, however, conspire to keep Sardanapalus from adjourning to his pavilion of delight and collaborate to extinguish that refuge. In doing so they are acting from impulses that are neither Whig nor Tory but liberal (Myrrha's Greek heritage stamps her with liberalism's pedigree). Although they propose to emancipate Sardanapalus from slavery to his perverse impulses, they methodically bring his uncalculated expense of passion into reciprocal, economic balance with the public world. Salamenes' crucial rhetorical question, 'Were it less toil to sway his nations than consume his life?' (1, 21–2), presupposes the political economist's postulate that all human activity is labour, in order that consuming can be measured against swaying, as unproductive toil is measured against productive. Acting on that premise, the conspirators retrieve that *habitus* of dalliance and delight from its offstage, closeted darkness by captivating luxurious waste in a publicly available image of consumption – thereby embodying the interior world of the despot, bringing it to light, 'orbing' it within a system of reflections that makes it available for identification by Sardanapalus as by others (see 3, 90–2; 5, 62–9). The path of action repeatedly urged on Sardanapalus only appears political: no other end is in view but the economic end of preserving the regime, which is identified with the image of the despot, an image which Sardanapalus is aroused to display. In the economy of the play as of the regime, stimulation is followed by no act except another stimulus. Arousal *is* the dramatic action, which is carried out by reasons, examples, precepts and illustrations.

The play's rhetorization of politics – the evaporation of both its coercive and its ethical dimensions – enables a thoroughgoing sexualization of its plot. The economy of sex is the play's modern equivalent for unity of action. Gone are beginning, middle and end; there is only arousal, arousal, arousal and, finally, consummation. Myrrha's contingent 'yet' lures Sardanapalus on to the apocalyptic 'now', where happiness and sacrifice are fused beyond separation in act or thought by a consummate phrase stated without qualification: 'I come' (5, 498). The phrase announces a *modern* despotism, one which powerfully condenses the manifold articulations that traverse social life. Beginning, middle, and end are republican, Greek, classical – those distinctions belong to the world of deliberation, politics and tragedy. The engine of arousal and consummation is despotic, Assyrian, baroque and British – the systematic breakdown of distinctions announces the triumph of political economy and thus of liberalism, whose legitimating social doctrine it is. It is not clear, however, that Constant could take any comfort from a drama that may ultimately point the right moral – the individual despot falls – but that in getting to its point exploits the despot's catastrophe to reinvest the despotic aim with a modern pathos.

Constant's downright opposition between a commercialized West and a despotic East looks somewhat quaint when tested by the baroque twists of the Byronic dialectic. Recently, however, Colin Campbell, in his *The Romantic Ethic and the Spirit of Modern Consumerism*, has reclaimed romanticism for liberalism by refurbishing Weberian sociologial types in order to advance a hedonistic conception of pleasure, which descends less from the bourgeois Constant than from the baroque *Sardanapalus* (although the play is strangely unmentioned). Far more sanguine about the residual effect of anachronistic modes of thought than Constant, Campbell reinscribes romance (Freudianized as the hallucinatory system of infantile satisfaction) dead centre in the liberal mind. For Campbell the triumph of liberalism is not a function of men's eagerness for a death-like repose (which he calls 'satisfaction') but depends on their readiness to respond to continually renewed stimulation. In modern commercial society, according to Campbell, such experience occurs in anticipation of and as illusory substitute for a gratification that could only be inadequate to its advertisement. Consumerist society is sustained by the continual failure of the reality test to quell either the individual or the social production of illusions. The consumerist system acquires its formidable reproductive power by recasting the reality test (the moment of consumption) as *just another stimulus* to further daydreams of pleasure. For Campbell the modern, romantic consumer does not resist the lures of 'glory' because they are sterile (a positive attraction to a Malthusian) but because, though closeted, he can have in day-dream all the pleasure that glory might bring and with less toil than on the battlefield. 'The individual', Campbell affirms, 'is both actor and audience in his own drama, "his own" in the sense that he constructed it, stars in it, and constitutes the sum total of the audience.'[18] Consumer society is the projection of the principles informing romantic drama, what Byron called 'mental theatre'.

Constant's greatest fear is the commission of anachronism. Campbell envisions a global mental theatre where such fears are themselves anachronistic. 'Traditional hedonism', as he calls it, the elect individual's endeavour to maximize pleasurable sensations, has 'an inherent tendency toward despotism . . . toward acquiring greater and greater control over all that surrounds him'. 'Modern hedonism', on the other hand,

> presents all individuals with the possibility of being their own despot, exercising total control over the stimuli they experience, and hence the pleasure they receive. . . . In addition, the modern hedonist possesses the very special power to conjure up stimuli in the absence of any externally generated sensations. . . . This derives not merely from the fact that there are virtually no restrictions upon the faculty of imagination, but also from the fact that it is completely within the hedonist's own control.[19]

Childe Harold III narrates the progress of Campbell's types: the poem moves from the world of real despots to a modern world represented by the portentous career of Napoleon, who anachronistically attempts to realize what is only a day-dream. Bonaparte fails because he lacks what Campbell calls 'the distinctively modern faculty, the ability to create an illusion which is known to be false but felt to be true' – because, that is, he is no poet.[20] Modern hedonism begins in earnest with the Byronic representation of traditional despotism as an oriental day-dream available to all readers/purchasers of Byron's poems. Napoleon's career both illustrates the despotism to which all men aspire and exemplifies the consequences of madly refusing to accept that such power is only a fantasy. Campbell narrows the moment of consumption to a theoretical point, as if the 'disillusionment' with a 'so-called "new" product', though 'largely irrelevant', were nonetheless intolerable. The strategists of consumption aim to control the rhythm of day-dream and consumption (its seasons or its metre) and to exile all that is irrelevant to the 'moment'. Consequently, both the day-dream and its disillusion will be stereotyped, transformed into pictures that pornographically induce the wish to which they 'respond', as in *Sardanapalus*, where all 'reasons' for arousing Sardanapalus are stimuli designed to arouse him.

To say that such stereotyping is pornographic entails a tactical alignment with Lady Byron. It was Lady Byron who famously called the author of *Childe Harold III* 'the absolute monarch of words, [who] uses them, as Bonaparte did lives, for conquest'. However bloodless, Byron's conquests are conquests just the same. For Lady Byron, there is little to choose between getting people to do what one wants by military violence or by symbolic violence, little difference between subduing or swaying. To the aggrieved woman who has learned her philosophy in Byron's bedroom, the difference supposed between a swaying that impels wives and readers into 'mutual agreement' and a subduing that compels them to accept what they cannot hope to change is made merely rhetorical by the identity of ends. Lady Byron stands as a strong critic of Byronism by reminding the liberal that an economy sexualized is an economy that has transformed the very impulses of pleasure into a systematic violence.[21]

Lady Byron might have added that in the consumerist society heralded by Byronism triumphant day-dreaming loses its effortless charm by being assigned a *value* as a kind of forced labour. Campbell helps us see that the lively debate among political economists over the usefulness of Adam Smith's category of unproductive labour responded to just this transformation. What could the opposition of productive/unproductive mean in a society where day-dreaming has become a form of labour, which, like sex, must be made to pay off? Nothing, argued J.R. McCulloch, who urged the abandonment of the distinction in his entry on political economy in the *Encyclopedia Britannica*. McCulloch's heresy roused Thomas Malthus to a defence of the continued merit of Smith's distinction on the grounds that productivity must involve the increase 'of the quantity or value of material products'; therefore, the labour of servants (to use the classic example) is unproductive. Malthus nonetheless insists that the term 'unproductive' is a technical term employed without the intention of '*stigmatizing*' the kinds of labour to which it was applied. In his attempt to preserve the Smithian definition, the conciliatory Malthus seems to dissolve the distinction between production and consumption. He concludes that 'one of the most powerful causes of wealth must be the general prevalence of such a taste for material products as will occasion the employment of a great and increasing quantity of that kind of labour which produces them'.[22] Servants are unproductive and the higher classes' desire for servants equally so. But the taste for ornate furniture is productive because it entails the increase of labour. Under Malthus's dispensation, then, wanting, desiring, longing are unified under the sign of consumption and given value as productive labour; it is just a matter of desiring things rather than persons. This manoeuvre adumbrates the breakdown of the opposition between production and consumption on which political economy implicitly rests.[23] Such a 'deconstructive' move is made progressive, *economic*, by Malthus's earlier unexamined commission of the anachronism that violates both Constant's optimistic vision of repose and Campbell's seamless subjectivism: he claims that 'the labour which commodities will *command* may be considered as a standard measure of their natural and exchangeable value . . .'.[24] Labour measures value; but commodities command labour. To imagine a consumer society (a society where consumption is productive and taste directed toward proper ends) is to require a command economy, an economy, that is, in which fashionable commodities – as opposed to invisible servants or plain-Jane governesses – can command the labour of day-dreaming that gives them value in a market where the legitimacy of a price is determined by its ability to command a purchase. Every market transaction is thus an act of conquest, every act of swaying a kind of subduing.[25] No consumer has his pleasure completely under his control; every despot dreams as he is bid.

Because the moment of consumption is imaginary, it can be repeated indefinitely: each moment of arousal leads to another and then another. The final scene of the play which ends with the suicide of the vanquished Sardanapalus and Myrrha on a grand funeral pyre metaphorically consummates this sequence of arousals. That is, the funeral pyre condenses the whole play into a single emblematic moment which, however poetically just, seems not so much to dramatically conclude but to lyrically annihilate all that has gone before. The final solution of *Sardanapalus'* rhetorical problem, 'he must be roused', ruins the play. The reviewer for *Blackwood's* complains: 'There is a great deal of power in Sardanapalus . . . but as a play, it is an utter failure; and in God's name, why call a thing a tragedy, unless it be meant to be a play?' (*RR* B, 1, p. 177). The reviewer is answered in the next issue: 'Tragedies are made to be acted', it is declared; 'if not, they . . . resemble the razors recorded by the facetious Peter Pindar, – not made to shave, but to sell' (*RR* B, 1, p. 182). Not to shave but to sell: *Blackwood's* shrewdly remarks on the complicity of Romantic drama's repudiation of the hurly-burly of stage representation with a certain homeostasis characteristic of the commodity, which, unlike the advertising for the commodity, owes its marketable charm to its recessive self-closure. In its purity the commodity lacks any purpose except to be sold; unsold it is incomplete and temptingly vulnerable to any false use that could damage its appeal. Considered in its purity the commodity will only be sold if buying befalls it as a fulfillment of it, as a rapt apprehension that owns the right to bring forth this vulnerable thing from its closet for the brief moment of its consumption. It is the participation of *Sardanapalus* in the equivocal status and destiny of the commodity that elevates it above the stagecraft of previous generations and allows the drama to reabsorb its own vulnerability to representation as an element serving the extension of its sway.

To the traditional questions asked of *Sardanapalus* (What good is a tragedy not made for acting? What good is a king not made for governing?) might be added: What good is a slave not exploited for sexual pleasure? The slave is good for burning. Ritual cremation has long

fascinated the Western imperial imagination.[26] Its canonical locale was
India, where, under the Western eyes of J.G.E. Herder, the cult of the
suttee served the political end of insuring the allegiance of wives to their
despotic husbands. With no hope of surviving their lord, Herder writes,
the wives could have no motive for plotting his overthrow:

> The men [of Hindustan] were incapable of securing from sparks the
> inflammable tinder, which their voluptuousness had [gathered in the
> harem]; and too weak and indolent, to unravel the immense web of
> female capacities and contrivances, and turn them to better purposes:
> accordingly, as weak and voluptuous barbarians, they sought their
> own quiet in a barbarous manner; and subjected by force those, whose
> artfulness their understanding was unable to sway.[27]

Myrrha, however, is not an oriental wife but a freed Greek concubine.
And her death is not coerced but consensual. She goes 'freely and
fearlessly' to the pyre (5, 465). Indeed, her self-sacrifice climactically
vindicates Sardanapalus's ability to sway the one subject whose consent
counts, because she is the one subject who sees with Western eyes, who
can buy rather than merely obey. The play triumphs in its imagination of
its ability to command a purchase as if it were freely willed. Fully
specular, the play reinforces its rule by imagining the consumption of its
own consumer – an effect epitomized by Myrrha's last equivocal
utterance, 'I come', which, by simultaneously *promising* her leap onto the
consuming fire and *declaring* an orgasmic consummation, finely suspends
all finalities. The moment of consumption displays both expectation and
fulfillment, a fulfillment enriched by the expectation of more to come.[28]

Myrrha's equivocation is as overdetermined as is Sardanapalus'
swaying, which may be a means of exercising social control, but which
also expresses an effeminate style that is itself the symptom of some
vacillation about the appropriate sexual object of choice.[29] The
consummation thus at once raises the question of Myrrha's gender (Does
the tyrant construct her as male or female? Does the playwright intend
for her to be played by a woman or a boy?) by suspending it. She is
either male or female, depending on whether the play is adjudged
destined for closet or stage. Insofar as she is the *visible* vehicle of a final
identification, Myrrha must be female, so that the sexual declaration, 'I
come', may be as empirically unfalsifiable as the rhetorical promise, 'I
come'. If an actress says she comes no gaze can confute her. Indeed the
appearance of a woman mitigates the pun, allows assertion to fade into
promise. The woman is the public image of the perfect consumer, fully
responsive to the dictates of the market.

Insofar as the play is interred in the closet and read in a book, where
the claim to come is not subject to visual verification, Myrrha can be and

is as male as Salamenes. Her masculinization is the precondition of her capacity to consent. In a book the indecorous pun on 'come' becomes legible as the reason for keeping the drama from the stage. Gender, then, does not make any difference except as a nuance that invigorates the appeal of Myrrha as our (readers and spectators, subjects and objects, guys and gals) equivocal stand-in, an appeal which Delacroix deftly illustrates by depicting Myrrha from behind. Gender equivocation is the open secret of the closet lurking suggestively in every performance on the British stage, just as the possibility of stage representation deliciously enlivens every closeted reading. As for producer and consumer, master and slave, one option inverts the other: the female can be understood as consenting to the consummatory moment insofar as she can be imagined in some closeted region to be really male; the masculine prerogative to grant or withhold consent can be effectively overridden insofar as a man can be effeminized as the object of an imperious and public desire. The pun on 'come' decisively proves the play's ability to swing both ways, between closet and stage, private and public, homo and hetero – to swing between poles, to subdue difference, and thereby to *sway*. The play both flaunts and fulfills the ambitions of global comprehensiveness that political economy could only countenance in its dreams.[30] *Sardanapalus* is the *Wealth of Nations* in drag.

Ernesto Laclau and Chantal Mouffe have defined the onset of totalitarianism as that moment when

> the state raises itself to the status of the sole possessor of the truth of the social order . . . and seeks to control all the networks of sociability. In the face of the radical indeterminacy which democracy opens up, this involves an attempt to reimpose an absolute centre, and to re-establish the closure which will thus restore unity.[31]

Sardanapalus efficiently *contains* the leeway that endangers old-fashioned authoritarian regimes by a centreing trope of equivocation that sutures action and reflection in the same fashion that genders fortuitously come together, that myrrha and mirror are apparently seamed, that consumption and labour are economically combined, and that lyric and drama are romantically hybridized. That equivocation makes possible the rendition of all ostensible fractures in 'the network of sociability' as mere nuances and enables the deployment of all nuances as the means to sway; it establishes a volatile centre that wavers from side to side on the breezes of a public opinion which it reflexively frames. The theatrical technology by which the despot represents his right to rule fails because no despot can go everywhere. Sardanapalus ultimately wins by making everyone come to him. He succeeds in exemplifying a sovereignty which, unlike the laborious and wasteful conquest of his ancestors, has become nothing other than the sheer power of exemplification. This 'light to lesson ages' illuminates the end of history (5, 440–1). By this light we can appreciate commercial society's triumphant troping of conquest as repetition compulsion and can liberally endorse repetition compulsion as the economical consumption of commodities in serial moments of choice.

In more traditional terms, the climactic suspension of the sexual and the rhetorical in *Sardanapalus* exemplifies Schlegel's notion of romantic poetry:

> It alone can become, like the epic, a mirror of the whole circumambient world, an image of the age. And it can also – more than any other form – hover at the midpoint between the portrayed and the portrayer, free of all real and ideal self-interest, on the wings of poetic reflection, and can raise that reflection again and again to a higher power, can multiply it in an endless succession of mirrors.[32]

This is the moment that 'I come' tries to grasp – the raising of the Myrrha-stage to a higher power. *Sardanapalus* instantiates romantic poetry as the perfection of the commodity form by rendering the aestheticizing of politics as fulfilled in an act of consumption. Whether one chooses Delacroix's trenchant *Death of Sardanapalus* or John Martin's grandiloquent *Fall of Nineveh* as the best pictorial illustration of the closing consummation is immaterial.[33] The play concludes by offering itself as a thing subject to perfect illustration, as a work of art that can see itself becoming a picture and which authorizes the pictorial part to stand for an imaginary whole. *Sardanapalus'* suspended consummation does, then, illustrate the 'law of literature' as promised in the Preface; but it is a new law for a modern literature, an edict which determines that what is unified is that which, like the realistic novel, continually promises its susceptibility to perfect illustration, a world-view.

As fully objectified as his play (and thus reciprocally occupying both the position of himself *and* his mirror, of master and slave, actor and audience), Sardanapalus need never die and nevermore must exert himself in the harem or the throne room. His 'sovereignty' is exempt from challenge because it is grounded in the consent not of the governed but of the consumer, whose consent to be ceaselessly aroused is signalled by her/his absorption in a social imaginary* anchored by the idea of him/

---

* The term *social imaginary* is derived from Jacques Lacan's concept the *Imaginary* order, which he distinguishes from the Symbolic and the Real. The 'mirror-stage' (see Headnote) is a moment or feature of this order, in which the kind of relation that predominates is that of identification, which may be jubilant or aggressive, with the image of a counterpart. The term 'social imaginary' describes the experience of the social world as determined by this phase or aspect of the

herself as an oriental despot. *Sardanapalus* imagines the transformation of a baroque state of emergency into a modern *culture* of emergency where every man is her own despot, and every despot continuously roused to the moment of consumption. As Constant eloquently warned, 'There is no limit to the tyranny that seeks to exact the signs of consent.' What Constant could not see is that the 'counterfeiting of liberty' he ascribed to the despotism of 'the Grand Turk' inheres in every act of consumption by which liberal society maintains its sway.[34]

Commiting anachronism

What could be more felicitous than this triumph of economics over politics and aesthetics over ethics? Approval by the reviewers was, however, fitful and faint. Some of the objections were generic, such as Francis Jeffrey's complaint in the *Edinburgh Review* that 'instead of the warm and native and ever-varying graces of a spontaneous effusion, the work acquires the false and feeble brilliancy of a prize essay in a foreign tongue' (*RR* B, 2, p. 920). In the *Quarterly*'s response to *Sardanapalus*, however, Byron's foreign tongue gets a new twist. Reginald Heber denounces the prefatory attempt to impose the unities as a 'law of literature' and urges that

> when . . . these usurpations find an advocate in one who is himself among the most illustrious living ornaments of English poetry, it is time to make up our minds, either to defend the national laws, or to submit to the 'Code of Napoleon'; and to examine whether there be really, in favour of this last, so much extrinsic authority or so much intrinsic excellence, as to call on us to adopt it, in place of that ancient licence of pleasing and being pleased in the manner most effectual and most natural, which the poets and audiences of England have, till now, considered as their birthright.
>
> (*RR* 5, p. 2059).

Sardanapalus may hoodwink his Grecian, but, as Hobhouse foresaw, Lord Byron breeds resistance. Here the Tory reviewer resorts to the Whiggish ideology of ancient licences, updating the Norman yoke as a Napoleonic invasion. Lord Byron's attempt at authoritarian legislation is

---

constitution of the individual. On the mirror-stage, the Imaginary, and their relation to the social, see Fredric Jameson, 'Imaginary and Symbolic in Lacan', especially pp. 349–68 and p. 377. Two accounts of the social imaginary of modern society are Ernesto Laclau and Chantal Mouffe, *Hegemony and Socialist Strategy* (see Christensen's note 31) and Slavoj Zizek, *The Sublime Object of Ideology* (London: Verso, 1989).

met with the rousing cries of 'Nature and country'. Nature (or Shakespeare), not abstract codes, it is urged, is the law for English drama. Paradoxically, the clearest threat to the integrity of English literature is mounted by that speaker who is English poetry's most 'illustrious living ornament'. It is as if the reviewer sickens at the preface as a *surplus* of exemplification which destabilizes the perfectly balanced apparatus of reflection and displaces the example, precept, or illustration from subordination to any law that could give it reason. The unequivocal registration of this displacement by the *Quarterly* reviewer indicates a flaw in the play's economy. It marks the resurgence of the political as a style of assertion that exceeds the closure of the commodity.

Although the *Quarterly* reviewer responds to the preface, the displacement is not confined there. Reviewers' objections to Lord Byron's Napoleonic usurpation were matched by complaints about his various anachronisms: the reference in the Assyrian court to the so-called practices of 'oriental' rulers, the portrayal of a Greek slave before the time enslavement of the Greeks had begun, and Sardanapalus' speculations regarding the contents of pyramids about which he could know nothing. The complaints about anachronism might seem especially odd, for in a certain sense they align Lord Byron with a fine old Shakespearian foible – one of those most ridiculed by his French detractors. Those and other faults might be eliminated with ease and would be by a writer who took care over his compositions. Lord Byron's neglect is rendered more troublesome by the linkage between such vicious details and Sardanapalus' own perverse addendum to the cities he founded, the verse that, as he says, contains 'the history of all things human':

> Sardanapalus
> The king, and son of Anacyndaraxes,
> In one day built Anchialus and Tarsus.
> Eat, drink, and love; the rest's not worth a fillip.

> (1, 296–9)

The *Quarterly* observes that

> the strange story variously told, and without further explanation scarcely intelligible, which represents him as building (or fortifying) two cities in a single day, and then deforming his exploits with an indecent image and inscription, would seem to imply a mixture of energy with his folly not impossible, perhaps, to the madness of absolute power, and which may lead us to impute his fall less to weakness than to an injudicious and ostentatious contempt of the opinions and prejudices of mankind.

> (*RR* B, 5, p. 2066)

Sardanapalus defaces his own best work. It is a deformation characteristic, as it were, of a poet out of step with the times. The *London Magazine* notices the pattern and, yoking the poet and Sardanapalus, indicts Lord Byron as a "chartered libertine", who has made humanity a jest':

> 'Once a jacobin, always a jacobin', was formerly a paradox; 'but now the time gives it proof'. 'Once an aristocrat, always an aristocrat' might pass, with as little question, into a proverb. Lord Byron, who has sometimes sought to wrap himself in impenetrable mystery, who has worn the fantastic disguises of corsairs, giaours and motley jesters, now comes out in all the dignity of his birth, arrayed in a court suit of the old French fashion, with the star glittering on his breast, and the coronet overtopping his laurels. The costume only has been changed, the man has been the same from the first.
>
> (*RR* B, 4, p. 1611)

The man who has stayed the same in the face of changes of taste is a man who shows contempt for what Emerson would later call 'the voice of humanity'.[35] He limps out of the closet onto the stage in a costume that cannot hide that he remains hidden, secretly degrading mankind as he deforms his own best works. Once an aristocrat always an aristocrat idntifies that one who troubles the self-identity of humanity by persisting as chronic disturbance to mankind's synchronism. 'Once an aristocrat always an aristocrat' marks out the noble poet – as it once had marked the scurrilous jacobin – for inveterate antagonism and eventual sacrifice. But if self-identity does belong to humanity, it cannot belong to the aristocrat, whose charter has no legitimacy, whose contempt has no grounds, and whose anachronistic existence has no historical being. Who then is this scapegoat? Or, paraphrasing Keats, who exactly *is* this coming to the sacrifice?

Sardanapalus raises the question himself in the passage that immediately precedes the firing of pyre and that has offended both critics and directors of the play (it was struck, for good dramatic reasons, from the excellent 1990 performance at Yale University):

> In this blazing palace,
> And its enormous walls of reeking ruin,
> We leave a nobler monument than Egypt
> Hath piled in her brick mountains, o'er dead kings,
> Or *kine*, for none know whether those proud piles
> Be for their monarch, or their ox-god Apis;
> So much for monuments that have forgotten
> Their very record!
>
> (5, 480–7)

Profoundly anachronistic and profoundly unnecessary, this is a
meditation which could not have happened over something which did
happen but has been forgotten.[36] What has been forgotten is whether the
pyramid memorialized the actual sacrifice of the scapegoat or instead the
sacrifice of a scapegoat (scapebull in this case) for the scapegoat.
Humanity has forgotten what it could not help forgetting: that which is
encrypted in and by the pyramid in its very construction. The solemn
encryption is, in effect, a deforming inscription which punningly scatters
what it monumentally centres. It is as if Sardanapalus has not only
impossibly read Herodotus but as if he has read *Childe Harold I*, which
links the death of the bull to the death of the aristocrat; and it is as if he
has read Coleridge's *Biographia Literaria*, which uses the pyramid to
illustrate the brickbound, canonical unity of a Shakespeare or a Milton. 'I
was wont boldly to affirm', Coleridge reminisces, 'that it would be
scarcely more difficult to push a stone out from the pyramids with the
bare hand, than to alter a word, or the position of a word, in Milton or
Shakspeare, (in their most important works at least) without making the
author say something else, or something worse, than he does say'.[37]
Sardanapalus goes beyond the *Biographia* to engage the sacrificial
investment that endows such authorities with value – an aboriginal
violence that Coleridge was unable to face, whether in this version of
Milton and Shakespeare or in his treatment of Wordsworth's 'Thorn'. But
Sardanapalus also goes beyond sceptically undermining Coleridge's
nervous idealization; it 'remembers' the pyramids as memorials of
neither the real nor the symbolic death of kings or of kine, but precisely
as the 'memorial' of the primordial alteration of that sacerdotal word
which names what is encrypted in order to motivate the architectural
construction.

Sardanapalus could be imagined to have read Coleridge because he
seems to read English: the dramatic fiction that the Assyrian speaks his
own language is violated by a slippage not between things (the kind of
empirical problem that could be settled by archaeologists or historicists,
who might dismantle the pyramid to remove the bones to determine the
facts to deliver a lecture), but by a slippage between *letters* which could
only occur in English untranslated. Sardanapalus wanders into English
as the *g* of king wanders into the *e* of kine, transgressing kind.
Sardanapalus comes out in a world all but completely civilized and,
therefore, according to Lord Byron, never to be completely civilized
because (to our good fortune) never completely subject to unification
under the sign of humanity. Neither king nor kine, Lord Byron's
strength is demotic and democratic: it 'does not reside in his full
positivity as a subject, [therefore] any attempt, no matter how refined, to
enslave (including his own) him will fail because there is within him
something that escapes objectification'.[38] English *appears* in *Sardanapalus*

as if encrypted within itself as an inextirpable wandering or deformation that cannot be resolved by sacrifice.[39] It appears as that romantic strength which cannot be captured by a picture and therefore cannot be consumed.

Notes

1. ADAM SMITH, *Theory of Moral Sentiments*, quoted in J.C.D. CLARK, *English Society 1688–1832* (Cambridge: Cambridge University Press, 1985), p. 102.

2. *Byron's Bulldog: The Letters of John Cam Hobhouse to Lord Byron*, ed. Peter W. Graham (Columbia: Ohio State University Press, 1984), pp. 258–9. Hobhouse (later Lord Broughton), was a member of Byron's intimate circle at Cambridge, became his travelling companion (he compiled extensive notes to the first two and fourth cantos of *Childe Harold*) and, the poet's friend in and out of season, represented Byron's interests in England during his self-imposed exile. That friendship was most tested by Hobhouse's principled abandonment of the Whigs for the cause of reform. Hobhouse's increasing political celebrity as well as his alliance with so-called 'vulgar' advocates of popular democracy excited Byron's envy, aroused his prejudices, and drew his satiric fire. On the other side, the daring and so-called 'prurient' aspects of *Don Juan* flushed out Hobhouse's prudery and timorousness – qualities which he would later exercise by co-operating with Lady Byron and John Murray (Byron's publisher) in the burning of the poet's supposedly scandalous memoirs.

3. See, for example, the plea of John Murray, Lord Byron's publisher, that the poet abandon the indecencies of *Don Juan* and return to 'the tone of Beppo' (LESLIE A. MARCHAND, *Byron: A Biography* 3 vols (New York: Knopf, 1957), Vol. 3, p. 1040).

4. *The Romantics Reviewed*, ed. Donald H. Reiman (New York: Garland, 1972), Part B: *Byron and Regency Society Poets*, vol. 2, p. 896. Hereafter identified as *RR* in text.

5. BENJAMIN CONSTANT, *The Spirit of Conquest and Usurpation in Their Relation to European Civilization* (1814) in *Political Writings*, ed. Biancamaria Fontana (Cambridge: Cambridge University Press, 1988), p. 93.

6. CONSTANT, *Conquest*, p. 55.

7. CONSTANT, *Conquest*, p. 100. Constant has specifically in mind Napoleon's expedition in Egypt during 1798–99. But as his accompanying reference to the contemporary attempt 'to revive a style fallen into desuetude since Cambyses and Xerxes' make clear, his political mythography recognizes no significant distinction between Africa and the Levant, both of which fall under the rubric of Asia.

8. For a critique of Marx's employment of the category of 'Asiatic mode of production', see ANTHONY GIDDENS, *A Contemporary Critique of Historical Materialism* (Berkeley: University of California Press, 1981), pp. 81–8.

9. Scott and Byron's prematurity is discussed in relation to the imperial project of English literature in JEROME CHRISTENSEN, *Lord Byron's Strength: Romantic*

Writing and Commercial Society (Baltimore: Johns Hopkins University Press, 1992), Chapter 4.

10. According to Claude Lefort, there is an 'essential difference' between 'political liberalism, as formulated by Tocqueville, and economic liberalism'. The latter 'may ally itself with despotism; the view that free institutions and respect for the rights of individuals are indissociable is part of his critique of omnipotent power' (*Democracy and Political Theory*, trans. David Macey (Minneapolis: University of Minnesota Press, 1988), p. 166).

11. *The Correspondence of Edmund Burke*, Vol. 6, ed. Alfred Cobban and Robert A. Smith (Chicago: University of Chicago Press, 1967), pp. 72–3.

12. CONSTANT, *Conquest*, p. 53.

13. *Byron's Letters and Journals*, ed. Leslie A. Marchand, 12 vols (Cambridge, MA: Harvard University Press, 1973–82), Vol. 8, p. 66.

14. For the case that Byron can be identified as a 'romantic liberal' see PETER THORSLEV, 'Post-Waterloo Liberalism: The Second Generation', *Studies in Romanticism*, **28** (Fall 1989): 437–61.

15. See EDMUND BURKE, *Reflections on the Revolution in France* (Harmondsworth: Penguin, 1969), pp. 175–6.

16. On the use of technological justifications to mystify the political motivation for retaining hierarchical structures of authority in the supposedly rationalized industrial workplace, see STEPHEN A. MARGLIN, 'What Do the Bosses Do? The Origins and Functions of Hierarchy in Capitalist Production', in *Classes, Power, and Conflict*, ed. Anthony Giddens and David Held (Berkeley: University of California Press, 1982), pp. 285–98.

17. See J.G.A. POCOCK, *The Machiavellian Moment: Florentine and the Atlantic Republican Tradition* (Princeton: Princeton University Press, 1975), Chapters 13 and 14.

18. COLIN CAMPBELL, *The Romantic Ethic and the Spirit of Modern Consumerism* (Oxford: Basil Blackwell, 1987), p. 78.

19. Ibid., p. 76.

20. Ibid., p. 78. For a similar argument in defence of liberalism, see Richard Rorty, *Contingency, Irony, and Solidarity* (Cambridge: Cambridge University Press, 1989), especially Chapters 1 and 2.

21. See JEAN BAUDRILLARD on sex and productivity, *Seduction*, trans. Brian Singer (New York: St Martins Press, 1990), pp. 37–49.

22. THOMAS ROBERT MALTHUS, 'On Political Economy', *The Quarterly Review* (1824) in *The Works of Thomas Robert Malthus*, ed. E.A. Wrigley and David Souden, 8 vols (London: William Pickering, 1986), Vol. 7, pp. 261, 263.

23. See Thomas De Quincey's attempt to overcome this opposition in the first chapter of his treatise *The Logic of Political Economy* (1844) in *The Collected Writings of Thomas De Quincey*, ed. David Masson, 14 vols (London: 1897), Vol. 9, pp. 122–200.

24. MALTHUS, 'The Measure of Value' (1823), *Works*, Vol. 7, p. 180 (emphasis added).

25. Lord Byron to Douglas Kinnaird: '[D]o not all men try to abate the price of all

they buy? – I contend that a bargain even between brethren – is a declaration of war' (*Byron's Letters and Journals*, Vol. 8, p. 153).

26. DEIRDRE DAVID, 'Grilled Alive in Calcutta', unpublished lecture delivered at the Johns Hopkins University (December 1988).

27. JOHANN GOTTFRIED HERDER, *Outlines of a Philosophy of the History of Man* (1784), trans. T. Churchill (New York: Bergman, 1966), p. 213.

28. Cf. Marjorie Levinson's interesting allegorization of John Keats as representative of the *'eternally coming'* middle class in her *Keats's Life of Allegory: The Origins of a Style* (Oxford: Basil Blackwell, 1988), p. 24 (p. 204 above). The difference here, and it is considerable, is that the orgasmic vocabulary is not merely descriptive, such as it is in Keats's 'coming musk rose', but performative as well. Moreover Byron's play dramatizes that equivocation as the 'middle class's' hovering reflection on itself: that is, Byron's scene includes the 'Levinson' position as well as the 'Keats' position.

29. Susan J. Wolfson shrewdly investigates the implications of Sardanapalus's effeminacy in '"A Problem Few Dare Imitate": *Sardanapalus* and "Effeminate Character",' *ELH*, **58** (1991): 867-902.

30. For a discussion of the despotic dreams of political economy as they play out in the exemplary *agon* between David Hume and Jean Jacques Rousseau, see JEROME CHRISTENSEN, *Practicing Enlightenment: Hume and the Formation of a Literary Career* (Madison: University of Wisconsin Press, 1987), pp. 243–73.

31. ERNESTO LACLAU and CHANTAL MOUFFE, *Hegemony and Socialist Strategy: Towards a Radical Democratic Politics* (London: Verso, 1985), p. 188.

32. *Friedrich Schlegel's* LUCINDE *and the Fragments*, trans. Peter Firchow (Minneapolis: University of Minnesota Press, 1971), p. 174.

33. On the pairing with Martin, see MARTIN MEISEL, *Realizations: Narrative, Pictorial, and Theatrical Arts in Nineteenth-Century England* (Princeton: Princeton University Press, 1983), p. 174.

34. CONSTANT, *Conquest*, p. 95.

35. RALPH WALDO EMERSON, 'Heroism', *Essays, First Series* in *Emerson's Works* (New York: Bigelow and Brown, n.d.), p. 161.

36. For a Hegelian vindication of the 'necessary anachronism' in the novels of Walter Scott, which 'consists . . . simply in allowing his characters to express feelings and thoughts about real, historical relationships in a much clearer way than the actual men and women of the time could have done', see GEORG LUKACS, *The Historical Novel*, trans. Hannah and Stanley Mitchell (Harmondsworth: Penguin, 1962), pp. 67–9.

37. SAMUEL TAYLOR COLERIDGE, *Biographia Literaria*, ed. James Engell and W. Jackson Bate, Vol. 7 of the *Collected Coleridge*, 2 vols (Princeton: Princeton University Press, 1983), Vol. 1, p. 23.

38. LEFORT, *Democracy*, p. 181.

39. The point could be pursued by attending to the linguistic scattering that exceeds the sacrificial centring, particularly in terms of the way the doubling of Myrrha into the visual order of mirror is supplemented and destabilized by the olfactory sense of her as 'myrrh' ('Bring frankincense and myrrh' (5, 280).

10 Unbinding Words: *Prometheus Unbound**

Carol Jacobs

An interpretation of Shelley's *Prometheus Unbound* has very high
stakes. One is reading a poem about revolution and the transformation of human society by a great poet whose radical political views
meant that this was for him (as for many modern readers) a vital
subject. It would be a mistake to deny that this is the situation. One
wrongly tries to evade or minimize it in taking the text less seriously
than it takes itself – say, elucidating it chiefly through reference to
the received meanings of its chief themes or figures in Shelley's
period, or (more subtly) making sense of it through implicit reference
to the meanings of revolution or apocalypse within a known philosophical or historical tradition. What one has to do in the case of this
text is to read it, in the sense of taking it seriously as statement and
argument (and prophecy). That the poem is a lyrical drama precludes
none of those functions, far from it (the poem at least in that respect
is typical of 'Romantic literature').

Carol Jacobs's essay exemplifies the disquieting process and the
strange results that follow from such a conclusion. *Prometheus
Unbound* is extremely hard to read, not simply because of its 'complexity' but because of the way it sets up and thwarts expectations of
certain patterns of intelligibility: renunciation, self-recovery through
recollection, prefiguration or prophecy, orientation toward a final
goal or telos. Jacobs's reading traces the unravelling of these interpretive premises. A reading of *Prometheus Unbound* also irreversibly
complicates or disqualifies, one could argue in the wake of her essay,
the notion of a Romantic withdrawal from politics to poetic creation:
terms within the framework of which a literary historian might
interpret the very composition of such a poem – but at the price of

---

* Reprinted from Carol Jacobs, *Uncontainable Romanticism. Shelley, Bronte, Kleist*
(Baltimore and London: Johns Hopkins University Press, 1989), pp. 19–57.

overlooking what the poem says and demonstrates about a withdrawal: the withdrawal, not from 'the echoes of the human world'
(not from 'the *human* world', engaged never through unmediated
perception but through 'echoes'), but from the *guilt* and *pathos*
associated (to date) with 'self-differentiation' and with 'endless
mediation', with the discontinuity of history and the inadequacy of
language.

The essay printed here is a version, substantially cut, of a chapter
of Carol Jacobs's *Uncontainable Romanticism: Shelley, Bronte, Kleist.* (The
text was shortened partly by giving the line numbers of some of the
many passages in the poem discussed in the essay, rather than
quoting them in full. The reader will need to have beside her the text
of *Prometheus Unbound.*)

How does one begin to read the text entitled *Prometheus Unbound*? How
does one read the monologue that breaks the silence of the night in
which the first scene is set, a scene that explicitly promises the dawning
of a new day? For this monologue is spoken by the figure who 'gave man
speech' a 'speech [which then] created thought' (II, iv, 72–3).[1]

> He gave man speech, and speech created thought,
> Which is the measure of the Universe;
> And Science struck the thrones of Earth and Heaven
> Which shook but fell not; and the harmonious mind
> Poured itself forth in all-prophetic song.
>
> (II, iv, 72–6)

How to think this speech, how to measure it, caught as one is in the all
too familiar double-bind of thinking that which makes thought possible
and speaking the possibility of speech. The distress of this reader-baffling
situation is assuaged if not fully alleviated by the thrust of Prometheus's
words. For it seems to go without saying that Shelley's text is about the
release of the Titan – a restoration to his proper place and proper
authority, then, of the origin of speech and thought – and about the
downfall of all that menaces him.

In the opening lines, Prometheus himself speaks of nothing if not this.
For alongside his insistence on a temporality beyond measure in which
each endlessly divided moment seems the forever of long years (I,
12–15), alongside the stasis that promises 'No change, no pause, no
hope!' (I, 24), he is yet certain of the advent of the revolutionary hour to
come.

If the sway of teleology is to overcome an aimless passage of time,[2] the authority in whose name this revolution is to take place is, nevertheless, somewhat difficult to situate. The originary, compelling moment of this sequence of events took place thousands of years before the opening scene the reader is called to witness. And, although we may encounter it, belatedly, only through hearsay and a strange ritual of repetition, it would seem to attest to the fact that Prometheus's strength, then as now, lay in his voice. For, in contradistinction to Aeschylus's hero, Shelley's has not acted his defiance but rather spoken it. The mythological Promethean deed is transformed into an originary act of words, the annunciation of the curse.

At that critical juncture, then, Prometheus uttered his devastating curse and set the stage for all to come, for with these words, as Prometheus relates it, he placed his 'all-enduring will' against 'the fierce omnipotence of Jove' making 'his agony / the barrier' to the 'else all-conquering foe' (I, 114–19) of Earth and her sons. Prometheus's voice has ever since been treasured as a repository of power and value. Earth and her sons 'Preserve [that curse], a treasured spell' and 'meditate/In secret joy and hope those dreadful words' (I, 184–5). The Titan's words, then, shield and preserve and can be preserved in turn as a resource of power.

Yet as the elements of nature recount the effect of Prometheus's voice, they are entirely counter to any promise of deliverance from former sufferings. How are we to understand this double language that, it turns out, betrays others and itself, that brings with it the violence of madness and rending, that imposes a tyrannical voicelessness on those who would speak (I, 89–106)? Can such utterance be reconciled with the benevolent figure Asia later describes – he who gave man speech, thought and Science, a power, as she tells it, able to strike 'the thrones of Earth and Heaven' (II, iv, 74)?

But as no reader of *Prometheus Unbound* can fail to note that same figure that once defied the omnipotence of Jupiter had also empowered him (I, 381–2 and II, iv, 43–5); the same utterance that shielded those of the earth also called for their suffering.

> Aye, do thy worst. Thou art Omnipotent.
>   O'er all things but thyself I gave thee power,
> And my own will. Be thy swift mischiefs sent
>   To blast mankind, from yon etherial tower.
>   Let thy malignant spirit move
>   Its darkness over those I love:
>   On me and mine I imprecate
>   The utmost torture of thy hate

(I, 272–9)

What kind of voice is this that claims to be a barrier to the agony of others and also the source of the power to inflict it? And what is the only realm that Prometheus preserves here from the violence of Jove if not that of his own will (I, 274), the authority of his own words?

The economy of renunciation is such, however – isn't this what we are to understand and what so many of Shelley's readers have understood before us? – that the hatred and violence of the curse (an invocation that has brought suffering to Earth and Prometheus alike) have been rather Prometheus's greatest error. Its reiteration is, therefore, the path to conscious self-understanding and the means to undo the evil of that speech.

> *Prometheus*   It doth repent me: words are quick and vain;
> Grief for awhile is blind, and so was mine.
> I wish no living thing to suffer pain.
>
> (I, 303–5)

But if such a counter-current is easy to understand, there are others that make it quite difficult to define the almost unfathomable situation at the opening of the text. Prometheus, hero of the drama, knows that the curse took place but cannot recall its content. This lapse marks the loss of something beyond a particular moment of speech for if he fails to induce the Mountains, Springs, Air and Whirlwinds to repeat his curse of long ago, what is at stake is nothing less than the present power of his word.

> If then my words had power
> – Though I am changed so that aught evil wish
> Is dead within, although no memory be
> Of what is hate – let them not lose'it now!
> What was that curse? for ye all heard me speak.
>
> (I, 69—73)

Prometheus desperately seeks the repetition of those words as an affirmation of the power of his voice and it also signifies nothing less than the affirmation of his identity.

> I hear a sound of voices – not the voice
> Which I gave forth . . .
>
> . . . Know ye not me
> The Titan? . . .
>
> (I, 112–18)

What does it mean to have a figure who represents the origin of the spoken word and thought yet forgets his own most critical declamation – whose strange amnesia extends, moreover, to a loss of sense of self and of his own authority? What does it mean that Prometheus is not only bound to a ravine of icy rocks, as the stage directions would have it, but that *Prometheus Unbound* opens in the abyss between an obliterated originary moment that it takes 300 lines to recall and a revolution deferred for yet two acts?

Let us begin with the deferral. It is, in fact, where the text begins. If Prometheus's penitence is indeed the critical gesture of the drama, the inner revolution required to bring about a transformation of the outer realm, if the moment of recall seems pivotal in that it should summon the past, empty it of its morally negative content and precipitate us into a new era, how are we to explain the events that follow it? For no sooner does he bring about a repetition of the originary linguistic act, no sooner is the gap in memory accounted for, than Prometheus admits its failure to provide the sense of recognition he sought in hearing the voice which he gave forth: 'Were these my words, O Parent?' (I, 302).

Not only does the repetition of the curse fail to solve the crisis of self-identity and authority, the revolution itself is not measurably closer at hand. Mercury, messenger of Jupiter, immediately appears on the scene and his errand is revealing. Mercury has been accompanied by the Furies who joyously assault their victim as 'ministers of pain and fear' (I, 452). Prometheus's words it seems – willy-nilly – do indeed retain their power, for in the curse, as spoken by the phantasm of Jupiter, we read:

> Rain then thy plagues upon me here,
> Ghastly disease and frenzying fear;
> And let alternate frost and fire
> Eat into me and be thine ire
> Lightning and cutting hail and legioned forms
> Of furies, driving by upon the wounding storms.

> (I, 266–71)

If his tormentors appear as something of the perfectly literal fulfillment of Prometheus's original curse,[3] what has happened to his will to recall that moment of blind fury? 'The Curse / Once breathed on thee I would recall' (I, 58–9), Prometheus announced in his opening monologue. He wishes, of course, not only to remember his words but also to revoke them. Yet their recitation not only prompts no genuine recall in the sense of recollection, it also fails to bring about the desired nullification. Prometheus, it seems, is as little able to empty his words of their power as he is to guarantee their fullness.

And how could it be otherwise when the crucial term in question is 'recall'? It is this word that has set the critics by the ears creating a turmoil with regard to fixing the Titan's exact intent.[4] For 'recall', here as often in Shelley, performs with all the complexity – and none of the ordered control – of the Hegelian term *Aufhebung*. It suggests a calling back to memory, and even a more general summoning back, a restoration, a making present once again. How to reconcile this with its sense as revoking or annulling the purport of a text – and this again with its sense as recall, to call again, a second time?[5] None of these meanings is able to hold its own in the strategy of Shelley's first act. The curse is summoned back, in a manner of speaking, but never is made present enough to mind to become remembrance. It is called again, but hardly just as it was uttered three thousand years earlier. And the will to revoke it seems, at least for now, is as doomed as the desire to recall it precisely.

Prometheus, then, cannot effect his revolution with the gesture of 'recall'. What takes place, however, when Prometheus finally comes into his own? Does this mean that he will come to know his own voice, his self, his past, his future? When all we know of him is liberated, he is indeed unbound: but how are we to understand such unbinding? In this text so concerned with tyrants and slaves, the Titan has met – if not his master, at least – his match, one who is neither Jupiter nor his representatives, but rather an adversary that even in its name is the counter force to Pro-metheus (fore-thought). For it is on the figure of 'recall' in all its implications that this crucial scene hangs. It is this that unbinds Prometheus, makes his relationship to words no longer, necessarily, binding – and not only those of the curse. This is not to say that the intentional link between authority, knowledge and language is definitively severed. On the contrary. Far more unsettling is that Prometheus may never know if he is in a position to recall either as confirmation – to remember, restore, re-call – or as annullation – to revoke, or, for that matter, to find a language that might fulfill the promise of his own name by naming that which is to come.

The immediate revolution that Prometheus's readers might like to foresee, then, does not take place, not least of all because the conventional temporality of revolution is unhinged. For if the difference between annulling the past and restoring it cannot be designated, how is one to know if one is coming or going? There is, however, no question that a revolution of sorts is what *Prometheus Unbound* is about, and this is, at least in part, the temporal and linguistic apocalypse that 'recall' exemplifies. The moment of recall, then, is indeed, in a sense, the critical force of revolution, but it fulfills neither the desires of Prometheus nor those of his readers. Prometheus wishes to repent and to thereby prove the power of his words, to reaffirm his own identity or even to become conscious of his past errors in order to transcend them. But he cannot authentically renounce his will-to-power, not least of all because the very desire for repentance reasserts that will: 'The Curse / Once breathed on thee I *would* recall' (I, 58–9, emphasis mine). Prometheus cannot give up his power but his words can and do unsay their speaker.[6] If the moment of recall operates as the vortex of a revolution, it is because another notion of language is at play in which the authority of the speaker's will is thoroughly disordered. Recalling cannot at this moment continue to serve as the remembrance of a particular consciousness, the repetition of a particular voice, or a revocation brought about by the will of a particular subject. The radical renunciation that first begins to take place here will later reverberate in Prometheus's proleptic description of the cave (III, iii), in the 'harmonies divine', the 'difference sweet', and the 'echoes of the human world' (III, iii, 38, 39, 44). It is not that one will there transcend the contra-diction – such double-talk as that we saw in Prometheus's original curse. It is just that such 'difference' will no longer bear the onus of moral inconsistency.

Not only is *recall* a word that performs the dissemination of its varied meanings, these meanings oddly recapitulate some of our most treasured (if mutually exclusive) theories about how language functions – as a making present in full restoration of that which it names, or as a bringing to mind of that which is, nevertheless, recognized as past, or as that which annuls that of which it speaks. Much of Act I becomes an echo-chamber for these questions – for the questions of relationship between a subject and its language, between its language and the thing it names – and also for the question of dialogue. The complex problematic of the recall, a language which may well revoke itself in the moment of its affirmation, takes over the entire scene. Earth's ultimate response to Prometheus's desire to take possession of his own words says more than she can know, for she speaks with an irony that can hardly be intentional.

Prometheus	But mine own words, I pray, deny me not.
The Earth	They shall be told. – Ere Babylon was dust,
	The Magus Zoroaster, my dead child,
	Met his own image walking in the garden.
	That apparition, sole of men, he saw.
	For know, there are two worlds of life and death:
	One that which thou beholdest, but the other
	Is underneath the grave, where do inhabit
	The shadows of all forms that think and live
	Till death unite them, and they part no more;
	Dreams and the light imaginings of men
	And all that faith creates, or love desires,
	Terrible, strange, sublime and beauteous shapes,
	There thou art, and dost hang, a writhing shade

> 'Mid whirlwind-peopled mountains; all the Gods
> Are there, and all the Powers of nameless worlds,
> Vast, sceptred phantoms; heroes, men, and beasts;
> And Demogorgon, a tremendous Gloom;
>
> (I, 190–207)

This other world is fundamentally one of language, inhabited as it is by images, the images of 'all forms that think and live'. Prometheus's desire to maintain the power of his voice in having his past words made present to him ('If then my words had power . . . let them not lose it now!'), his desire to confirm his self-identity, is answered by the necessary confrontation with a denial of such possibilities. A form can meet its image, a subject its dreams and imaginings, only by way of death. As always in Shelley's texts, this is no literal death but a death within life. The passage demands maintaining the disjunction between the image and that which it shadows forth. At the very moment of their union, the world of shades is a realm of no will to power: here reside names without power and powers without names ('all the Powers of nameless worlds' are there).

Thus the attempt to unite power and name, to give speech to a shape, or authority to an image, is a violent and unsuccessful ventriloquism. The figure who speaks the curse will experience that voice as total alterity, as the invasion of an other that rends him from within.

> *Phantasm of Jupiter*   What unaccustomed sounds
>   Are hovering on my lips, unlike the voice
>   With which our pallid race hold ghastly talk
>   In darkness?
>
>   A spirit seizes me, and speaks within:
>   It tears me as fire tears a thunder-cloud!
>
> (I, 242–5, 254–5)

Like Prometheus, the phantasm hears unaccustomed sounds unlike the voice that might assure him of his own identity. His words belie any possible coincidence between thought and speech – a disjunction that should give us pause, since Prometheus was said to have given speech which then created thought (II, 72).[7]

> *Prometheus*   Speak the words which I would hear,
>   Although no thought inform thine empty voice.
>
> (I, 248–9)

Such is the voice that has no thought to 'in-form' it, to give shape to the shape. For if the world of this phantasm can be said to consist of anything, it is empty shapes and shades, shadows and images, the violent questionability of representation performed by the figure of the recall.

The first act requires a confrontation with the realm of the dead and all that realm implies; it remains caught in the involutions of recalling the past. However, the second act moves forward, it would seem, with a sense of momentum to the point of transformation and actual revolution. Asia is joined by Panthea and together they follow the call of Echoes to Demogorgon's abode. There they are carried away by the Car of the Hour in the apocalyptic passage that concludes with Asia's monologue: 'My soul is an enchanted Boat.'

For all this the opening lines of the second act seem an uncanny repetition of the crises of Act I. The setting of the earlier scene pledged the dawning of a new day ('Morning slowly breaks' (I, scene description)) only to be followed by a peculiarly inexorable temporal dilemma. In the second act Asia too announces what seems to be the coming of a new era. This Spring, however, is a season more immediately bound to memory than regeneration. The entire act moves between an imperfect recuperation of past dreams and the dream of a future that is not quite realized.

> Yes, like a spirit, like a thought which makes
> Unwonted tears throng to the horny eyes
> And beatings haunt the desolated heart
> Which should have learnt repose, – thou hast descended
> Cradled in tempests; thou dost wake, O Spring!
> O child of many winds! As suddenly
> Thou comest as the memory of a dream
> Which now is sad because it hath been sweet. . . .
>
> (II, i, 2–9)

Spring comes 'suddenly', cradled in the tempests and blasts of Heaven – an awakening that ruptures repose rather than guaranteeing new fullness. Spring's abruptness is 'like a thought' (II, i, 2), like a movement 'of the human mind' (Preface, p. 133) that undoes the valence of its object, a reflection on past operations of the mind, a memory that inverts the value of that which it reflects, turning sweetness to sadness. If, as Asia goes on to proclaim 'This is the season, this the day, the hour' (II, i, 13), it is the season of poorly camouflaged violence as it swiftly descends, less it would seem as the spirit of new beginnings than as a disfigurement of the past – of past dreams and of reality.

> Like genius, or like joy which riseth up
> As from the earth, clothing with golden clouds
> The desert of our life . . .
> This is the season, this the day, the hour. . . .
>
> (II, i, 10–3)

But is this the season, the day, the hour? When spring appears as a memory that fails to recapture the dream of the past, the advent of the long awaited moment seems, nevertheless, at hand. Such immediacy, however, quickly gives way to a temporality of delay.

> This is the season, this the day, the hour;
> At sunrise thou shouldst come, sweet sister mine,
> Too long desired, too long delaying, come!
> How like death-worms the wingless moments crawl!
>
> (II, i, 13–16)

As in Act I, the present moment is caught between the loss of the past and a deferral of the future – as though it had no other definition of its own.

> How late thou art! the sphered sun had climbed
> The sea, my heart was sick with hope, before
> The printless air felt thy belated plumes.
>
> (II, ii, 32–4)

Panthea's arrival marks the coming of an 'Aeolian music' (II, ii, 26). Yet this music, created as Panthea's plumes winnow the crimson dawn (II, ii, 27) appears, strangely enough, also as a writing. It is this displacement that takes shape over and over throughout the scene. The slide is between plume and plume, from nature to text and from the promise of immediate perception ('I feel, I see') to a more questionable print produced in the temporality of delay ('The printless air felt thy belated plumes'), marked upon the otherwise blank page of the printless air.

If this music is not offered to view, there is another kind of text which Asia wishes to read – a text she is sure that Panthea carries with her. For if spring implied a transvaluation of past dreams, most of the scene now turns on the narration of half-remembered dreams.

> *Panthea*   Pardon, great Sister! But my wings were faint
> With the delight of a remembered dream

> Asia   Lift up thine eyes
>   And let me read thy dream.
>
> > (II, i, 35–6, 55–6)

How does one read in the eyes of another? What kind of reading is this
and what can one hope to find there? It is as though Asia expects to take
in that dream as something one can really sense. When Panthea insists
on the spoken word, upon telling the story of her dream, such mediating
converse is lost upon Asia who declares words the empty equivalent of
air.

> Asia   Thou speakest, but thy words
>   Are as the air. I feel them not. . . . oh, lift
>   Thine eyes that I may read his written soul!
> Panthea I lift them, though they droop beneath the load
>   Of that they would express – what canst thou see
>   But thine own fairest shadow imaged there?
>
> > (II, i, 108–13)

The written soul, the text that Asia searches for in place of the
disconcerting narration is, nevertheless, an ambiguous creature of
shadow or shade. Perhaps 'thine own fairest shadow', as Panthea calls it,
an image of Asia herself, or of Panthea whom Prometheus had called the
shadow of Asia (II, i, 70), or of Prometheus, as Asia would have it, for
these three are image and shadow of one another.

> There is a change: beyond their inmost depth
> I see a shade – a shape – 'tis He, arrayed
> In the soft light of his own smiles which spread
> Like radiance from the cloud-surrounded moon.
> Prometheus, it is thou – depart not yet!
>
> > (II, i, 119–23)

If it is indeed Prometheus who appears, if Asia's desire for the immediate
'[reading of] his written soul' (II, i, 110) would seem fulfilled, this figure
is, nevertheless, just as immediately driven out by another, another
shape, another dream, whose content is the purest message of necessary
deferral and transience.

> Dream   Follow, follow!
> Panthea   It is mine other dream. –
> Asia   It disappears.
>
> > (II, i, 131–2)

Just prior to this Panthea had spoken of the dream Asia wishes to grasp within her sister's eyes. That discourse, had Asia been able to follow it, spoke of the necessary ambiguity of the direct presence that Asia seeks. As in Act I, no simple plenitude of recall is possible without the reverberations of loss: 'Then two dreams came. One I remember not' (II, i, 61). Yet it is not only the distance of its retelling that brings a forgetfulness and consciousness of obliteration. Panthea's dreamed experience of presence bespeaks loss of yet another kind.

> Then two dreams came. One I remember not.
> But in the other, his pale, wound-worn limbs
> Fell from Prometheus, and the azure night
> Grew radiant with the glory of that form
> Which lives unchanged within, and his voice fell
> Like music, which makes giddy the dim brain
> Faint with intoxication of keen joy:
> 'Sister of her whose footsteps pave the world
> With loveliness – more fair than aught but her
> Whose shadow thou art – lift thine eyes on me!'
> I lifted them –
>
> (II, i, 61–71)

Prometheus's call to Panthea to lift her eyes on him echoes those of Asia's insistent requests: 'Lift up thine eyes / And let me read thy dream – ' (II, i, 55–6 and also 109–10). Panthea's initial refusal, her determination to narrate her tale rather than allow it to be read directly, may reflect her understanding (for this is what the dream is about) that there is no light in this drama without shadow, no direct presence without the necessity of veiling and the risk of dissolution.

> I lifted them – the overpowering light
> Of that immortal shape was shadowed o'er
> By love; which, from his soft and flowing limbs
> And passion-parted lips, and keen faint eyes
> Steam'd forth like vaporous fire; an atmosphere
> Which wrapt me in its all-dissolving power
> As the warm ether of the morning sun
> Wraps ere it drinks some cloud of wandering dew.
> I saw not – heard not – moved not – only felt
> His presence flow and mingle through my blood
> Till it became his life and his grew mine
> And I was thus absorbed. . . .
>
> (II, i, 71–82)

Prometheus's power dissolves whatever it encounters and this absorption is not altogether one of ecstatic union: for his voice 'fell / Like music which makes giddy the dim brain' (II, i, 55–6) so that Panthea neither saw, nor heard, nor moved. And when Panthea's being is once again condensed, she finds her thoughts unable to articulate that which she has heard (II, i, 86–91).

The opening scene of *Prometheus Unbound* enacts the crisis of knowing one's own voice, of coming to terms with one's self, and places this dilemma in the broader matrix of a rupture in our conventional temporal and linguistic structures. Act II repeats these crises, in the context this time of a mystified sense of oneness with the other. For the relationship between Asia and Panthea, who, despite appearances, do not quite see eye to eye, is negatively echoed by that of Panthea to the dreamed shape of Prometheus, by that of the transfigured Asia to those around her (II, v, 51–71), as well as by that of Ione to Panthea (II, ii, 93–106). These intersubjective unions that fall dangerously short of simple ecstasy now give way to narrations that insistently juxtapose a temporality of incipience over against deferral, a promise of presence over against a writing that dislocates.

Once Asia has witnessed in Panthea's eyes the displacement of Prometheus by another shade, Panthea goes on to speak of this her second dream. Like that which Asia will soon relate, Panthea's dream concerns the meaning of their present encounter:

Dream	Follow, follow!
Panthea	It is mine other dream. –
Asia	It disappears.
Panthea	It passes now into my mind. Methought
	As we sate here the flower-infolding buds
	Burst on yon lightning-blasted almond tree,
	When swift from the white Scythian wilderness
	A wind swept forth wrinkling the Earth with frost . . .
	I looked, and all the blossoms were blown down. . . .

(II, i, 131–8)

Like that springtime that left the opening of Act II more a rupture than a period of generation (II, i, 1–7), the springtime of Panthea's dream is a bursting grafted onto that which is already blasted ('the flower-infolding buds / Burst on yon lightning-blasted almond tree'), a blossoming coincident, once again, with a violent wind. And not just any wind – nor just a wind that tears the flowers from the trees in the season of their unfolding, blowing them down in the very moment of their blowing.

But on each leaf was stamped – as the blue bells
Of Hyacinth tell Apollo's written grief –
O *follow, follow!*

(II, i, 139–41)

How are we then to understand the message on each leaf, the doubly
inscribed leaf that forces us from the botanical realm of organic continuity
to that of the written text: how are we to read this volume of scattered
pages? The mode of their stamping, we are told, is like the grief of
Apollo inscribed on the blue bells of Hyacinth. Whatever the echoed call
to follow may indicate, in recalling the plight of Apollo, it cannot offer
the promise of fulfillment. For that myth reiterates the inevitably failed
attempt to eradicate the difference between self and other, and reiterates
it with a vengeance. This is a vengeance, tellingly enough, both by and
on he who would presume to take language as his medium – and to take
it in a particular sense. Apollo, it seems, as the first god to desire one of
his own sex[8] fell in love with the lad Hyacinthus. Apollo incurs the
jealousy of the West Wind, and like the wind of Panthea's dream that
tears each blossom from the branch and stamps it with words of
dislocation, the West Wind of the myth is the force of a brutally
significant and complex transformation. For as Apollo instructs
Hyacinthus in the throw of the discus, the Wind changes that object
hurled away from the youth into something of a boomerang that strikes
him dead with his own missile.[9]

Hyacinthus's blood is changed into the flower that bears the same
name. Indeed it bears several senses of the same name. Just as the discus
is made to retrace its path and recoil on its author, Apollo must learn to
write in a mode of language that simultaneously affirms and denies the
object of his desire. On its petals Apollo, who is now metamorphosed
into a poet of another order, inscribes the letters αι that at once name his
lover and tell his written grief. For alpha iota are the initial letters of
Hyacinthus' name, a seeming call to presence, at the very least an
insistence on memory, and also, the cry of woe that acknowledges the
irrevocability of his loss.

Panthea's dream leaves the reader in a rather baffling situation. For if it
is presented in the unmistakable guise of the prophetic dream, as a
scenario whose interpretation is bound to clarify the future, everything in
its structure and content belies that possibility. Whereas the traditional
prophetic dream presupposes a correlation between dream text and
event, a memory before the event, so to speak, this particular prophetic
moment nearly defies that link. Not only does the dream first figure as a
blank in consciousness, not only does its appearance finally take shape as
the displacement of Prometheus's presence to Asia,[10] as a disjunction
rather than a prophecy of their future union, the very content of that

253

dream warns of misreading fulfillment where there is none, of misreading apparent signs of generation as the harbingers of a plenitude to come. Panthea's dream tells of undercutting the continuity on which the structure of organic growth as well as the structure of prophecy are based. The bursting of buds upon the almond trees does not unfold the first flowers of spring but takes place rather with a double rupture in our expectations. Those blossoms are blown down by the natural if seemingly perverse force of the wind from the Scythian wilderness. But perhaps more significant is the at first imperceptible displacement from leaf to leaf, from vernal growth to the printed page. And yet it is not the stamped message alone that makes the printed leaf a disruption of its natural counterpart, nor is it a simple crossing out of the kind of teleology associated both with organic nature and successful prophecy. What is printed on the leaf, as the text will go on to say, is a mocking of their voices rather than their realisation (II, i, 162–3), one that is emphatically and appropriately made to rhyme with *hollow* (II, i, 175). '*O follow, follow!*' (II, i, 141) is at once the structure of prophecy and its denial, a pointing towards or a call to move in the direction of – but without an endpoint. The leaves of Panthea's dream are like 'the blue bells / of Hyacinth [that] tell Apollo's written grief' (II, i, 139–40) because each tells the tale of the impossibility of its telling. The substitution of the flower for the boy takes place with an inscription whose double register denies the voice of lyrical affirmation that might recuperate the past and with it the gesture of the metaphor. Thus the substitution of the prophetic text for imminent reality comes about in a narration that insists on the dislocation of such continuities. What becomes predictable, then, if predictability were to remain a viable concept, is nothing more and nothing less than the production of the peculiar kind of writing encountered in these metaphors for the impossibility of metaphor.

But, it seems to go without saying, Panthea's dream is, despite all, about that which is to follow. Such writing appears at the critical moment of the revolution, or – at least, at the moment of revolution in Shelley's text – at what seems to be the beginning of a new era that could well be read as the substitution of a new authority in the place of a morally degenerate one. At the juncture of Jupiter's downfall, a certain cry reverberates, a cry whose syllables are printed nowhere else in all of Shelley's poetry, but a cry that echoes, nevertheless, significantly. For what Jupiter calls is that same 'αι' that the god of wisdom and poetry must learn to write, the 'Ai!' of Apollo's written grief.

Ai! Ai!

The elements obey me not . . . I sink . . .
Dizzily down – ever, forever, down –

And, like a cloud, mine enemy above
Darkens my fall with victory! – Ai! Ai!

(III, i, 79–83)

If Panthea's dream is prophetic of the revolution to come, and such a
coincidence in Jupiter's spoken grief would seem to leave room for no
other interpretation, it is a revolution that teaches us to rethink the
nature of revolution. For the revolutionary wail and the revolutionary
script tell us the 'no longer now' of 'Ai!' or the 'not here, not yet' of
'follow'; they mark a questioning of the concept of revolution as teleology
and of language as metaphor.

What Panthea's narration leads Asia to partially remember is her own
dream, a dream which both alters and echoes that of her sister. Asia, too,
speaks of moments of incipience that give way to a written call to
deferral.

But, on the shadows of the morning clouds
Athwart the purple mountain slope was written
Follow, O follow! as they vanished by,
And on each herb from which Heaven's dew had fallen
The like was stamped as with a withering fire;
A wind arose among the pines – it shook
The clinging music from their boughs, and then
Low, sweet, faint sounds, like the farewell of ghosts
Were heard – *O follow, follow, follow me!*
And then I said: 'Panthea, look on me.'
But in the depth of those beloved eyes
Still I saw, *follow, follow!*

(II, i, 151–62)

The '*follow, follow*' of Asia's dream comes once again as the answer to
the desire to find immediate presence in her sister's eyes. Once again
Asia has asked Panthea to 'lift / [her] eyes' presumably so 'that . . . [she]
may read . . . [Prometheus's] written soul!' (II, i, 109–10), but her dream
insists on the 'withering fire' of another inscription. This refusal of 'a
[reassuring] shade – a shape' (II, i, 120), this other kind of inscription, is
undoubtedly a call to read differently. In a manner of speaking, Asia
follows its call, although what she follows are 'Echoes', voices whose
origins are not their own, voices dislocated from the source of authority.
But whether Asia has learned to read is yet to be answered.

Echoes   In the world unknown
            Sleeps a voice unspoken;

255

> By thy step alone
> Can its rest be broken,
>
> (II, i, 190–3)

Asia, it seems, is called to break the rest of a 'voice unspoken'. Will she then come to know the realm of Demogorgon that was formerly 'the world unknown'; will she bring the 'voice unspoken' to full speech, or will she merely break the rest of a voice that must forever remain, in some sense, unspoken, awakening its refusal of open voice?[11] It depends, of course, on how one reads what Shelley has to say.

The entrance to Demogorgon's abode, at any rate, is inauspicious enough, for it hurls an oracular vapour that intoxicates to a misapprehension of truth, that causes those who drink of it to cry in the Maenadic voice that accompanied the dismemberment of the prototypical lyric poet (II, iii, 1–10). To be sure all this seems put to rights once Jupiter is deposed (III, iii, 124–47) and Asia herself is not one to question, much less rend, the integrity of the lyrical utterance.

On the contrary. Her entire dialogue with Demogorgon is a celebration of the power of the word – albeit an ironized celebration. For if earlier Asia's concept of reading was the direct perception of Prometheus's 'written soul' (II, i, 110), 'a shape – . . . arrayed / In the soft light of his own smiles which spread / Like radiance from the cloud-surrounded moon' (II, i, 120–2), her confrontation with Demogorgon systematically inverts each value of that image.

> *Panthea*   I see a mighty Darkness
> Filling the seat of power; and rays of gloom
> Dart round, as light from the meridian Sun,
> Ungazed upon and shapeless – neither limb
> Nor form – nor outline.
>
> (II, iv, 2–6)

From the question of negative perception the text immediately shifts to that of knowledge, or, perhaps, quite literally, to that of knowledge as question.

> *Demogorgon*   Ask what thou wouldst know.
> *Asia*   What canst thou tell?
> *Demogorgon*   All things thou dar'st demand.
>
> (II, iv, 7–8)

What Asia is slow to grasp is that Demogorgon may bid her ask, but promises only to 'tell' rather than answer. And what he will tell is no more and no less than what she will ask.[12] It seems fitting then that the guides to Demogorgon's realm are echoes. For Demogorgon's particular form of oracular pronouncement is ultimately not unlike the echo, however misunderstood that form of expression must necessarily be. Thus at the close of their dialogue Asia admits that Demogorgon can only echo what her own soul would answer (II, iv, 121–6).

To the end, however, Asia remains blinded by a desire for a certain kind of knowledge.[13] From the very beginning of their encounter, Asia has sought a means to name power.

Asia	Who made the living world?
Demogorgon	God.
Asia	Who made all
	That it contains – thought, passion, reason, will,
	Imagination?
Demogorgon	God, Almighty God.
	(II, iv, 9–11)

Apparently satisfied with the self-evident significance of Demogorgon's response, Asia goes on to seek a name for the authority behind the forces of evil. But here Demogorgon offers no name but rather a force as action.

Asia	And who made terror, madness, crime, remorse?
Demogorgon	He reigns.
Asia	Utter his name – a world pining in pain
	Asks but his name; curses shall drag him down.
Demogorgon	He reigns.
	(II, iv, 19, 28–31)

More precisely, it is not the name *per se* that Asia desires, for the long speech that follows proves she too could pronounce it if she wished. What Asia seeks is the control that accompanies naming, domination through the curse, language as authority: she thus reiterates the various calls to and recalls of power of Prometheus and Mother Earth in Act I.

If Demogorgon refuses to answer, if he insists on performing the unspokenness of his own voice, Asia fills in that void abysm of the refusal of a language of power with her own narration. Her long speech (II, iv, 32–109) recounts the historical tale of the beginning of the world, its rule by Saturn, and, through Prometheus's gift of wisdom, its fall to Jupiter during whose reign Prometheus has done all possible to give men dominion over the world around them, to grant 'The birthright of their being, knowledge, power' (II, iv, 39). The Titan may stand at the origin of speech that creates thought, prophetic song and music, he may stand at the origin of science that challenges 'the thrones of Earth and Heaven

(II, iv, 74), but Asia's description is peculiarly punctuated by a replication of those same structures of false power.

> And he tamed fire, which like some beast of prey
> Most terrible, but lovely, played beneath
> The frown of man, and tortured to his will
> Iron and gold, the slaves and signs of power. . . .
>
> (II, iv, 66–9)

Prometheus, as she would have it, has instituted new relations of power and slavery in place of old ones. Asia, too, is less interested in abolishing thrones altogether than in establishing a new hierarchical order.

> Asia   [W]hile yet his [Jupiter's] frown shook Heaven, aye when
> His adversary from adamantine chains
> Cursed him, he trembled like a slave. Declare
> Who is his master? Is he too a slave?
> Demogorgon   All spirits are enslaved who serve things evil:
> Thou knowest if Jupiter be such or no.
> Asia   Whom calledst thou God?
> Demogorgon   I spoke but as ye speak –
> For Jove is the supreme of living things.
> Asia   Who is the master of the slave?
>
> (II, iv, 106–14)

Just what is at stake in Demogorgon's continued refusal to answer? To be sure the imperative that drives him here has nothing to do with an unwillingness to upset the mastery of Jupiter. This, after all, is the crucial event that takes place only one scene later. Demogorgon's reticence arises rather from Asia's fundamental misapprehension of the nature of truth and language.

> Demogorgon   – If the Abysm
> Could vomit forth its secrets: – but a voice
> Is wanting, the deep truth is imageless;
> For what would it avail to bid thee gaze
> On the revolving world? what to bid speak
>
> Fate, Time, Occasion, Chance and Change? To these
> All things are subject but eternal Love.
>
> (II, iv, 114–20)

Demogorgon's 'deep truth' is that of the abysm. It has no ground, no voice, no possibility of being represented. One can gaze on the revolving world ruled by 'Fate, Time, Occasion, Chance and Change'. Indeed poetry's 'figured curtain', as Shelley calls it elsewhere, [14] a realm of images, is just this world – and the only realm, in one form or another, to which we may have access. But nowhere, and certainly not by way of Demogorgon, can 'the deep truth' be voiced as Asia wishes, as a presence, as the present, as a here and now that endures.

But, surely, there is a 'far goal of Time' (III, iii, 174), a resting place, promised by the Spirit of the hour (II, iv, 173), announced by Asia at the end of Act II and the Earth in Act III, and implicit, most certainly, in the overall trajectory of the drama. Asia and Panthea arrive at the Caucasus. Prometheus is unbound by Hercules, and, in the moment of his unbinding, he performs the fore-thought promised by his name. For here Prometheus tells of an era, now only ever so slightly deferred, when he and Asia, Panthea and Ione will pass their time out of time in a place that escapes the conventional parameters of locality.

Still it is not that Prometheus envisions space and time as finally becoming the stable here and now after which Asia so longed, for, while he may claim to speak of a state of permanence, the passage describes a perpetual interchange between the cave and two realms that define it through their otherness – the abode of nature and the realm of man.

> And there is heard the ever-moving air
> Whispering without from tree to tree, and birds,
> And bees; and all around are mossy seats
> And the rough walls are clothed with long soft grass;
> A simple dwelling, which shall be our own,
> Where we will sit and talk of time and change
> As the world ebbs and flows, ourselves unchanged. . . .
>
> (III, iii, 18–24)

The difference between the cave and its exterior is easy to define but difficult to maintain. The world ebbs and flows, the air is ever-moving as are the bees and birds; and yet, those within remain 'unchanged'. This same natural world, nevertheless, is at once outside the cave and inside the cave (III, iii, 20–1), at once both of these and the border that separates the two.

> There is a Cave
> All overgrown with trailing odorous plants
> Which curtain out the day with leaves and flowers. . . .
>
> (III, iii, 10–12)

This curtain, like so many veils in Shelley, rises less to reveal than to insist on a blindness. It curtains out the day, but curtains it in as well – 'the . . . walls clothed with long soft grass', and curtains in not only the verdant growth of that realm without but also, apparently, its perpetual change.

> A simple dwelling, which shall be our own,
> Where we will sit and talk of time and change
> As the world ebbs and flows, ourselves unchanged –
> What can hide man from Mutability? –
> And if ye sigh, then I will smile, and thou
> Ione, shall chant fragments of sea-music,
> Until I weep, when ye shall smile away
> The tears she brought, which yet were sweet to shed;
> We will entangle buds and flowers, and beams
> Which twinkle on the fountain's brim, and make
> Strange combinations out of common things
> Like human babes in their brief innocence;
> And we will search, with looks and words of love
> For hidden thoughts, each lovelier than the last,
> Our unexhausted spirits, and like lutes
> Touched by the skill of the enamoured wind,
> Weave harmonies divine, yet ever new,
> From difference sweet where discord cannot be.

(III, iii, 22–39)

If the natural world ebbs and flows, if man cannot escape Mutability, what Prometheus envisages for himself, nevertheless, is also mutability, a permanent, if entirely 'sweet' mutability. When Asia sighs, he will smile. When Prometheus weeps, Asia will smile, a differentiation to be brought about by Ione's chanting of sea-music. For the entire experience takes place under the aegis of music and poetry: the group will 'talk of time and change', making 'Strange combinations out of common things', 'search[ing] with looks and words of love / For hidden thoughts', 'weav[ing] harmonies divine'. It marks a break from what preceded it for Prometheus has moved from the theatre of political struggle in which 'discord' displays a decisive will to authority to that of an apparently will-less interior scene of poetic creation.

Nevertheless, the fixed closure implied by the metaphor of withdrawal is belied not only by the unremitting interchange with the world outside, but also by the difference sweet of the perpetual activity within. The flowers and birds of the natural realm enter into strange combination with the beams of the fountain in a creation that takes place as ever new juxtapositions and harmonies. Here, however, a flower is never treated as a flower for nothing can remain itself or maintain its self-identity: every element enters into play only in relation to its other. Like that other flower that could not be itself, the syllable αι written by the god of poetry that named the flower and much else as well, the poetry of the cave brings about endless self-differentiation – but without the pathos of desire and grief. Nothing is uttered here without the difference implicit in a recall that is at once repetition and renunciation, restoration and revocation.

The natural object enters the cave to lose all semblance of organic unity – a non-violent version of the rupture-into-text of the leaves in Asia and Panthea's dreams. For the cave, on the other hand, the unremitting interchange with that outside world signifies the surrender of any illusory claim to a poetic enterprise that might evade all relation to the natural. And yet this hardly enables the recuperation of nature as essence in the name of a poetry that might pretend to escape the dislocations of representation: the passage is constructed with a startling symmetry that sets everything off-balance.

For no sooner are we assured of the difference sweet and harmonies divine that arise from within than Prometheus turns to the other sounds that come to the cave from without: 'the echoes of the human world' (III, iii, 44). Unlike the natural sounds, what enters from the human world comes by way of 'mediators' (III, iii, 58). All sounds and shapes come forth as 'echoes', murmurs, 'apparitions', 'phantoms', 'shadows' (III, iii, 44–57). A new version, then, of 'Mont Blanc's' 'cave of the witch Poesy' where the 'ceaseless motion' and unremitting interchange lead to a meditation on the phantasy of the human mind.[15] As in that earlier text, a 'legion of wild thoughts', 'swift shapes and sounds', (III, iii, 60) seem murmured in a voice too low and too 'unresting'[16] to be grasped.

The apparitions that visit Prometheus are bound to disquiet any seduction into a poetics of immediacy or duration. The imagery that earlier denoted the world outside the cave – winds, bees, flowers – here returns as the apparently incidental matter of description and simile. But what could be more unsettling to the natural earthly realm to which such imagery refers than a mythological allusion to Enna, the meadow whose ground collapsed at the moment Hades carried off Persephone. And as the myth tells us, when the god of the underworld abducted Demeter's daughter, the goddess of fruit and harvest went into mourning, so that Hades carried off the earth's natural plenitude as well.[17]

> And hither come, sped on the charmed winds
> Which meet from all the points of Heaven, as bees
> From every flower aerial Enna feeds
> At their known island-homes in Himera,

The echoes of the human world, which tell
Of the low voice of love. . . .

(III, iii, 40–5)

It is not a question here of simply counterbalancing two realms of
absolutes outside the cave, the one the here-and-now of natural
substance, the other the space of pure representation. It is not that
Prometheus's naming of the human implies the displacement of reality
by image and art. The human world performs, in the structure of an
echo, the menace to the natural realm. Thus Prometheus recalls the
elements of nature in a gesture that, simultaneously, causes the bees and
flowers of 'aerial Enna' to stand in the service of a myth that underscores
their potential disappearance.

This echo chamber of representation is, for Prometheus, now no cause
for grief, no sign of loss like the earlier attempt at recall nor a sign of
empty deferral like the 'follow' of prophecy in Act II. It is rather

The wandering voices and the shadows these
Of all that man becomes, the mediators
Of that best worship, love, by him and us
Given and returned, swift shapes and sounds which grow
More fair and soft as man grows wise and kind,
And veil by veil evil and error fall. . . .

(III, iii, 57–62)

Evil and error may fall here, veil by veil, but, as in 'A Defence of Poetry',
no inner core of essential truth results. What remains is, forever, 'swift
shapes and sounds' that simply grow more fair as shapes and sounds.

All this takes place in the name of (the mediators of) love and leads us
back to the admonishment of Demogorgon.

      – If the Abysm
Could vomit forth its secrets: – but a voice
Is wanting, the deep truth is imageless;
For what would it avail to bid thee gaze
On the revolving world? what to bid speak
Fate, Time, Occasion, Chance and Change? To these
All things are subject but eternal Love.

(II, iv, 114–20)

If eternal Love is not subject to 'Fate, Time, Occasion, Chance and
Change', this is because Love is not a thing but precisely the force that
drives eternal change as endless mediation.

We have reached a moment of uncontainable self-reflection – in the case of *Prometheus Unbound*, what might rather be called a landscape of limitless recall. For as Prometheus describes 'the cave and place around' (III, iii, 63), he both reiterates and transforms several of the most critical moments of the text that precedes it. The abyss of Demogorgon, the 'revolving world' of shapelessness as perpetual transformation, Demogorgon's refusal to be reified, his refusal to speak a language that delimits its referent, now appears as the very possibility of art.

> And lovely apparitions dim at first
> Then radiant . . .
>
> Shall visit us, the progeny immortal
> Of Painting, Sculpture and rapt Poesy
> And arts, though unimagined, yet to be.
>
> (III, iii, 49–50, 54–6)

As in the opening scene of recall that violates the structure of origin and repetition, here too the production of these apparitions is such that phantoms of forms take temporal precedence over reality.

> And lovely apparitions dim at first
> Then radiant – as the mind, arising bright
> From the embrace of beauty (whence the forms
> Of which these are the phantoms) casts on them
> The gathered rays which are reality –
>
> (III, iii, 49–53)

But whereas the earlier disruption was one of crisis, a crisis of authority, of the power of words, and a crisis in the concept of linear temporality, the dissolution at the cave is a matter for rapture in which no will to self-identity takes place. Thus the human realm of echoes outside the cave doubles and transforms the realm of the dead as Earth described it earlier: for there too it was a question of 'beauteous shapes' and the power of man's imagination (I, i, 195–202, cited earlier).

If representation casts the spell of death on reality in that earlier moment of the drama, it is now indistinguishable from reality's point of origin (III, iii, 51–3). Nevertheless, art at this juncture is not an absolute, neither the absolute emptiness of empty shade nor the fullness of that error Shelley calls life (III, iv, 190). The 'echoes of the human world', the scene of production of art as love, is one of a series of gestures that unbalances the weight of the absolute. If the earlier pages of *Prometheus Unbound* were fraught with the dangers of falling from power, of being bound to the earth, this moment in the pseudo-teleological structure is menaced with the threat of falling up. Thus Act III closes (and this was

Shelley's initial point of completion) with the threat, apparently circumvented, of being 'Pinnacled dim in the intense inane' (III, iv, 204). For as *Prometheus Unbound* was meant to close, man is:

> Nor yet exempt, though ruling them like slaves,
> From chance and death and mutability,
> The clogs of that which else might oversoar
> The loftiest star of unascended Heaven
> Pinnacled dim in the intense inane.
>
> (III, iv, 200–4)

Only man's mortality (all that is suggested by Earth's description of the 'two worlds of life and death', and by Demogorgon's 'revolving world') prevents him from a fate far worse than death, an oversoaring that would rob him of his reason and his definition. For if his death unsettles him in another sense, it does not allow him to fall up into delusions of the absolute.

Chance, death, and mutability, as we saw, are the ruling forces in the scene of the cave, not only because mutability by that other name of difference might seem far sweeter but because the entire performance of that scene is structured on a system of perpetual unbalance. Just as man's mutability prevents him from soaring to the intense inane of a seemingly heavenly absolute, so each of the three realms that Prometheus specifies, nature, the cave of harmonies, man's realm of poetic image, is that which trips the balance of the others.

But the cave, after all, does not mark the end point of the text. Act III goes on to celebrate the coming of the revolution to man, a revolution that liberates from the structure of hierarchy so completely that even the revolution's own claim to have created Heaven on Earth (III, iv, 160) is counterweighted, as we have seen. Act IV is its heavenly counterpart: it takes place, if not strictly speaking in Heaven, nevertheless with all the aura of a cosmic perspective. It is a perspective, however, that sings and dances of the impossibility of its own totalizing gesture. For this celebration repeats with more grandiose stakes the disbalance that preceded it.

And yet, this act begins like the first one with the promise of an era come to an end, this time a promise already fulfilled. Time is borne 'to his tomb in eternity' (IV, 9–14) and this signals (as *Prometheus Unbound* has suggested from the beginning) the end of traditional temporal concepts: but what replaces those concepts is an 'eternity' that only the closing lines of the text can account for.

Act IV begins with a dirge and continues with a wedding song, but what it buries is not quite what one thinks and the marriage it celebrates will never achieve duration. What starts as 'dear disunion' in Panthea's words (IV, 200) and moves to a celebration of oneness will be effaced by 'a mighty Power' (IV, 510) to which all resolution in *Prometheus Unbound* must give way. If Earth and Moon do indeed unite, their coming together is predicated on a ritual of delight in Jupiter's fall (IV, 350–5) and the celebration of man's new powers.

> All things confess his strength. –
>
> Language is a perpetual Orphic song,
> Which rules with Daedal harmony a throng
> Of thoughts and forms, which else senseless and shapeless were.
>
> > (IV, 412–17)

But Jupiter's relegation to the deep and man's shape-giving rule of thoughts and forms through language are quite explicitly eclipsed by a power far mightier than the momentary harmony of Earth and Moon.

> Peace! peace! a mighty Power, which is as Darkness,
> Is rising out o' Earth, and from the sky
> Is showered like Night, and from within the air
> Bursts, like eclipse which had been gathered up
> Into the pores of sunlight. . . .
>
> > (IV, 510–4)

Demogorgon, figure of shapelessness ('neither limb / Nor form – nor outline', II, iv, 5–6) replaces the 'stream of sound' of moon and earth (IV, 506) with 'a sense of words' (IV, 517). This is a language that is anything but the 'perpetual Orphic song' and 'Daedal harmony' attributed to man, that guaranteed the sense and shape of thought.[18]

Here the dance is broken and the song scattered as indeed they must be. For even the liberation from hierarchy on earth, the differential harmony in heaven and the virtue of perpetual displacement in Prometheus's cave run the danger of reification, of becoming that other virtue of the morally fixable – of becoming place as a ground to stand on. This is why the text insists not only on the cosmic eclipse of the marriage of Earth and Moon but also on the terrible and strange proximity, the coincidence rather that no good reader has missed, of the locus of the cave and the entrance to Demogorgon's abode. At this point there is the possibility once again of an oracular vapour hurled up to intoxicate to naive belief in 'truth, virtue, love, genius or joy' (II, iii, 4–10). 'Such virtue has the cave and place around' (III, iii, 63). For despite Earth's insistence on the transformation of that 'destined cave' (III, iii, 124–75), a new intoxication threatens to let one read 'this far goal of Time' (III, iii,

174) as telos, to let Prometheus and all he might come to symbolize assume a form of mastery less misplaced than that of Jupiter.

For where is Demogorgon in all of this – the anti-figure who refuses form and outline (II, iv, 5–6), demystifier of the power of conventional rhetoric, if not displaced just beneath that virtuous cave with Jupiter as his prisoner?

> This is the Day which down the void Abysm
> At the Earth-born's spell yawns for Heaven's Despotism,
>   And Conquest is dragged Captive through the Deep;
> Love from its awful throne of patient power
> In the wise heart, from the last giddy hour
>   Of dread endurance, from the slippery, steep,
> And narrow verge of crag-like Agony, springs
> And folds over the world its healing wings.
> Gentleness, Virtue, Wisdom and Endurance, –
> These are the seals of that most firm assurance
>   Which bars the pit over Destruction's strength. . . .
>
>   (IV, 554–64)

At the very juncture of conquering Jupiter, at the very moment when, in Asia's words, the master seems to have become a slave (II, iv, 109), what is dragged 'Captive through the Deep' is less he who can be named 'Jupiter' (as Asia might have preferred) than 'Conquest' itself (IV, 556). Love may have sprung forth but the abysm beneath remains slippery and steep. The danger, however, is once again, not so much a fall below as a fall upwards. It is over and against this that Demogorgon serves as

> The clogs of that which else might oversoar
> The loftiest star of unascended Heaven
> Pinnacled dim in the intense inane.
>
>   (III, iv, 202–4)

Thus the seals of assurance against the strength of Destruction are less that which maintains the status quo (of Prometheus' or man's or Earth and Heaven's conquest) than that which brings about a new revolution:

> And if, with infirm hand, Eternity,
> Mother of many acts and hours, should free
>   The serpent that would clasp her with his length –
> These are the spells by which to reassume
> An empire o'er the disentangled Doom.
>
>   (IV, 564–9)

Demogorgon seems to close *Prometheus Unbound* with the spells of the
final stanza (IV, 570–8), to offer the power-filled words to put the
serpent, Jupiter, back in his place should he escape. The text that began
with the crisis of the curse would close then with a new 'spell', one
whose potency is presumably far better assured than the involutions of
Prometheus' original words and all their forms of 'recall'. But the spatial
and temporal disruptions of *Prometheus Unbound* require that, from the
beginning, even before the conquest of Jupiter, the Doom that threatens
to disentangle itself in Demogorgon's last monologue is already there.
For the spirits that guide Asia and Panthea to Demogorgon sing of it as
'underneath his throne'.

Song of Spirit	Resist not the weakness –
	Such strength is in meekness –
	That the Eternal, the Immortal,
	Must unloose through life's portal
	The snake-like Doom coiled underneath his throne
	By that alone!
	(II, iii, 93–8)

The necessity of Demogorgon is such that he 'Must unloose . . . / The
snake-like Doom'. For who figures forth 'Eternity' if not Demogorgon –
not only in the Song of the Spirits cited above but also in his own words.
At the moment when Jupiter is thrust from power Demogorgon has this
to say:

Jupiter	Awful Shape, what art thou? Speak!
Demogorgon	Eternity – demand no direr name.
	Descend, and follow me down the abyss. . . .
	(III, i, 50–2)

'Eternity' is the name assumed by Demogorgon, he who refuses to be
named. He is there as the potential power of otherness, the liberator of
the serpent (IV, 565–7), a liberation that at the apparent 'close' of the text
might just as well reinstate Jupiter or at least all the powers that he
embodies.

'Eternity' here implies anything but a state of permanence for it
operates rather as the perpetual disruption of temporal and spatial stasis,
a disruption already at play, in a sense, in Prometheus's first monologue.
As in 'The Necessity of Atheism', eternity (or necessity) is the
questioning of the concept of origin; it is the pronounced
incomprehensibility of first cause,[19] and, it goes without saying, then, of
telos. This is why if one asks what *Prometheus Unbound* is 'about', it is not
about a restoration to his proper place and proper authority of

Prometheus as the origin of speech and thought, a movement toward
apocalypse or utopia, a millenium or redemption, but rather the
performance of perpetual, if unpredictable, revolution.

Notes

1. References to *Prometheus Unbound* are indicated in the text by act, scene and
   line number. All citations are from *Shelley's Poetry and Prose*, ed. Donald H.
   Reiman and Sharon B. Powers (New York: Norton, 1977).

2. Quite understandably, almost all of Shelley's readers insist on the teleological
   structure of the drama, though many have been struck by the difficulties of
   locating the action. To name just two typical examples: MILTON WILSON,
   Shelley's Later Poetry (New York: Columbia, 1957), pp. 42, 50 and 56, and
   CARLOS BAKER (*Shelley's Major Poetry*, New York: Russell and Russell, 1961)
   who reads the first act as containing the complete 'moral reformation of
   Prometheus' (p. 98) and therefore 'the hour of the world's redemption' (p. 92).

3. See SUSAN HAWK BRISMAN's fine essay, '"Unsaying His High Language": The
   Problem of Voice in *Prometheus Unbound*', *Studies in Romanticism*, **16**, no. 1
   (1977): 61.

4. See PETER BUTTER, *Shelley's Idols of the Cave* (Edinburgh: Edinburgh University
   Press, 1954), p. 173, in conjunction with the interventions in the *Times Literary
   Supplement* 16 December 1955, 6 and 20 January 1957 and 15 February 1957.

5. *The Compact Edition of the Oxford English Dictionary* (New York: Oxford
   University Press, 1971), II, 2435.

6. See DANA POLAN, 'The Ruin of a Poetics: The Political Practice of *Prometheus
   Unbound*', *Enclitic*, **7** (1983): 38–9. Polan briefly recognizes the implications of
   the pun *recall* but sees *Prometheus Unbound* as a text that 'moves from stasis to
   stasis'. The full complexity of the play of *recall*, however, involves a refusal of
   any possibility of stasis.

7. Earl Wasserman reads this passage as Prometheus facing his former moral self
   in *Shelley: A Critical Reading* (Baltimore: Johns Hopkins University Press, 1971),
   p. 260. In a sense this is certainly true, but the confrontation is also between
   two modes of language, or, more accurately, between Prometheus's desire for
   a confirmation of self-identity through language and the figure's refusal.

8. ROBERT GRAVES, *The Greek Myths* (Aylesbury: Penguin, 1955), I, 78–9.

9. Ovid's version is that Hyacinthus catches the missile thrown by his lover – as
   though to mark the danger of catching that thrown by the god of poetry.

10. The second dream displaces the shape in Panthea's eyes (II, i, 131–3).

11. Baker ascribes to Asia the fullest powers of interpretation based on her
    encounter with Panthea, *Shelley's Major Poetry*, p. 104. Her dialogue with
    Demogorgon, however, would seem to belie this.

12. See WASSERMAN, *Shelley: A Critical Reading*, p. 322.

13. See TILOTTOMA RAJAN, *Dark Interpreter* (Ithaca: Cornell University Press, 1980),
    pp. 89–90.

14. 'A Defence of Poetry', *Shelley's Poetry and Prose*, ed. Donald H. Reiman and Sharon B. Powers (New York: Norton, 1977), p. 505.

15. *Prometheus Unbound* echoes in a sense, and most especially in this the third act, the situation of 'Mont Blanc'. However, what in the earlier poem is problematized as a crisis of epistemology and rhetoric is dramatized in *Prometheus Unbound* as a struggle for political power.

16. 'Mont Blanc', ll. 33, 41.

17. OVID, *Metamorphoses*, trans. Rolfe Humphries (Bloomington: Indiana University Press, 1955), p. 122.

18. The danger in Shelley (which is as much the comfort) is taking any one statement on the nature of language as the final word. Thus neither Asia's description of Prometheus's relation to language in Act II, iv, nor the Earth's insistence on man's orphic song, nor for that matter, ironically, the last ironical words of Demogorgon should be given the weight of their literal statements – out of context. See, for example, the opening pages of FREDERICK BURWICK's 'The Language of Causality in *Prometheus Unbound*', *Keats–Shelley Journal*, **31** (1982): 136–7, or Brisman's concept of the Promethean principle, 'Unsaying His High Language', pp. 58, 61.

19. 'The Necessity of Atheism', *The Complete Works of Percy Bysshe Shelley*, ed. Roger Ingpen and Walter Peck (New York: Gordian, 1965), v, p. 208.

Notes on Authors*

CATHY CARUTH (born 1955) took her PhD at Yale University, where she is Associate Professor of English. Her book *Empirical Truths and Critical Fictions: Locke, Wordsworth, Kant, and Freud* (1991) analyses the conceptual and rhetorical strategies of works which have been important in defining the category of empirical experience. She has edited two special issues of *American Imago* (**48**: 1, 4, 1991) entitled 'Psychoanalysis, Culture and Trauma', exploring the significance for reflection on culture of new research on trauma and memory. This project is reflected in her own essay 'Unclaimed Experience: Trauma and the Possibility of History' (*Yale French Studies, 79, 1991*). Her other writings include an essay on the referential aspect of language, 'The Claims of Reference' (*Yale Journal of Criticism*, October 1990) and an essay examining one conception of historical causality in *The Prelude*, 'Unknown Causes, Poetic Effects' (*Diacritics*, Winter 1987). She is also the editor, with Deborah Esch, of *Reviewing Deconstruction* (New Brunswick: Rutgers University Press, 1993).

JEROME CHRISTENSEN (born 1948) studied at Cornell and taught at Purdue University before moving to Johns Hopkins. He is the author of three books: *Coleridge's Blessed Machine of Language* (1981), *Practicing Englightenment: Hume and the Formation of a Literary Career* (Madison: University of Wisconsin Press, 1987) and *Lord Byron's Strength: Romantic Writing and Commercial Society* (1992). He has written essays on 'corporate populism' as well as on Wordsworth, Keats and the Romantic sublime, including a major essay on 'The Thorn' and the differences dividing Coleridge and Wordsworth ('Wordsworth's Misery, Coleridge's Woe', *ELH*, 46 (1979). Christensen interprets the style and rhetoric of Romantic texts in connection with questions of ideology and politics.

PAUL DE MAN (born Belgium, 1919) settled in the United States in 1947. He took his PhD in Comparative Literature at Harvard and taught at Cornell University, Johns Hopkins, and the University of Zurich before becoming Professor of French and Comparative Literature at Yale University. His essay 'The Rhetoric of Temporality' (1969) was a major early influence on the rethinking of Romanticism; his later writings and those of his students demonstrated the complexity of Romantic writing (illegitimating, moreover, such a term as 'Romantic'). De Man died in 1983. In addition to *The Rhetoric of Romanticism* (1984) and *Romanticism and Contemporary Criticism* (Baltimore: The Johns Hopkins University Press, 1992) –

---

* No publication information is given here for books which are listed under Further Reading.

posthumous collections of essays and lectures, which deal with texts of Wordsworth, Hölderlin, Rousseau, Shelley and Yeats – much of *Blindness and Insight* (1970, rev. edn 1983) and *Allegories of Reading* (1979) concerns Romantic authors (above all Rousseau) or categories and assumptions involved in writing the history of Romanticism. De Man's sustained elaboration of the concept of allegory impinges on the aims and procedures of literary interpretation and theory. Some early essays collected in *Critical Writings, 1953–1978*, ed. Lindsay Waters (Minneapolis: University of Minnesota Press, 1990) touch upon problems of Romanticism, as do the late essays of *Aesthetic Ideology*, ed. Andrzej Warminiski (Minneapolis: University of Minnesota Press, 1993), on materiality and the sublime in Kant and Hegel. A further collection is *The Resistance to Theory* (Minneapolis: University of Minnesota Press, 1986).

GEOFFREY H. HARTMAN (born 1929) took his PhD at Yale and taught at the University of Iowa before returning to Yale, where he is Karl Young Professor of Comparative Literature. Hartman was a pioneer of close reading and of modern studies of Wordsworth. His earliest books are *The Unmediated Vision: An Interpretation of Wordsworth, Hopkins, Rilke, and Valery* (1954) and *Wordsworth's Poetry, 1878–1814* (1964). Essays of two decades on Wordsworth are collected in *The Unremarkable Wordsworth* (1987); two further volumes, *Beyond Formalism* (1970) and *The Fate of Reading* (1975), include important writing on Romanticism. He has edited several volumes of English Institute essays and, with David Thorburn, *Romanticism: Vistas, Instances, Continuities* (Ithaca: Cornell University Press, 1978). Hartman has produced several works of literary theory: *Saving the Text: Derrida, Literature, Philosophy* (Baltimore: Johns Hopkins University Press, 1981) and *Criticism in the Wilderness* (New Haven: Yale University Press, 1980). In *Midrash and Literature*, edited with Sanford Budick (New Haven: Yale University Press, 1986), he has turned his attention toward a practice of interpretation in important respects different from what has been called 'the *Judaeo-Christian* tradition'. In recent years he has chaired the programme of Jewish Studies at Yale and edited *Bitburg: A Moral and Political Perspective* (Bloomington: Indiana University Press, 1986).

NEIL HERTZ (born 1932) is Professor in the Humanities Centre, Johns Hopkins University. He previously taught for many years at Cornell. His work, much of which is collected in *The End of the Line: Essays on Psychoanalysis and the Sublime* (1985), combines the attention to tone and stance characteristic of the best New Criticism with attention to the sorts of questions raised by psychoanalysis and post-structuralist theory. He is completing a book on George Eliot for Basil Blackwell's 'Rereading Literature' series. With Thomas Keenan and Werner Hamacher, he edited Paul de Man, *Wartime Journalism, 1939–1943* (Lincoln: University of Nebraska Press, 1988) and *Responses: On Paul de Man's Wartime Journalism* (Lincoln: University of Nebraska Press, 1989). He is the author of two important essays on the rhetoric of Paul de Man's Romantic criticism and theory: 'Lurid Figures', in *Reading De Man Reading* (Minneapolis: University of Minnesota Press, 1987), and 'More Lurid Figures', in *Diacritics* (Fall 1990).

MARGARET HOMANS (born 1952) took her PhD at Yale, where she is presently Professor of English. The essay reprinted here is a chapter of her second book, *Bearing the Word. Language and Female Experience in Nineteenth-Century Women's Writing* (1986), a wide-ranging study of the transformations of experience in literature by women, including the experience of being associated (as a woman) with a position outside of language. Homans' first book is *Woman Writers and Poetic Identity: Dorothy Wordsworth, Emily Bronte, and Emily Dickinson* (Princeton: Princeton University Press, 1980). Her 'Keats Reading Women, Women Reading

Keats' (*Studies in Romanticism*, **29**: 3 (Fall 1990)) won the Keats–Shelley Association prize for the best essay in 1991. She is presently working on a book on contemporary Black women writers.

CAROL JACOBS (born 1943) studied at Cornell and Johns Hopkins and is Professor of Comparative Literature at the State University of New York at Buffalo. She is the author of three books, analytical readings of texts of the Romantic and modern period. Her first book, *The Dissimulating Harmony: The Image of Interpretation in Nietzsche, Rilke, Artaud, and Benjamin* (Baltimore: Johns Hopkins University Press, 1978), includes a foreword by Paul de Man on the procedures of critical reading. *Uncontainable Romanticism. Shelley, Bronte, Kleist* (1989) considers the problems of grounds and of limits posed by the works she examines. Her third book, *Telling Time* (Baltimore: Johns Hopkins University Press, 1992), considers the question of time in works including Lessing's *Laocoon* and Ford Madox Ford's *The Good Soldier*. Among Jacobs's other writings is a reading of Walter Benjamin's 'The Task of the Translator' ('The Monstrosity of Translation', *MLN*, Winter 1978).

MARY JACOBUS (born 1944) was educated at Oxford and was Fellow and Tutor and University Lecturer in English at Lady Margaret Hall. Since 1980 she has taught at Cornell University, where she holds the Anderson Chair in the Department of English. Her first book, *Tradition and Experiment in Wordsworth's 'Lyrical Ballads'* (1976), was a work of interpretive scholarship. A growing engagement with feminist theory issued first in the collective volume *Women Writing and Writing About Women* (London: Croom Helm, 1979), which she edited. Her *Reading Woman: Essays in Feminist Criticism* (London: Methuen, 1986) and *Romanticism, Writing, and Sexual Difference: Essays on 'The Prelude'* (1989) exemplify the provocative and productive intersection of feminism, psychoanalysis and post-structuralism in the study of Romantic literature and modern thought. She is at work on a book of essays on theories and fantasies of reproductive origins and on questions relating to the representation of the maternal body in a variety of literary and non-literary texts.

MARJORIE LEVINSON (born 1951) took her PhD at the University of Chicago. She is Professor of English at the University of Pennsylvania and author of *The Romantic Fragment Poem: A Critique of a Form* (1986), *Wordsworth's Great Period Poems: Four Essays* (Cambridge: Cambridge University Press, 1986), and *Keats's Life of Allegory* (1988). One of the most astute participants in the New Historicism, she offers in her Introduction and her essay 'The New Historicism: Back to the Future', in the collective volume *Rethinking Historicism: Critical Readings in Romantic History* (1989), provocative critical examinations of the mode.

KAREN SWANN (born 1952) received her degrees from Oberlin College and Cornell University. She teaches in the English Department and the Women's Studies Programme, of which she is the Chair, at Williams College, Williamstown, Massachussetts. Her writing, which brings feminist and psychoanalytic insights to bear in close readings of texts of Wordsworth, Coleridge, Keats and their reception, includes 'Public Transport: Adventuring on Wordsworth's Salisbury Plain', *English Literary History*, **55** (1988); 'Harassing the Muse', in Anne Mellor's *Romanticism and Feminism* (1988); 'Suffering and Sensation in "The Ruined Cottage"' (*PMLA*, 1991); 'The Sublime and the Vulgar' in *College English* (January 1990); and, a companion piece to the essay reprinted here, '"Christabel": The Wandering Mother and the Enigma of Form', *Studies in Romanticism*, **23** (Winter 1984). She is completing a book entitled *Public Transport: Romantic Experiments in Sensationalism*.

Further Reading

Collections

ABRAMS, M.H. (ed.) *English Romantic Poets: Modern Essays in Criticism*. New York: Oxford University Press, 1960. (Includes such classic essays as Lovejoy's 'On the Discrimination of Romanticisms' and Wimsatt's 'The Structure of Romantic Nature Imagery.')

BLOOM, HAROLD (ed.) *Romanticism and Consciousness: Essays in Criticism*. New York: Norton: 1970. (Captures the beginnings of a new understanding of Romanticism.)

BROMWICH, DAVID (ed.) *Romantic Critical Essays*. Cambridge: Cambridge University Press, 1987. (Outstanding introduction accompanying texts by Wordsworth, Shelley, Lamb, Hazlitt and others, in the best collection of Romantic criticism.)

GALLANT, CHRISTINE (ed.) *Coleridge's Theory of Imagination Today*. New York: AMS Press, 1969. (Essays of interest by Catherine Wheeler, Susan Wolfson, and John Beer.)

GLECKNER, ROBERT F. and GERALD ENSCOE (eds) *Romanticism: Points of View*. Englewood Cliffs, N.J.: Prentice Hall, 1970. (Essays from Walter Pater to Abrams and Hartman.)

JOHNSTON, KENNETH R., et al. (eds) *Romantic Revolutions: Criticism and Theory*. Bloomington: Indiana University Press, 1990. (Essays focusing on recent critical debates surrounding British and American Romanticism.)

LEVINSON, MARJORIE, MARILYN BUTLER, JEROME McGANN and PAUL HAMILTON *Rethinking Historicism: Critical Readings in Romantic History*. Oxford: Blackwell, 1989. (Essays of and on new historicism.)

MELLOR, ANNE K. (ed.) *Romanticism and Feminism*. Bloomington: Indiana University Press, 1988.

REED, ARDEN (ed.) *Romanticism and Language*. Ithaca: Cornell University Press, 1984. (Essays by Christensen, Parker, Jacobus, Ferguson, Chase, and others of this generation.)

Guide

JORDAN, FRANK (ed.) *The English Romantic Poets: A Review of Research and Criticism*. 4th edn. New York: MLA, 1985.

Monographs

Abrams, M.H. *The Mirror and the Lamp: Romantic Theory and the Critical Tradition.* Oxford: Oxford University Press, 1953. (Pioneering study of the revolution of Romantic critical theory and its modern legacy.)

——*Natural Supernaturalism: Tradition and Revolution in Romantic Literature.* New York: Norton, 1971. (Interprets central Romatic themes and concepts as secularized versions of traditional theological notions.)

——*The Correspondent Breeze: Essays on English Romanticism.* New York: Norton, 1984. (Classic essays, including 'English Romanticism: The Spirit of the Age' and 'Structure and Style in the Greater Romantic Lyric'.)

Bahti, Timothy 'Figures of Interpretation, the Interpretation of Figure: A Reading of Wordsworth's "Dream of the Arab."' *Studies in Romanticism*, **18** (1979): 601–28.

Blanchot, Maurice 'The Athenaeum.' *Studies in Romanticism*, **22** (1983): 163–72. (See Introduction, p. 40 n52.)

Bloom, Harold *The Visionary Company: A Reading of English Romantic Poetry.* Ithaca: Cornell University Press, 1961. (Written before Bloom developed his theory of poetic influence; contains readings of many important Romantic poems.)

——*The Ringers in the Tower.* Chicago: University of Chicago Press, 1971. (Important essays, including 'The Internalization of Quest Romance'.)

——*The Anxiety of Influence: A Theory of Poetry.* New York: Oxford University Press, 1973. (A theory based on a conception of the strong Romantic poet who misreads his predecessors to make space for his own writing.)

——*Poetry and Repression.* New Haven: Yale University Press, 1976. (Chapters on Wordsworth, Shelley and others.)

Brinkley, Robert A. 'The Incident in the Simplon Pass: A Note on Wordsworth's Revisions', *The Wordsworth Circle*, **12**: 2 (Spring 1981): 122–5. (An excellent summary of readings of the crossing of the Alps passage in Book VI of *The Prelude* as well as a careful consideration of the implications of the several versions.)

Brisman, Leslie *Milton's Poetry of Choice and Its Romantic Heirs.* Ithaca: Cornell University Press, 1973.

——*Romantic Origins.* Ithaca: Cornell University Press, 1978. (On the Romantic 'self' and myths of origin.)

Burke, Kenneth 'Symbolic Action in a Poem by Keats.' *A Grammar of Motives.* New York: Prentice-Hall, 1945, pp. 447–63. (A bold, iconoclastic reading of 'Ode on a Grecian Urn.')

Butler, Marilyn *Romantics, Rebels, and Revolutionaries: English Literature and Its Background: 1760–1830.* London: Oxford University Press, 1981. (A study of the varied concerns and controversies engaging writers of the age.)

Carlson, Julie 'An Active Imagination: Coleridge and the Politics of Dramatic Reform.' *Modern Philology*, **86** (1988): 22–33.

CARUTH, CATHY *Empirical Truths and Critical Fictions: Locke, Wordsworth, Kant, Freud*. Baltimore: Johns Hopkins University Press, 1991. (A brilliant reading of her chosen philosophical and literary texts as transformations of a narrative of 'experience' and of the work of mourning.)

CHANDLER, JAMES *Wordsworth's Second Nature: A Study of the Poetry and Politics*. Chicago: University of Chicago Press, 1984.

CHASE, CYNTHIA *Decomposing Figures: Rhetorical Readings in the Romantic Tradition*. Baltimore: Johns Hopkins University Press, 1986. (Rhetorical readings of works by Wordsworth, Keats, Baudelaire and Rousseau, among others.)

CHRISTENSEN, JEROME *Coleridge's Blessed Machine of Language*. Ithaca: Cornell University Press, 1981.

——*Lord Byron's Strength: Romantic Writing and Commercial Society*. Baltimore: Johns Hopkins University Press, 1992.

CULLER, JONATHAN 'The Mirror Stage', in Lawrence Lipking (ed.), *High Romantic Argument: Essays for M.H. Abrams*. Ithaca: Cornell University Press, 1981. (A deconstructive interpretation of *The Mirror and the Lamp*.)

CURRAN, STUART *Poetic Form and British Romanticism*. New York: Oxford University Press, 1986.

DE MAN, PAUL Introduction. *The Selected Poetry of Keats*. New York: New American Library, 1966, pp. ix-xxxvi.

——*Allegories of Reading: Figural Language in Rousseau, Nietzsche, Rilke, and Proust*. New Haven: Yale University Press, 1979. (In addition to the six essays on Rousseau, other essays are pertinent to problems in the modern study of Romanticism.)

——'The Rhetoric of Temporality', in *Blindness and Insight*. rev. edn. Minneapolis: University of Minnesota Press, 1983. (Revises the notions of allegory and irony and their place in Romantic literature.)

——*The Rhetoric of Romanticism*. New York, Columbia University Press, 1984. (Important essays on Wordsworth, Hölderlin, Shelley, Yeats and Kleist.)

DERRIDA, JACQUES 'Economimesis', in Sylviane Agacinski et al., *Mimesis: Des articulations*. Paris: Flammarion, 1975, pp. 55–93. (On Kant and the paradoxes of mimesis which structure Romantic and post-Romantic criticism and theory.)

——'The Parergon', *The Truth in Painting*. Chicago: University of Chicago Press, 1987, pp. 15–148. (On Kant's Third Critique, the aesthetic frame, and the Sublime.)

DONATO, EUGENIO 'Divine Agonies: Of Representation and Narrative in Romantic Poetics', *Glyph*, **6** (1977): 90–122.

——'The Ruins of Memory: Archeological Fragments and Textual Artifacts', *MLN*, **93** (1978): 575–96.

EMPSON, WILLIAM 'Sense in *The Prelude*'. *The Structure of Complex Words*. London: Chatto, 1969, pp. 289–305. (A exploration of the remarkable effects of the multiple meanings of this word.)

ESCH, DEBORAH 'A Defence of Rhetoric / The Triumph of Reading: de Man, Shelley, and the Rhetoric of Romanticism', in Wlad Godzich and Lindsay

Waters (eds), *Reading de Man Reading*. Minneapolis: University of Minnesota Press, 1989.

FERGUSON, FRANCES *Wordsworth: Language as Counter-Spirit*. New Haven: Yale University Press, 1977. (A study of Wordsworth's implicit and explicit reflection on language.)

——'Historicism, Deconstruction, and Wordsworth', *Diacritics* (Winter 1987): 33–43.

FURET, FRANCOIS *Interpreting the French Revolution*. Cambridge: Cambridge University Press, 1981. (The best book on the political significance of the French Revolution.)

——and MONA OUZOUF (eds) *Critical Dictionary of the French Revolution*. Cambridge: Harvard University Press, 1989.

GLEN, HEATHER *Vision and Disenchantment: Blake's 'Songs' and Wordsworths 'Lyrical Ballads'*. Cambridge: Cambridge University Press, 1983. (Reads the two collections as distinctive responses to social and cultural pressures.)

HAMILTON, PAUL *Coleridge's Poetics*. Stanford: Stanford University Press, 1988.

HARTMAN, GEOFFREY H. *The Unmediated Vision: An Interpretation of Wordsworth, Hopkins, Rilke, and Valery*. New Haven: Yale University Press, 1954.

——'Romantic Poetry and the Genius Loci', in *Beyond Formalism: Literary Essays 1958–1970*. New Haven: Yale University Press, 1970.

——*Wordsworth's Poetry, 1787–1814*. Cambridge, Mass.: Harvard University Press, 1971. (This study of 1964 initiated a new phase of Wordsworth criticism. The 1971 edition contains a 'Retrospect 1971'.)

——*The Fate of Reading, and Other Essays*. Chicago: University of Chicago Press, 1975. (Includes important essays on Keats.)

——*The Unremarkable Wordsworth*. Minneapolis: University of Minnesota Press, 1987. (Important essays from two decades.)

HERTZ, NEIL *The End of the Line: Essays on Psychoanalysis and the Sublime*. New York: Columbia University Press, 1985. (In addition to the essay reprinted here, studies of scenarios of the sublime in Wordsworth, Freud, and others.)

HOGLE, JERROLD 'Shelley's Poetics: The Power as Metaphor'. *Keats–Shelley Journal* (1982): 159–97.

——*Shelley's Process: Radical Transference and the Development of His Major Works*. New York: Oxford University Press, 1988. (An impressive reading of the basic rhetorical mode of Shelley's poetry.)

HOMANS, MARGARET *Women Writers and Poetic Identity: Dorothy Wordsworth, Emily Bronte, and Emily Dickinson*. Princeton: Princeton University Press, 1980.

——*Bearing the Word. Language and Female Experience in Nineteenth-Century Women's Writing*. Chicago: University of Chicago Press, 1986. (In addition to the chapter reprinted here, contains essays on representation and woman's place in language.)

JACOBS, CAROL *Uncontainable Romanticism. Shelley, Bronte, Kleist*. Baltimore and London: Johns Hopkins University Press, 1989. (A shortened version of one chapter reprinted here.)

JACOBUS, MARY *Tradition and Experiment in Wordsworth's Lyrical Ballads (1798)*. London: Oxford University Press, 1976. (A pre-post-structuralist discussion.)

——*Romanticism, Writing, and Sexual Difference: Essays on 'The Prelude'*. Oxford: Clarendon Press, 1989. (A re-reading of *The Prelude* in the light of post-structuralist and feminist theory.)

JANOWITZ, ANNE *England's Ruins: Poetic Purpose and the National Landscape*. Oxford: Basil Blackwell, 1990. (Study of how various aesthetics of the ruin serve the ideology of nationalism.)

KLANCHER, JON *The Making of English Reading Audiences: 1790–1832*. Madison: University of Wisconsin Press, 1987.

KROEBER, KARL *Romantic Narrative Art*. Madison: University of Wisconsin Press, 1960. (Chapters on balladry, and 'realistic adventure', the poetic tale, the personal epic, and other narrative modes in Romantic poetry and the novels of Scott.)

KNAPP, STEVEN *Personification and the Sublime: Milton to Coleridge*. Cambridge: Harvard University Press, 1985.

LACOUE-LABARTHE, PHILIPPE and NANCY, JEAN-LUC *The Literary Absolute: The Theory of Literature in German Romanticism*. Trans. Philip Barnard and Cheryl Lester. Albany: State University of New York Press, 1988. (A powerful study of the origins in romanticism of the modern idea of literature and of the philosophical and critical dimensions of romanticism in general.)

LEVINSON, MARJORIE *The Romantic Fragment Poem: A Critique of a Form*. Chapel Hill: University of North Carolina Press, 1987.

——*Keats's Life of Allegory*. Oxford: Basil Blackwell, 1988. (The Introduction is reprinted here.)

LIU, ALAN *Wordsworth: The Sense of History*. Stanford: Stanford University Press, 1989. (A massive New Historicist study and serious reflection on how history makes an appearance in Wordsworth.)

MARSHALL, DAVID *The Surprising Effects of Sympathy: Marivaux, Diderot, Rousseau, and Mary Shelley*. Chicago: University of Chicago Press, 1988. (On the eighteenth-century concern with theatricality and with sympathy.)

McFarland, Thomas *Romanticism and the Forms of Ruin: Wordsworth, Coleridge, and the Modalities of Fragmentation*. Princeton: Princeton University Press, 1981.

McGANN, JEROME J. *The Romantic Ideology: A Critical Investigation*. Chicago, University of Chicago Press, 1983. (Argues that ideologies embodied in Romantic poetry and theory have shaped the criticism of Romanticism.)

——'Byron, Mobility, and the Poetics of Hysterical Ventriloquism'. *Romanticism Past and Present*, **9** (1985): 67–82.

——'The Book of Byron and the Book of a World', in Neal Fraistat (ed.) *Poems in Their Places: The Intertextuality and Order of Poetic Collections*. Chapel Hill: University of North Carolina Press, 1986, pp. 254–72.

PARKER, REEVE *Coleridge's Meditative Art*. Ithaca: Cornell University Press, 1975.

——'"Oh could you hear his voice!": Wordsworth, Coleridge, and Ventriloquism'. *Romanticism and Language*, ed. Arden Reed. Ithaca: Cornell University Press, 1985, pp. 125–43.

——'Reading Wordsworth's Power: Narrative and Usurpation in *The Borderers*.' *ELH*, **54** (1987): 299–331.

——'"In some sort seeing with my proper eyes": Wordsworth and the Spectacles of Paris.' *Studies in Romanticism*, **27** (1988): 369–90.

PARRISH, STEPHEN *The Art of the 'Lyrical Ballads'*. Cambridge: Harvard University Press, 1973. (Groundbreaking reading of poetic technique.)

POOVEY, MARY *The Proper Lady and the Woman Writer: Ideology as Style in the Works of Mary Wollstonecraft, Mary Shelley, and Jane Austen*. Chicago: University of Chicago Press, 1984.

QUINNEY, LAURA 'Skepticism and Grimness in Shelley'. *Colloquium Helveticum*, **11/12** (1990): 169–81.

RAJAN, TILOTTAMA *Dark Interpreter: The Discourse of Romanticism*. Ithaca: Cornell University Press, 1980.

——*The Supplement of Reading: Figures of Understanding in Romantic Theory and Practice*. Ithaca: Cornell University Press, 1990.

ROSS, MARLON *The Contours of Masculine Desire: Romanticism and the Rise of Women's Poetry*. New York: Oxford University Press, 1989.

SACKS, PETER *The English Elegy*. Baltimore: Johns Hopkins University Press, 1985. (Fine discussion of Shelley's 'Alastor'.)

SHAFFER, ELINOR *'Kubla Khan' and the Fall of Jerusalem: The Mythological School in Biblical Criticism and Secular Literature, 1770–1880*. Cambridge: Cambridge University Press, 1975.

SIMPSON, DAVID *Irony and Authority in Romantic Poetry*. London: Macmillan, 1979.

——'Criticism, Politics, and Style in Wordsworth's Poetry'. *Critical Inquiry*, **11** (1984): 52–81.

——*Wordsworth's Historical Imagination: The Poetry of Displacement*. New York: Methuen, 1987. (Interesting new historicist work.)

STILLINGER, JACK *The Hoodwinking of Madeleine and Other Essays on Keats's Poems*. Urbana: University of Illinois Press, 1971. (Discussion of poems' rhetoric by a leading Keats scholar.)

WARMINSKI, ANDRZEJ 'Missed Crossing: Wordsworth's Apocalypses'. *Modern Language Notes*, **99** (1984): 938–1006. (Brilliant rhetorical reading of Book V of *The Prelude* and discussion of Romanticism in terms of the tension between literal and figurative language.)

——*Readings in Interpretation: Hölderlin, Hegel, Heidegger*. Minneapolis: University of Minnesota Press, 1985. (Valuable first chapter on major Romantic tropes; important rhetorical reading of Hegel's *Phenomenology*.)

WASSERMAN, EARL *The Finer Tone: Keats's Major Poems*. Baltimore: Johns Hopkins University Press, 1967.

——*Shelley: A Critical Reading*. Baltimore: Johns Hopkins University Press, 1971.

WEISKEL, THOMAS *The Romantic Sublime: Studies in the Structure and Psychology of Transcendence*. Baltimore: Johns Hopkins University Press, 1976. (Combines psychoanalysis and semiotics.)

WILLIAMS, RAYMOND *Culture and Society 1780–1850*. New York: Harper & Row, 1958. (Includes 'The Romantic Artist' and 'Marxism and Culture'.)

——*The Country and the City*. Oxford: Oxford University Press, 1973. (A reflective essay in social history by a distinguished Marxist.)

WILNER, JOSHUA 'Romanticism and the Internalization of Scripture', in Geoffrey Hartman and Sanford Budick (eds) *Midrash and Literature*. New Haven: Yale University Press, 1986, pp. 237–51.

Index